Volume 40 is finally here*!!*

Plus, the fan book volume 40.5 is also on sale*!!* This character and that character from the Nationals are all covered. Of course, a special short story in full-color is also included*!!* Atobe's untold story revealed*?!* In any case, it goes beyond the realm of other fan books (*laugh*). Check it out*!!*

— Takeshi Konomi, 2007

About Takeshi Konomi

Takeshi Konomi exploded onto the manga scene with the incredible **THE PRINCE OF TENNIS**. His refined art style and sleek character designs proved popular with **Weekly Shonen Jump** readers, and **THE PRINCE OF TENNIS** became the number one sports manga in Japan almost overnight. Its cast of fascinating male tennis players attracted legions of female readers even though it was originally intended to be a boys' comic. The manga continues to be a success in Japan and has inspired a hit anime series, as well as several video games and mountains of merchandise.

THE PRINCE OF TENNIS
VOL. 40
SHONEN JUMP Manga Edition

STORY AND ART BY
TAKESHI KONOMI

Translation/Joe Yamazaki
Touch-up Art & Lettering/Vanessa Satone
Design/Sam Elzway
Editor/Daniel Gillespie

Printed in Canada

Published by VIZ Media, LLC
P.O. Box 77010
San Francisco, CA 94107

10 9 8 7 6 5 4 3 2 1
First printing, January 2011

SHONEN JUMP Manga

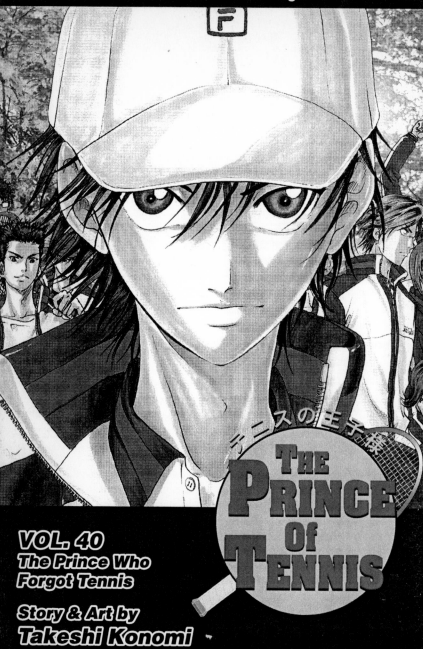

THE PRINCE OF TENNIS

VOL. 40
*The Prince Who
Forgot Tennis*

Story & Art by
Takeshi Konomi

ENNIS CLUB

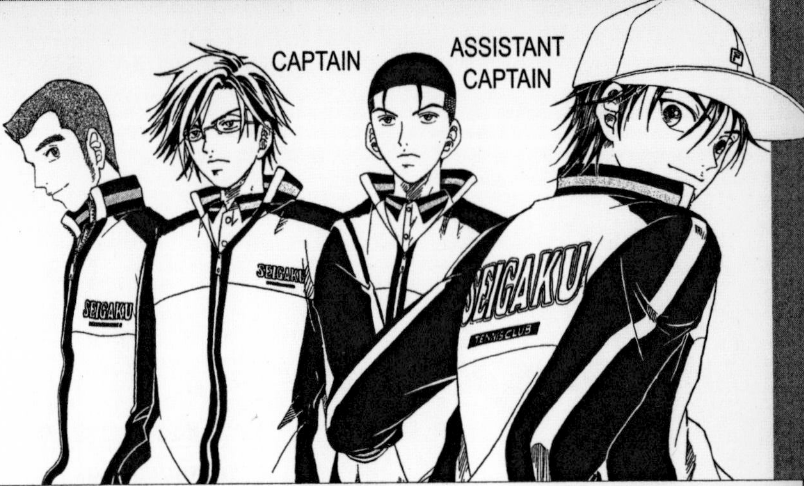
CAPTAIN
ASSISTANT CAPTAIN

• TAKASHI KAWAMURA • KUNIMITSU TEZUKA • SHUICHIRO OISHI • RYOMA ECHIZEN •

STORY & CHARACTERS

Seishun Academy student Ryoma Echizen is a tennis prodigy, with wins in four consecutive U.S. Junior Tennis Tournaments under his belt. He became a starter as a 7th grader and led his team to the District Preliminaries! Despite a few mishaps, Seishun won the District Prelims and the City Tournament, and earned a ticket to the Kanto Tournament. The team came away victorious from its first-round matches, but captain Kunimitsu injured his shoulder and went to Kyushu for treatment. Despite losing Kunimitsu and assistant captain Shuichiro to injury, Seishun pulled together as a team, winning the Kanto Tournament and earning a slot at the Nationals!

With Kunimitsu recovered and back on the team, Seishun enter the Nationals with their strongest lineup and defeat Okinawa's Higa Junior High in the opening round, Hyotei in the quarterfinals, and Shitenhoji in the semifinals. In the final round, they're up against Rikkai. Kunimitsu and Genichiro Sanada face off in the first match! These two top players have been anticipating this match for a long time. And now, the final phase of this ultimate showdown has finally arrived.

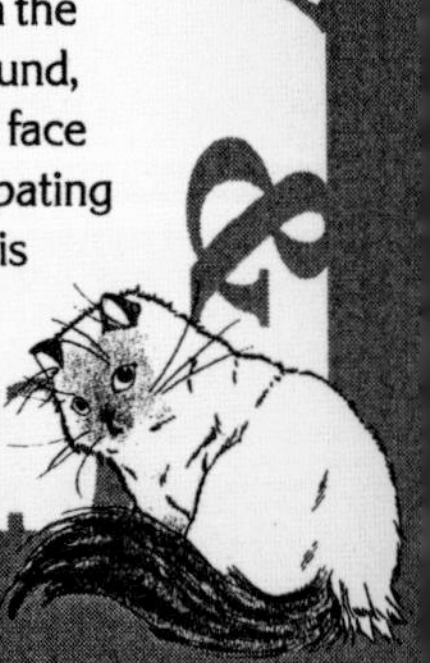

SEIGAKU T

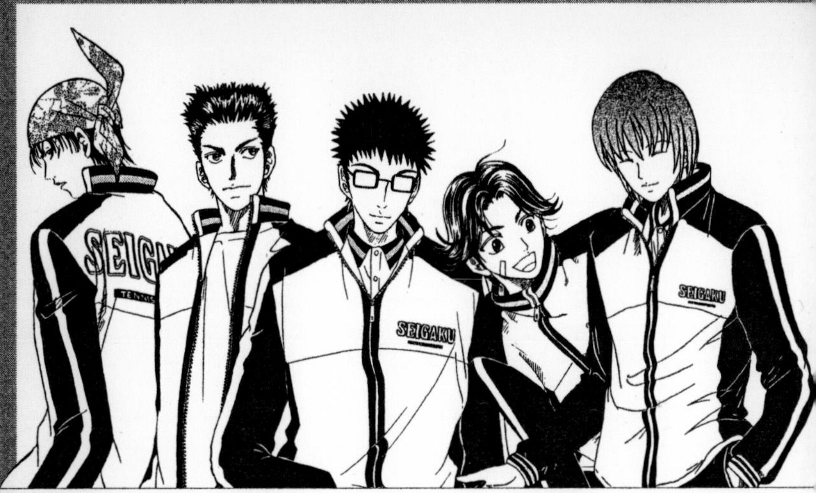

● KAORU KAIDO ● TAKESHI MOMOSHIRO ● SADAHARU INUI ● EIJI KIKUMARU ● SHUSUKE FUJI ●

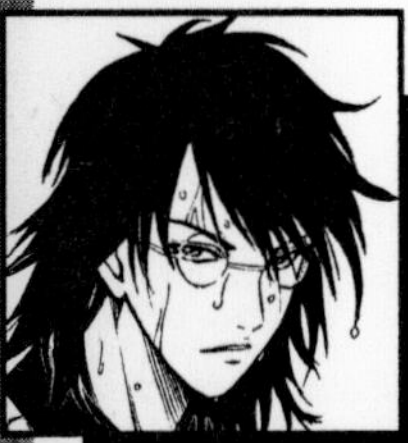

HYOTEI ACADEMY

YUSHI OSHITARI

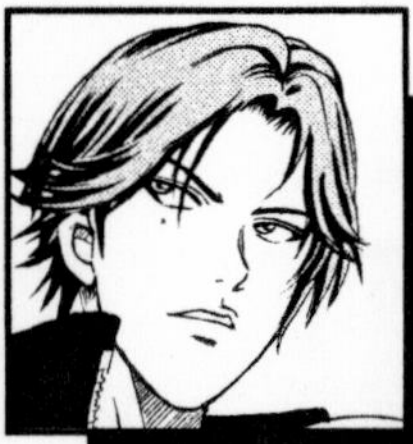

HYOTEI ACADEMY

KEIGO ATOBE

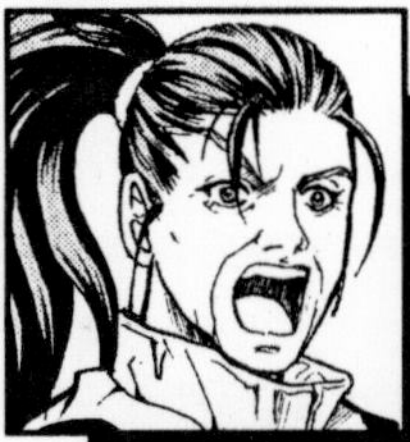

SEISHUN ACADEMY TENNIS COACH

SUMIRE RYUZAKI

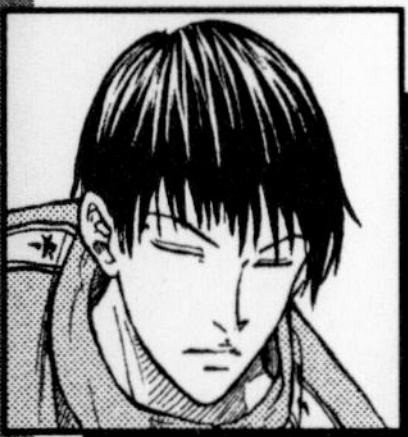

RIKKAI

RENJI YANAGI

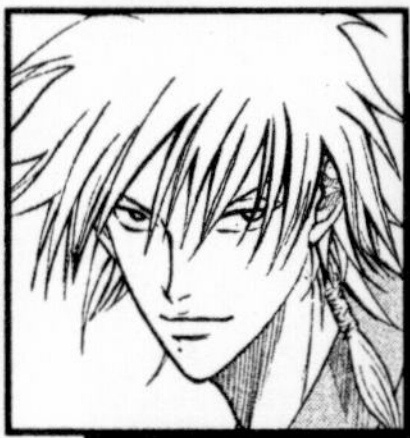

RIKKAI

MASAHARU NIO

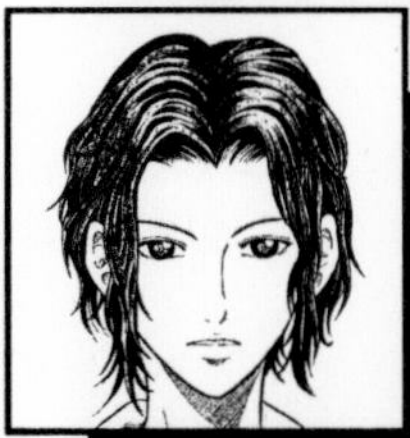

RIKKAI

SEIICHI YUKIMURA

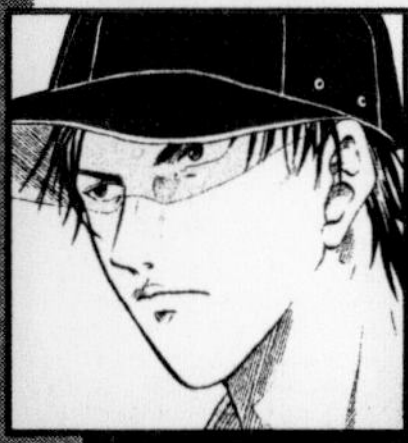

RIKKAI

GENICHIRO SANADA

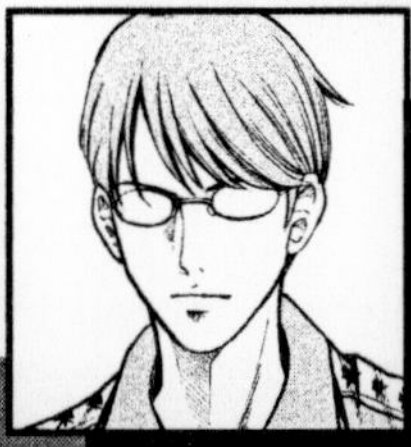

RIKKAI

HIROSHI YAGYU

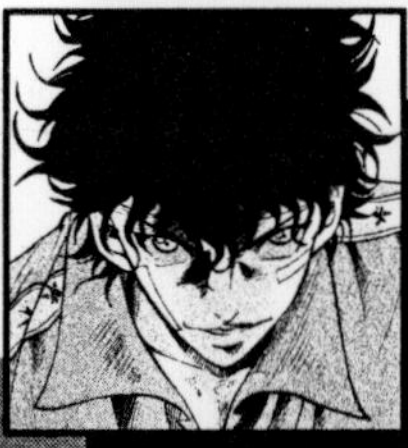

RIKKAI

AKAYA KIRIHARA

CONTENTS

Vol. 40
The Prince Who Forgot Tennis

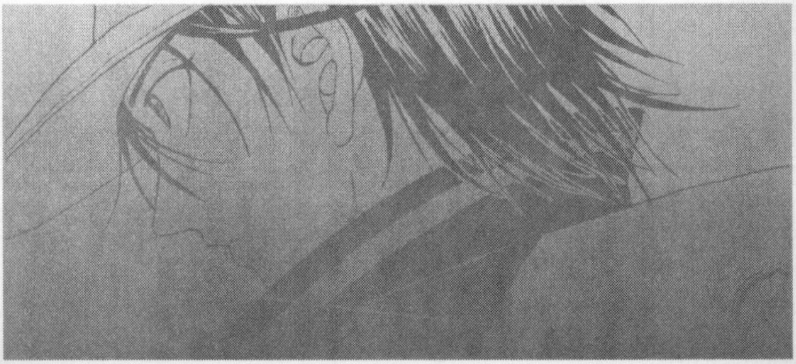

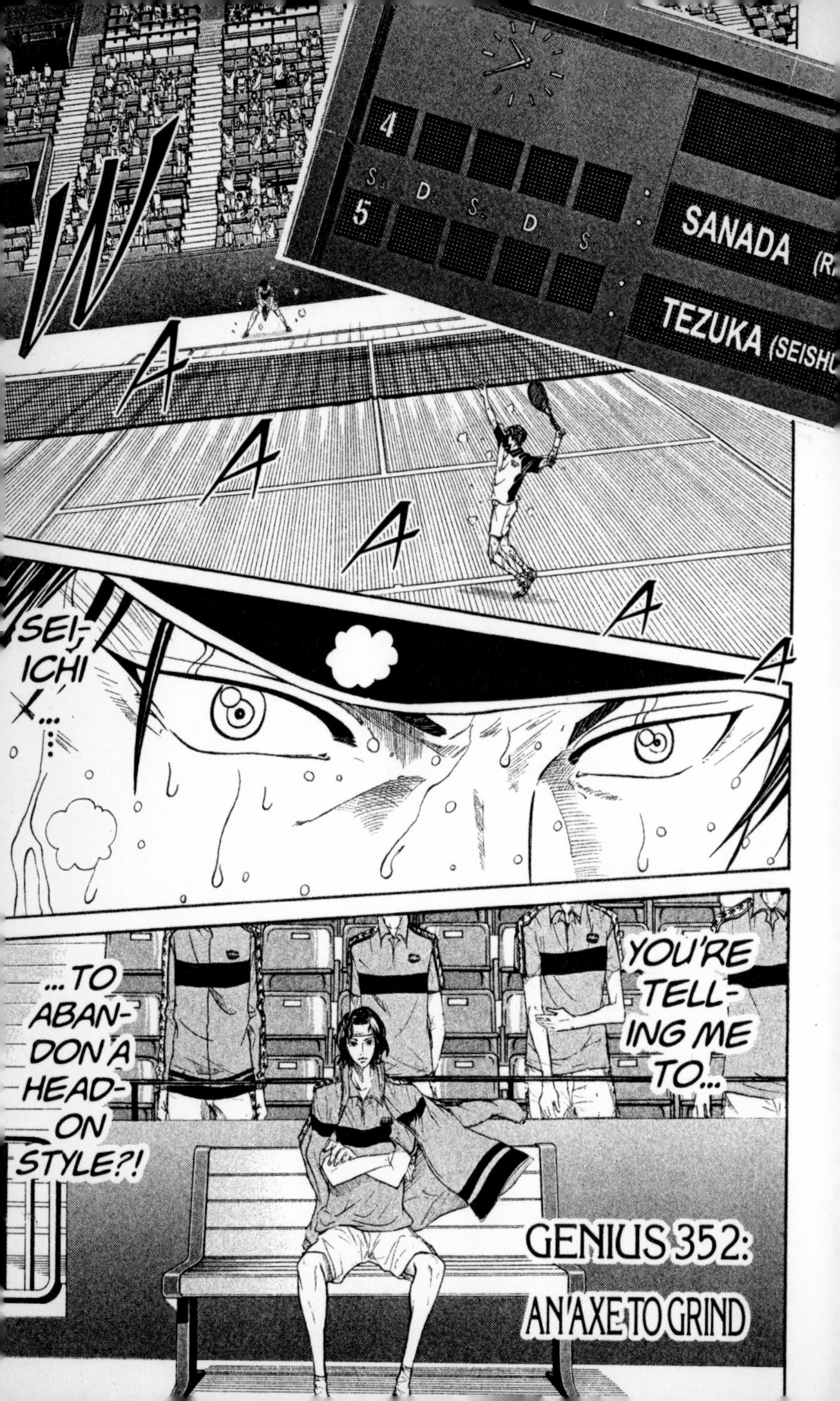
4
S D S D S
5
SANADA
TEZUKA
WAAAAAA
SEI-ICHI...
YOU'RE TELLING ME TO...
...TO ABANDON A HEAD-ON STYLE?!

GENIUS 352: AN AXE TO GRIND

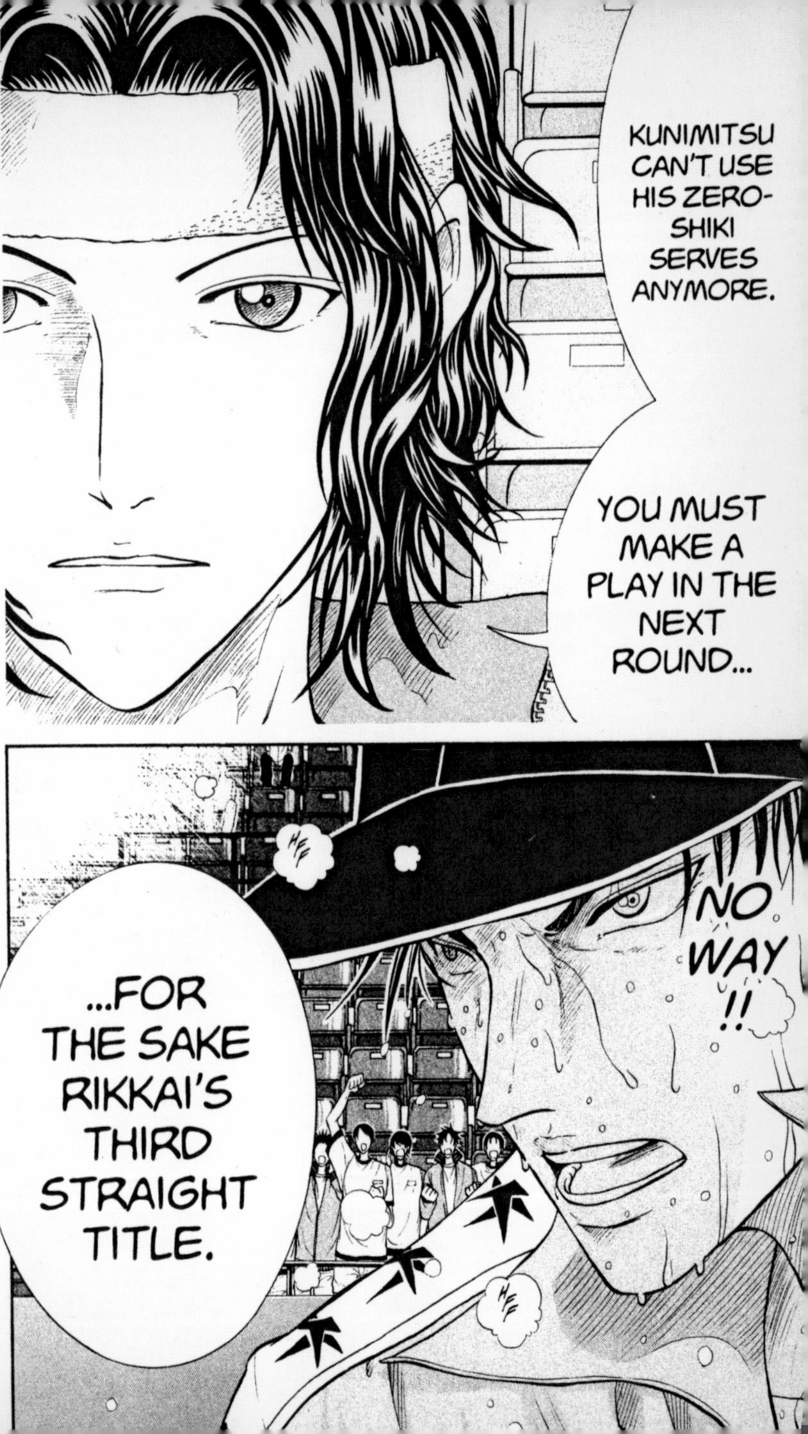
KUNIMITSU CAN'T USE HIS ZERO-SHIKI SERVES ANYMORE.
YOU MUST MAKE A PLAY IN THE NEXT ROUND...
NO WAY!!
...FOR THE SAKE RIKKAI'S THIRD STRAIGHT TITLE.

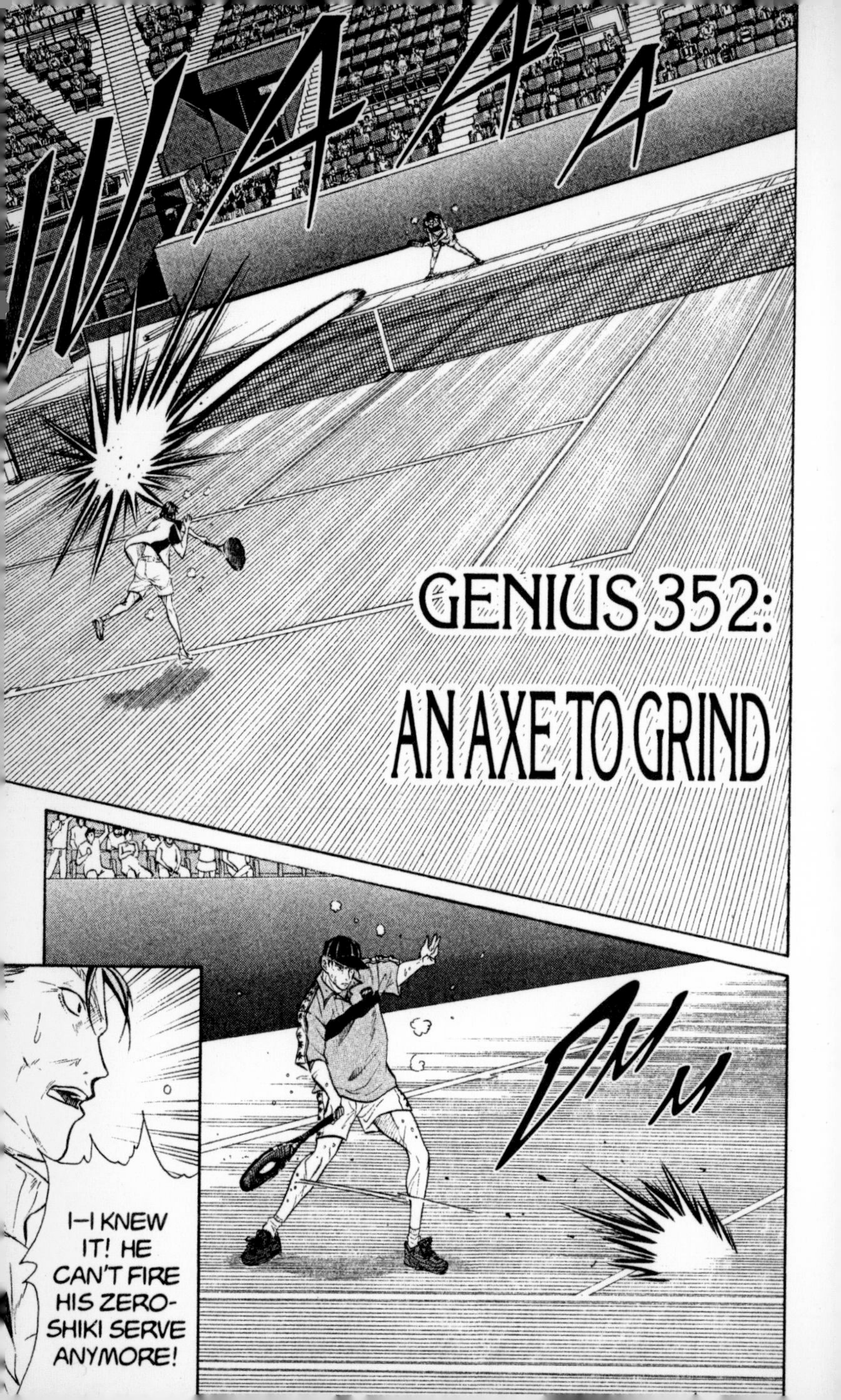
WAAA
GENIUS 352:
AN AXE TO GRIND
DMM
I-I KNEW IT! HE CAN'T FIRE HIS ZERO-SHIKI SERVE ANYMORE!

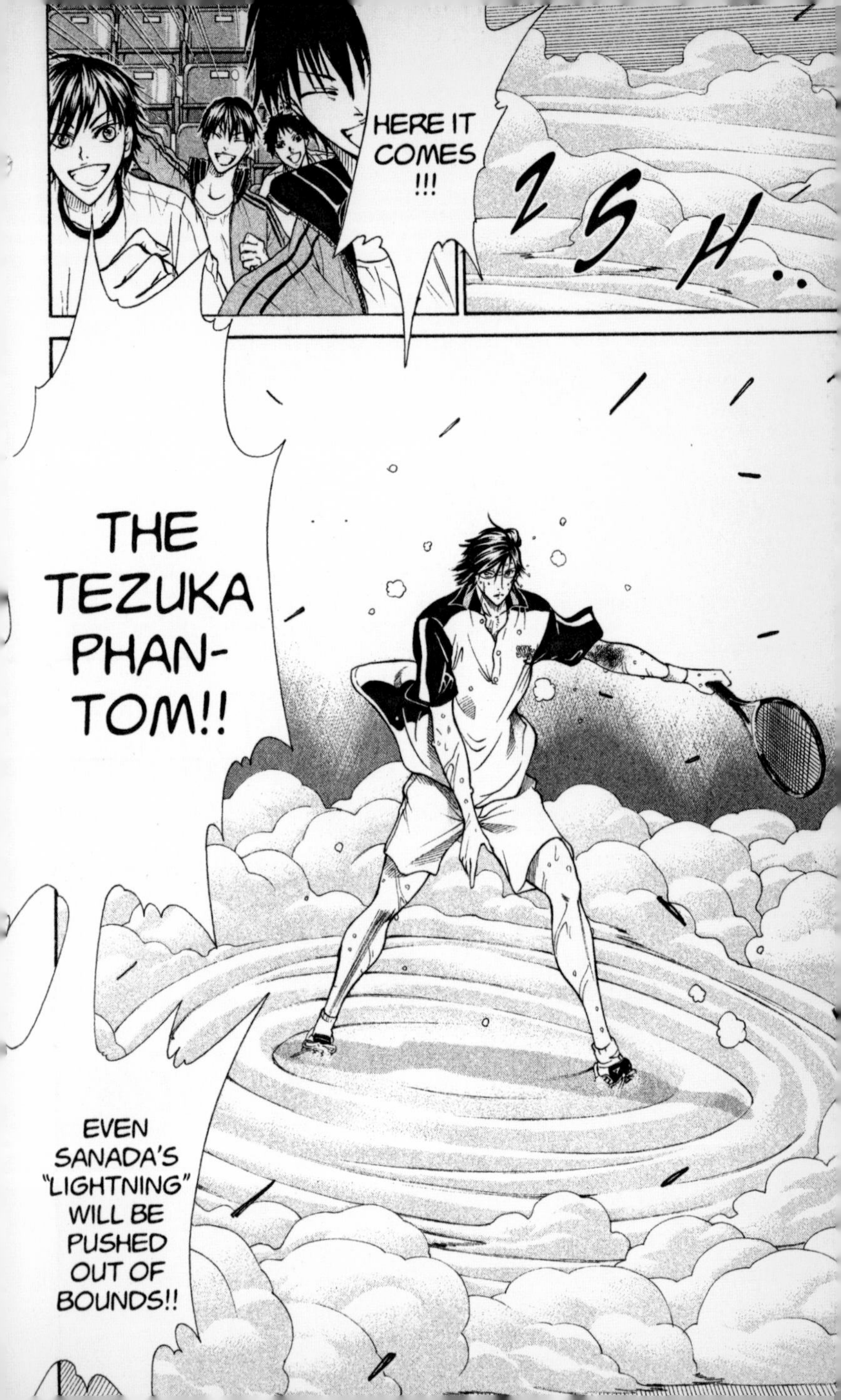
ZSH..
HERE IT COMES !!!
THE TEZUKA PHANTOM!!
EVEN SANADA'S "LIGHTNING" WILL BE PUSHED OUT OF BOUNDS!!

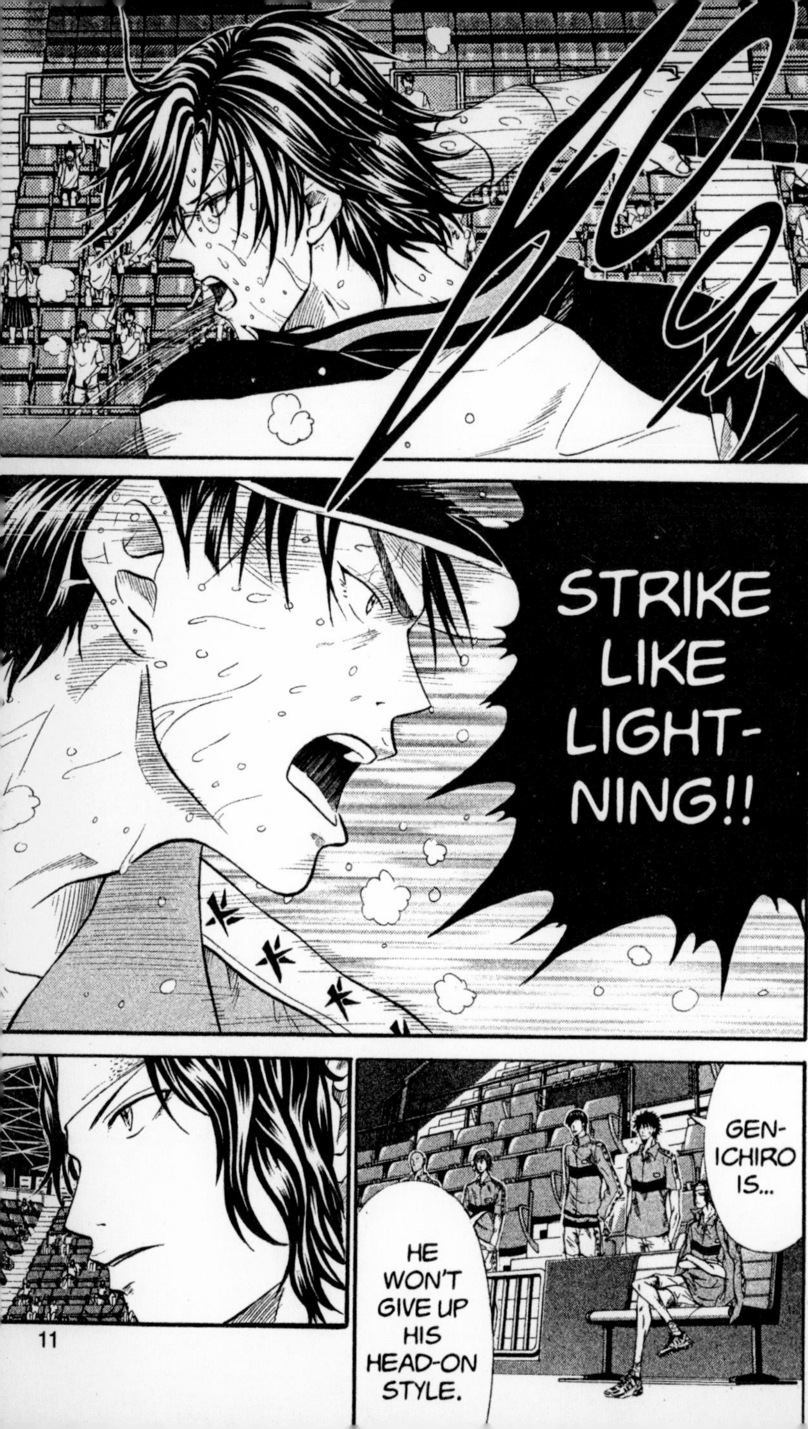
STRIKE LIKE LIGHT-NING!!
GEN-ICHIRO IS...
HE WON'T GIVE UP HIS HEAD-ON STYLE.

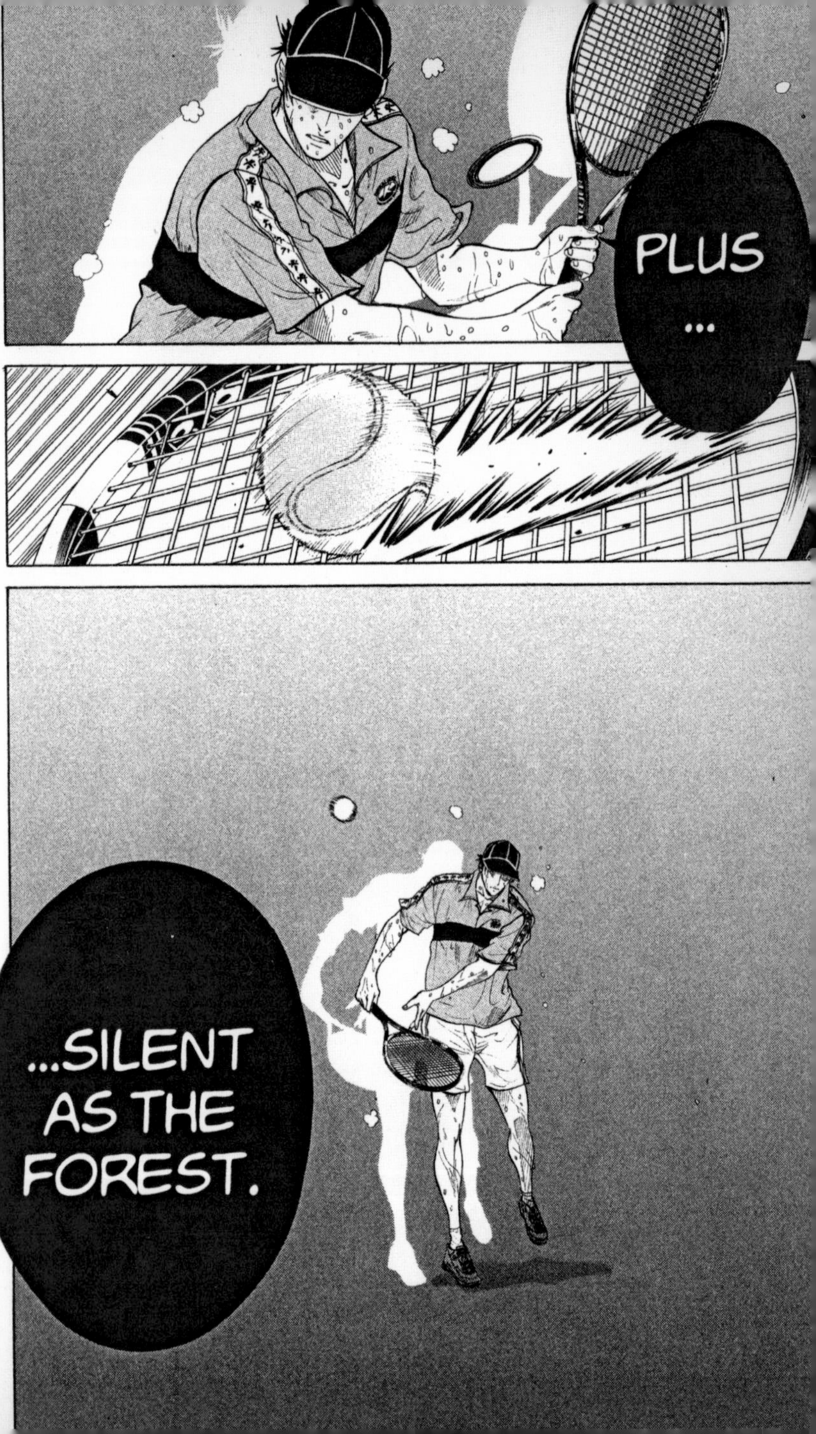
PLUS ...
...SILENT AS THE FOREST.

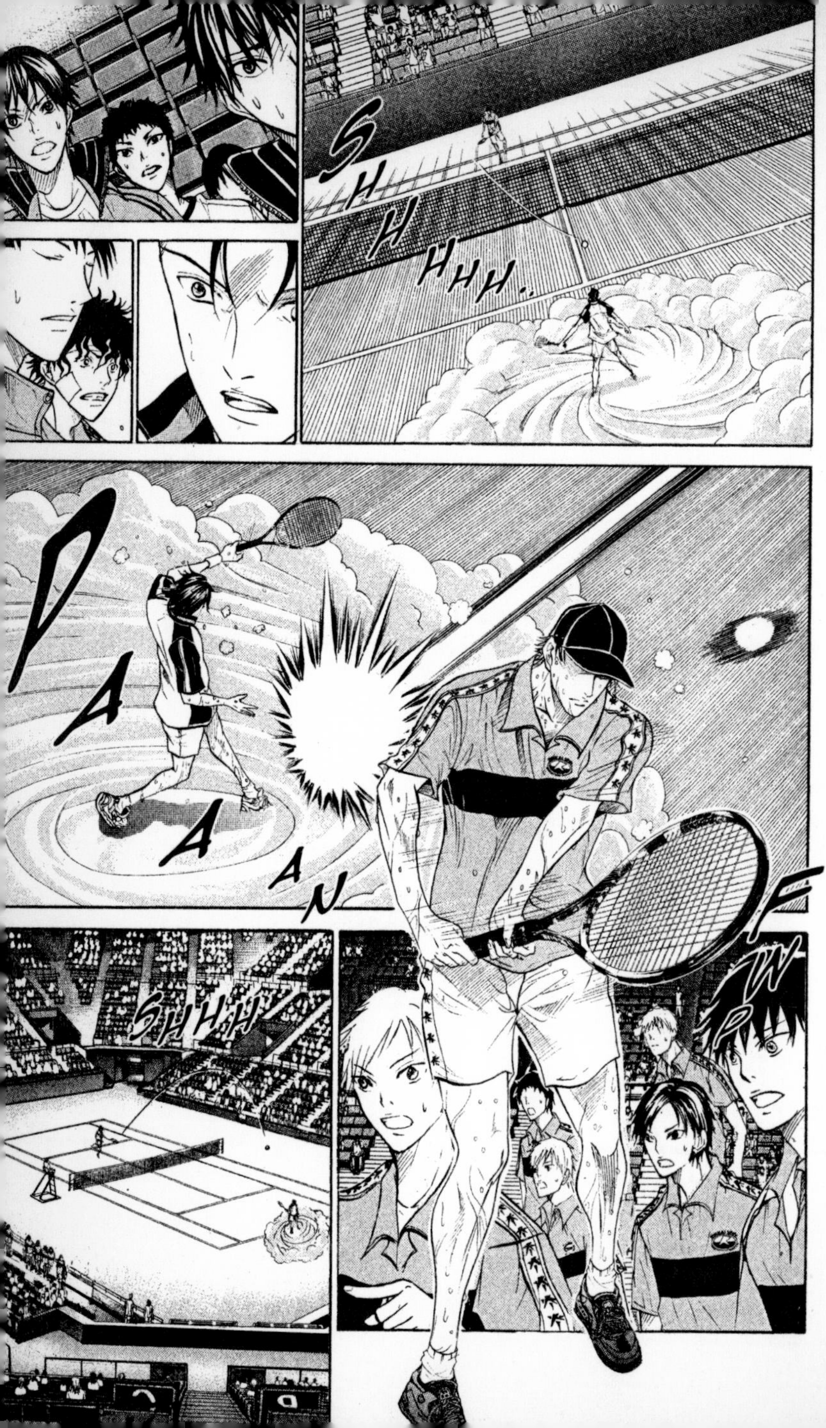
SHHHHH..
DAAAN
FWP
SHHH

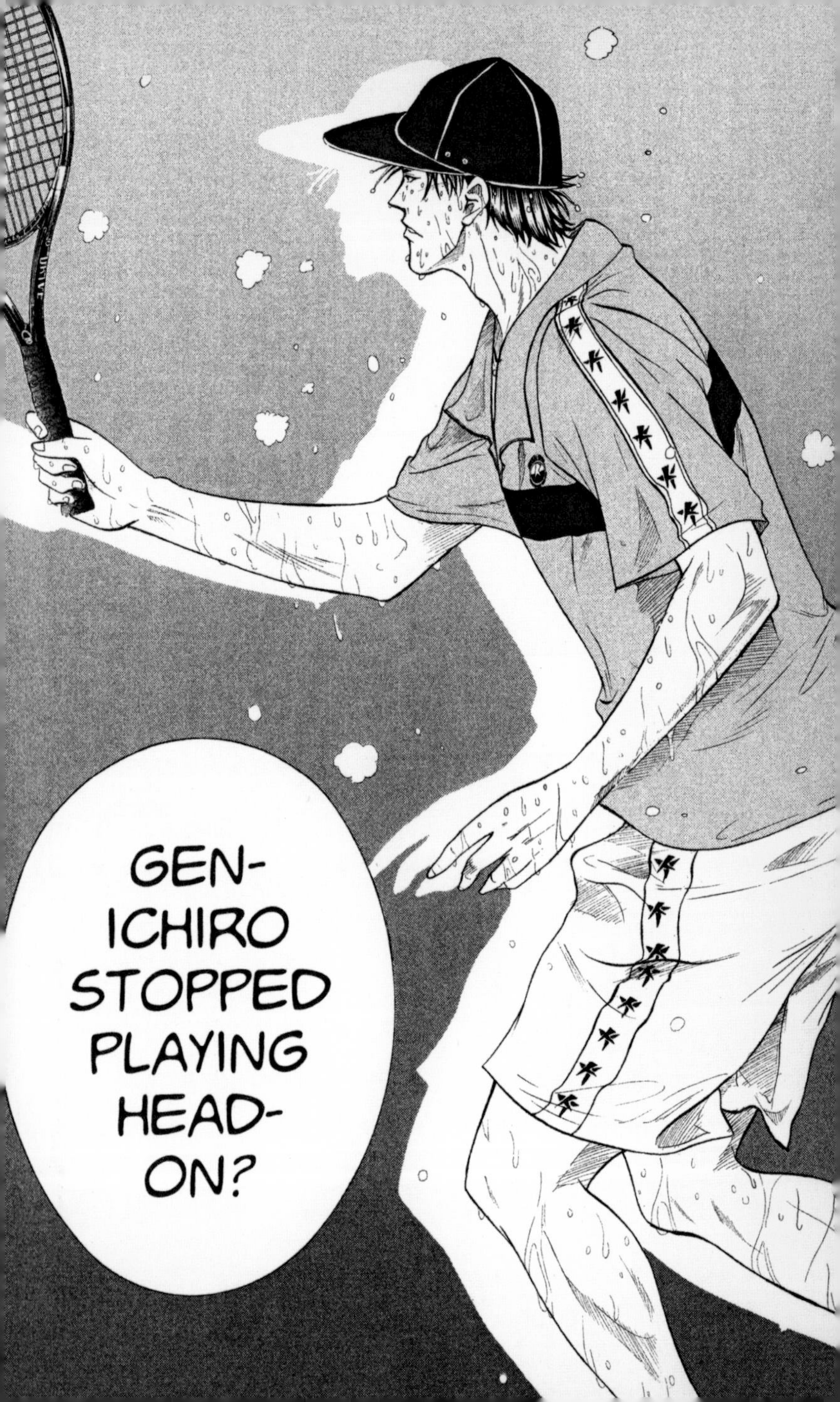
GEN-ICHIRO STOPPED PLAYING HEAD-ON?

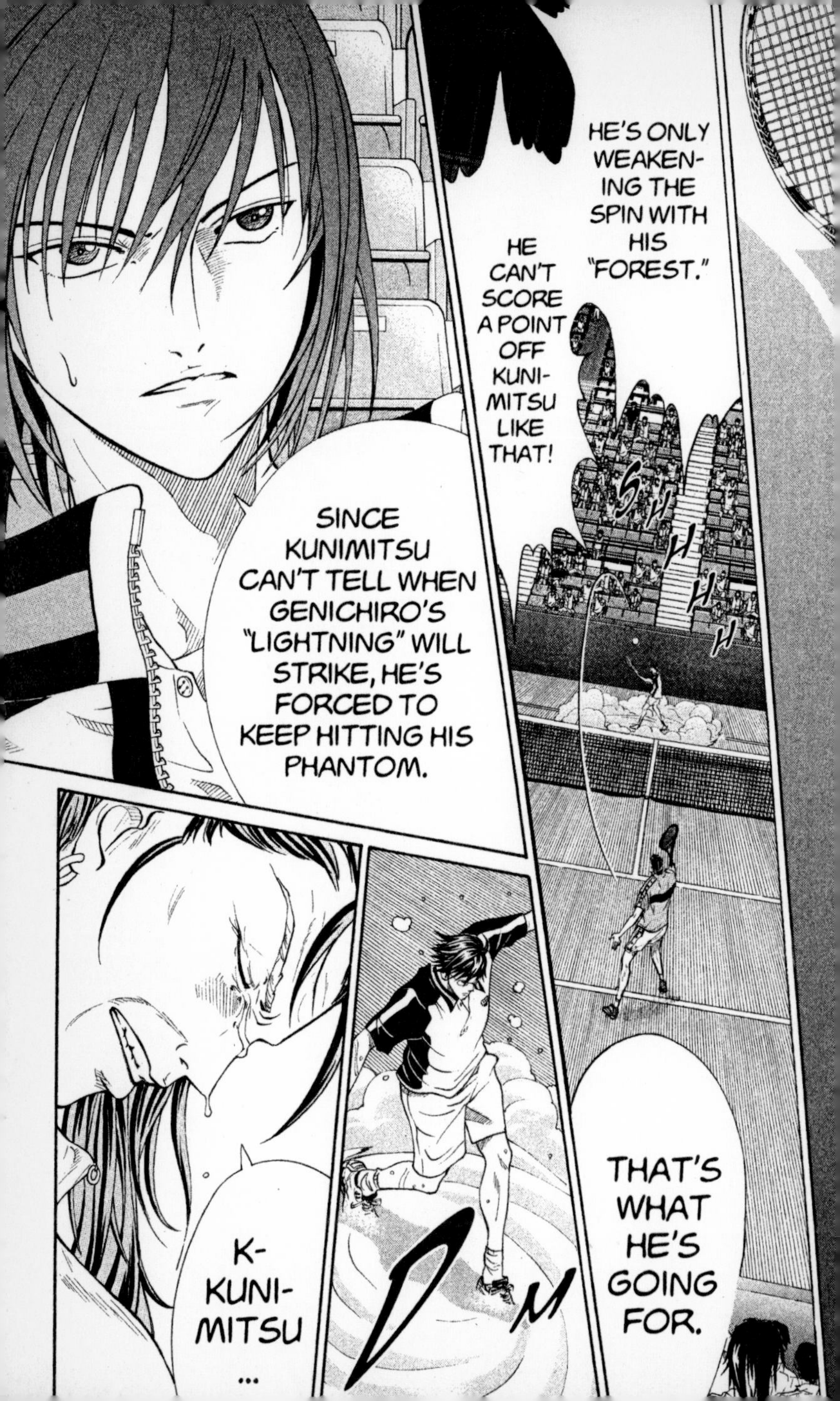
HE'S ONLY WEAKENING THE SPIN WITH HIS "FOREST."
HE CAN'T SCORE A POINT OFF KUNIMITSU LIKE THAT!
SHHHHH
SINCE KUNIMITSU CAN'T TELL WHEN GENICHIRO'S "LIGHTNING" WILL STRIKE, HE'S FORCED TO KEEP HITTING HIS PHANTOM.
THAT'S WHAT HE'S GOING FOR.
DM
K-KUNIMITSU...

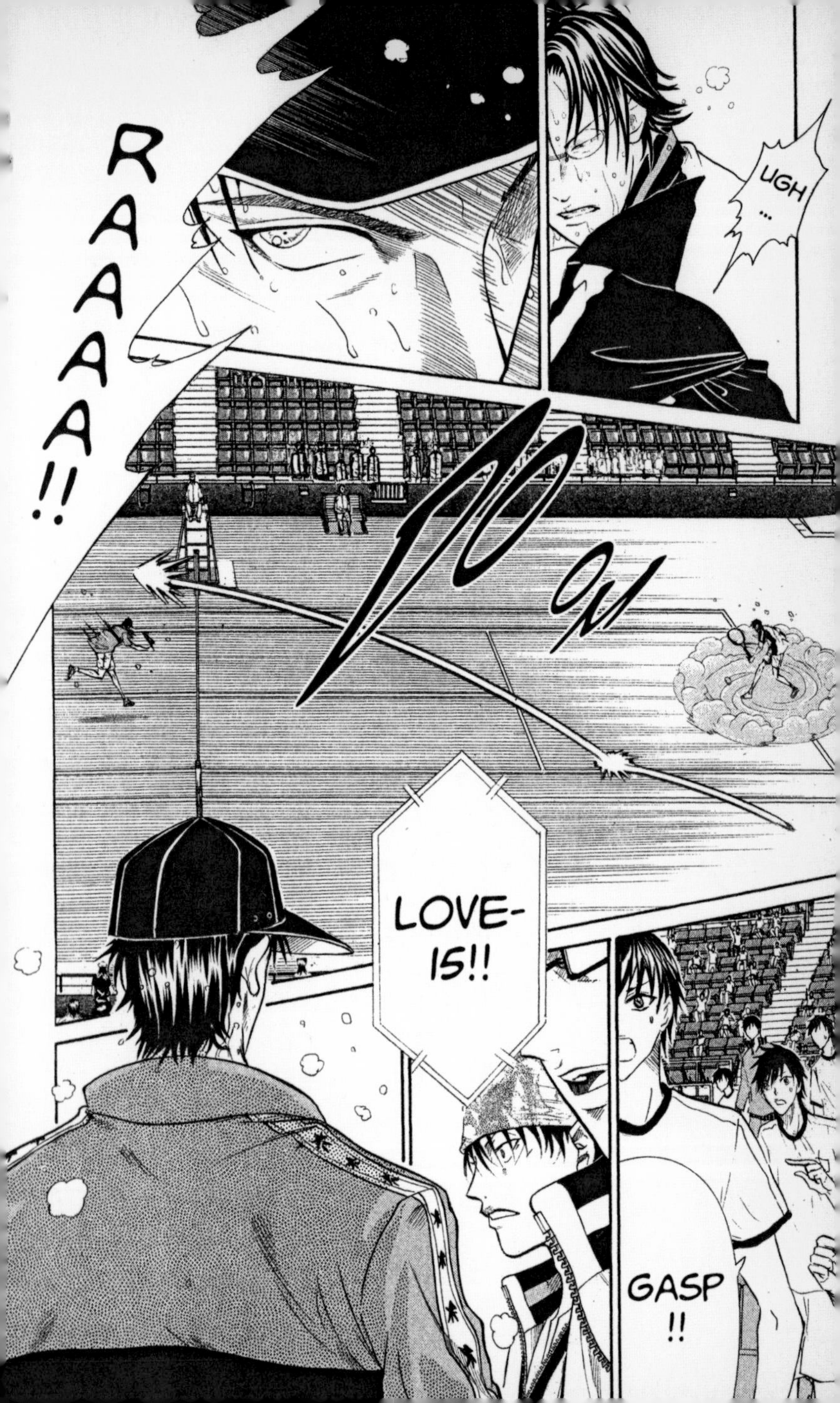
UGH ...
RAAAAA!!
LOVE-15!!
GASP !!

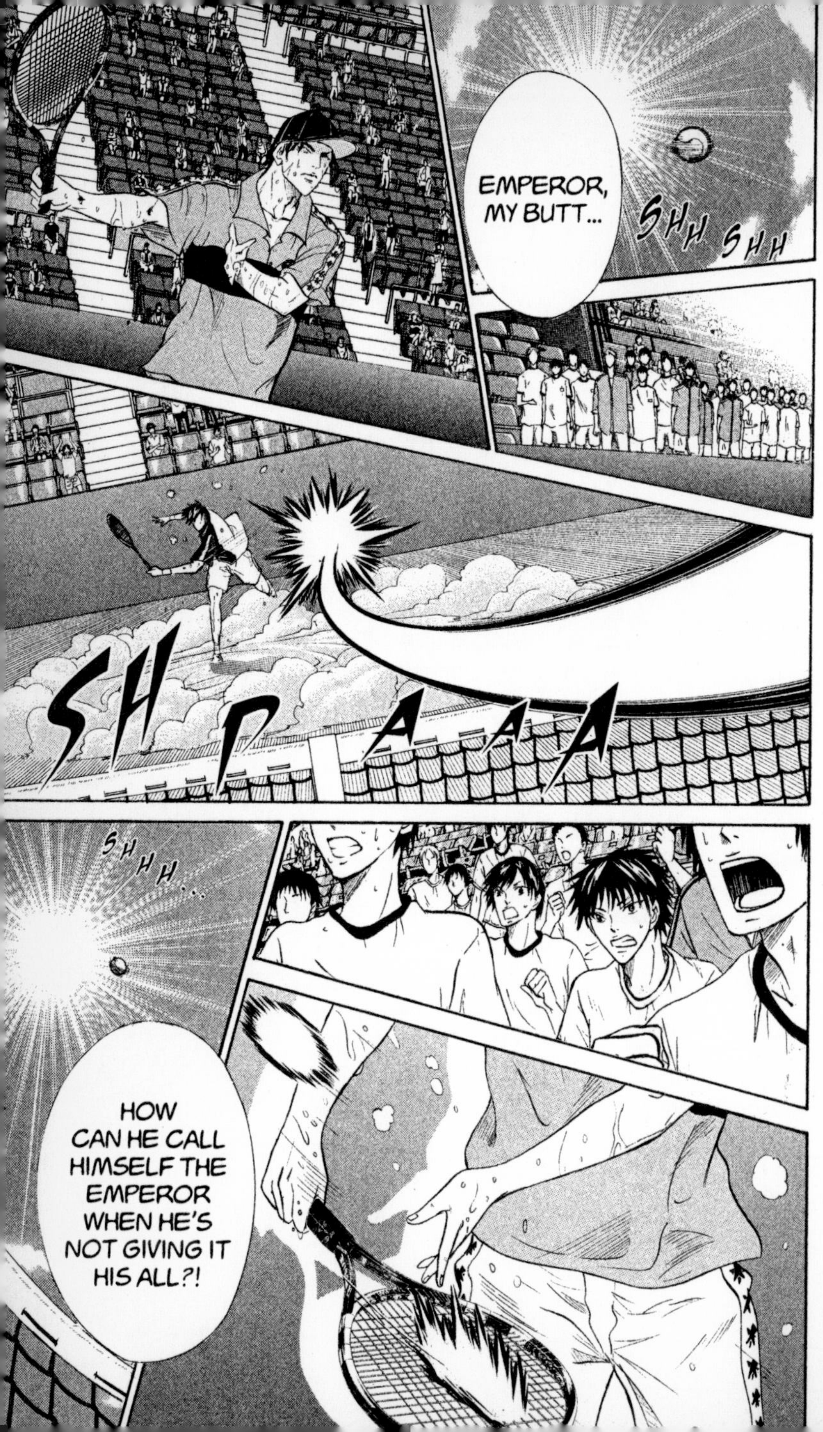
EMPEROR, MY BUTT...
SHH SHH
SHPAAA
SHHH...
HOW CAN HE CALL HIMSELF THE EMPEROR WHEN HE'S NOT GIVING IT HIS ALL?!

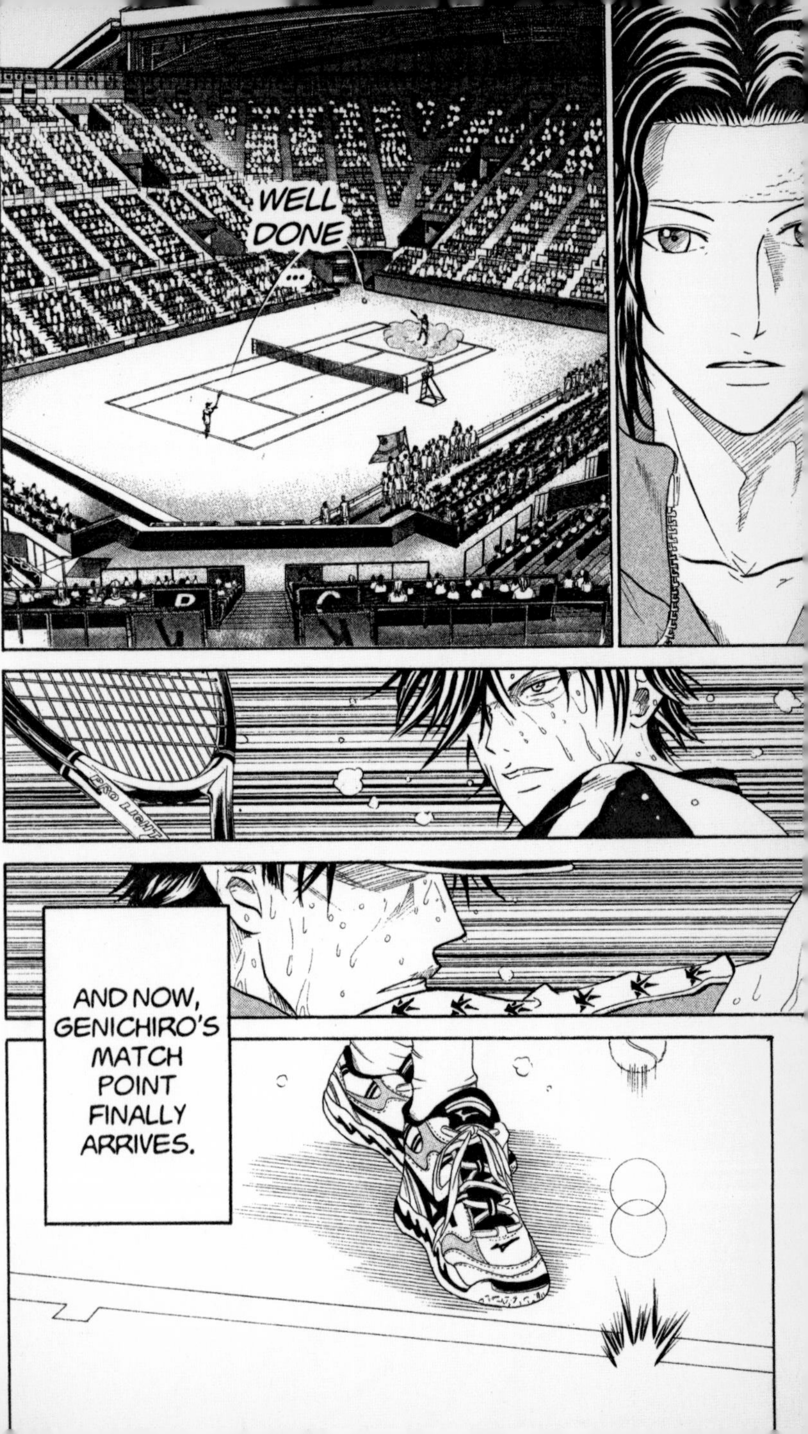
WELL DONE
...
PRO LIGHT
AND NOW, GENICHIRO'S MATCH POINT FINALLY ARRIVES.

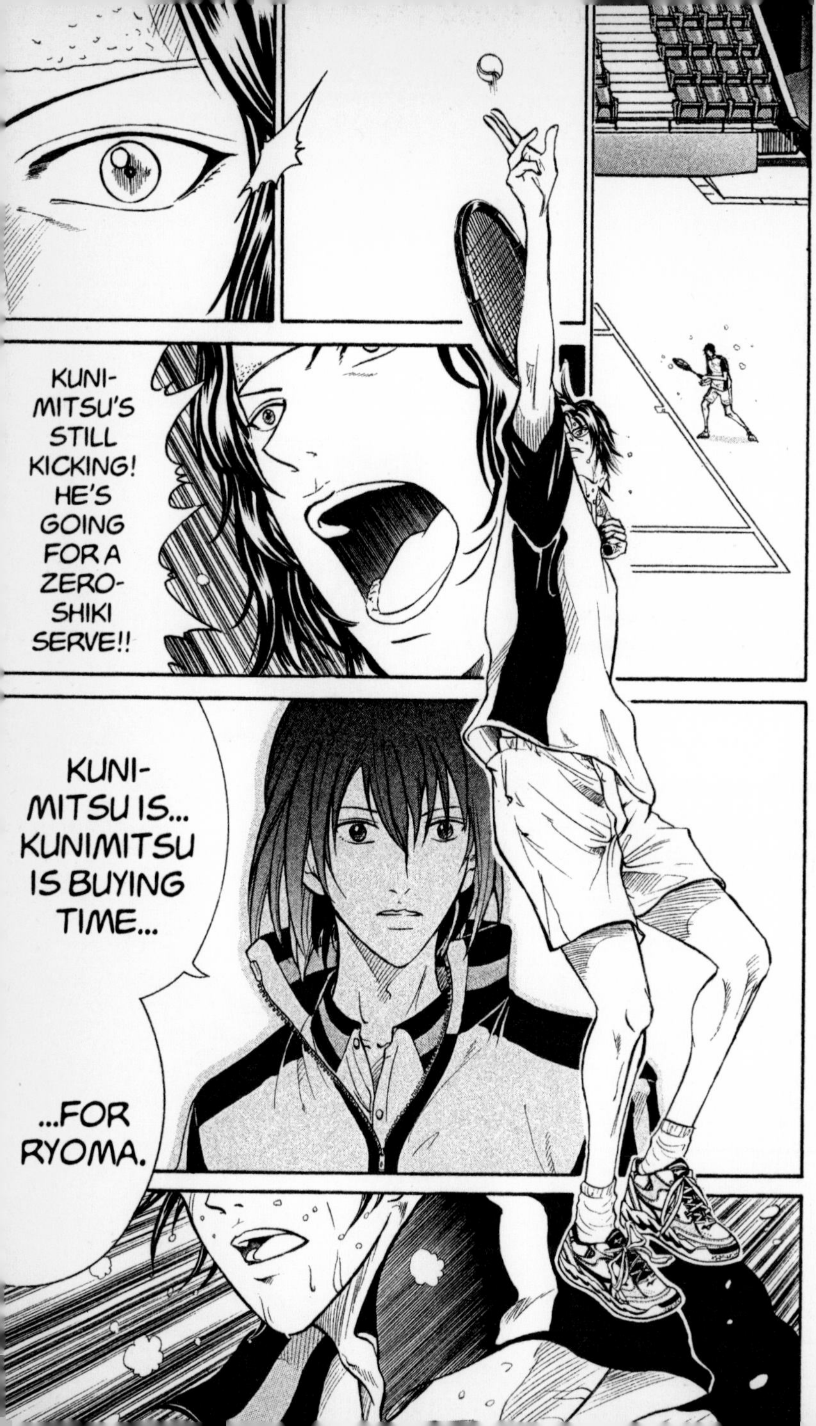
KUNI-MITSU'S STILL KICKING! HE'S GOING FOR A ZERO-SHIKI SERVE!!
KUNI-MITSU IS... KUNIMITSU IS BUYING TIME...
...FOR RYOMA.

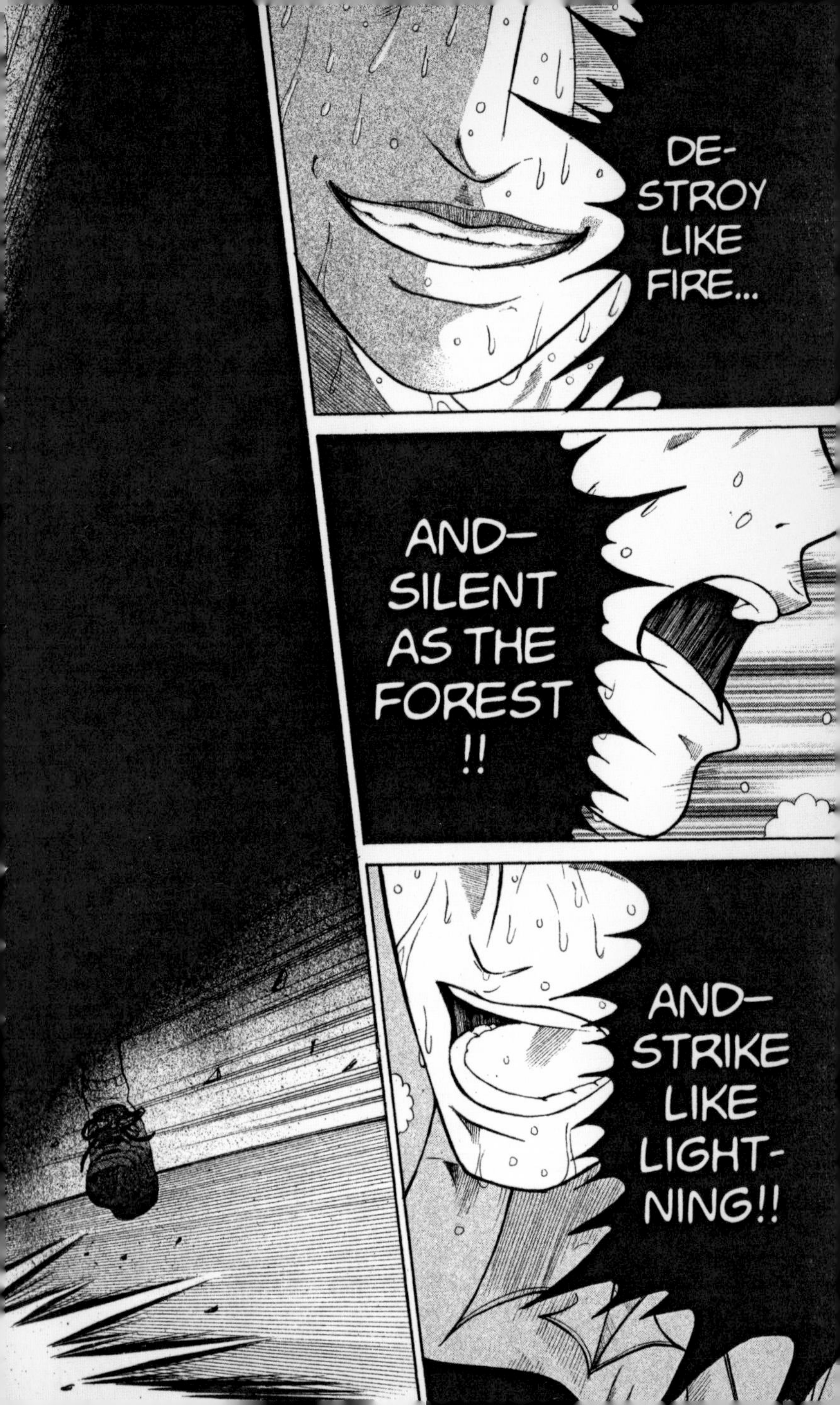
DE-STROY LIKE FIRE...
AND-SILENT AS THE FOREST !!
AND-STRIKE LIKE LIGHT-NING!!

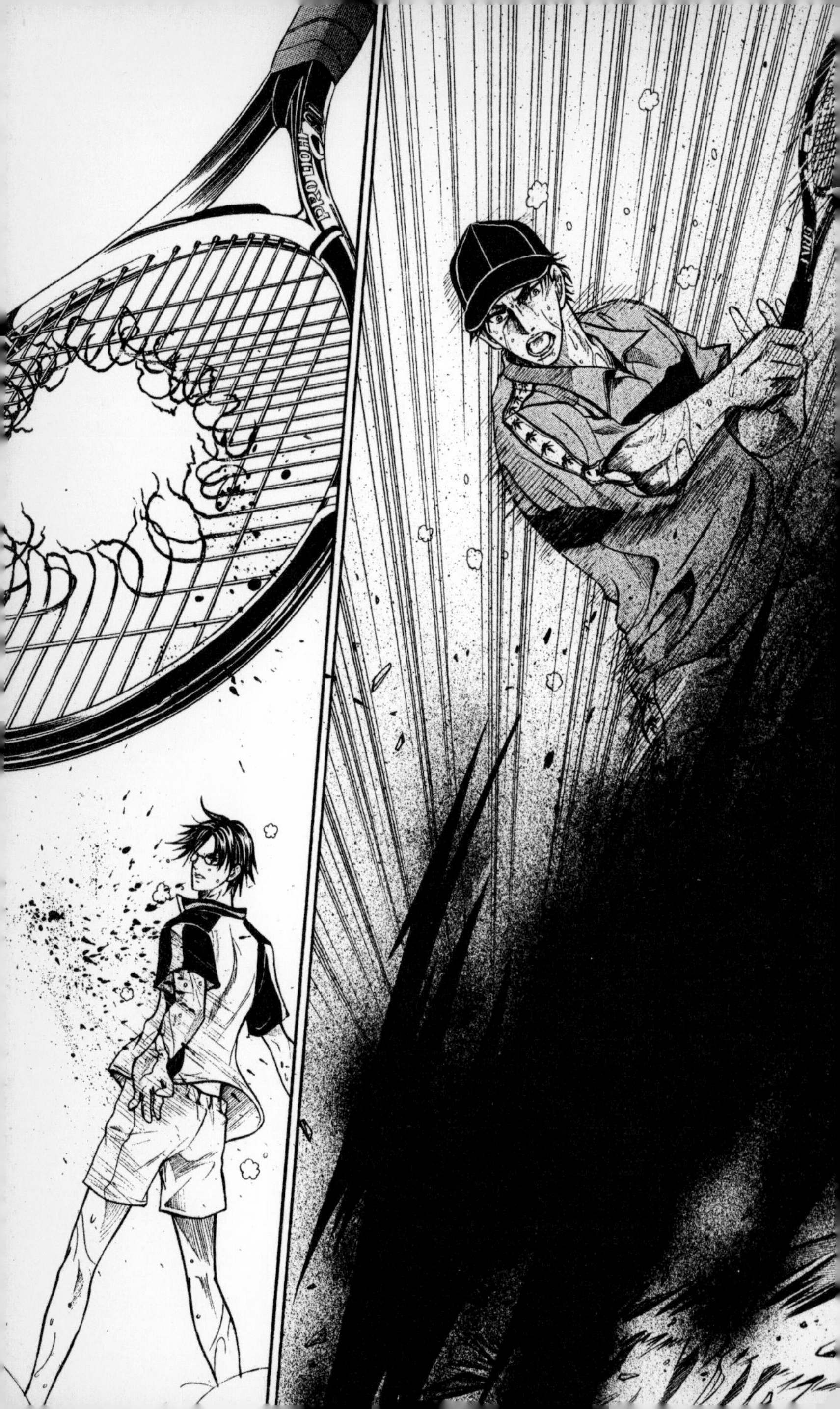

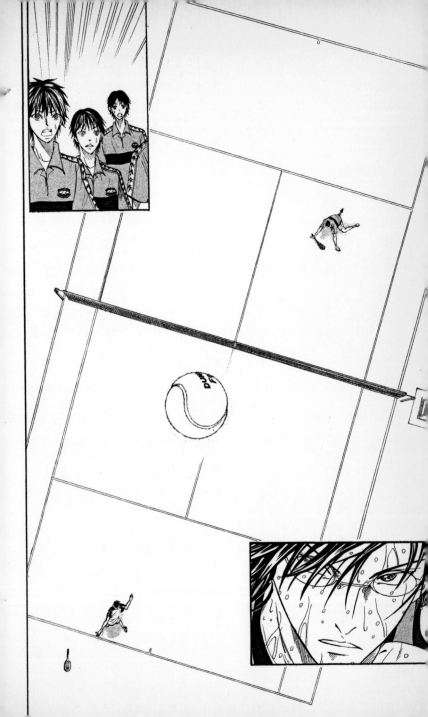

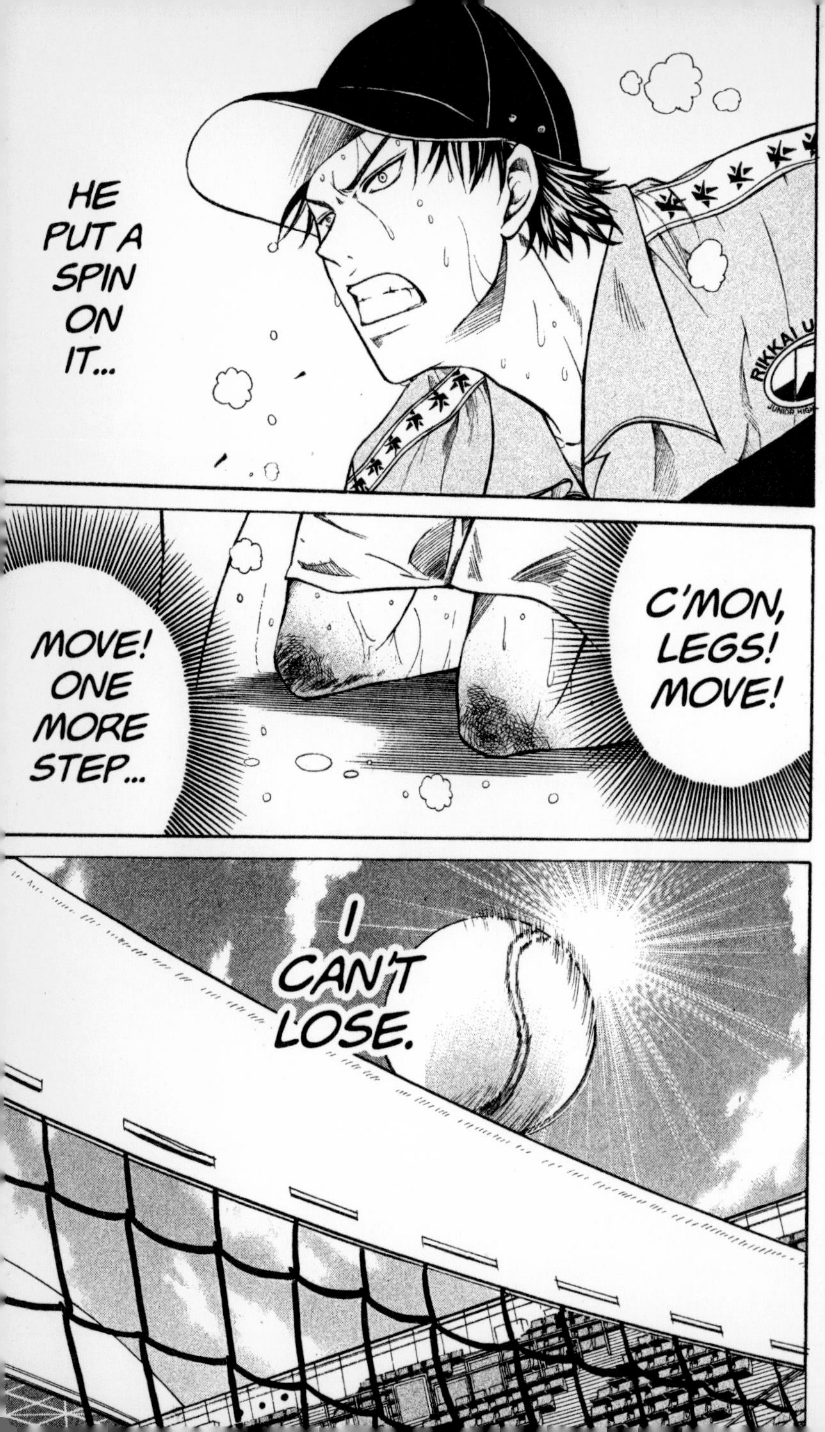
HE PUT A SPIN ON IT...
C'MON, LEGS! MOVE!
MOVE! ONE MORE STEP...
I CAN'T LOSE.

テニスの王子様

THE PRINCE OF TENNIS

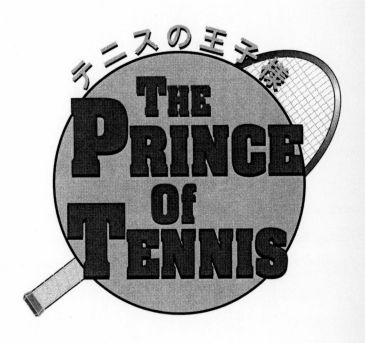

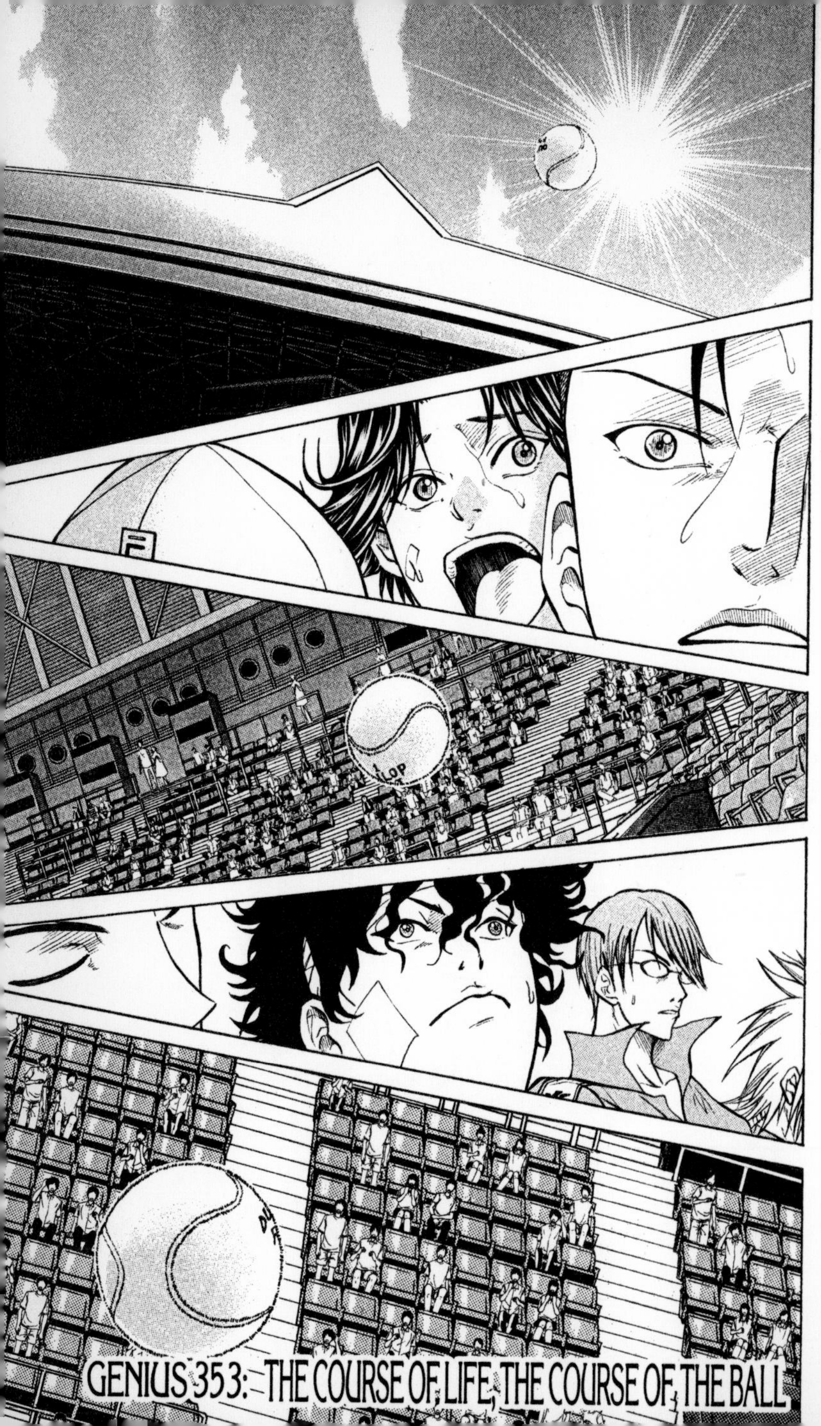
GENIUS 353: THE COURSE OF LIFE, THE COURSE OF THE BALL

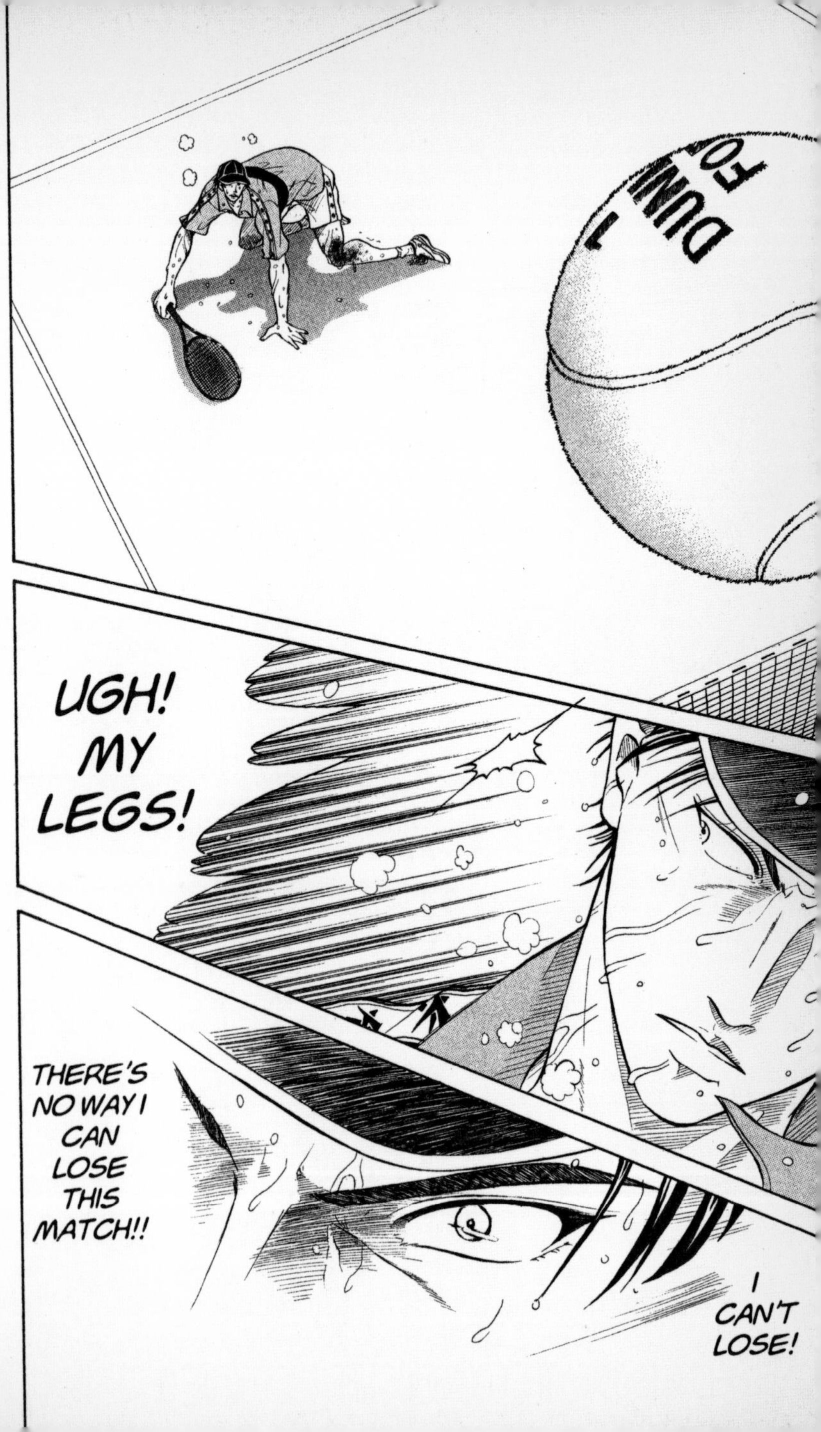
UGH! MY LEGS!
THERE'S NO WAY I CAN LOSE THIS MATCH!!
I CAN'T LOSE!

SEISHUN,
YOU'RE
SLACKING...

GENIUS 353:
THE COURSE
OF LIFE, THE
COURSE OF
THE BALL

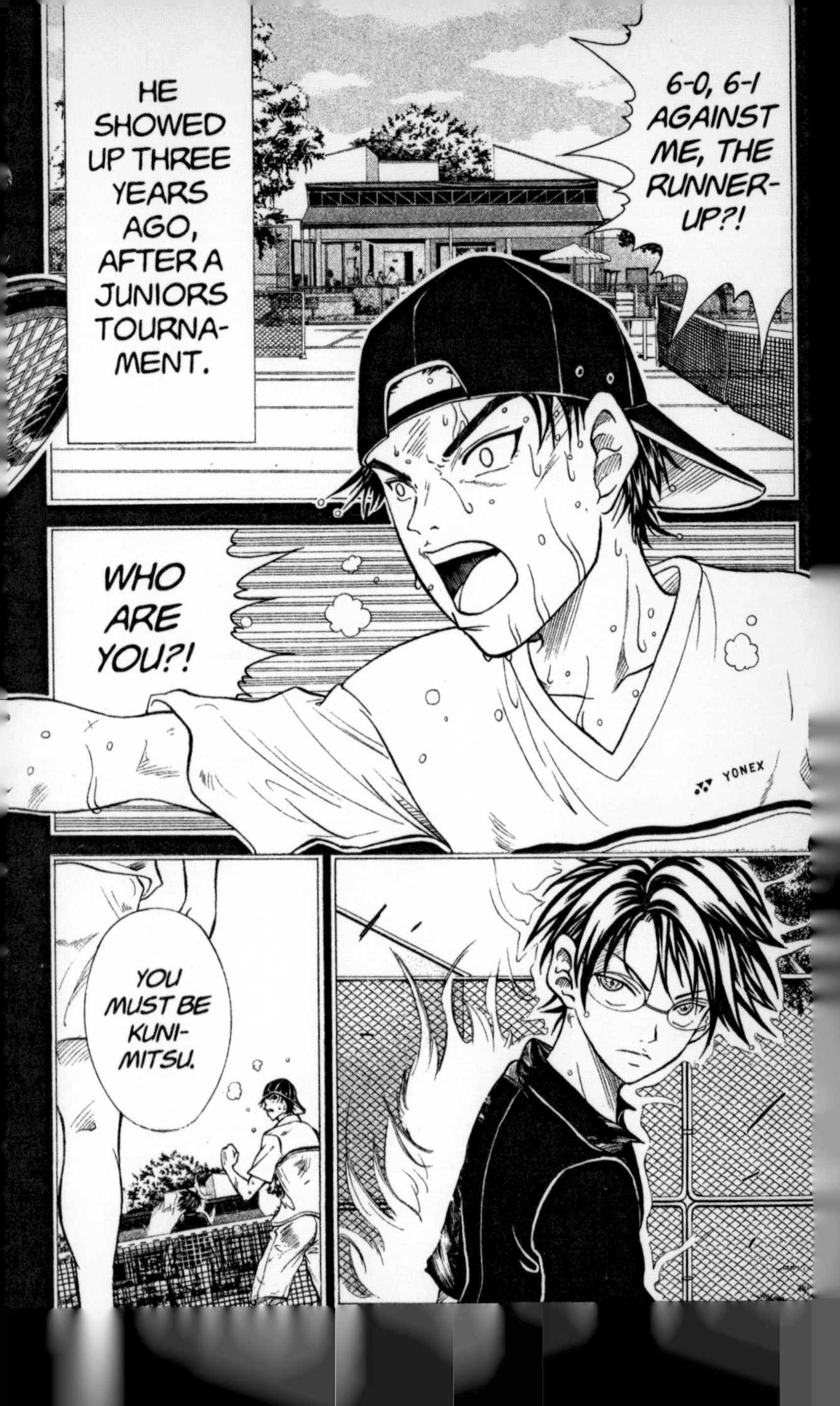
6-0, 6-1 AGAINST ME, THE RUNNER-UP?!
HE SHOWED UP THREE YEARS AGO, AFTER A JUNIORS TOURNAMENT.
WHO ARE YOU?!
YONEX
YOU MUST BE KUNIMITSU.

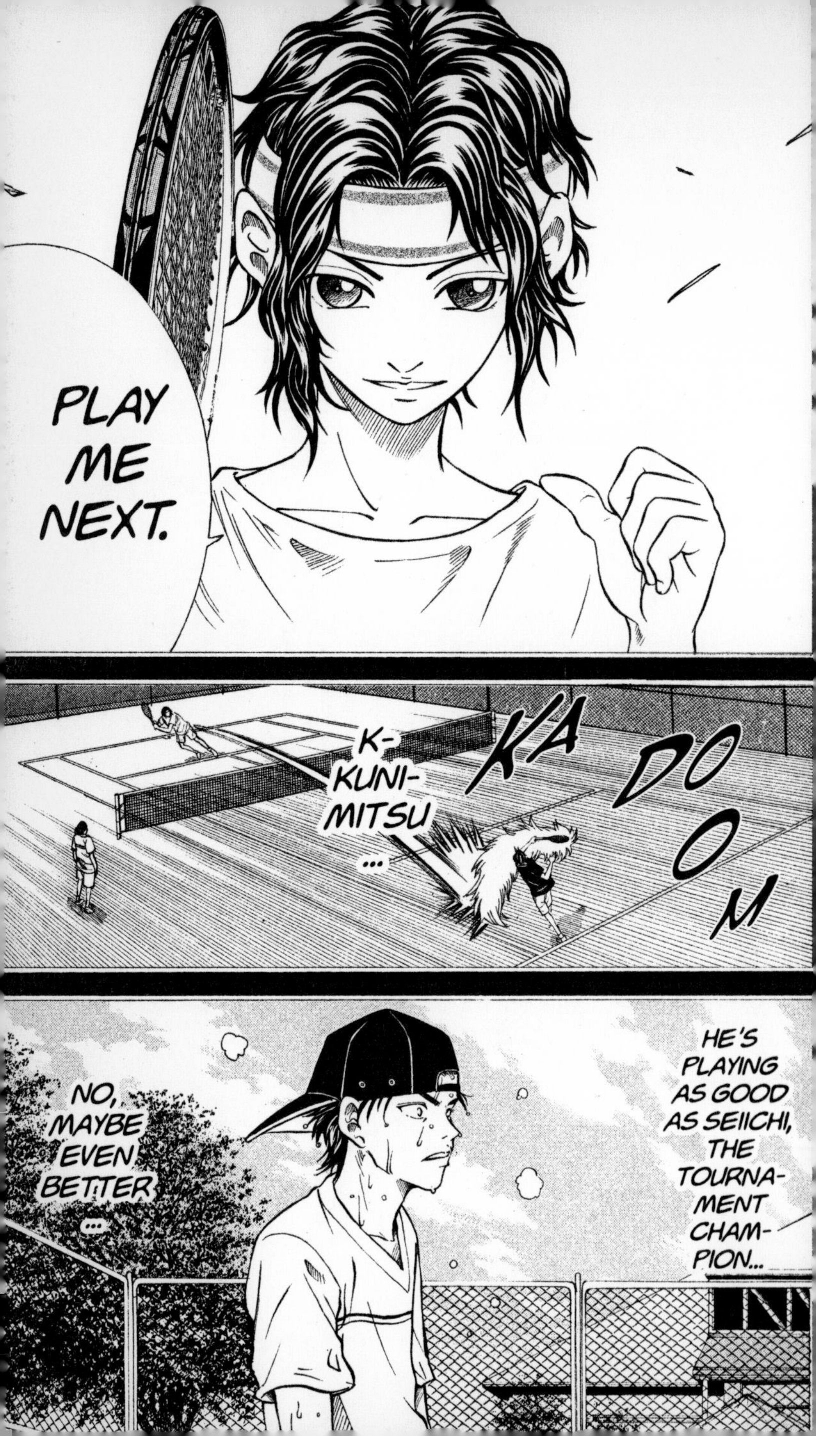
PLAY ME NEXT.
KADOOOM
K-KUNIMITSU...
HE'S PLAYING AS GOOD AS SEIICHI, THE TOURNAMENT CHAMPION...
NO, MAYBE EVEN BETTER...

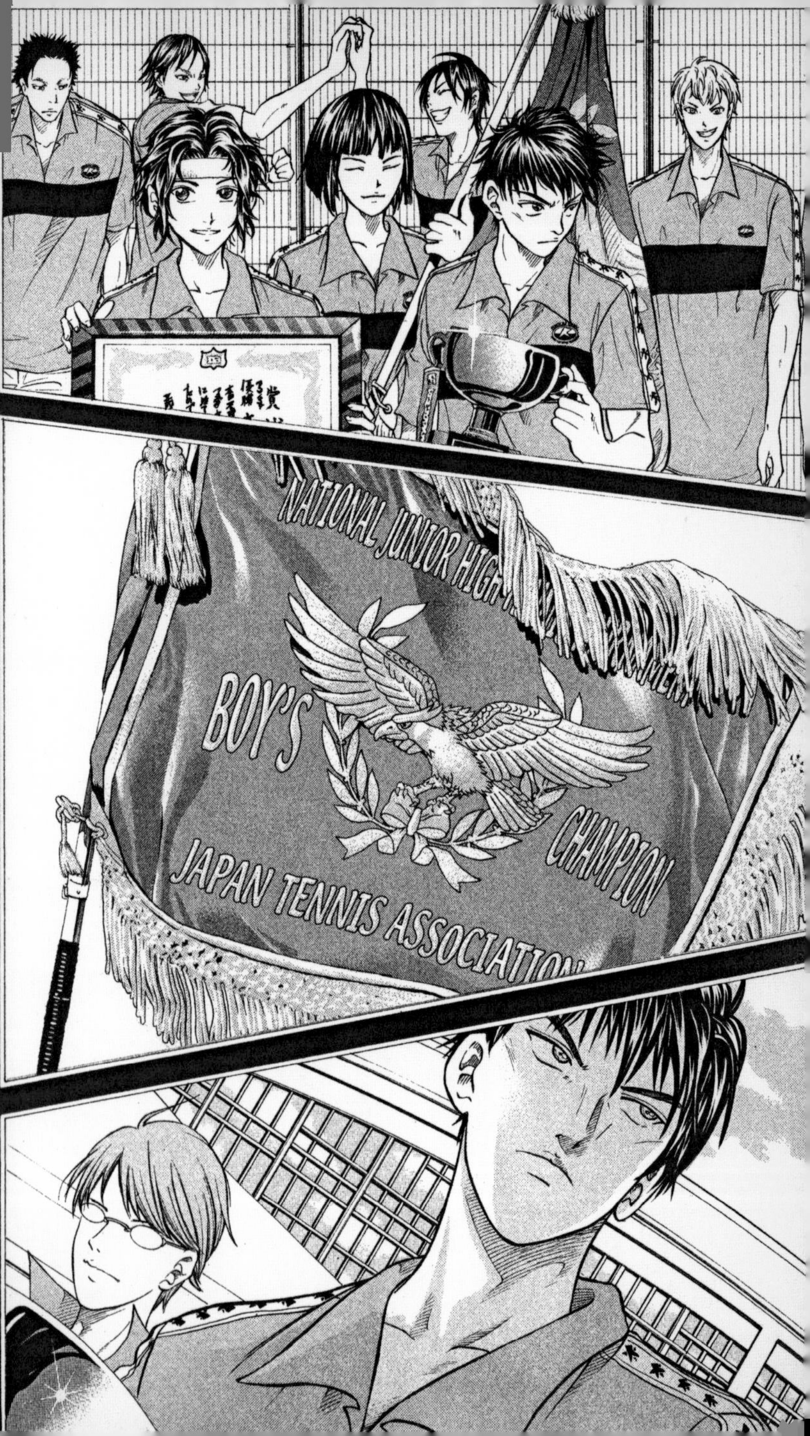
NATIONAL JUNIOR HIGH
BOY'S
CHAMPION
JAPAN TENNIS ASSOCIATION

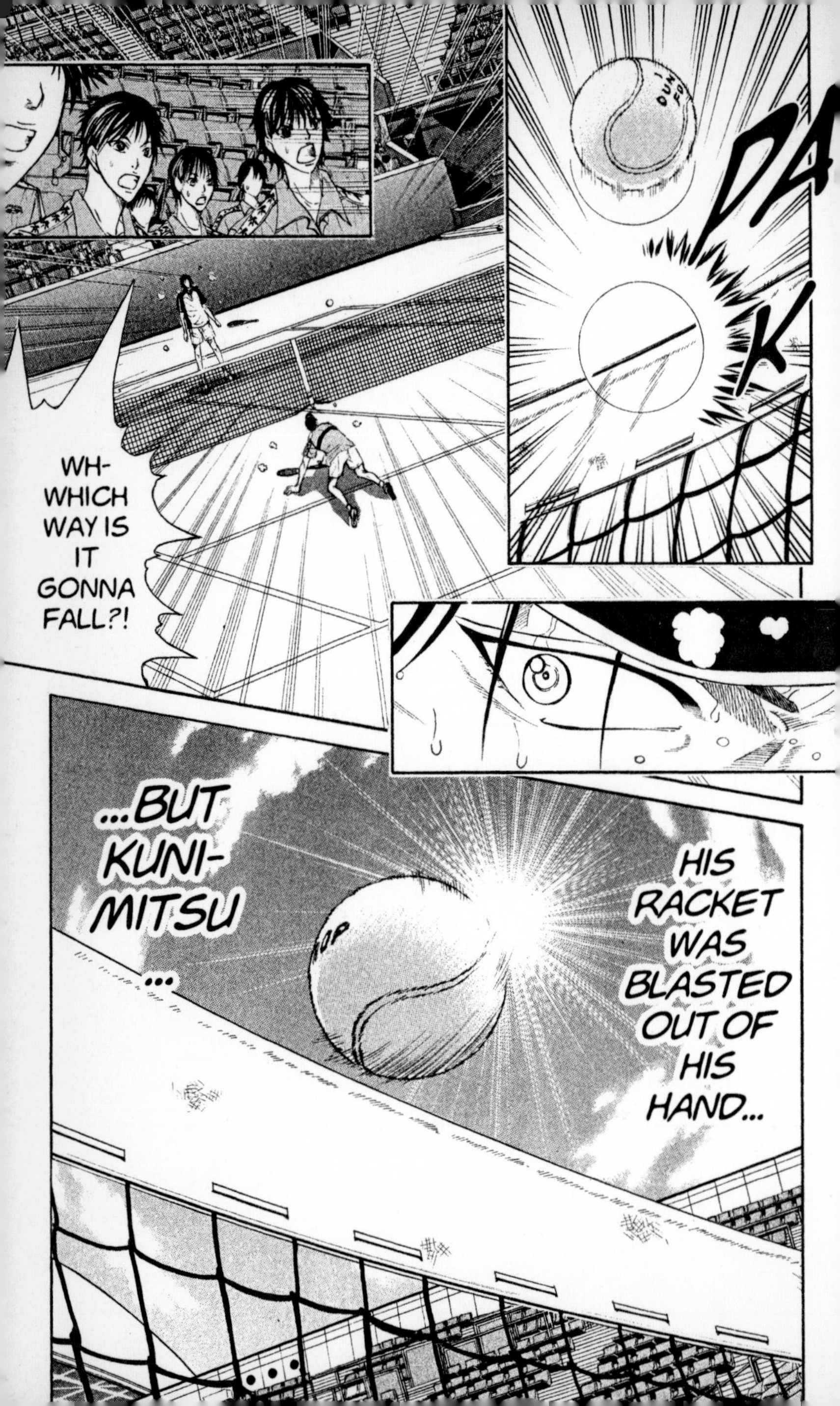
DAK
WH- WHICH WAY IS IT GONNA FALL?!
HIS RACKET WAS BLASTED OUT OF HIS HAND...
...BUT KUNI- MITSU ...

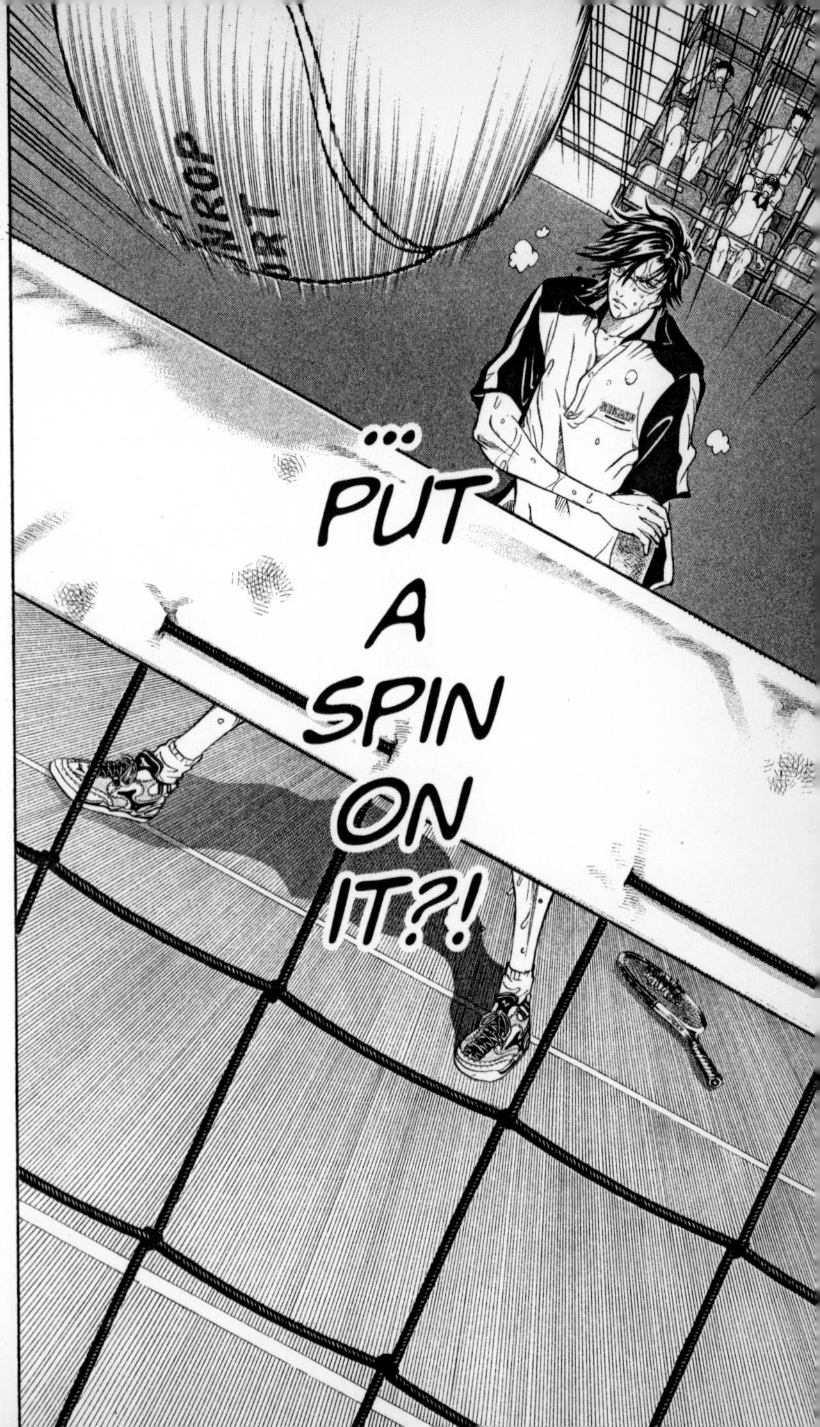
...PUT A SPIN ON IT?!

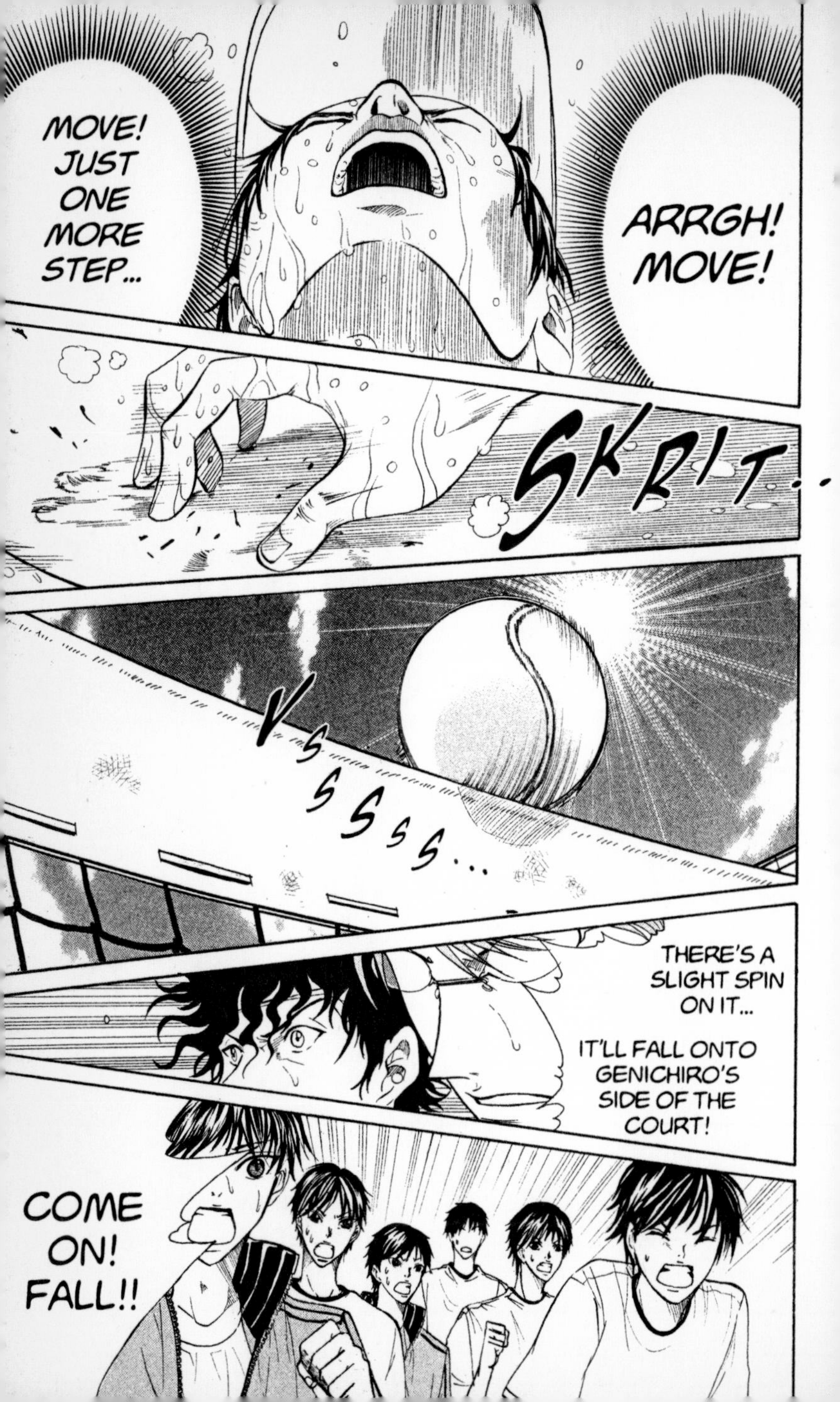
ARRGH! MOVE!
MOVE! JUST ONE MORE STEP...
SKRIT...
VSSSSS...
THERE'S A SLIGHT SPIN ON IT...
IT'LL FALL ONTO GENICHIRO'S SIDE OF THE COURT!
COME ON! FALL!!

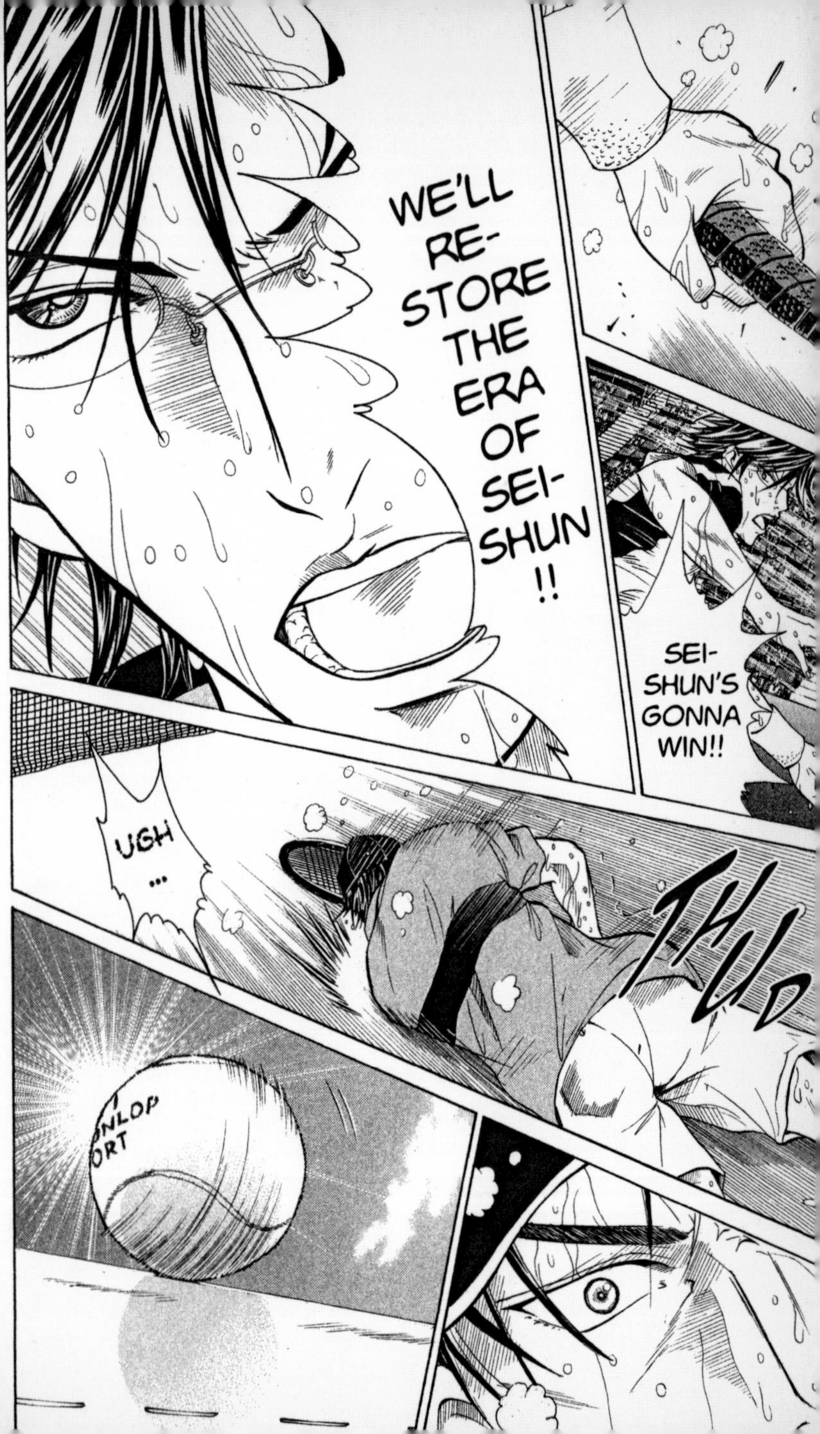
WE'LL RE-STORE THE ERA OF SEI-SHUN!!
SEI-SHUN'S GONNA WIN!!
UGH ...
THUD

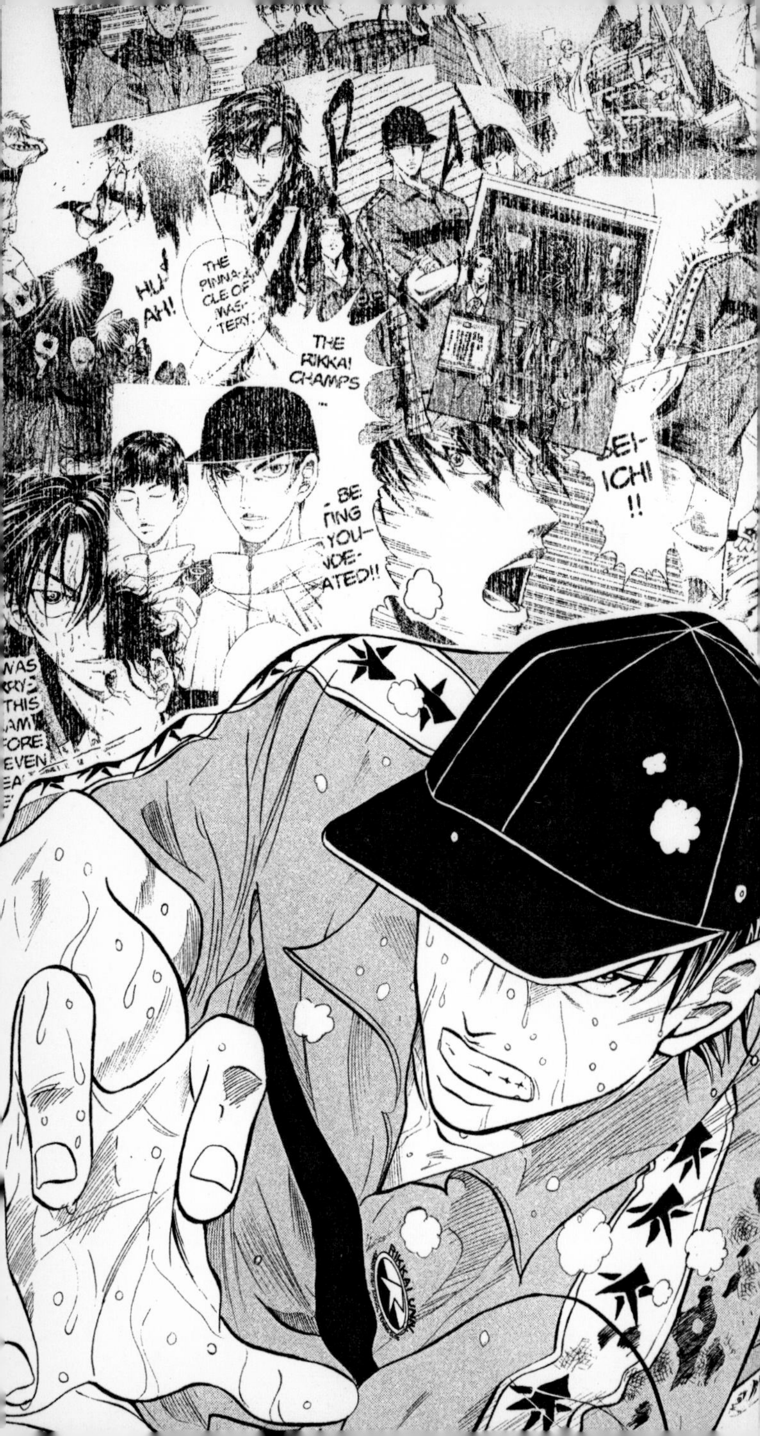
THE RIKKAI CHAMPS ...
THE PINNACLE OF MASTERY.
HU-AH!
SEI-ICHI!!
...BE-TING YOU-NDE-ATED!!
WAS RRY- THIS AM FORE EVEN EA

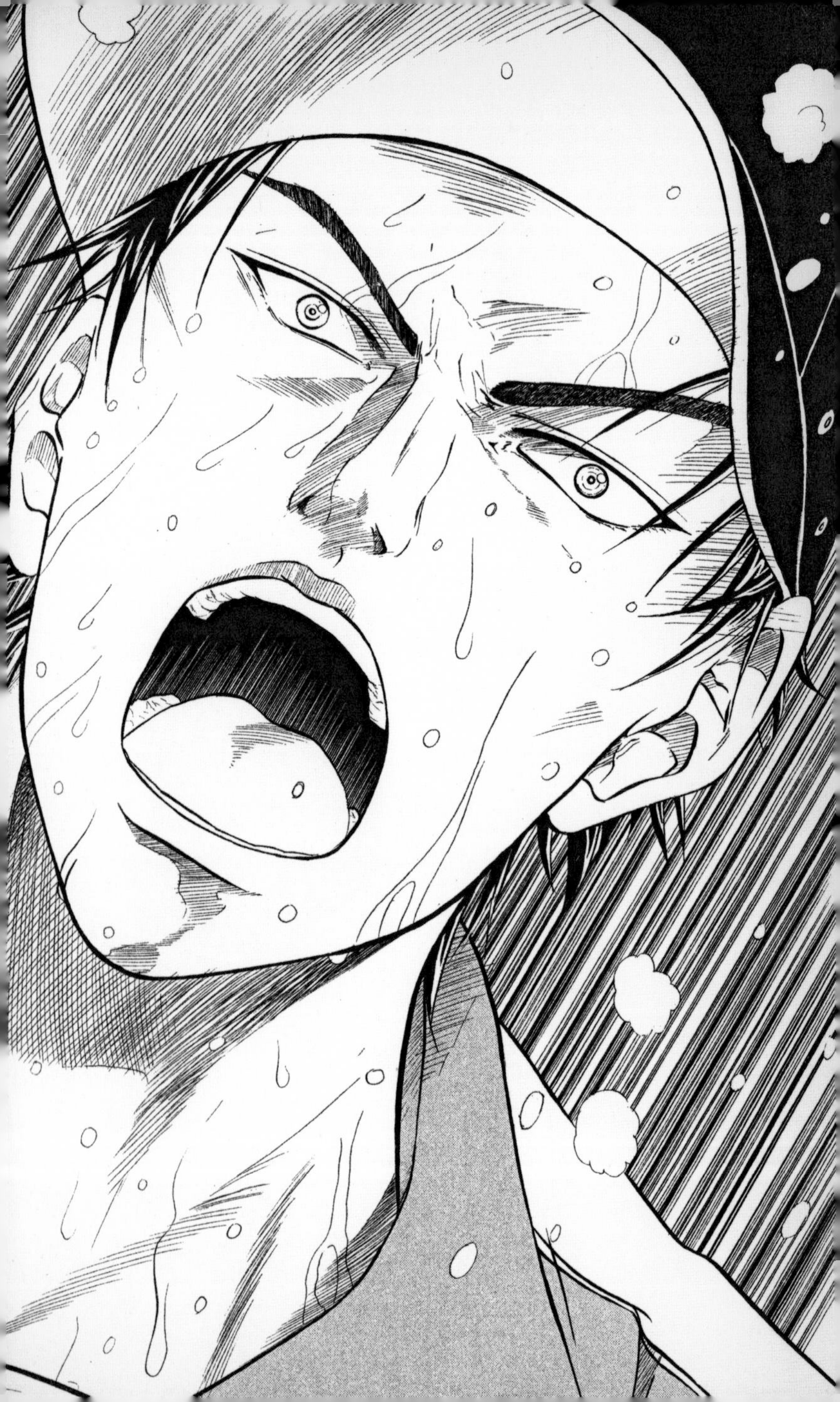

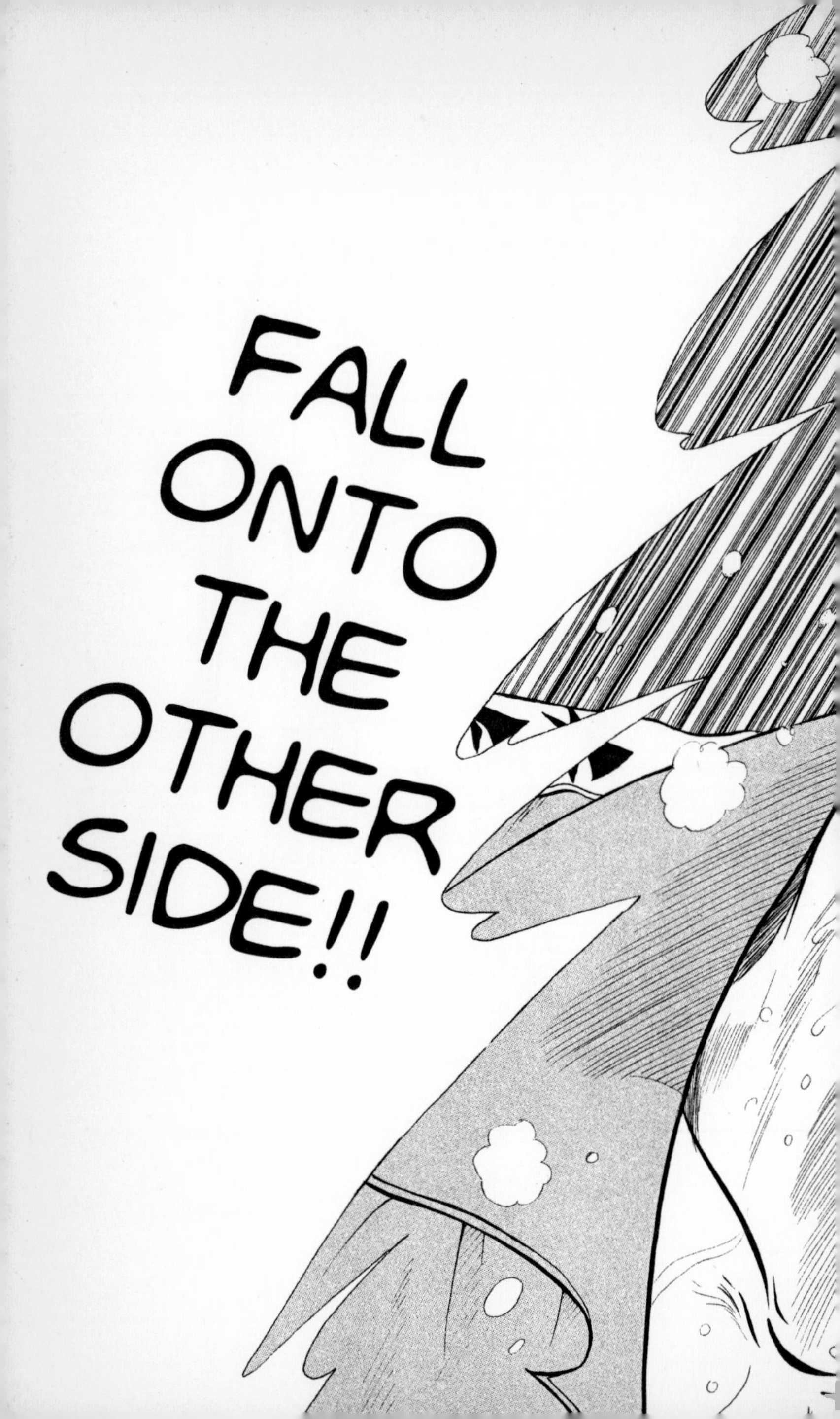
FALL ONTO THE OTHER SIDE!!

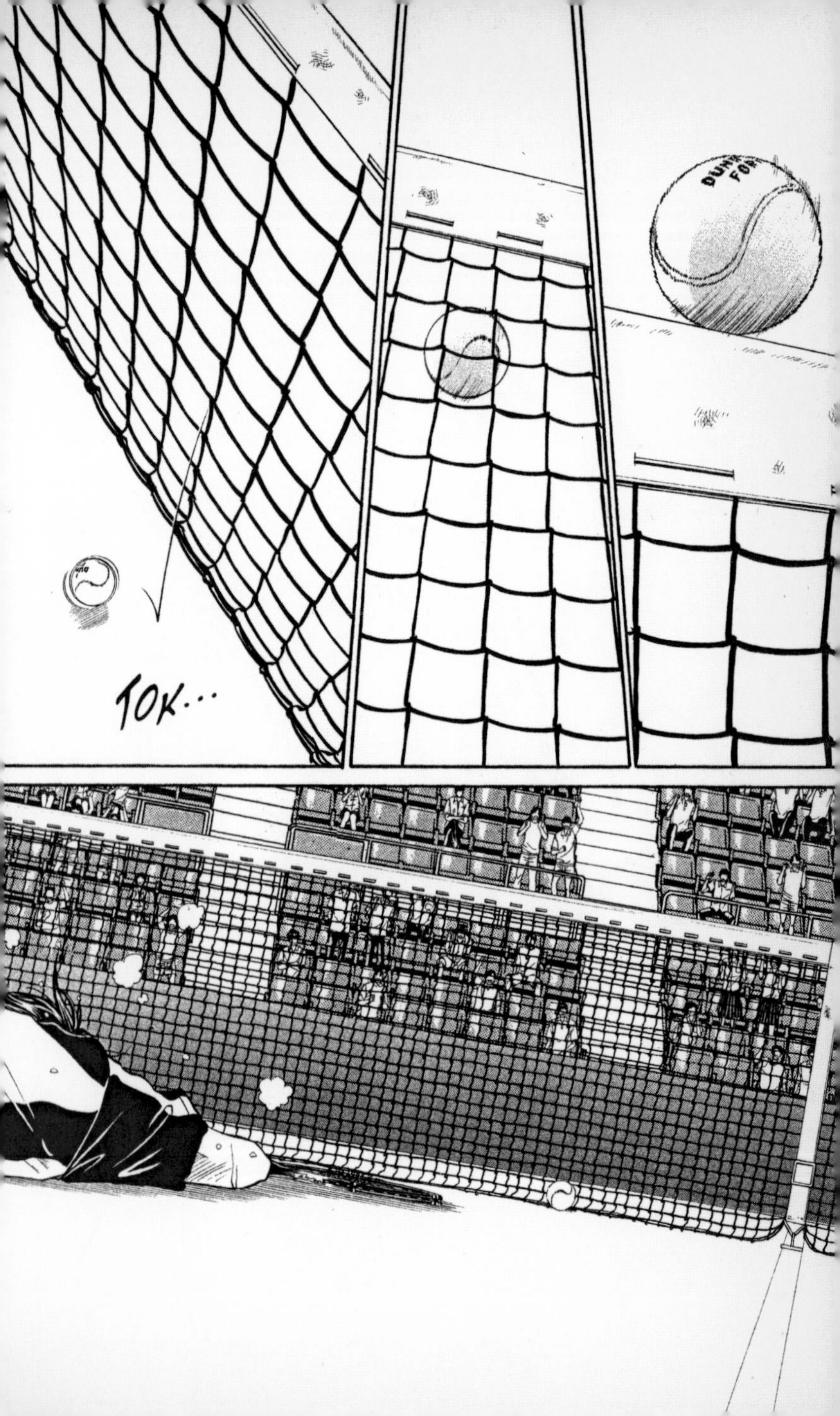
TOK...

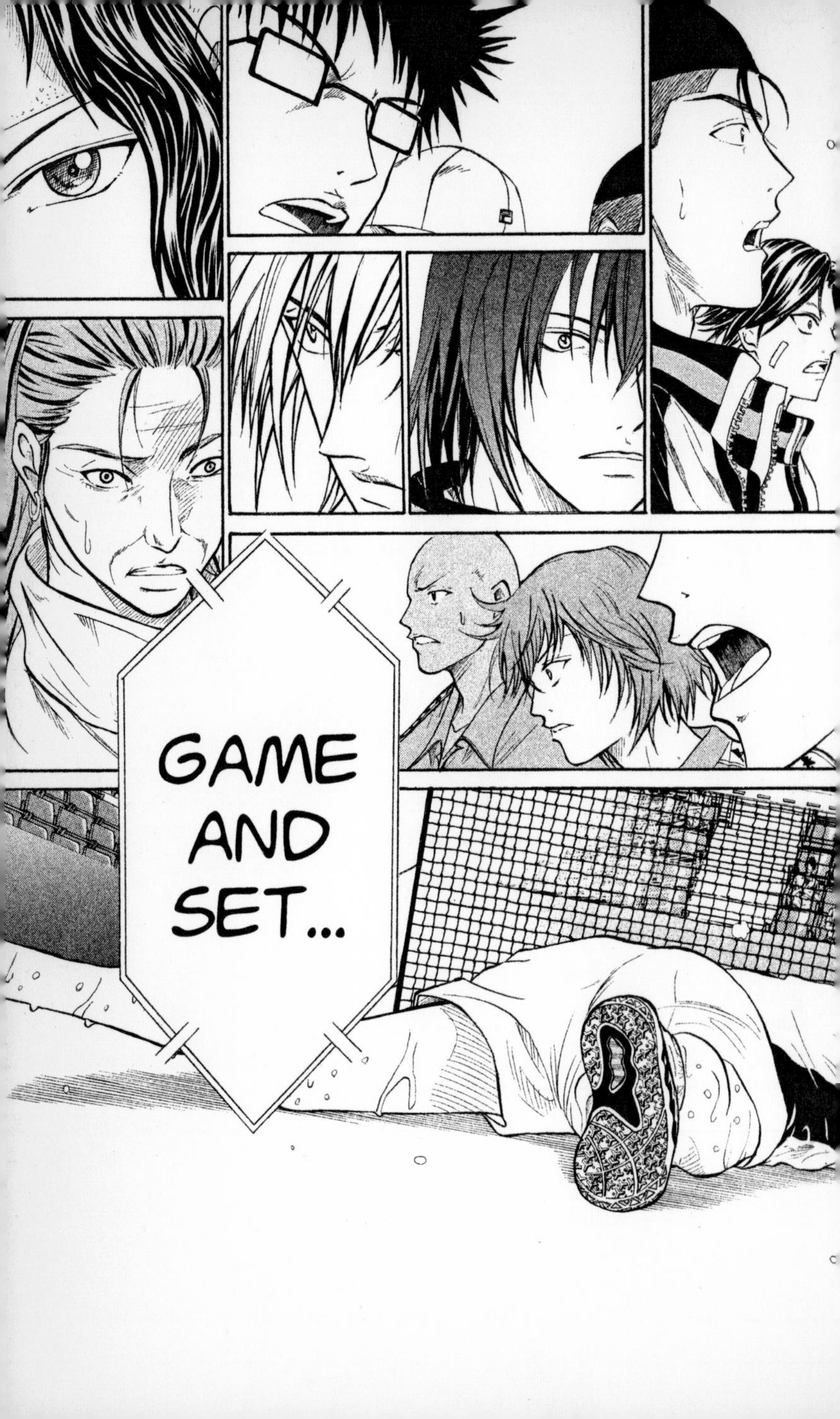
GAME AND SET...

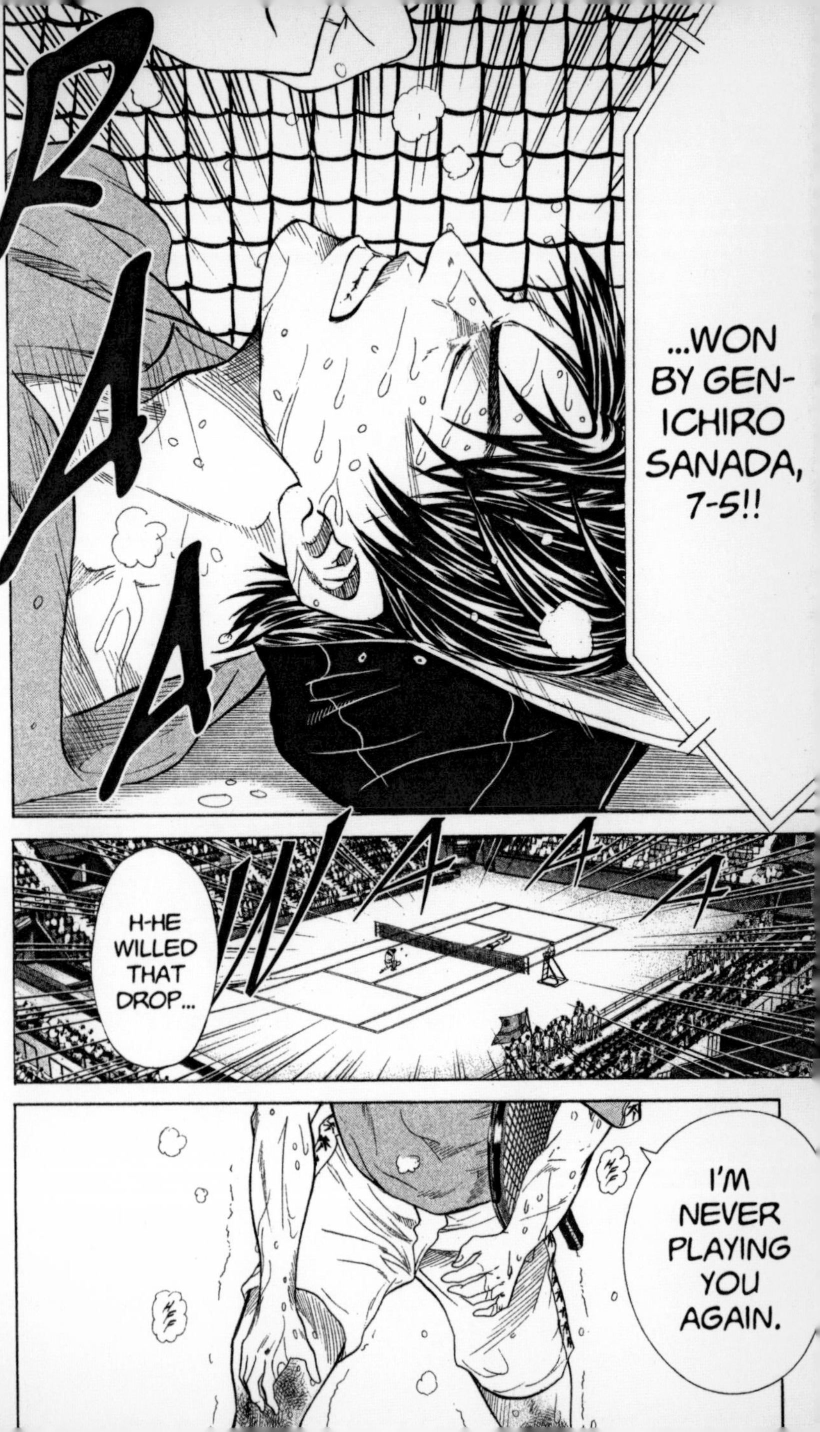

...WON BY GEN-ICHIRO SANADA, 7-5!!
WAAAA
H-HE WILLED THAT DROP...
I'M NEVER PLAYING YOU AGAIN.

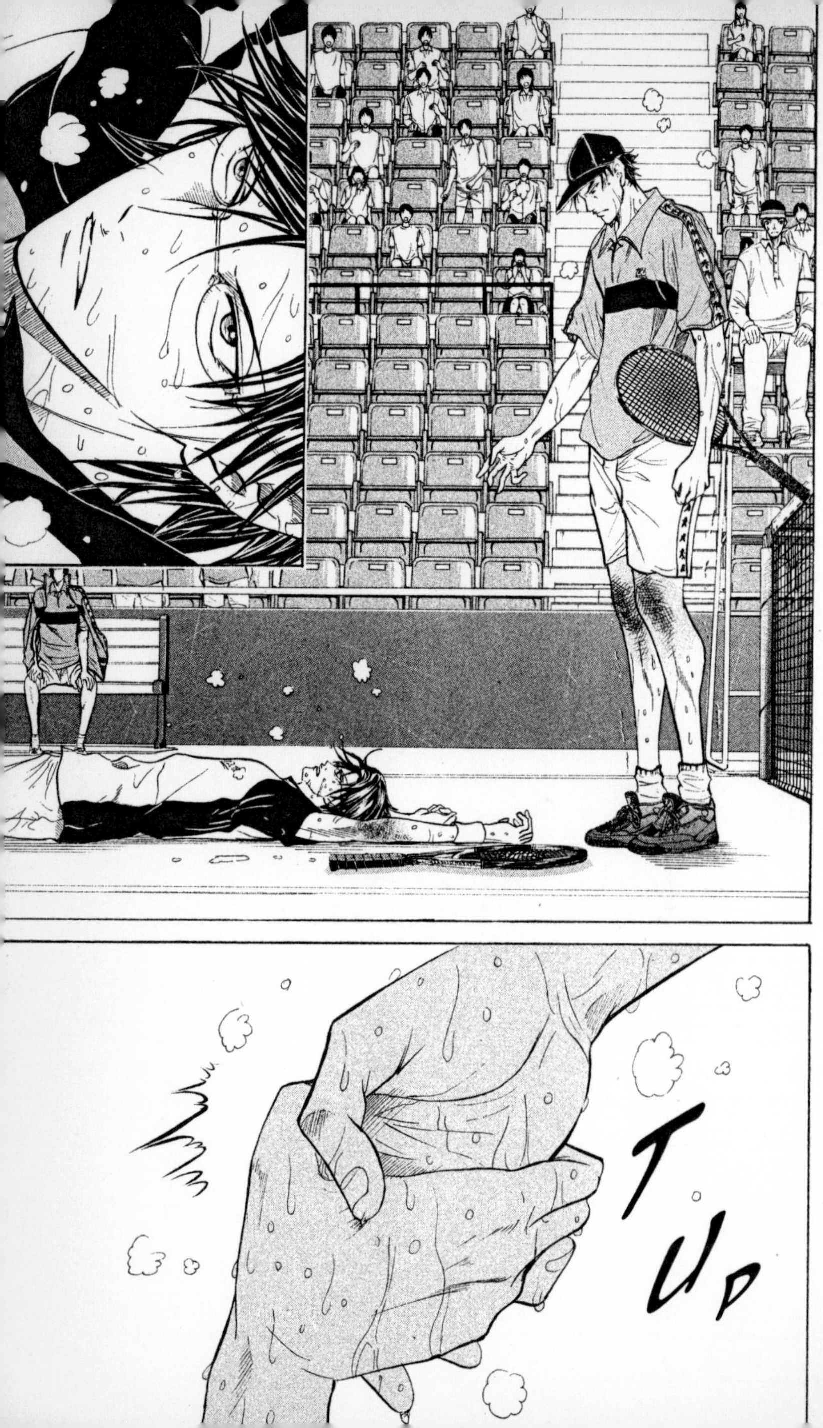
TUD

テニスの王子様

THE PRINCE OF TENNIS

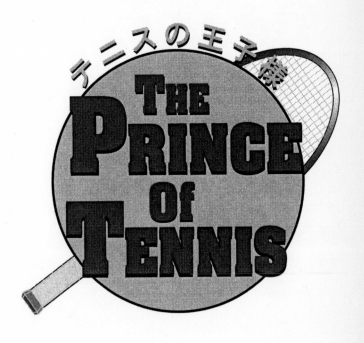

GENIUS 354: THE PRINCE WHO FORGOT TENNIS

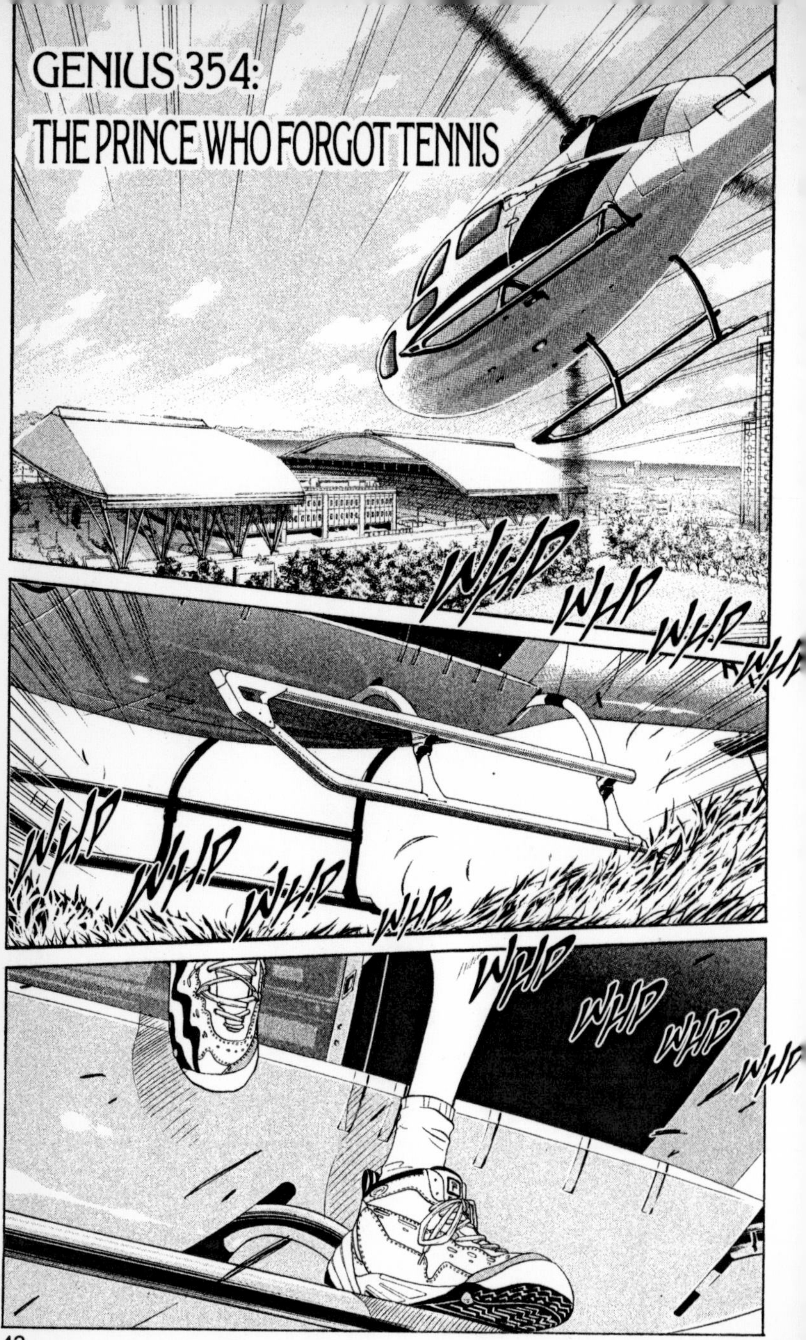
WHP
WHP
WHP
WHP
WHP
WHP
WHP
WHP
WHP
WHP
WHP
WHP

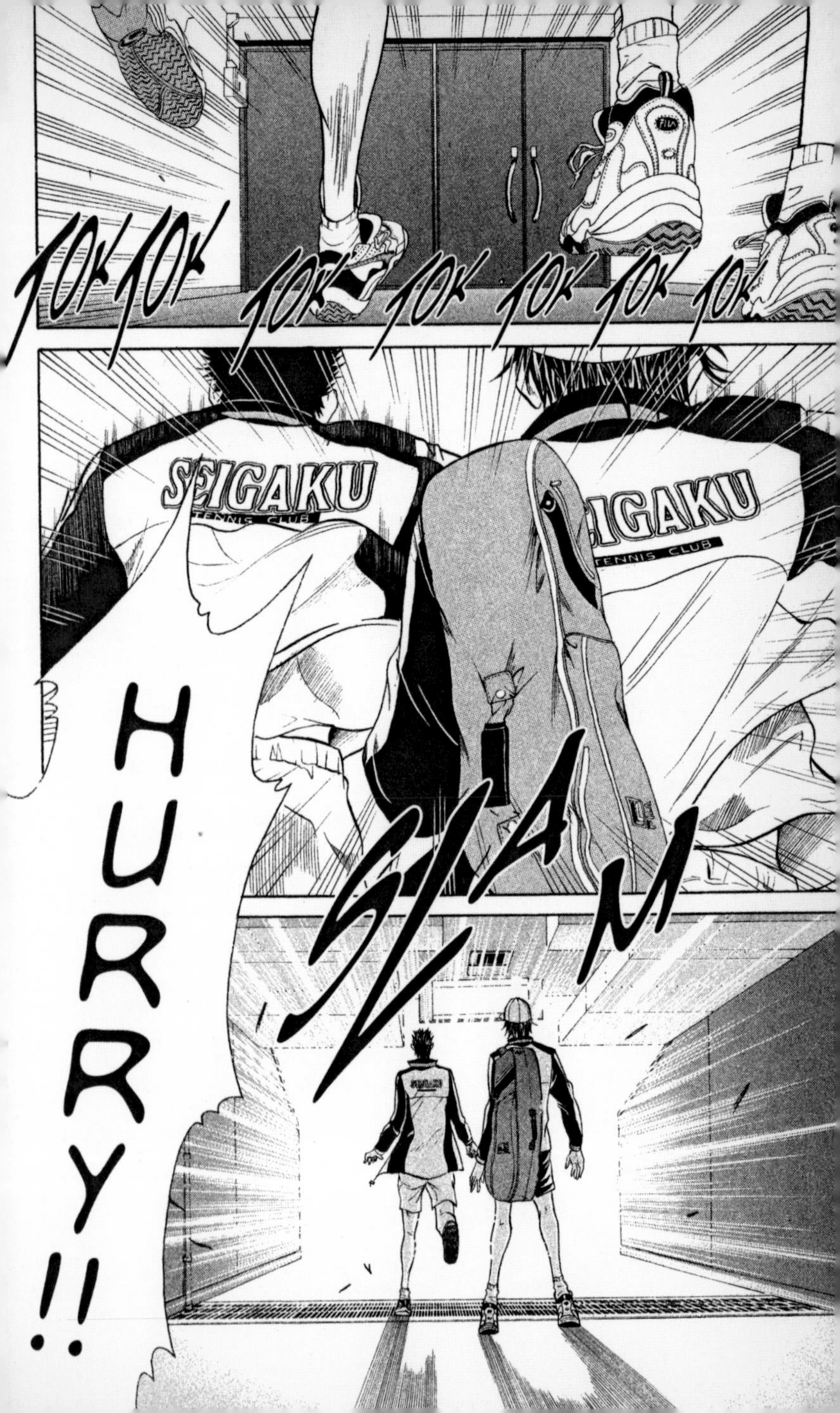
TOK TOK
TOK
TOK
TOK
TOK
TOK
SEIGAKU
TENNIS CLUB
HURRY!!
SLAM

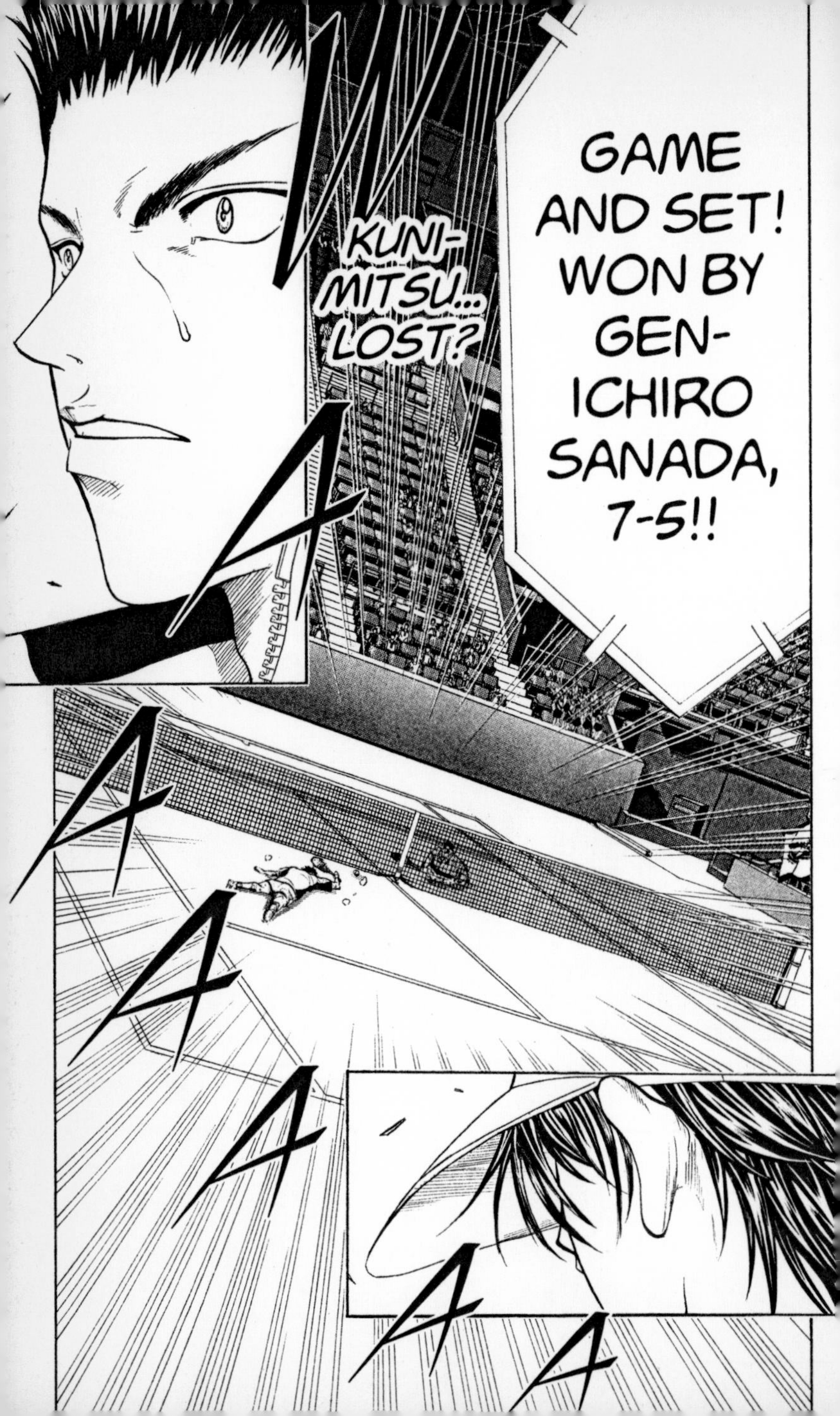
GAME AND SET! WON BY GEN-ICHIRO SANADA, 7-5!!
KUNI-MITSU... LOST?

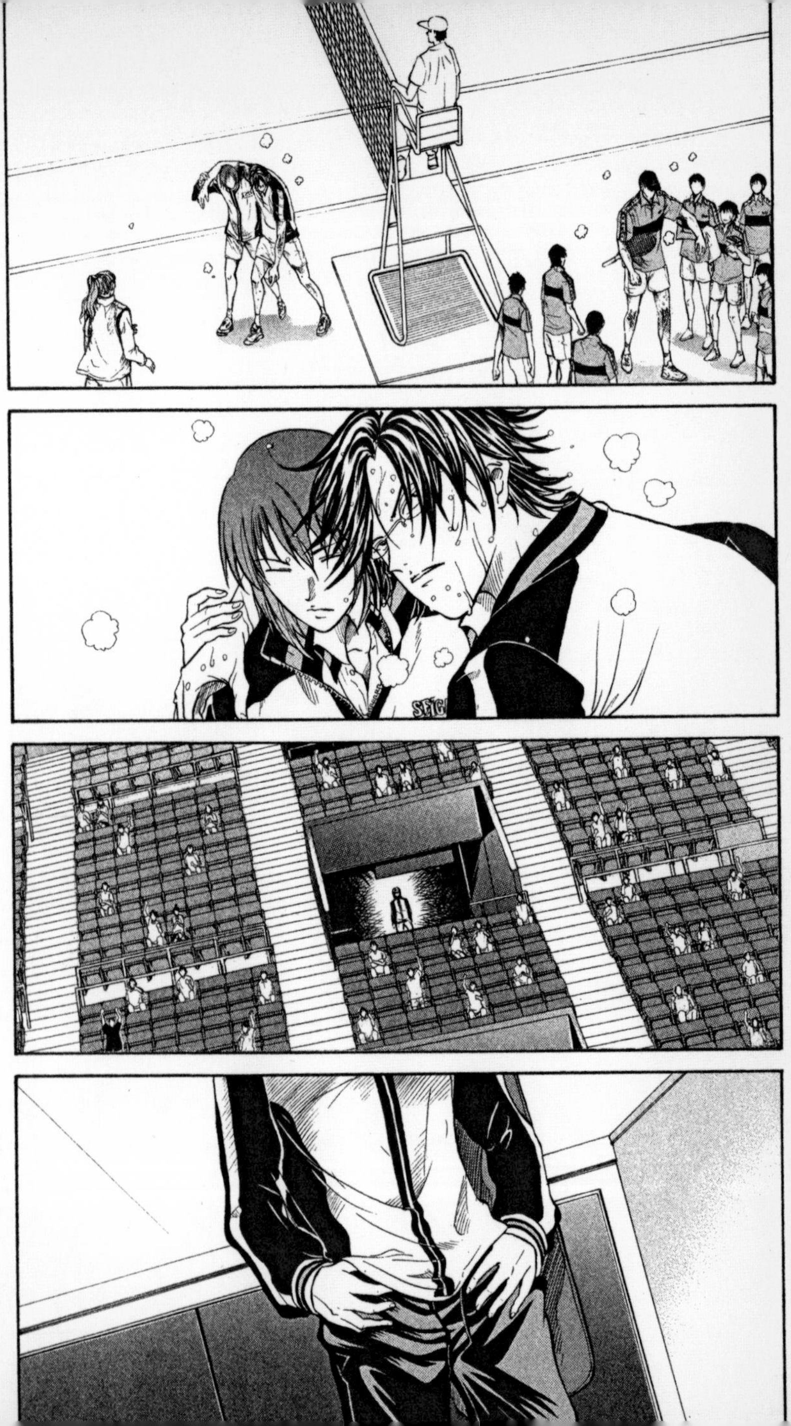

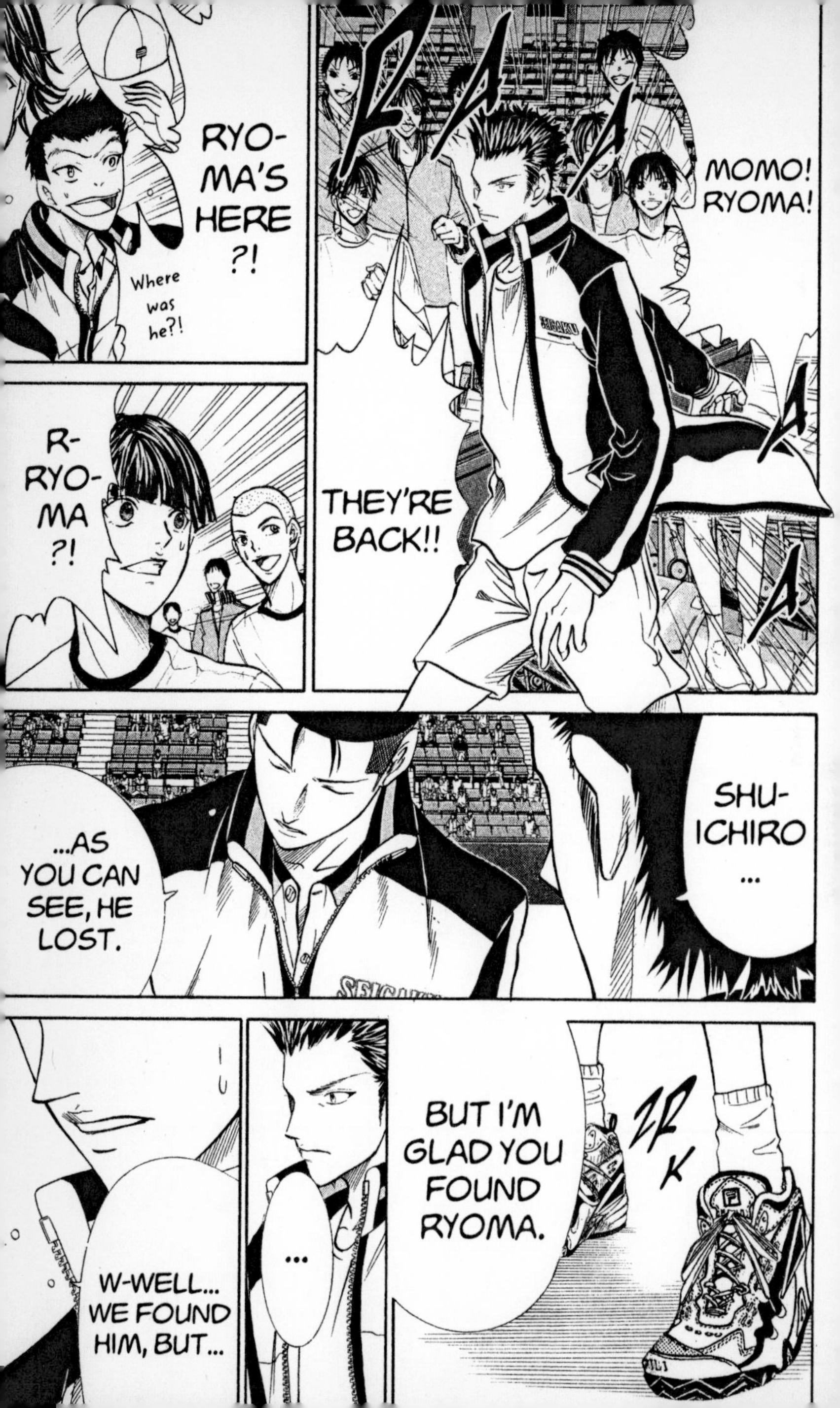
MOMO! RYOMA!
THEY'RE BACK!!
RYO-MA'S HERE?!
Where was he?!
R-RYO-MA?!
SHU-ICHIRO...
...AS YOU CAN SEE, HE LOST.
BUT I'M GLAD YOU FOUND RYOMA.
...
W-WELL... WE FOUND HIM, BUT...

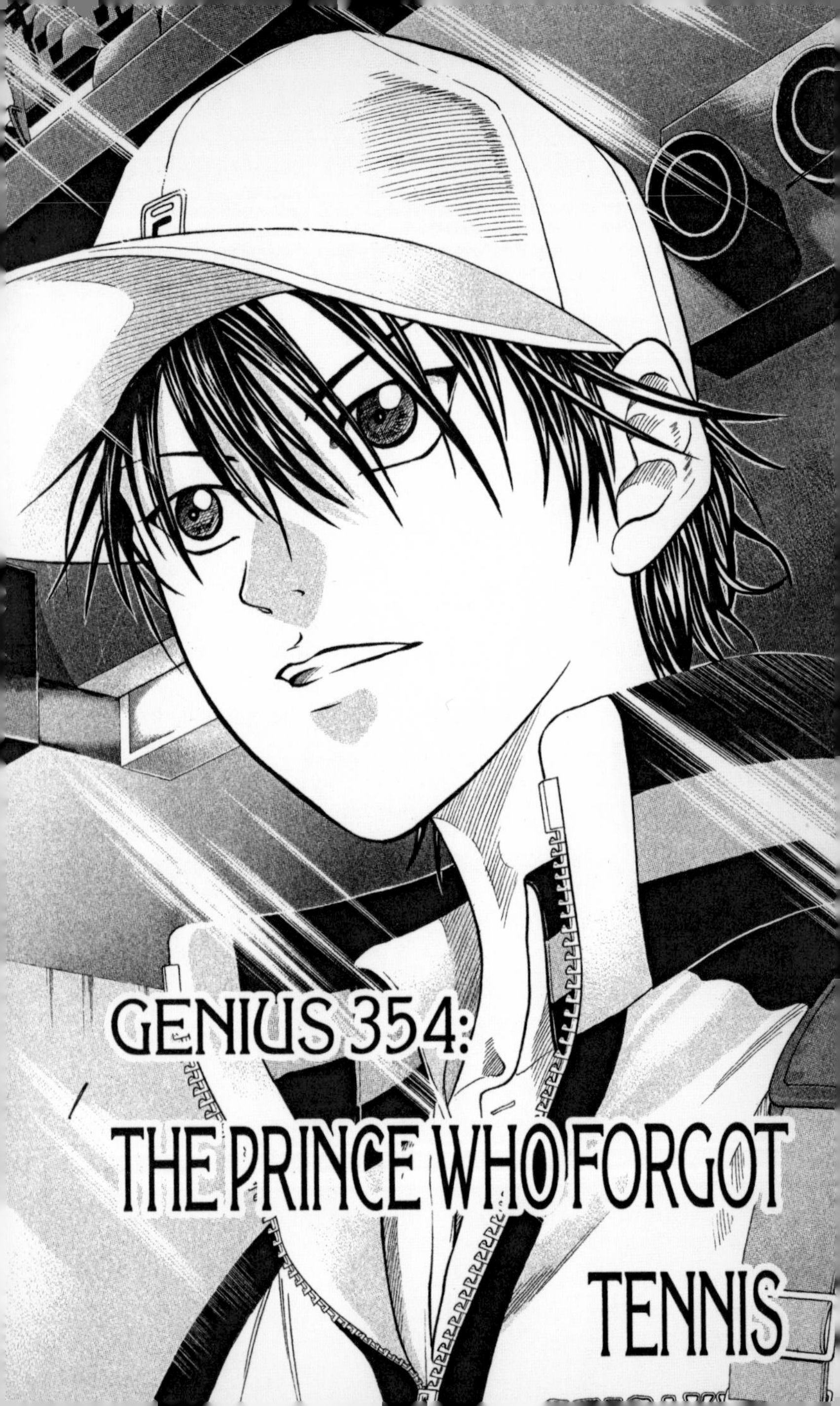
GENIUS 354:
THE PRINCE WHO FORGOT TENNIS

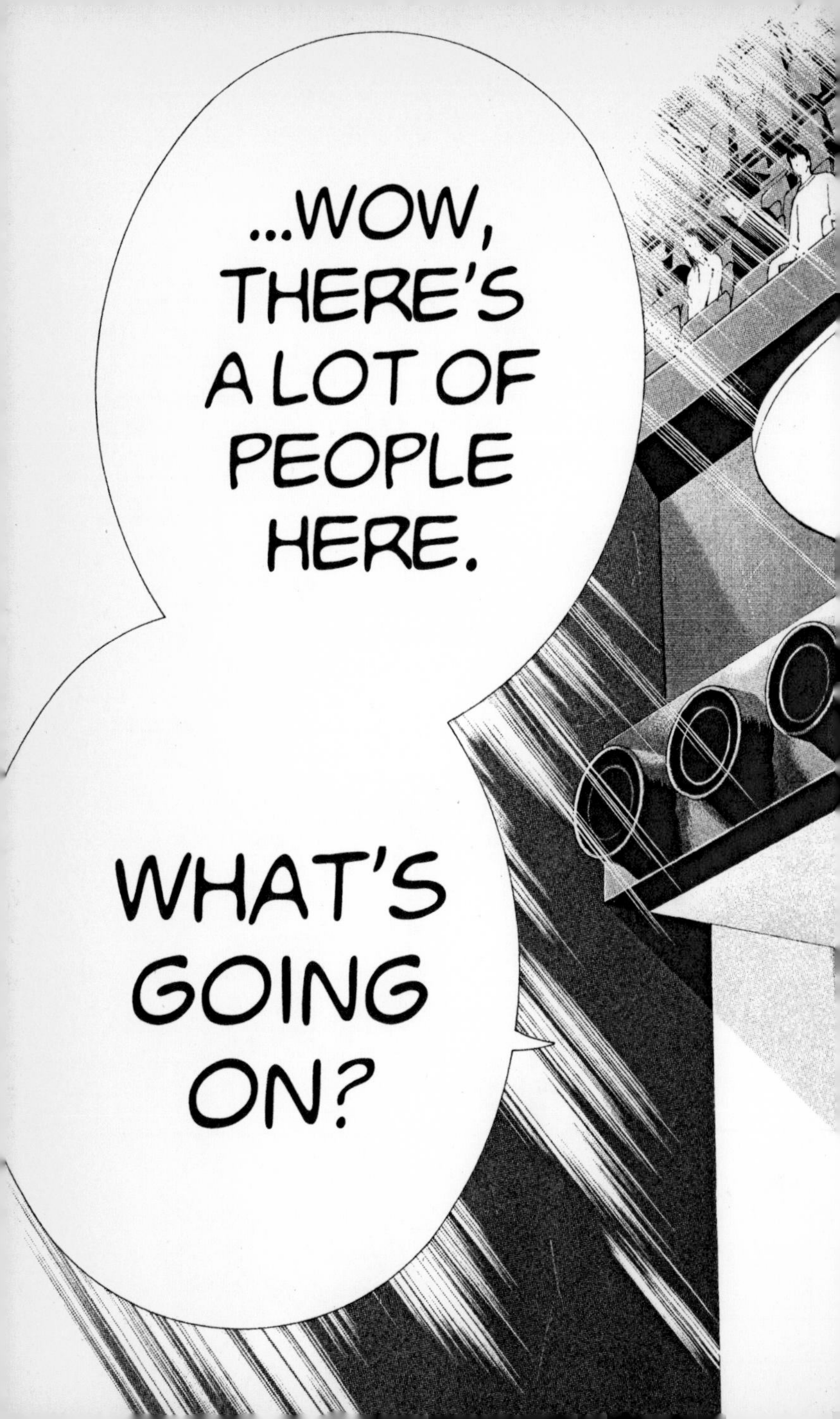
...WOW, THERE'S A LOT OF PEOPLE HERE.
WHAT'S GOING ON?

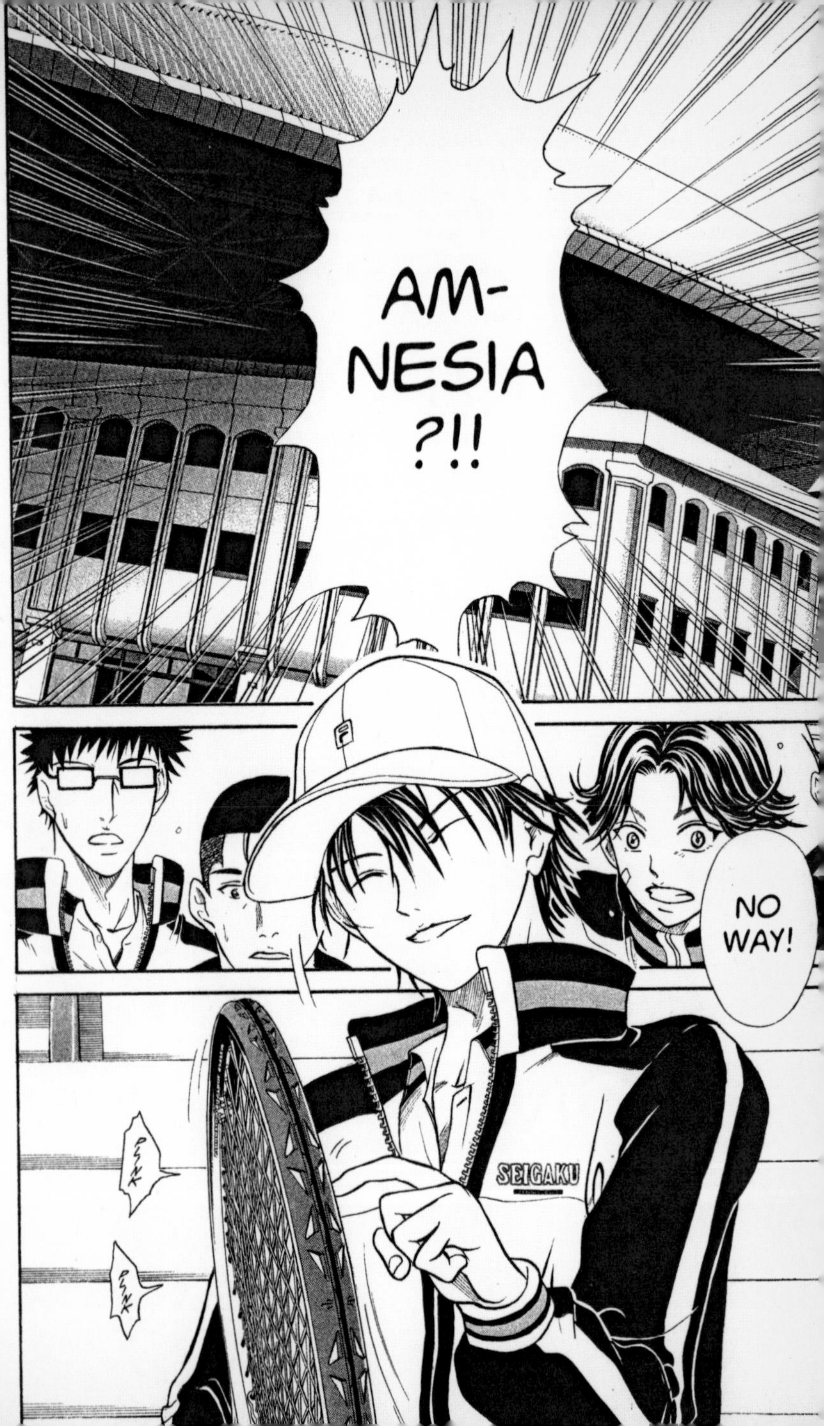
AM-NESIA ?!!
NO WAY!
PLINK
PLINK
SEIGAKU

READ THIS WAY

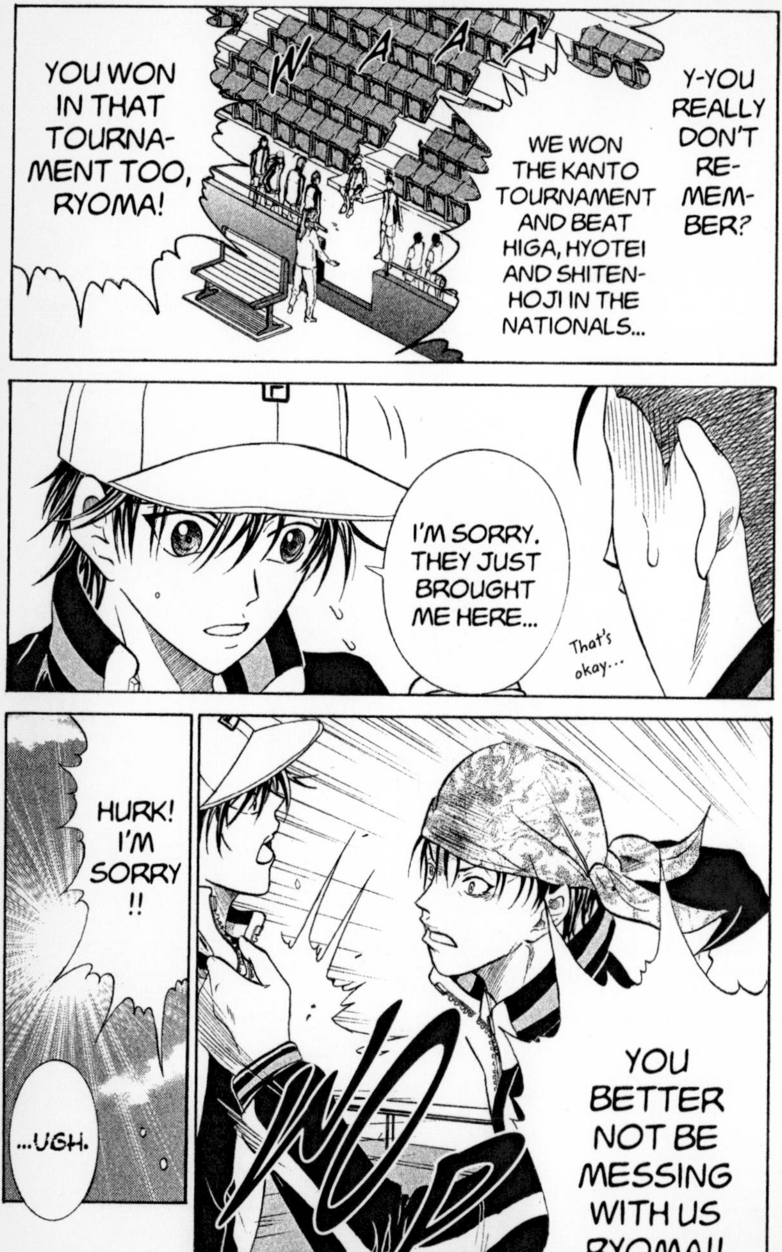
WAAA
Y-YOU REALLY DON'T RE-MEM-BER?
WE WON THE KANTO TOURNAMENT AND BEAT HIGA, HYOTEI AND SHITEN-HOJI IN THE NATIONALS...
YOU WON IN THAT TOURNA-MENT TOO, RYOMA!
I'M SORRY. THEY JUST BROUGHT ME HERE...
That's okay...
YOU BETTER NOT BE MESSING WITH US RYOMA!!
HURK! I'M SORRY !!
...UGH.

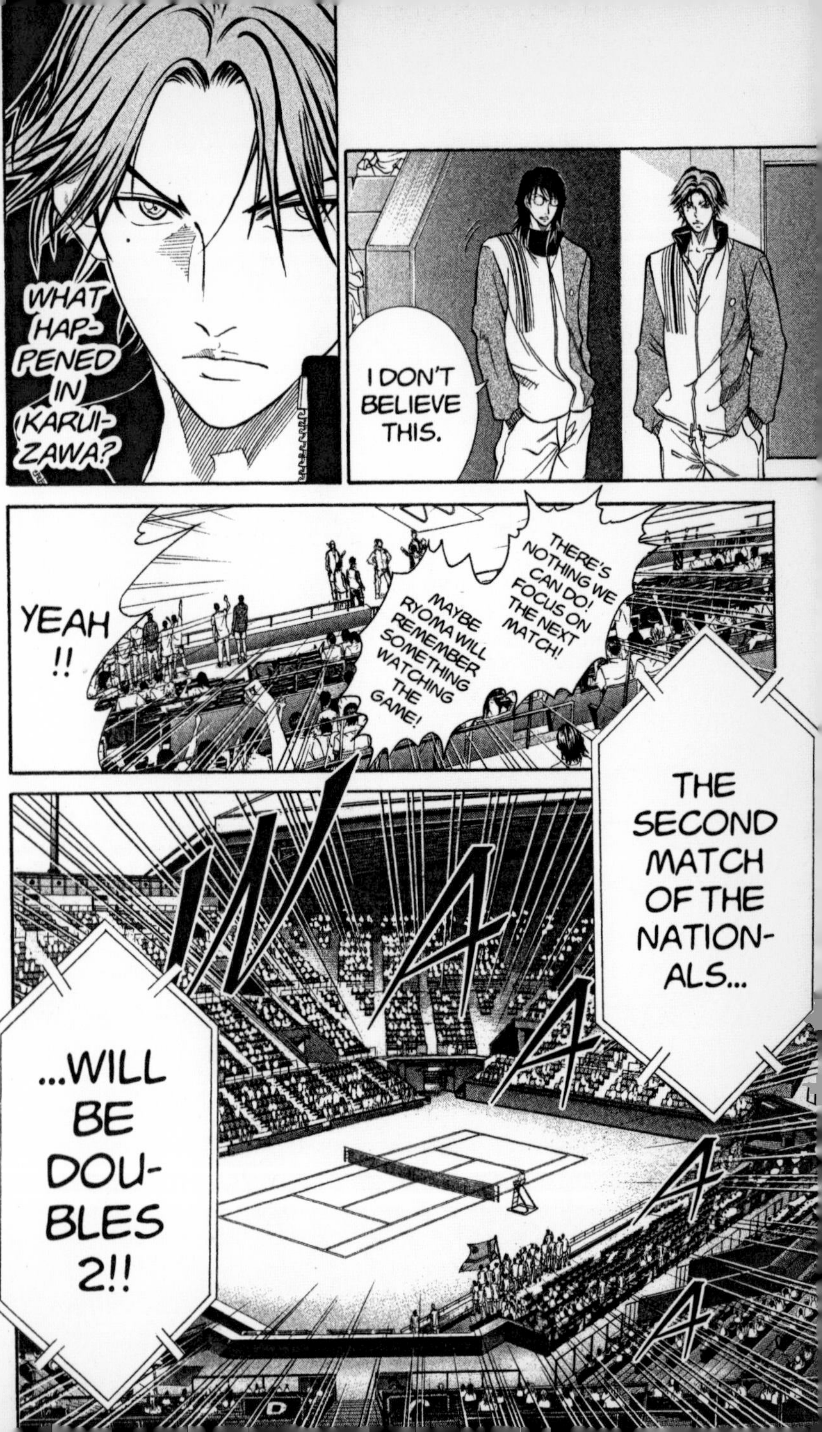
I DON'T BELIEVE THIS.
WHAT HAPPENED IN KARUIZAWA?
THERE'S NOTHING WE CAN DO! FOCUS ON THE NEXT MATCH!
MAYBE RYOMA WILL REMEMBER SOMETHING WATCHING THE GAME!
YEAH !!
THE SECOND MATCH OF THE NATIONALS...
WAAAA
...WILL BE DOUBLES 2!!

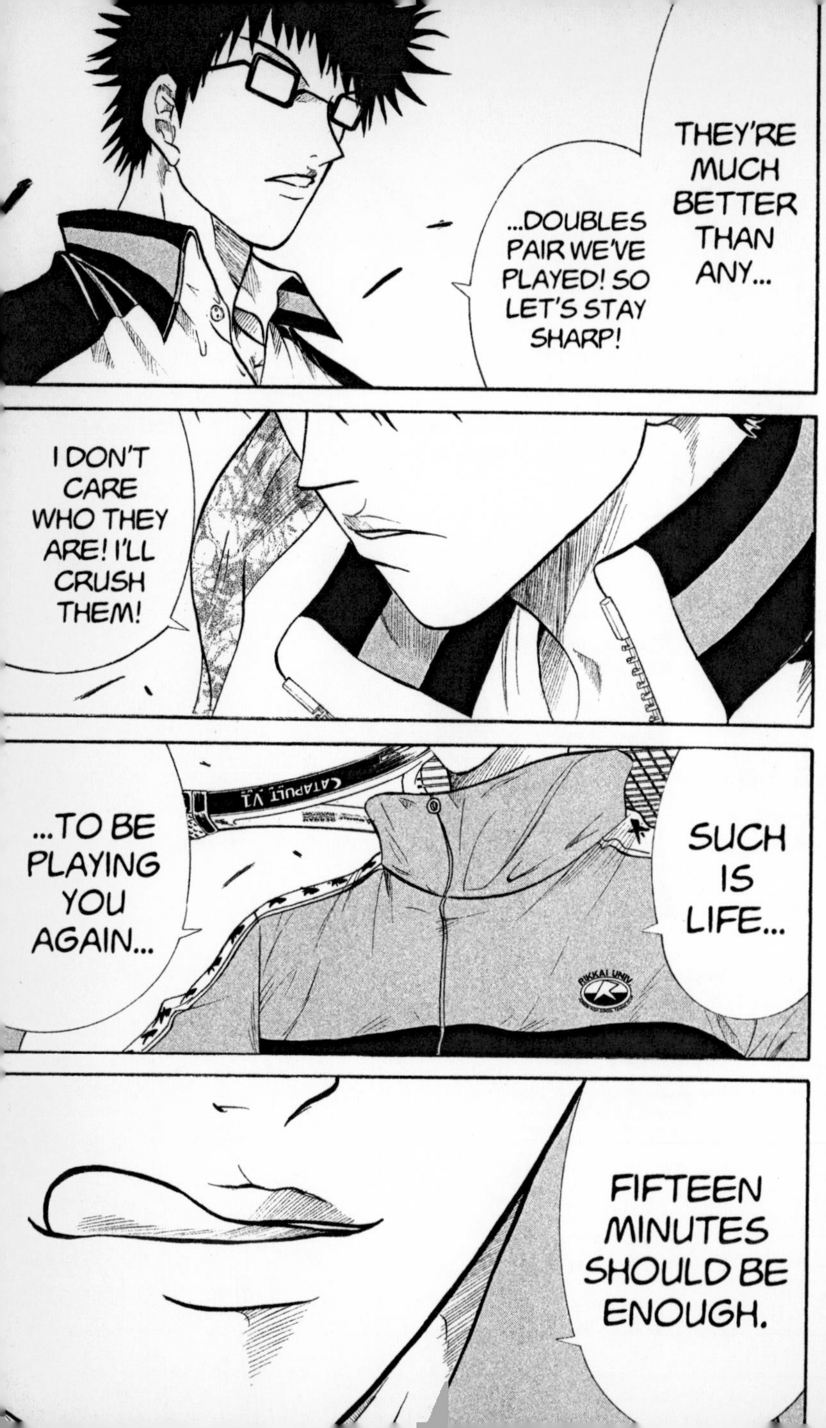
THEY'RE MUCH BETTER THAN ANY...
...DOUBLES PAIR WE'VE PLAYED! SO LET'S STAY SHARP!
I DON'T CARE WHO THEY ARE! I'LL CRUSH THEM!
SUCH IS LIFE...
...TO BE PLAYING YOU AGAIN...
RIKKAI UNIV
FIFTEEN MINUTES SHOULD BE ENOUGH.

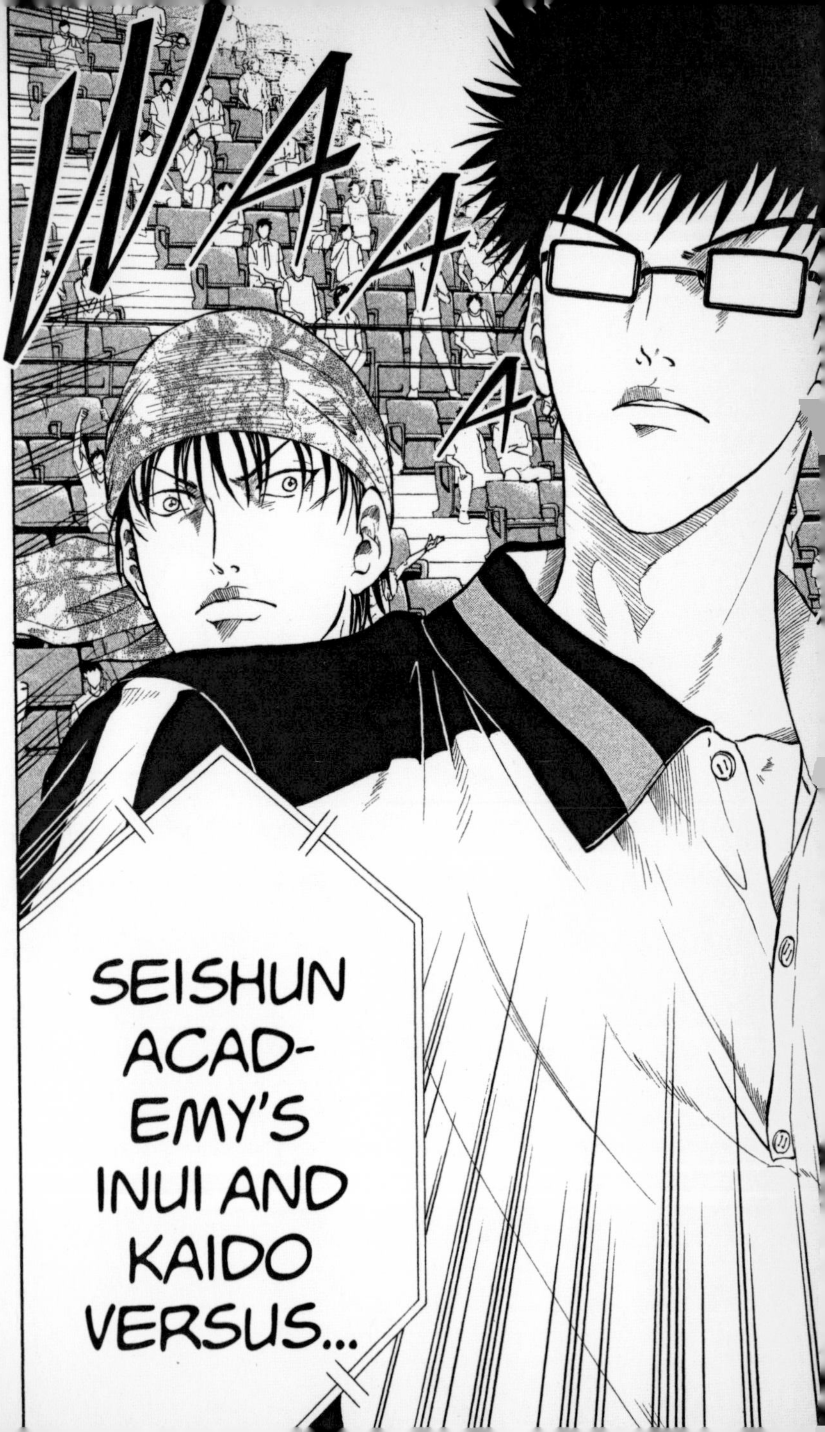
WAAAA
SEISHUN ACAD-EMY'S INUI AND KAIDO VERSUS...

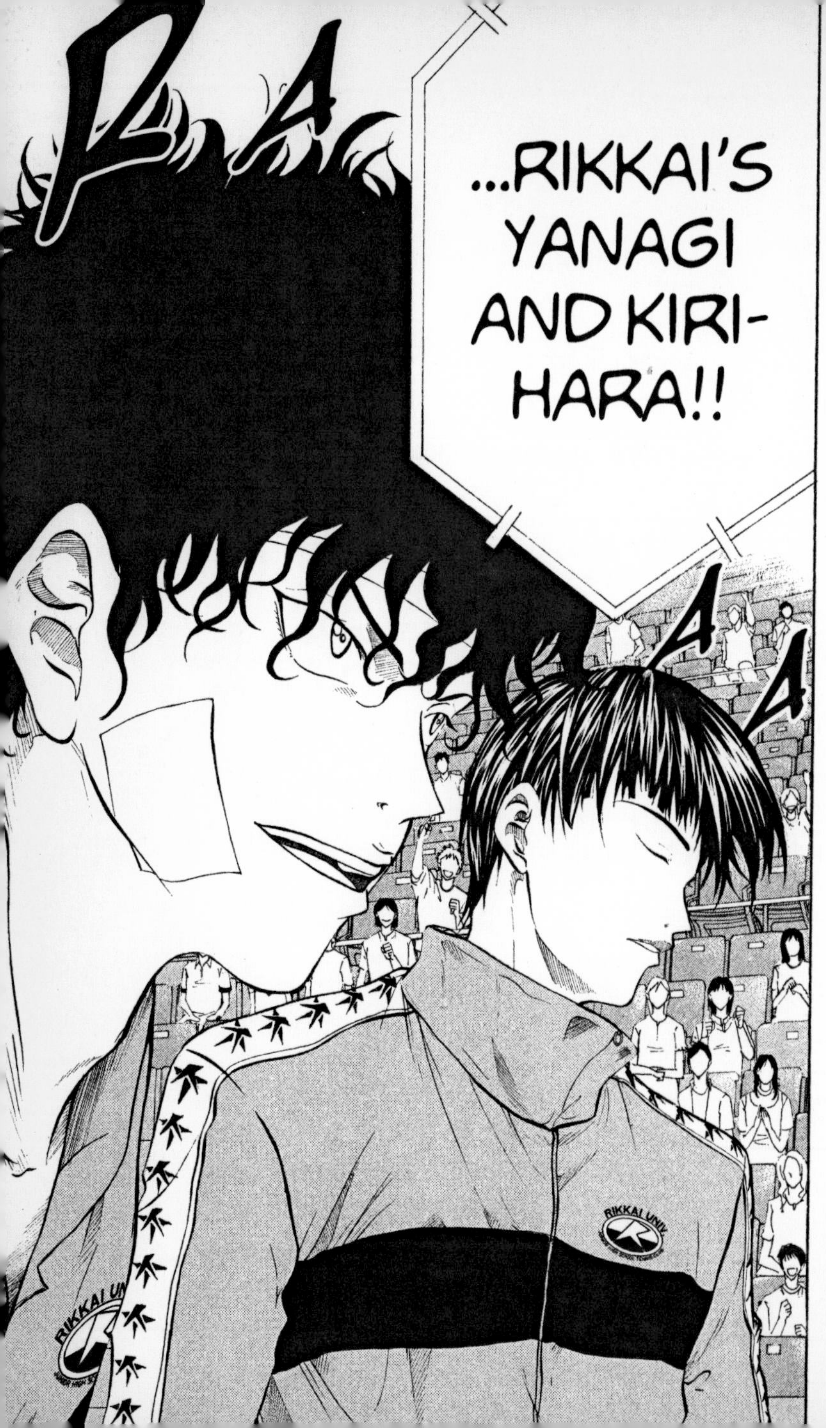
...RIKKAI'S YANAGI AND KIRI-HARA!!
RIKKAI UNIV

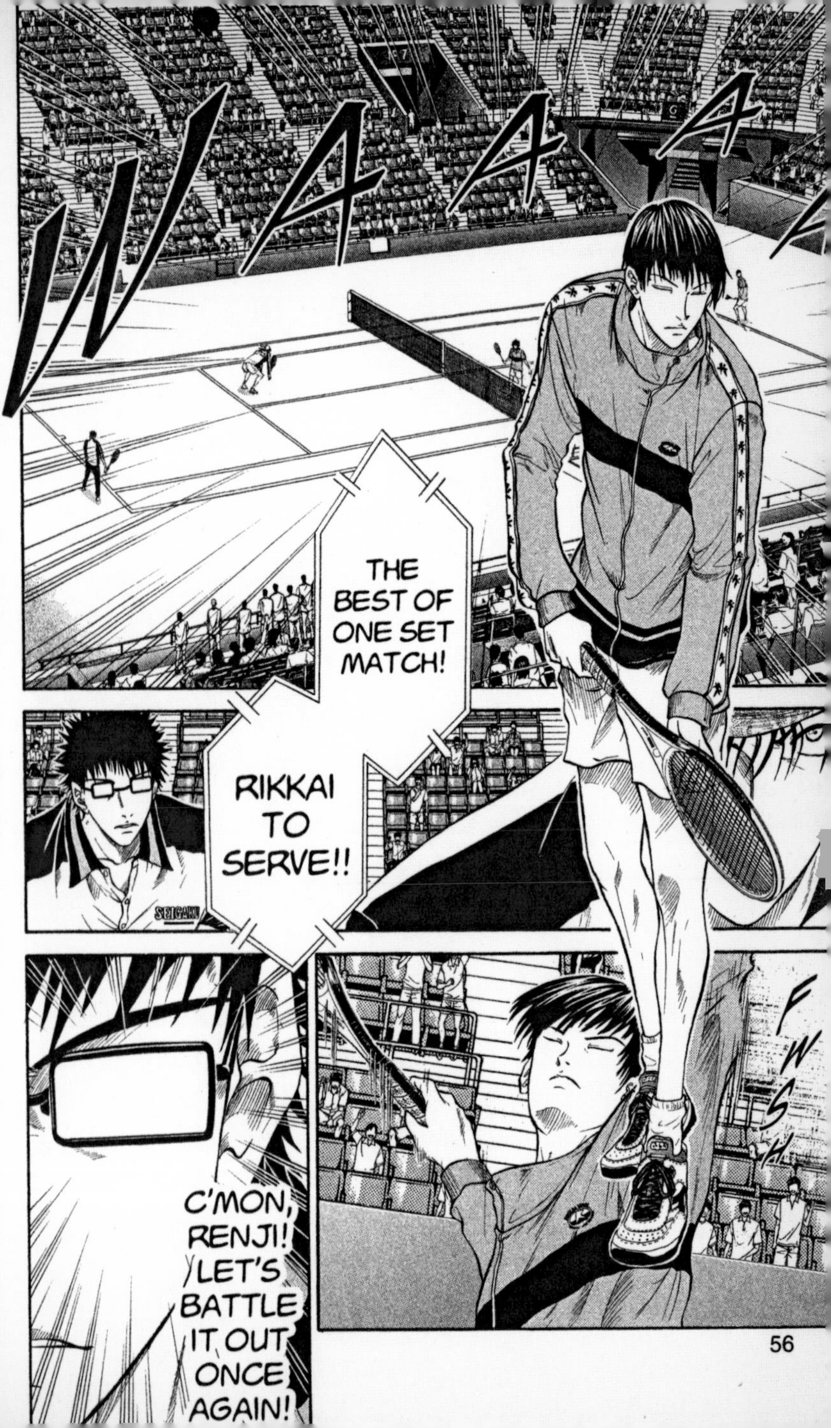
WAAAA
THE BEST OF ONE SET MATCH!
RIKKAI TO SERVE!!
SEIGAKU
FWSH
C'MON, RENJI! LET'S BATTLE IT OUT ONCE AGAIN!

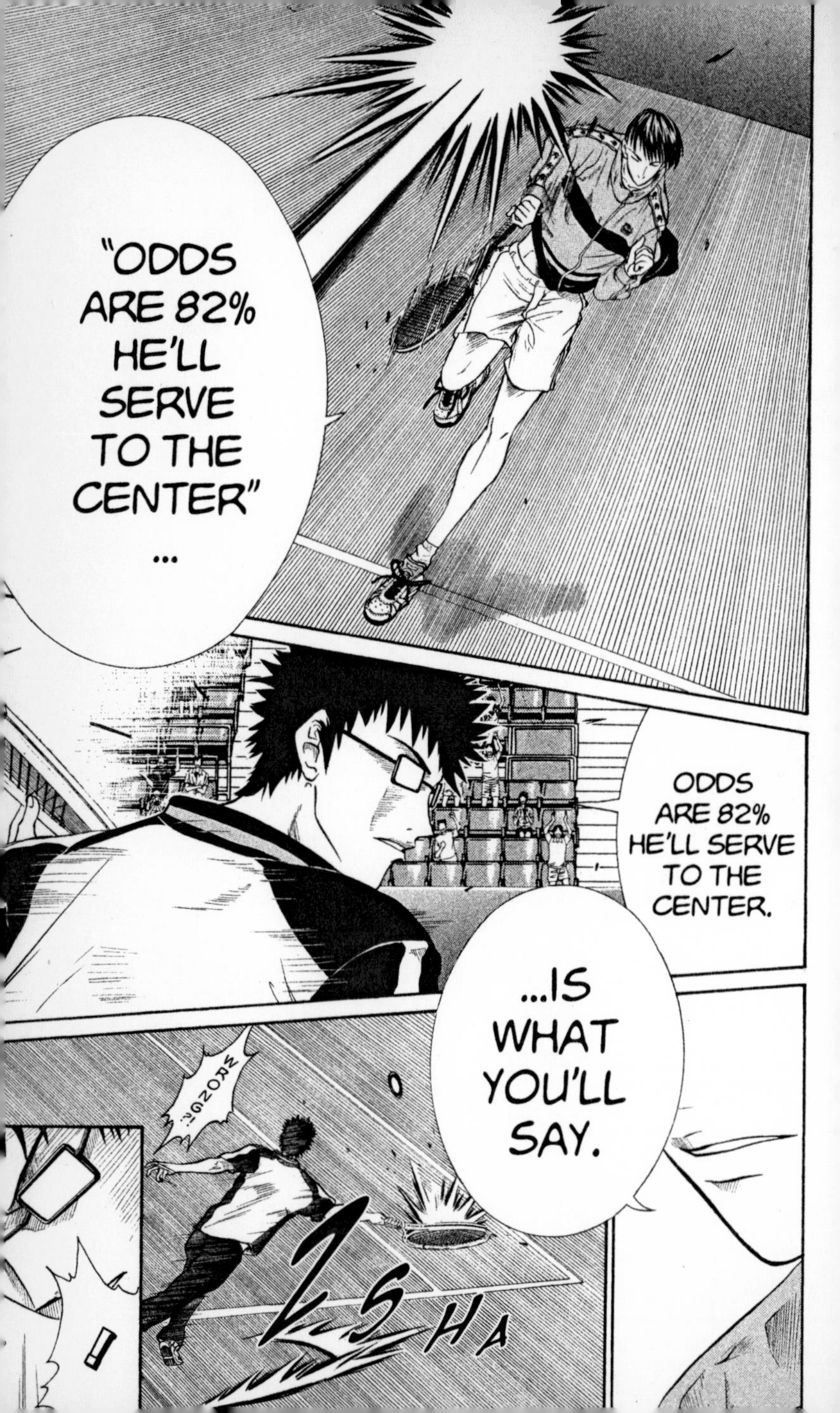
"ODDS ARE 82% HE'LL SERVE TO THE CENTER" ...
ODDS ARE 82% HE'LL SERVE TO THE CENTER.
...IS WHAT YOU'LL SAY.
WRONG?!
!
ZSHA

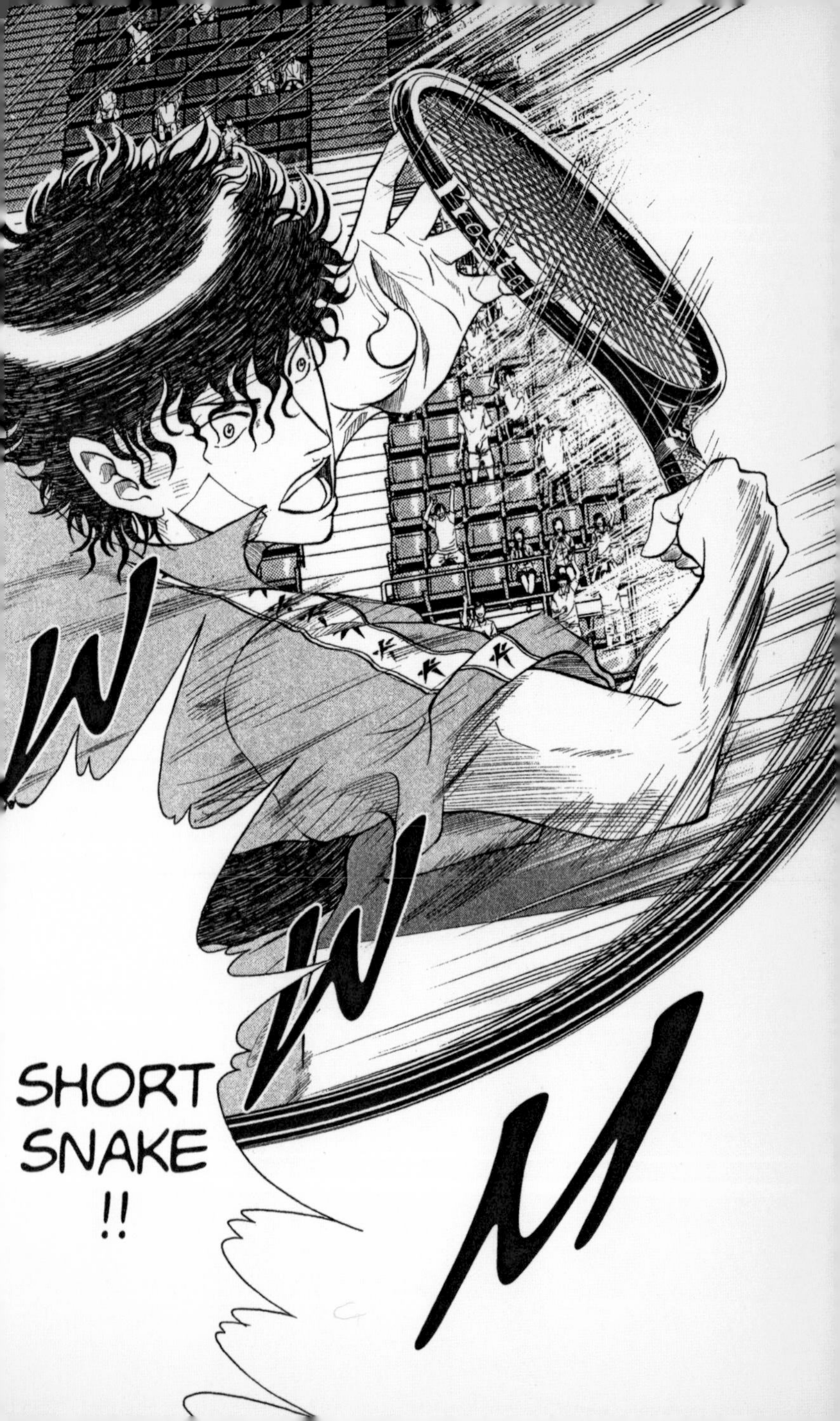
WWM
SHORT SNAKE !!

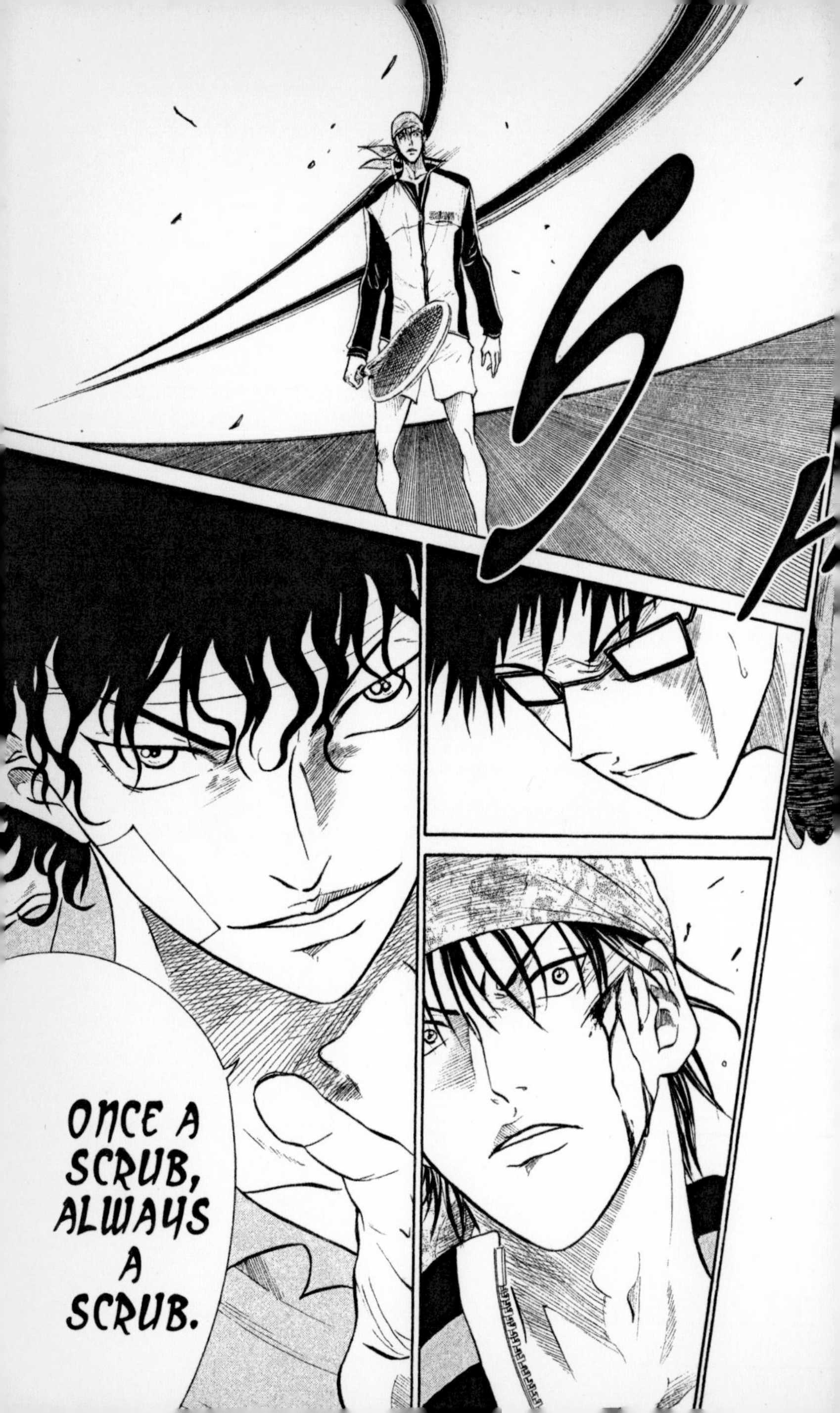
ONCE A SCRUB, ALWAYS A SCRUB.

テニスの王子様

THE PRINCE OF TENNIS

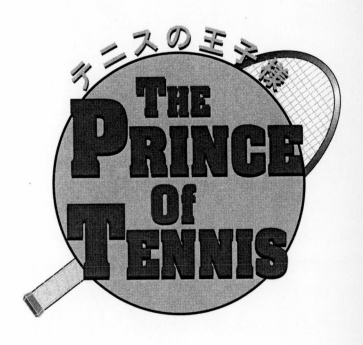

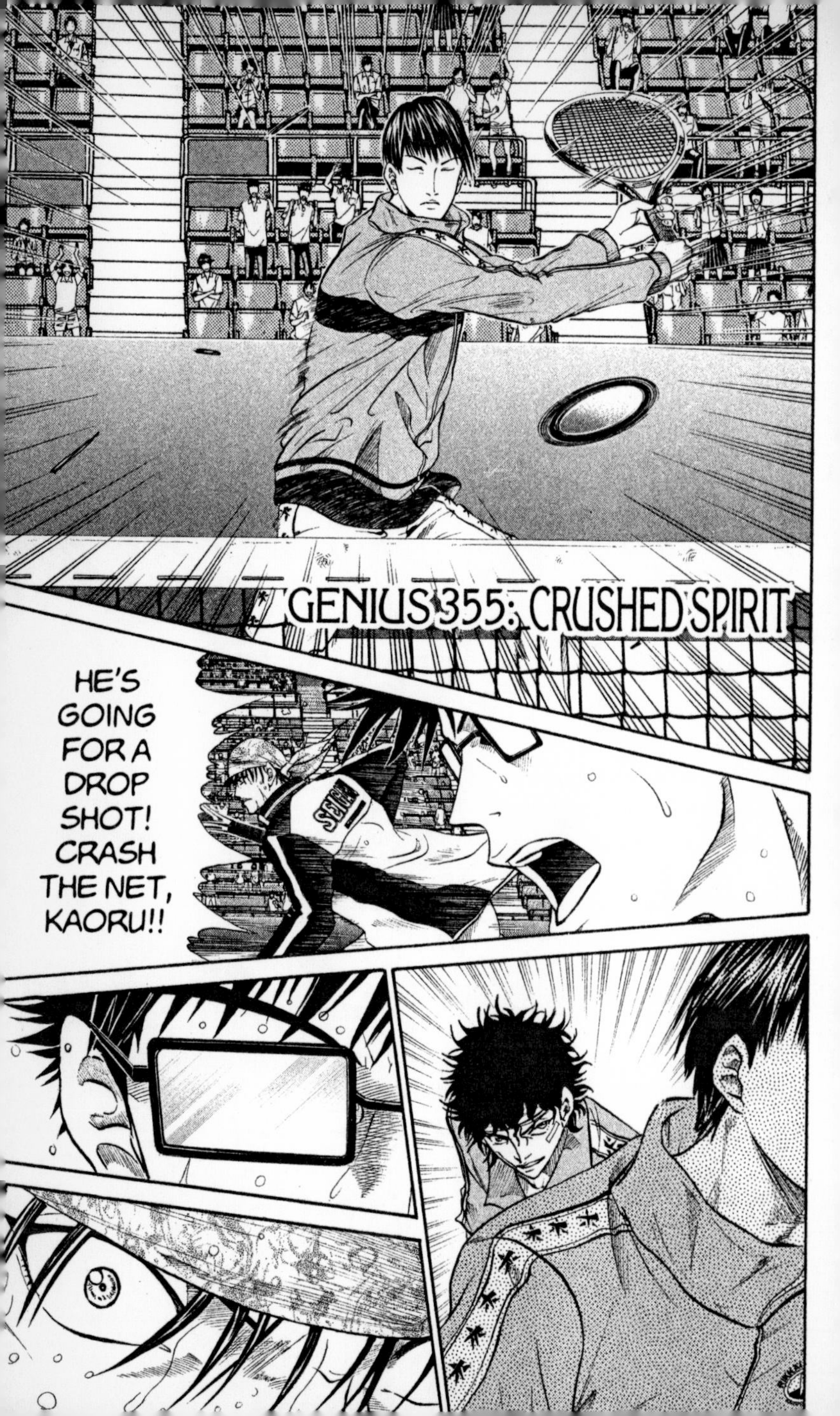
GENIUS 355: CRUSHED SPIRIT
HE'S GOING FOR A DROP SHOT! CRASH THE NET, KAORU!!

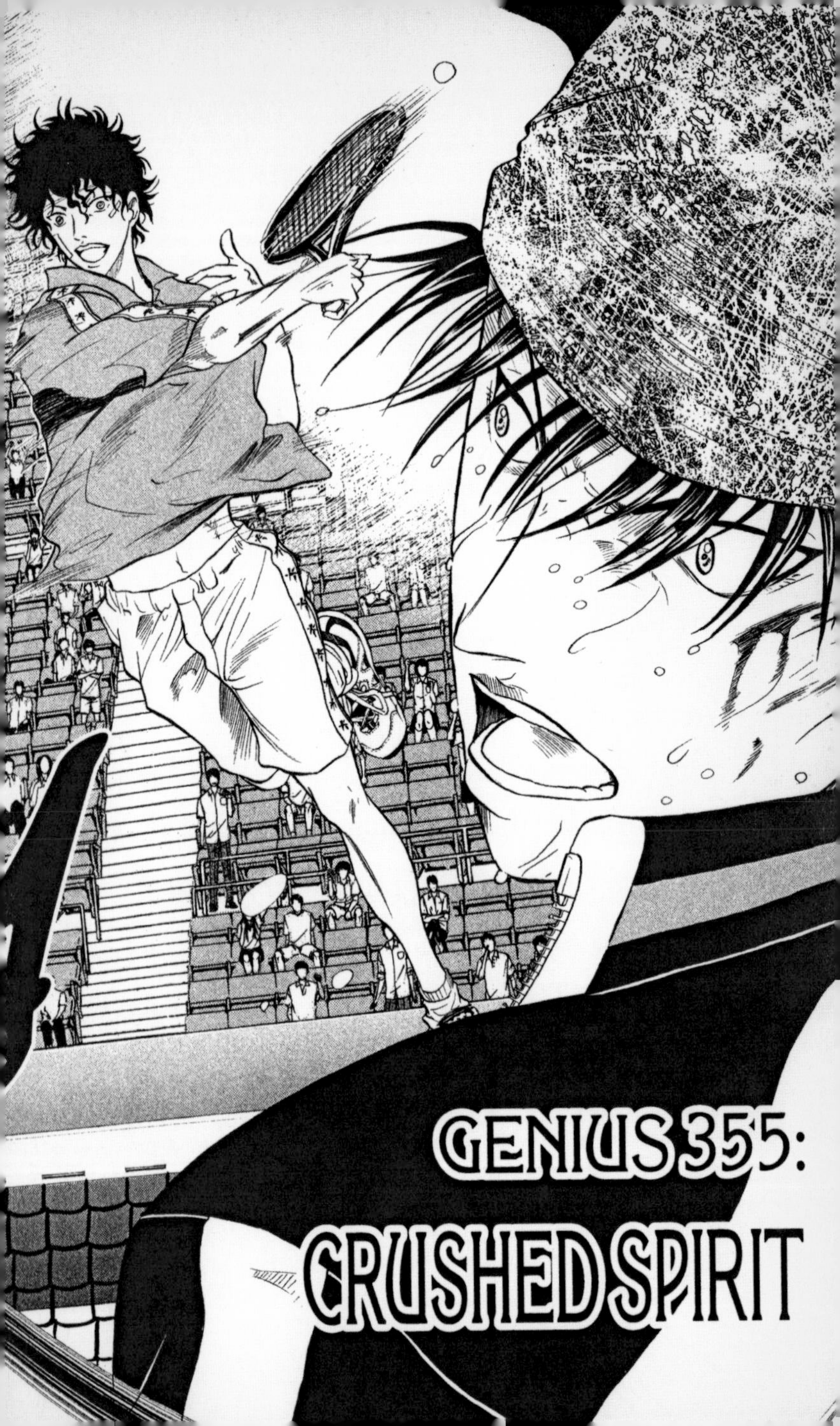
GENIUS 355:
CRUSHED SPIRIT

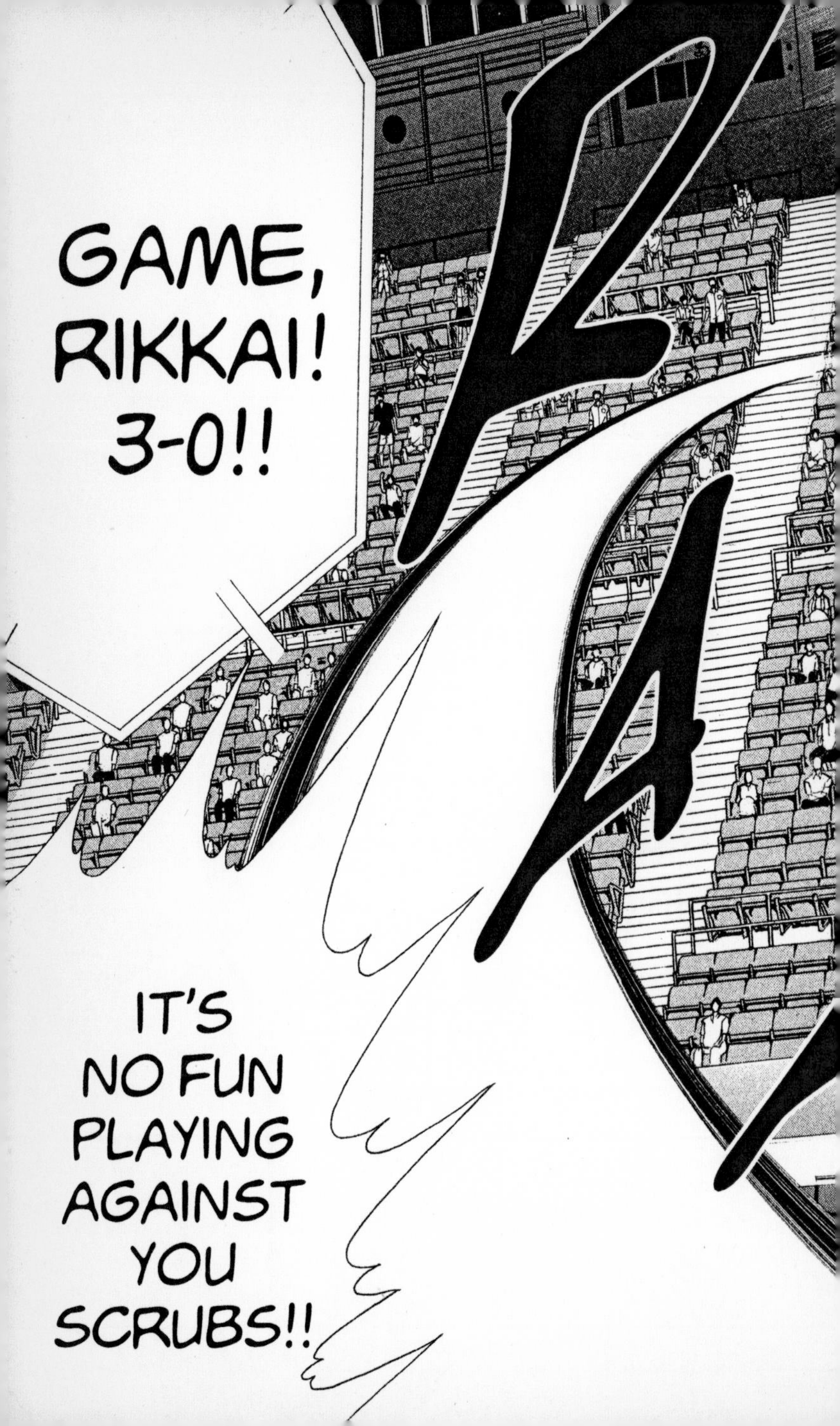
GAME, RIKKAI! 3-0!!
IT'S NO FUN PLAYING AGAINST YOU SCRUBS!!

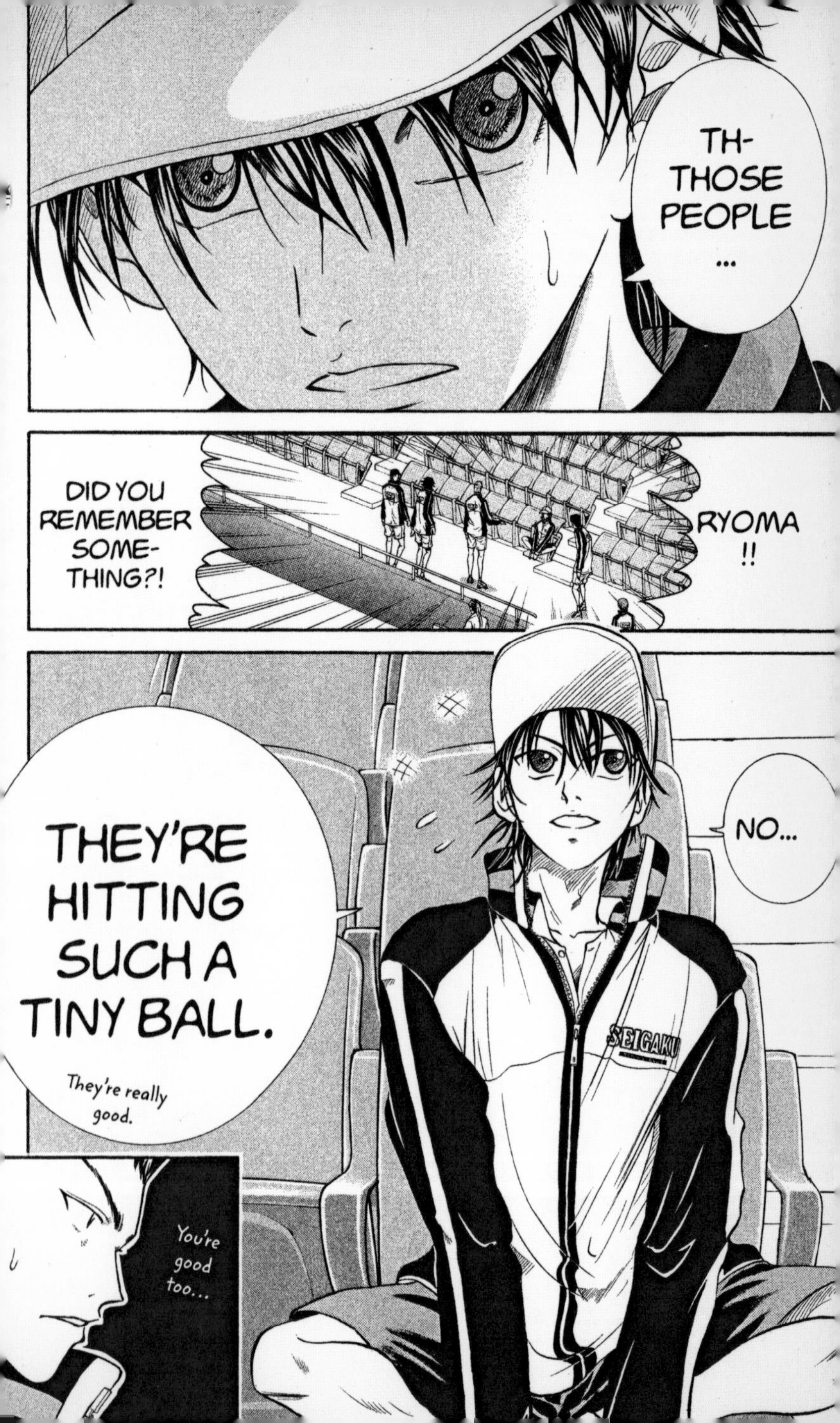
TH- THOSE PEOPLE ...
RYOMA !!
DID YOU REMEMBER SOME- THING?!
NO...
THEY'RE HITTING SUCH A TINY BALL.
They're really good.
You're good too...

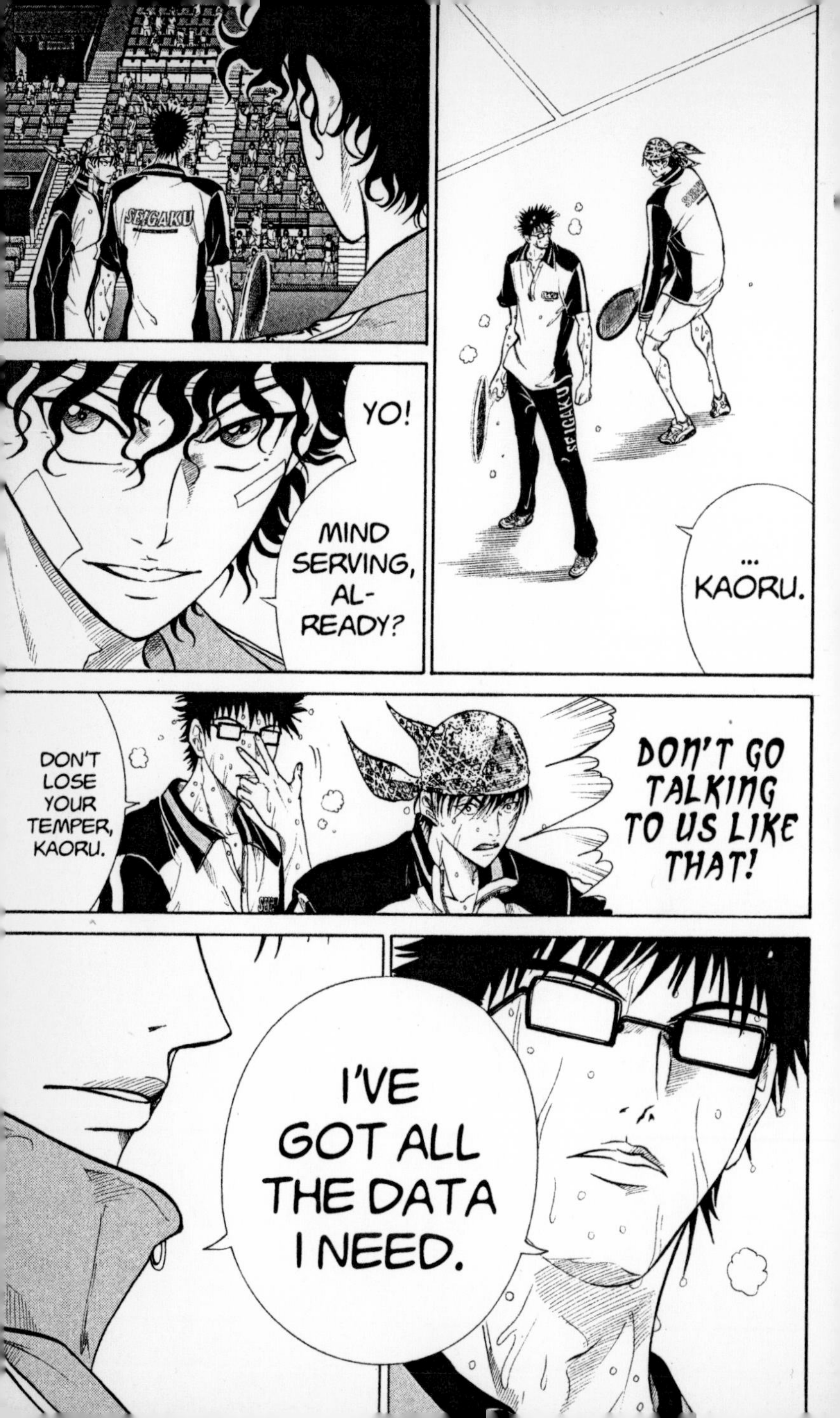

... KAORU.
YO!
MIND SERVING, AL-READY?
DON'T GO TALKING TO US LIKE THAT!
DON'T LOSE YOUR TEMPER, KAORU.
I'VE GOT ALL THE DATA I NEED.

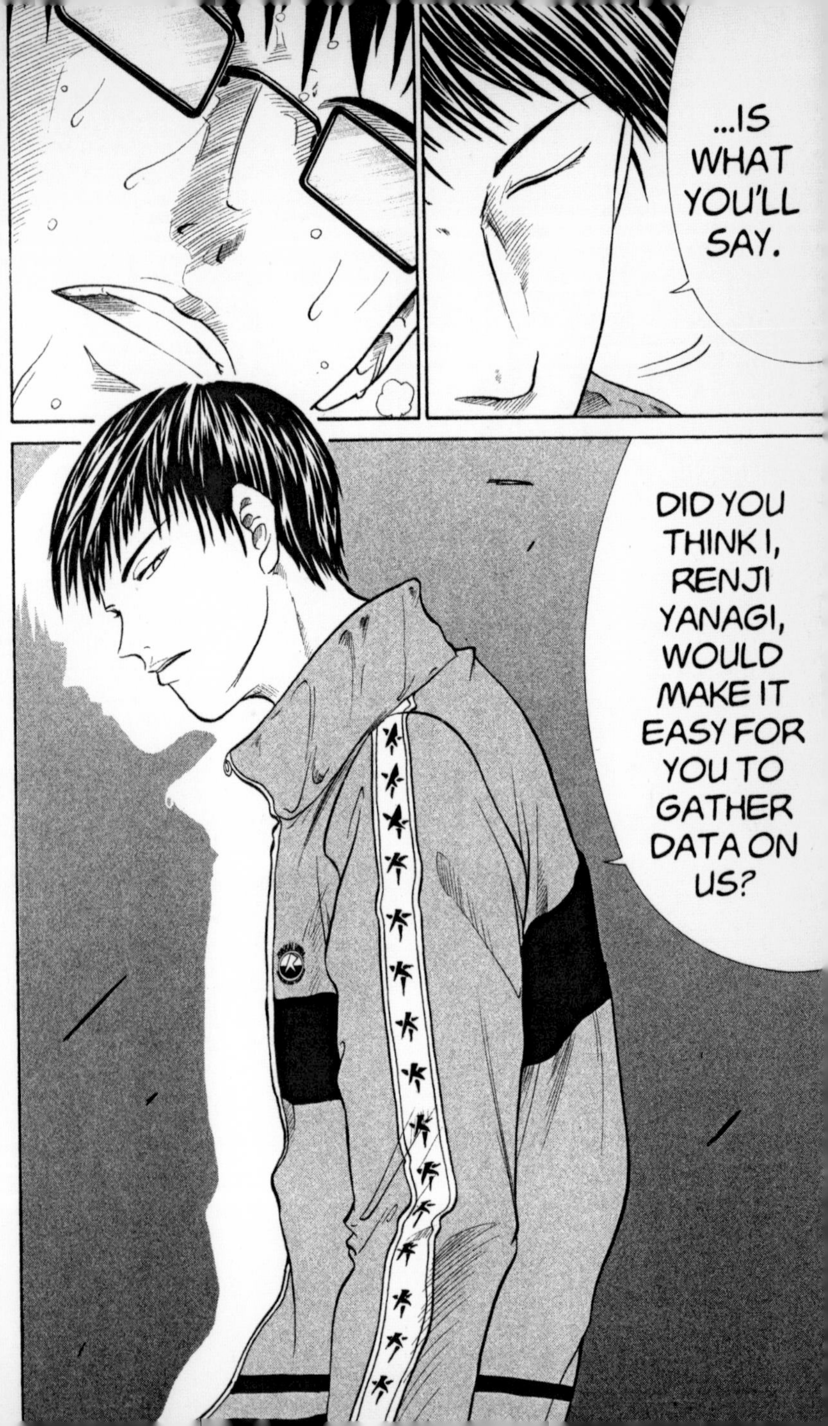
...IS WHAT YOU'LL SAY.
DID YOU THINK I, RENJI YANAGI, WOULD MAKE IT EASY FOR YOU TO GATHER DATA ON US?

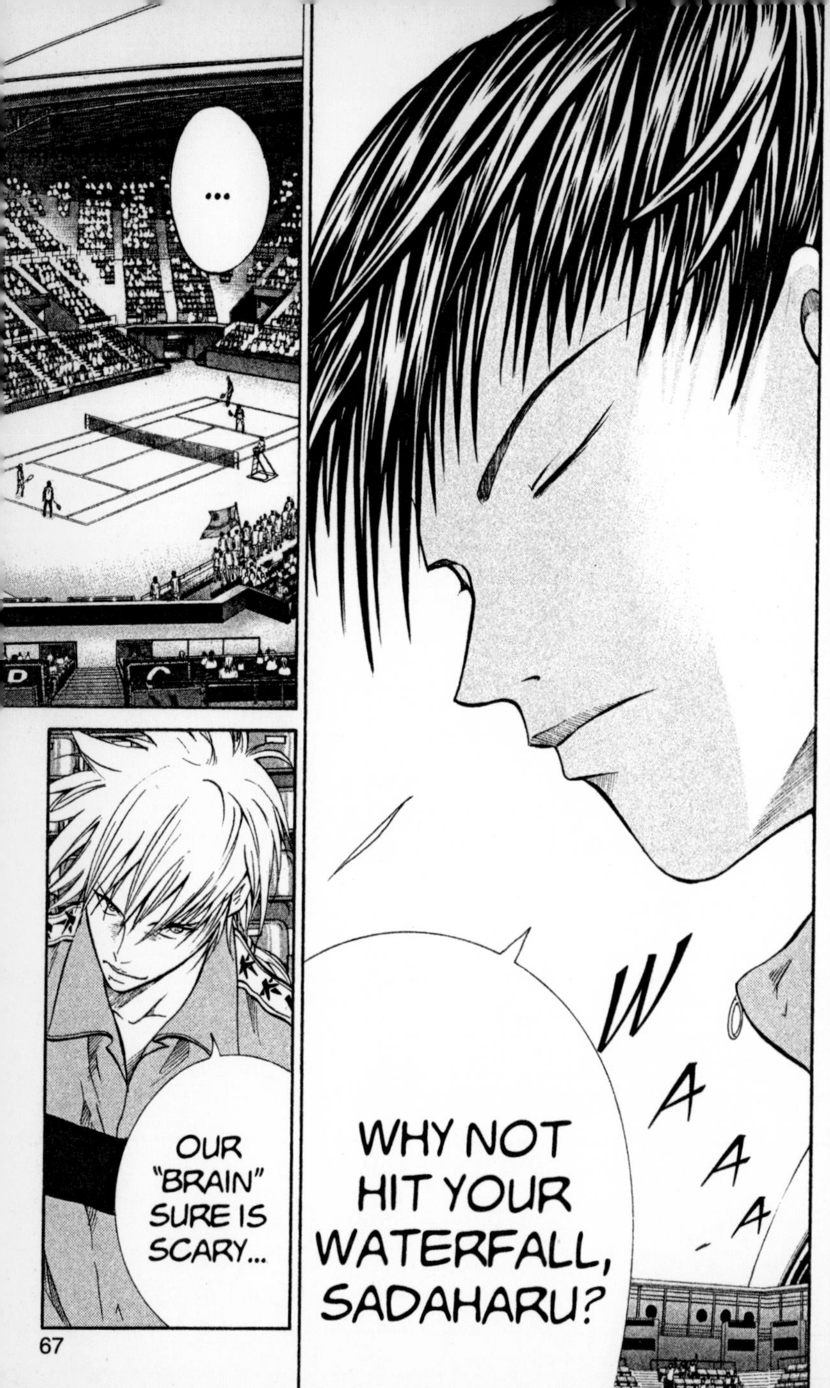
WHY NOT HIT YOUR WATERFALL, SADAHARU?
WAAAA
...
OUR "BRAIN" SURE IS SCARY...

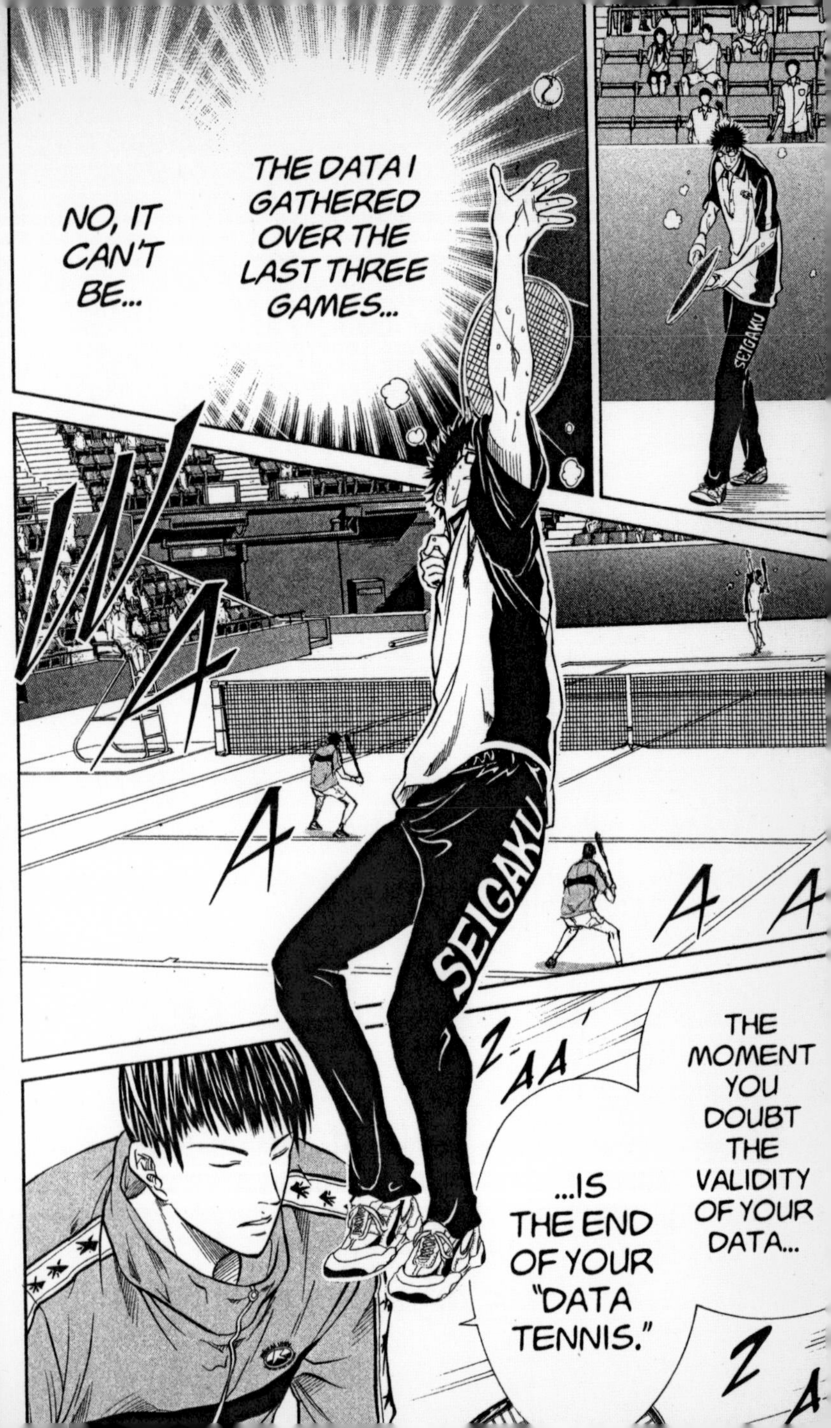

THE DATA I GATHERED OVER THE LAST THREE GAMES...
NO, IT CAN'T BE...
WAAAA
THE MOMENT YOU DOUBT THE VALIDITY OF YOUR DATA...
...IS THE END OF YOUR "DATA TENNIS."

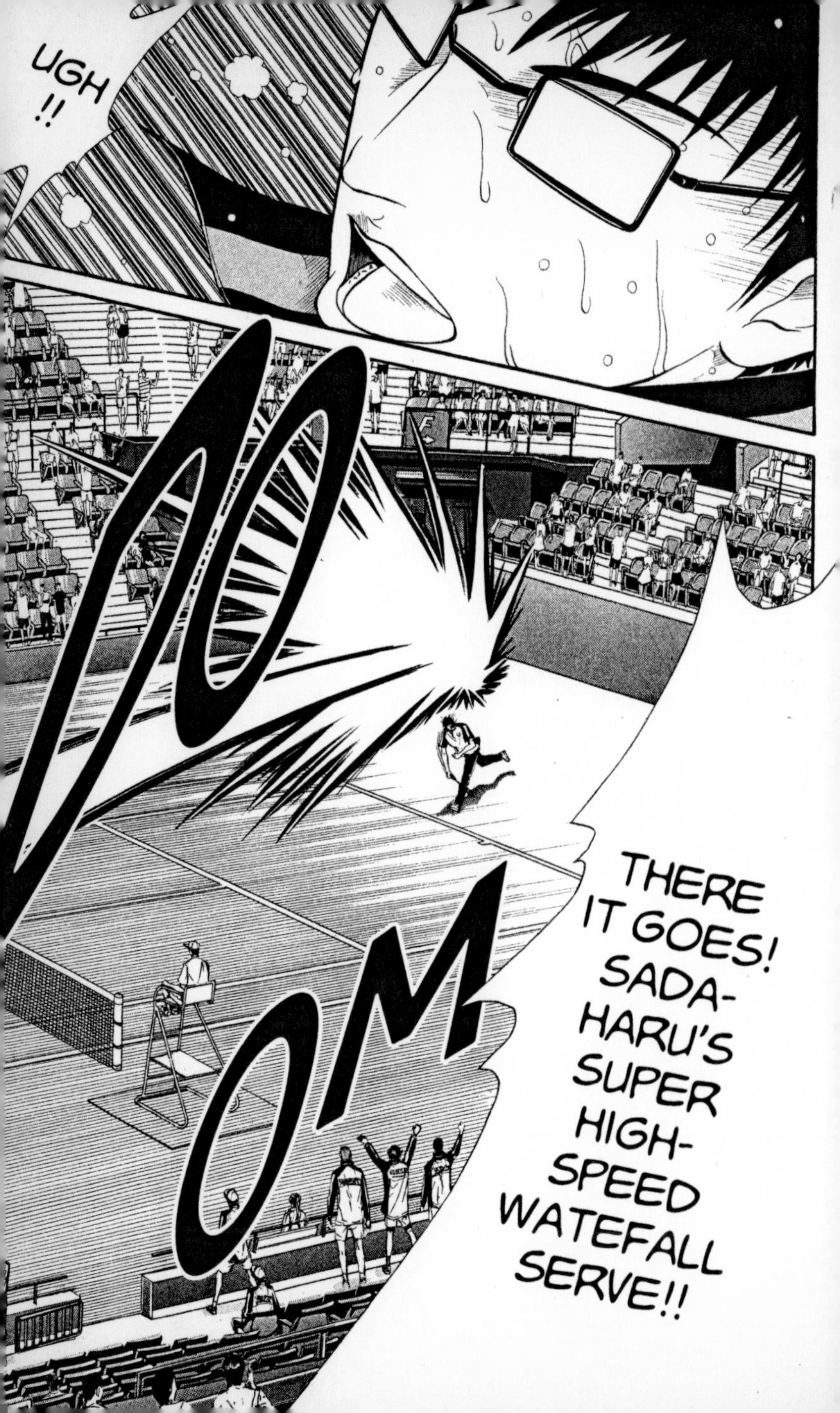
UGH !!
THERE IT GOES! SADA-HARU'S SUPER HIGH-SPEED WATEFALL SERVE!!
ZOOM

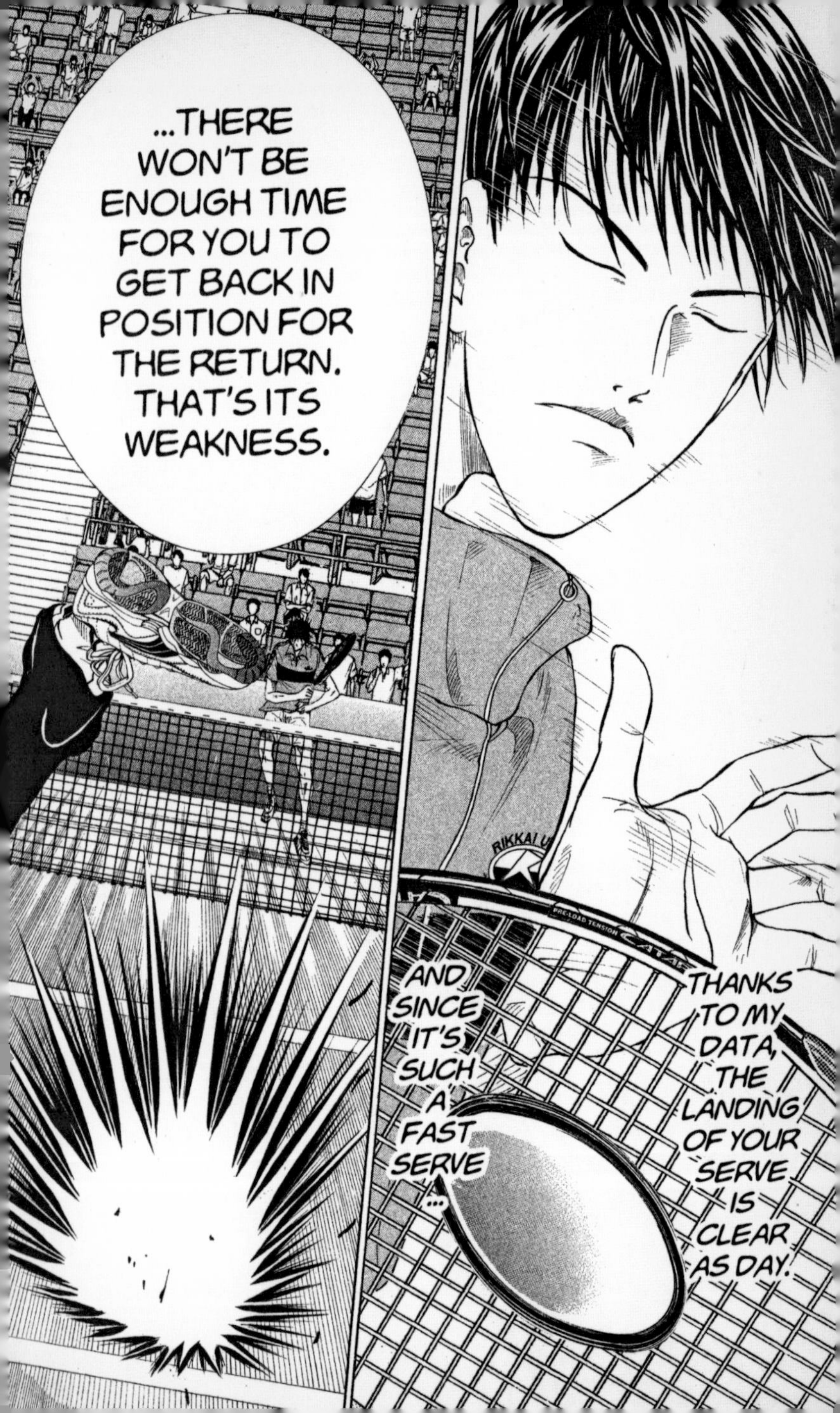
RIKKAI U
THANKS TO MY DATA, THE LANDING OF YOUR SERVE IS CLEAR AS DAY.
AND SINCE IT'S SUCH A FAST SERVE...
...THERE WON'T BE ENOUGH TIME FOR YOU TO GET BACK IN POSITION FOR THE RETURN. THAT'S ITS WEAKNESS.

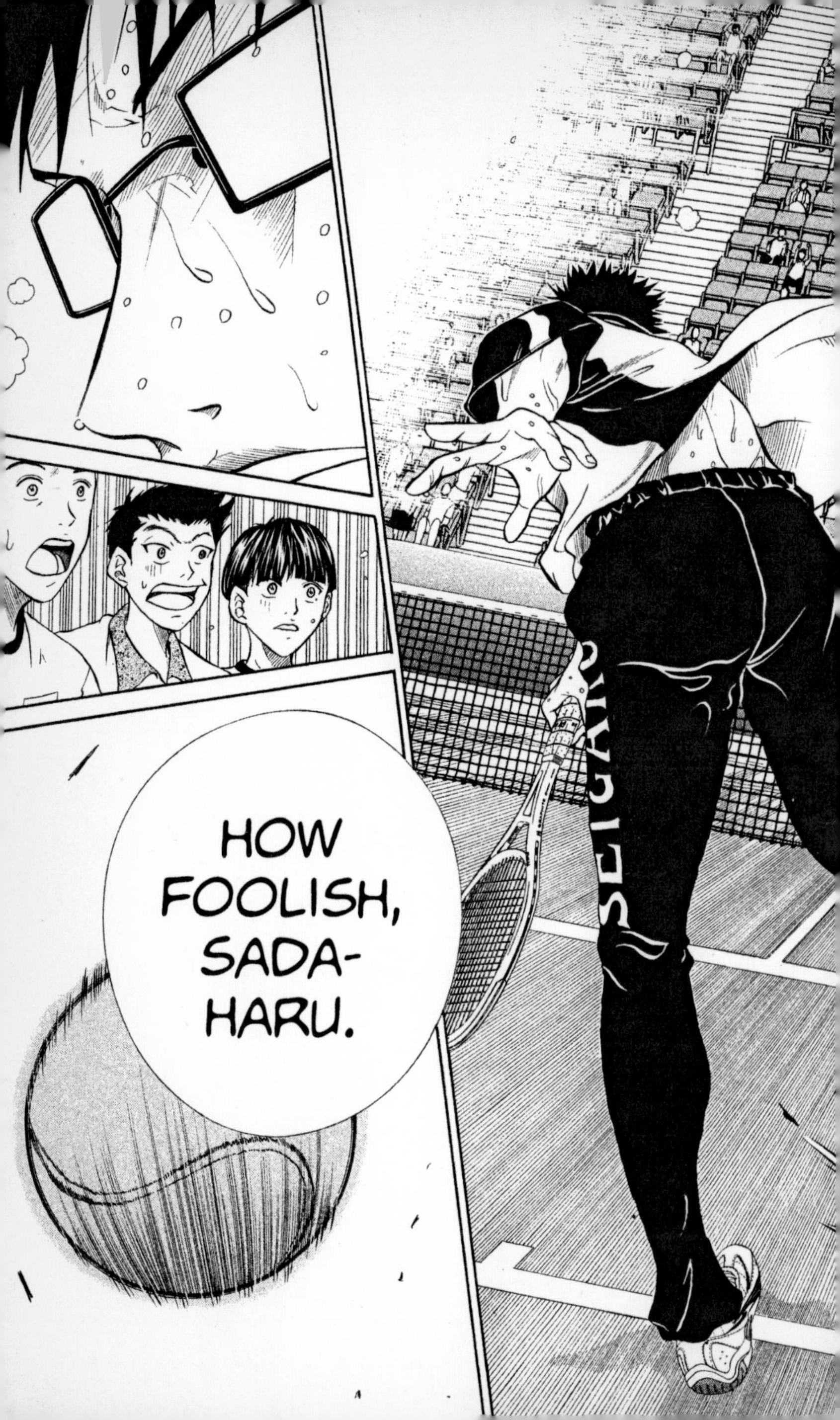
HOW FOOLISH, SADA-HARU.

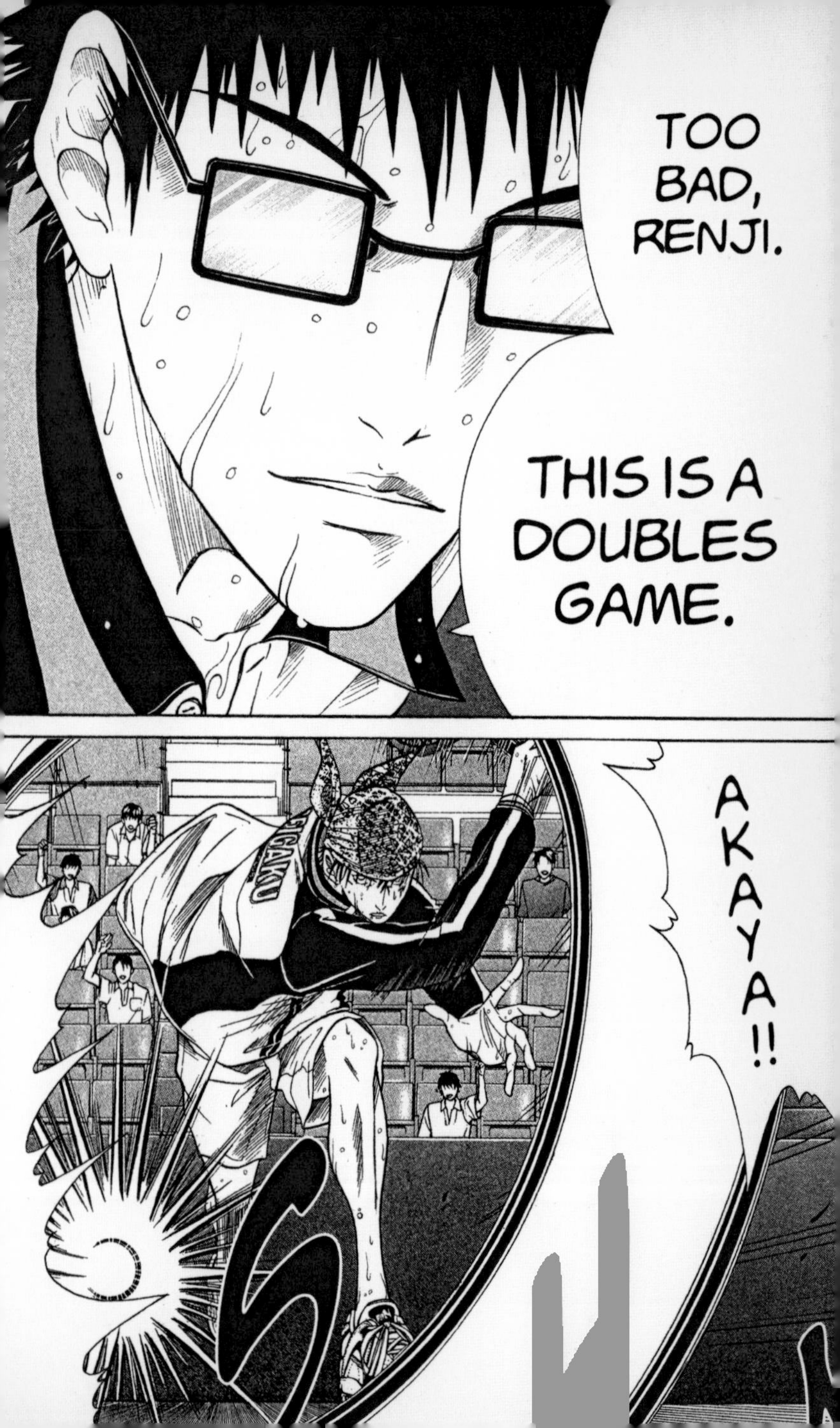
TOO BAD, RENJI.
THIS IS A DOUBLES GAME.
AKAYA!!

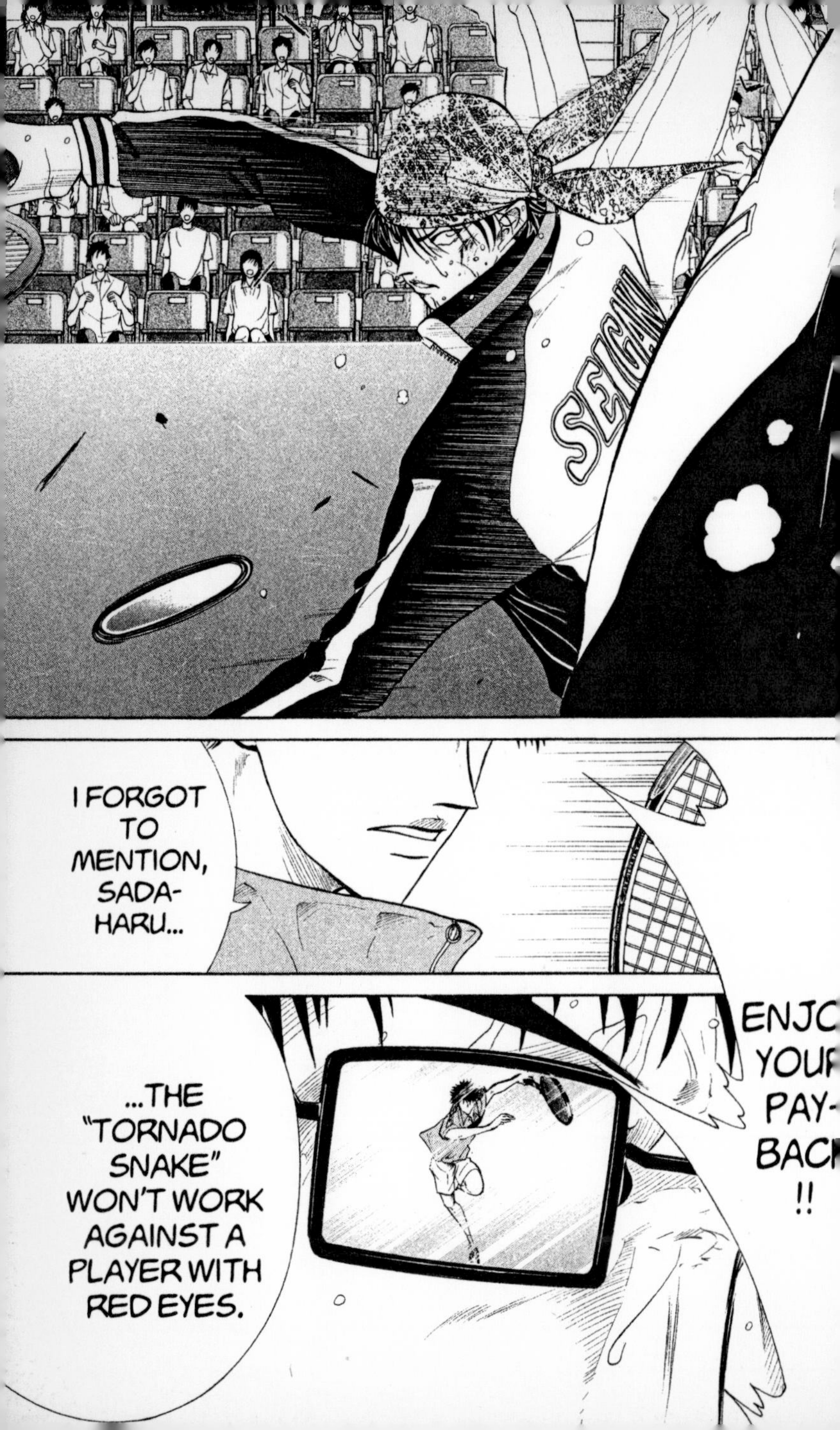
I FORGOT TO MENTION, SADA-HARU...
ENJO YOUR PAY-BACK !!
...THE "TORNADO SNAKE" WON'T WORK AGAINST A PLAYER WITH RED EYES.

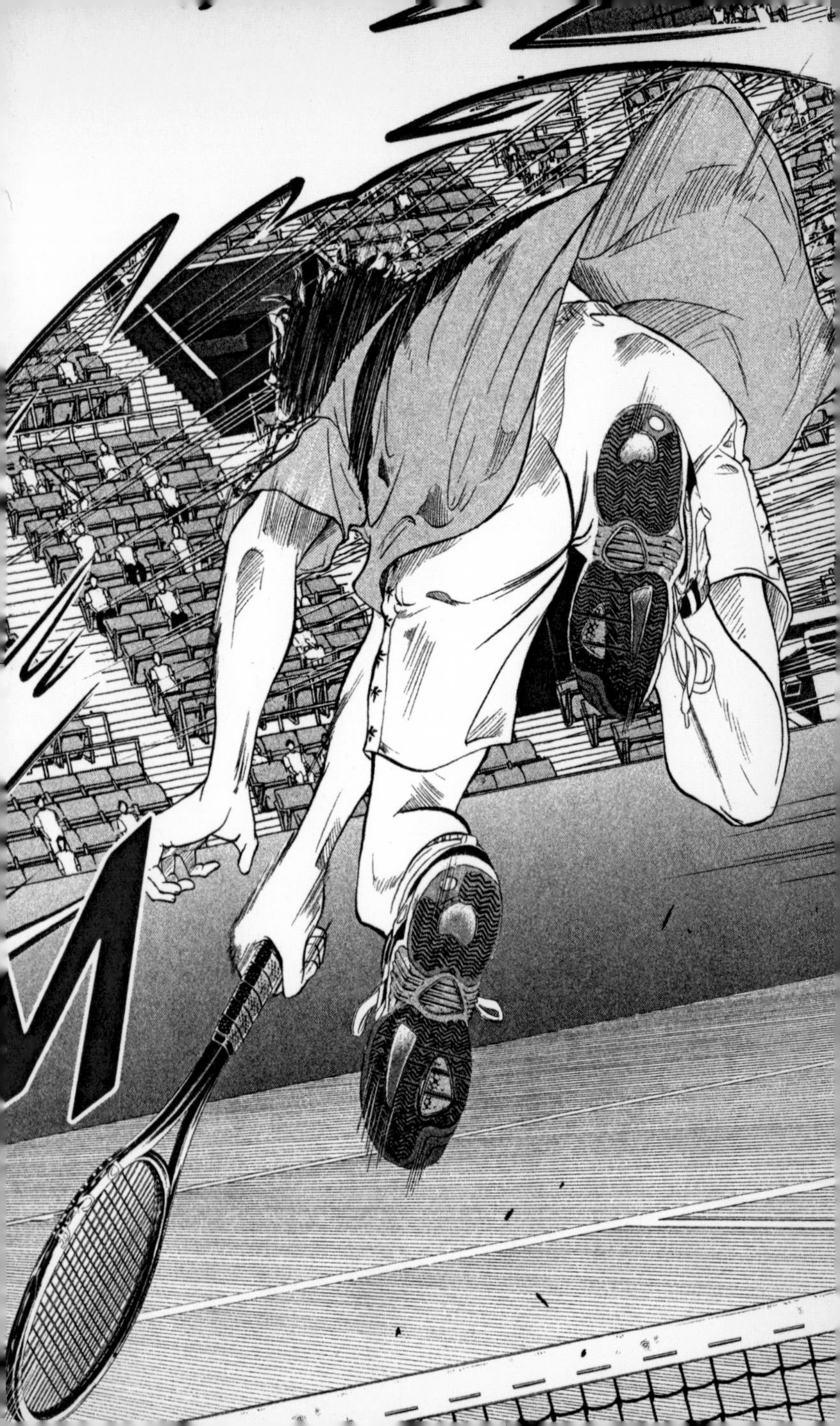

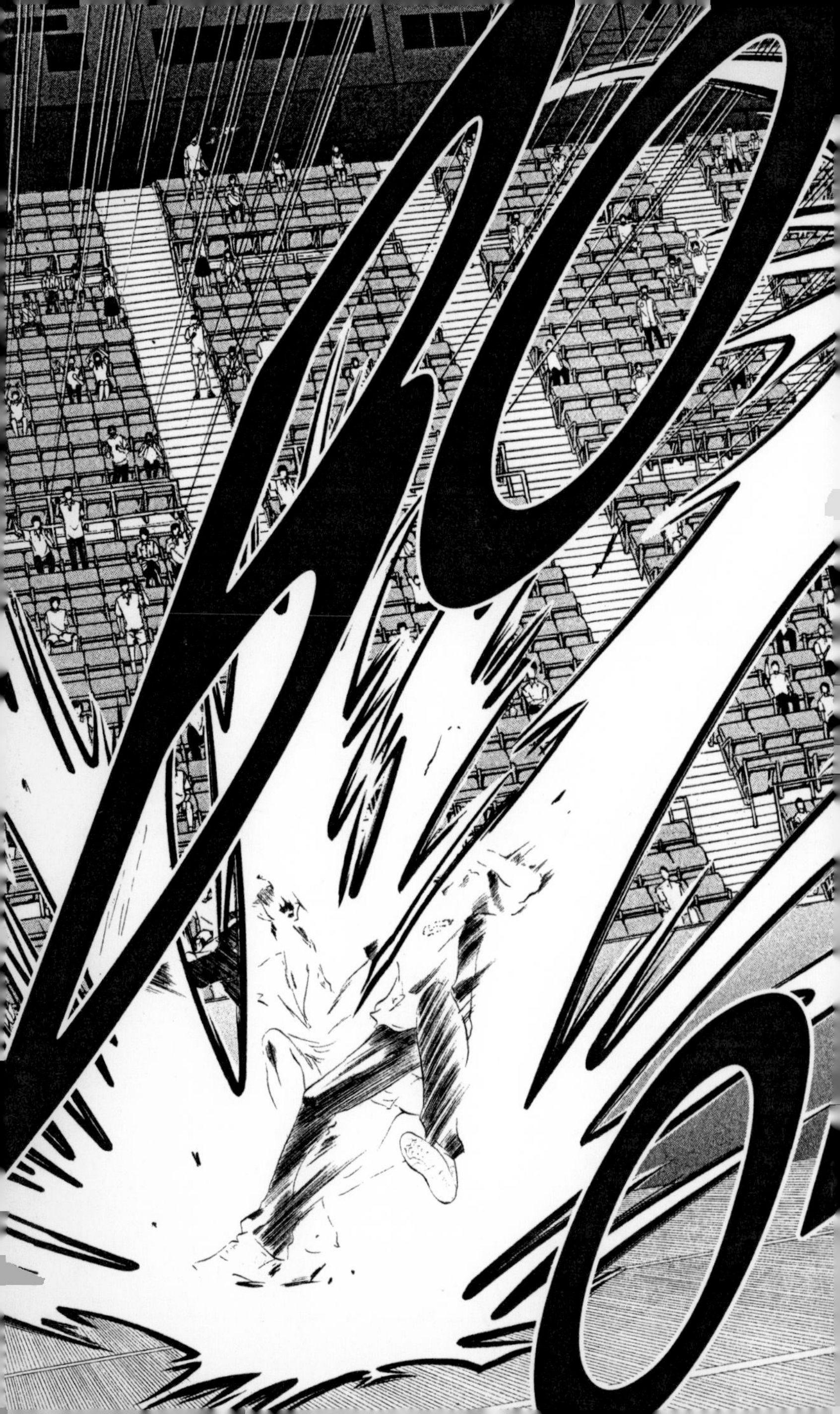

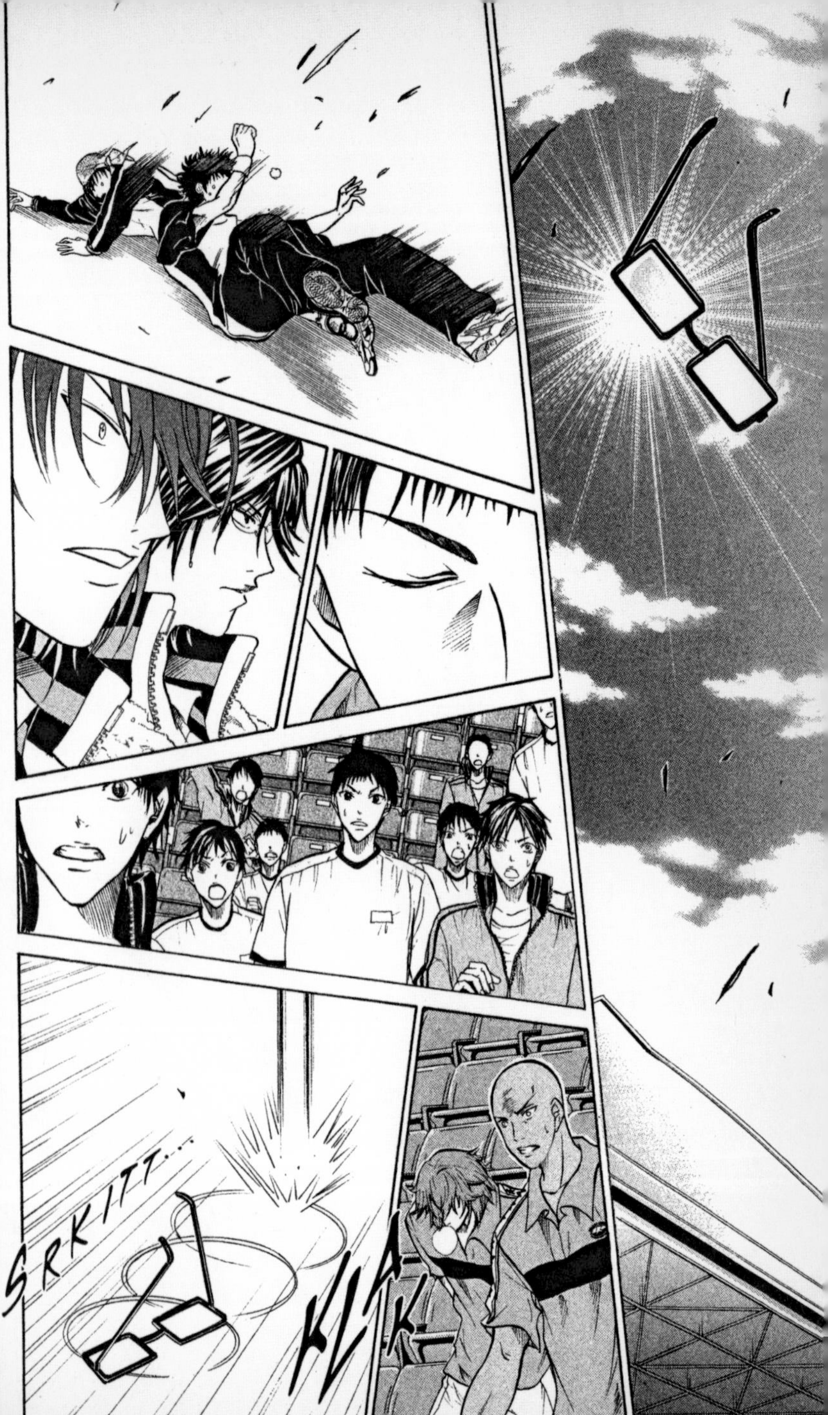
SRKITT....
KLAK

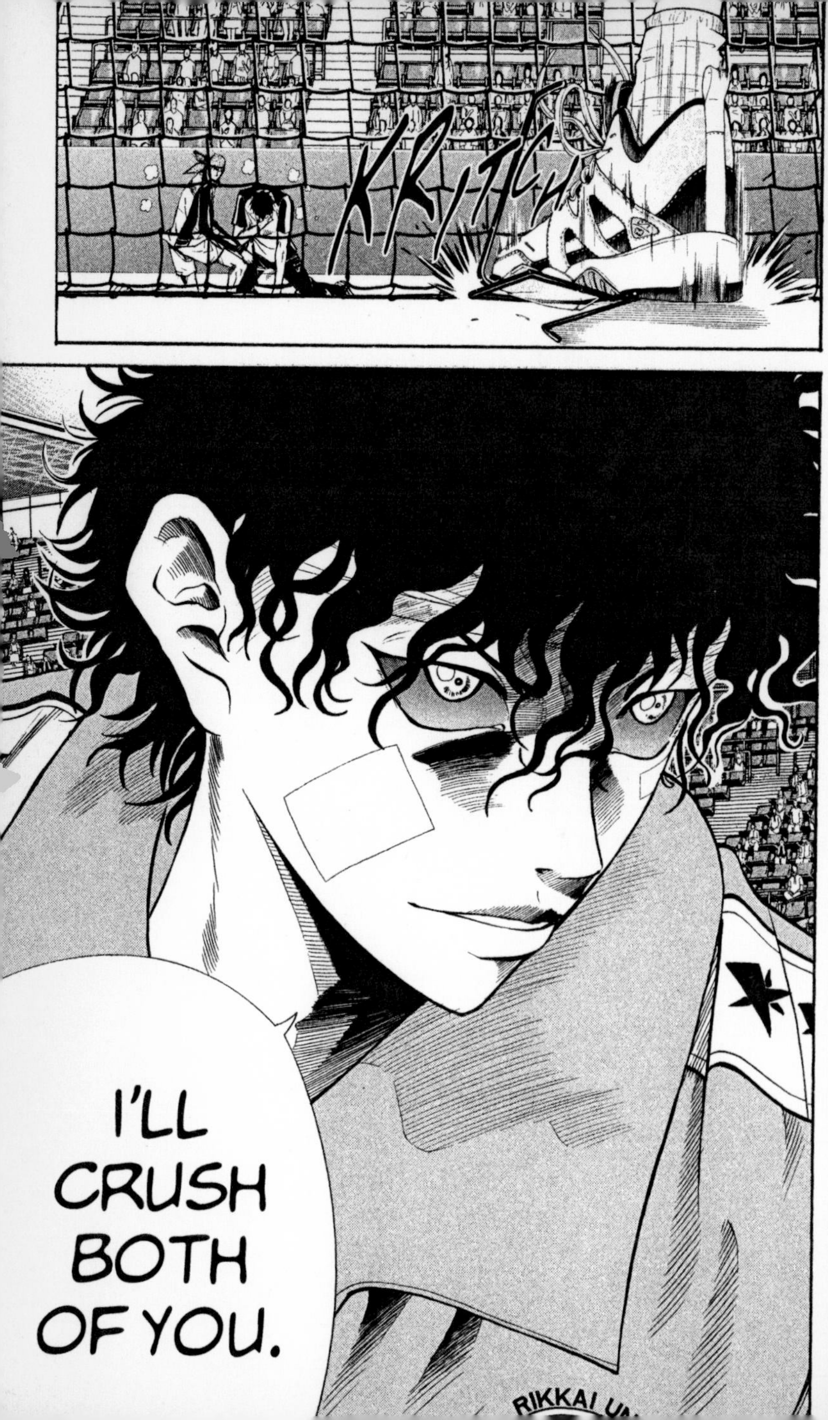
KRITCH
I'LL CRUSH BOTH OF YOU.

テニスの王子様

THE PRINCE Of TENNIS

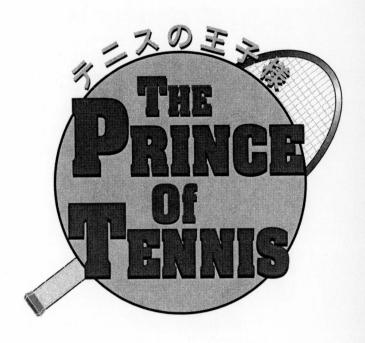

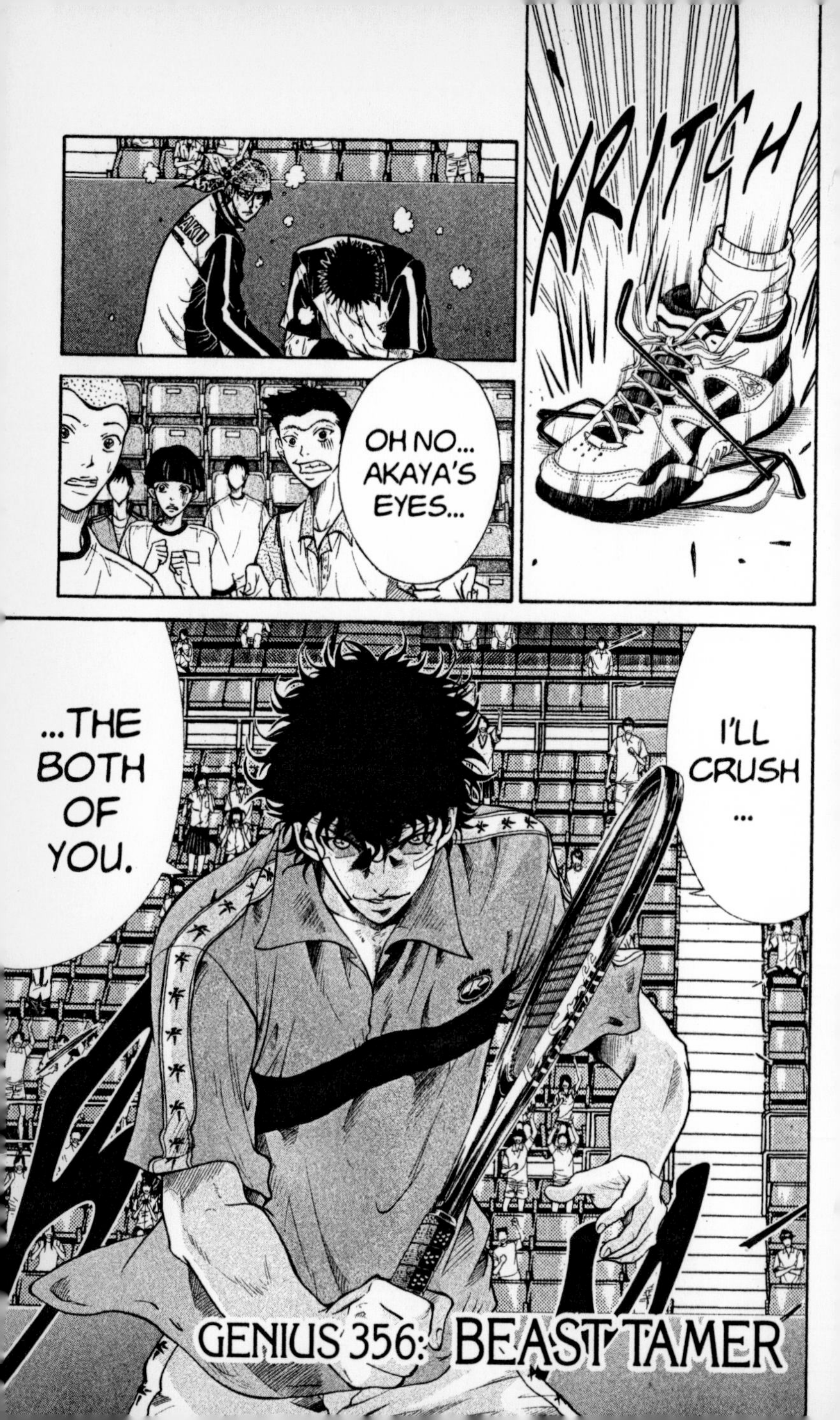
KRITCH
OH NO... AKAYA'S EYES...
I'LL CRUSH ...
...THE BOTH OF YOU.

GENIUS 356: BEAST TAMER

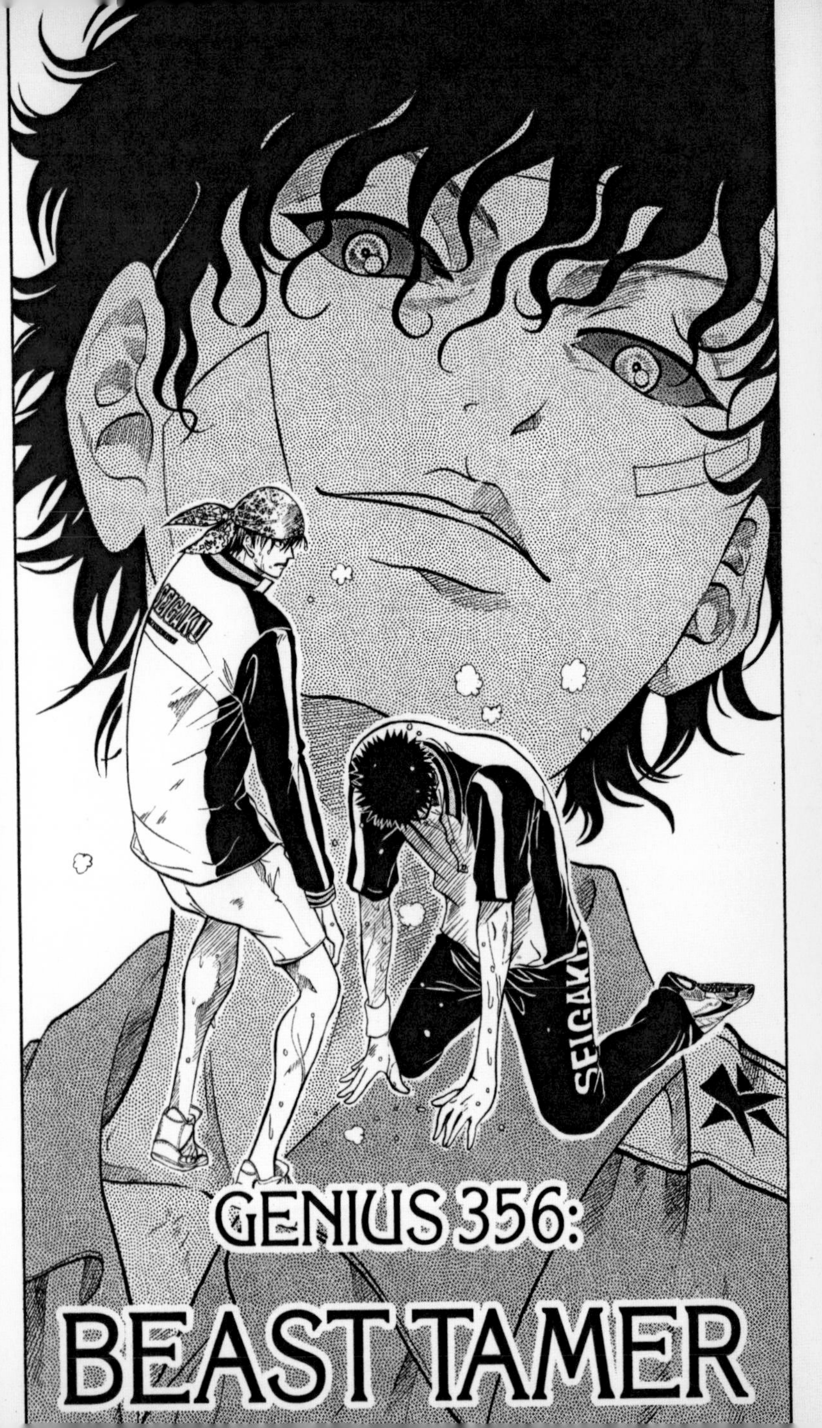
SEIGAKU
SEIGAKU
GENIUS 356:
BEAST TAMER

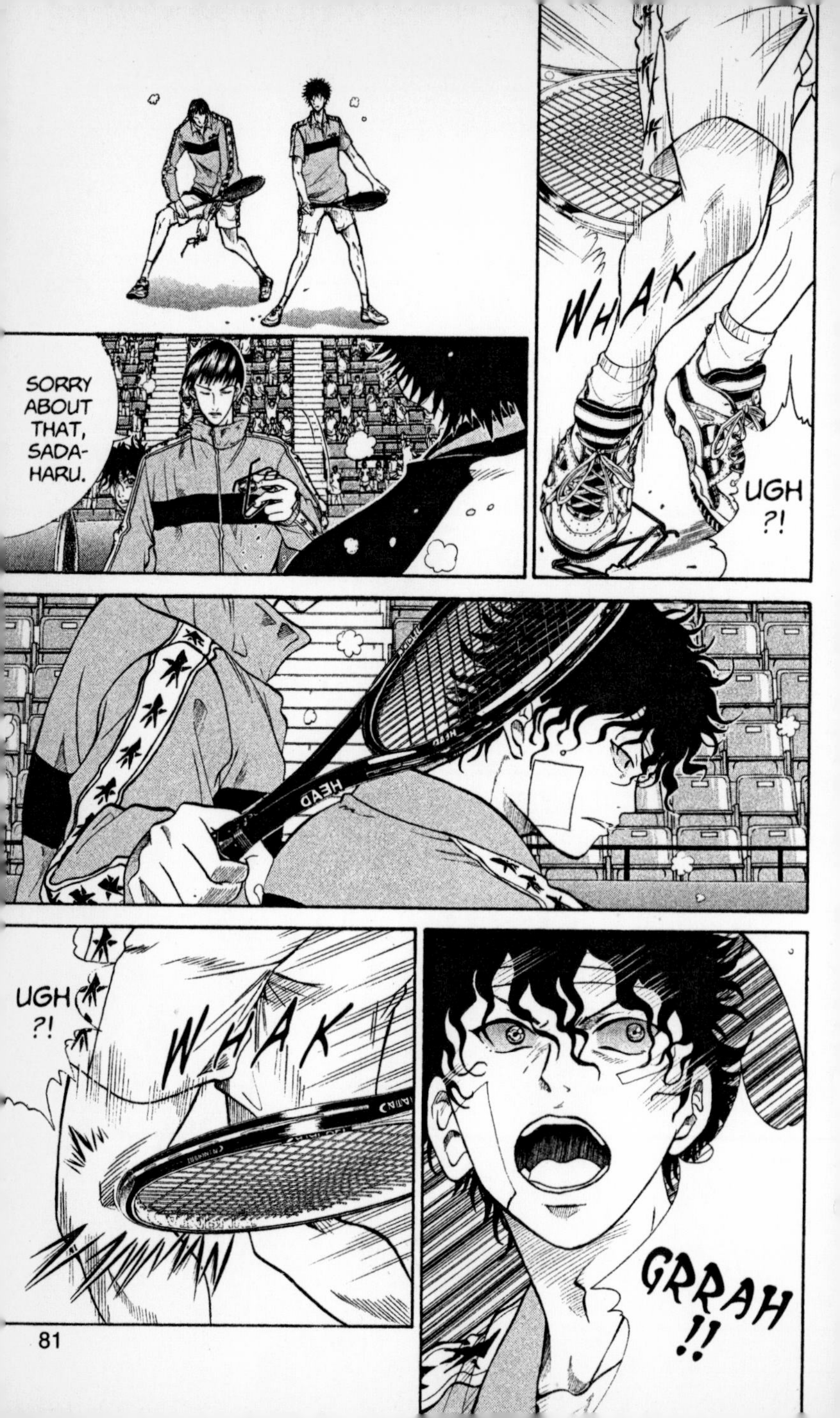
WHAK
UGH ?!
SORRY ABOUT THAT, SADAHARU.
GRRAH !!
UGH ?!
WHAK

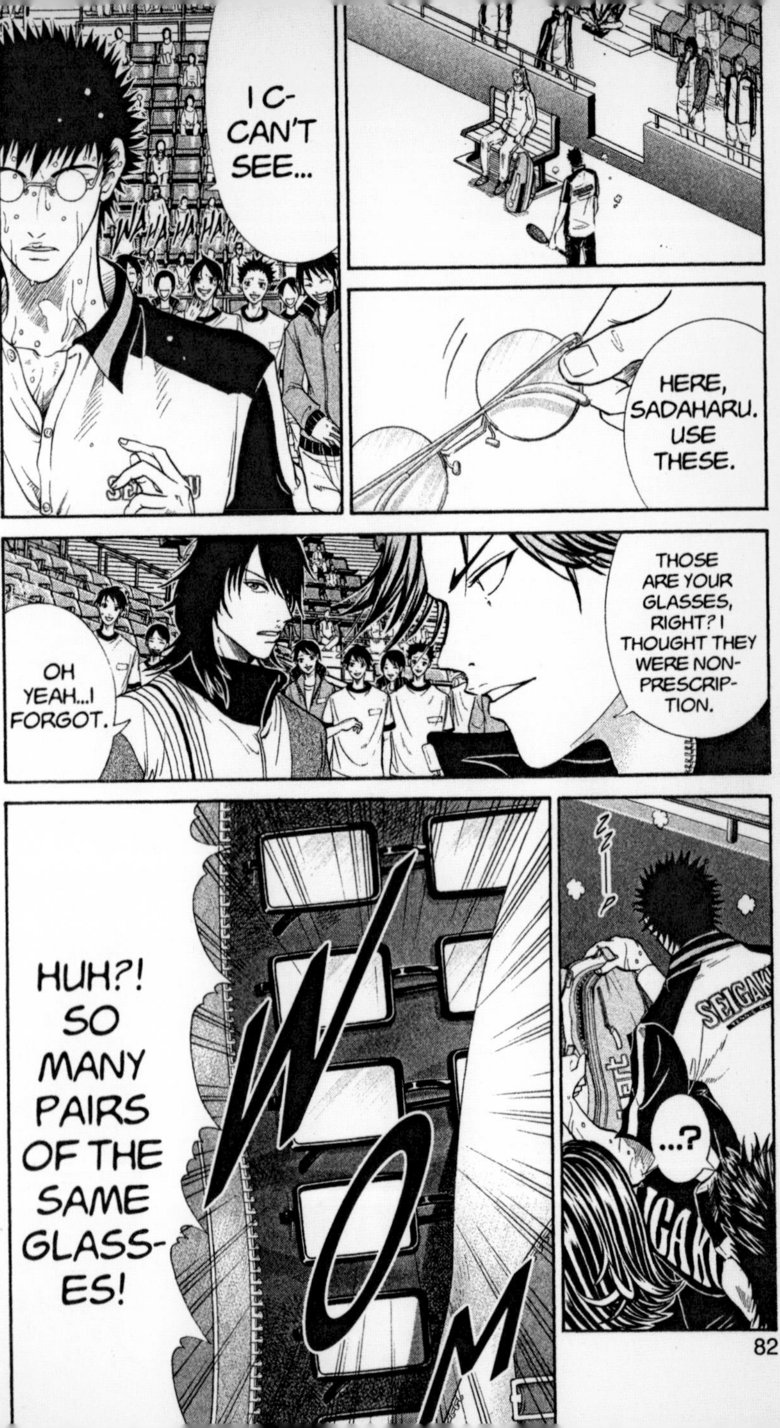
HERE, SADAHARU. USE THESE.
I C-CAN'T SEE...
THOSE ARE YOUR GLASSES, RIGHT? I THOUGHT THEY WERE NON-PRESCRIPTION.
OH YEAH...I FORGOT.
...?
HUH?! SO MANY PAIRS OF THE SAME GLASSES!
WOM

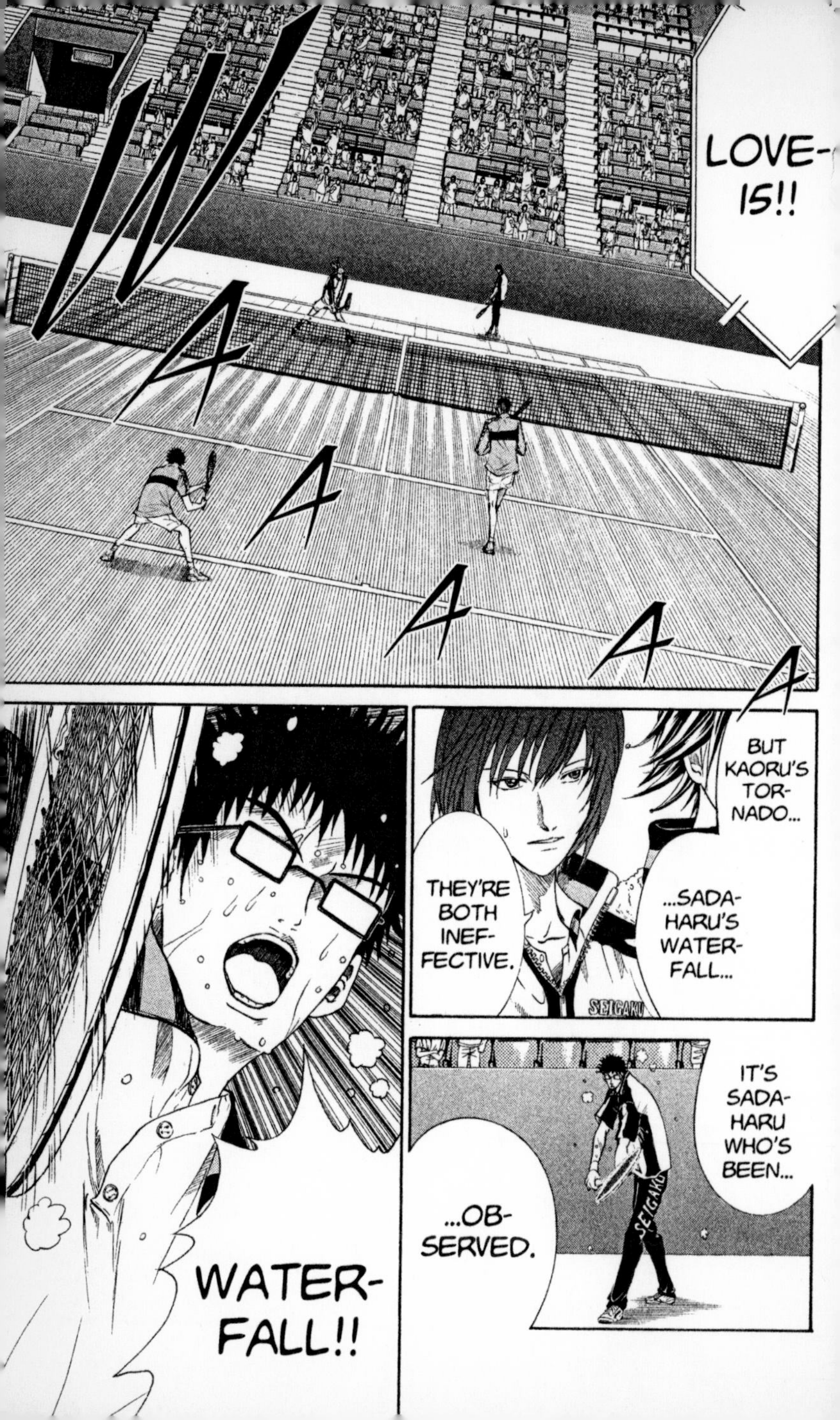

WAAAAA
LOVE-15!!
BUT KAORU'S TORNADO...
...SADAHARU'S WATERFALL...
THEY'RE BOTH INEFFECTIVE.
IT'S SADAHARU WHO'S BEEN...
...OBSERVED.
WATERFALL!!

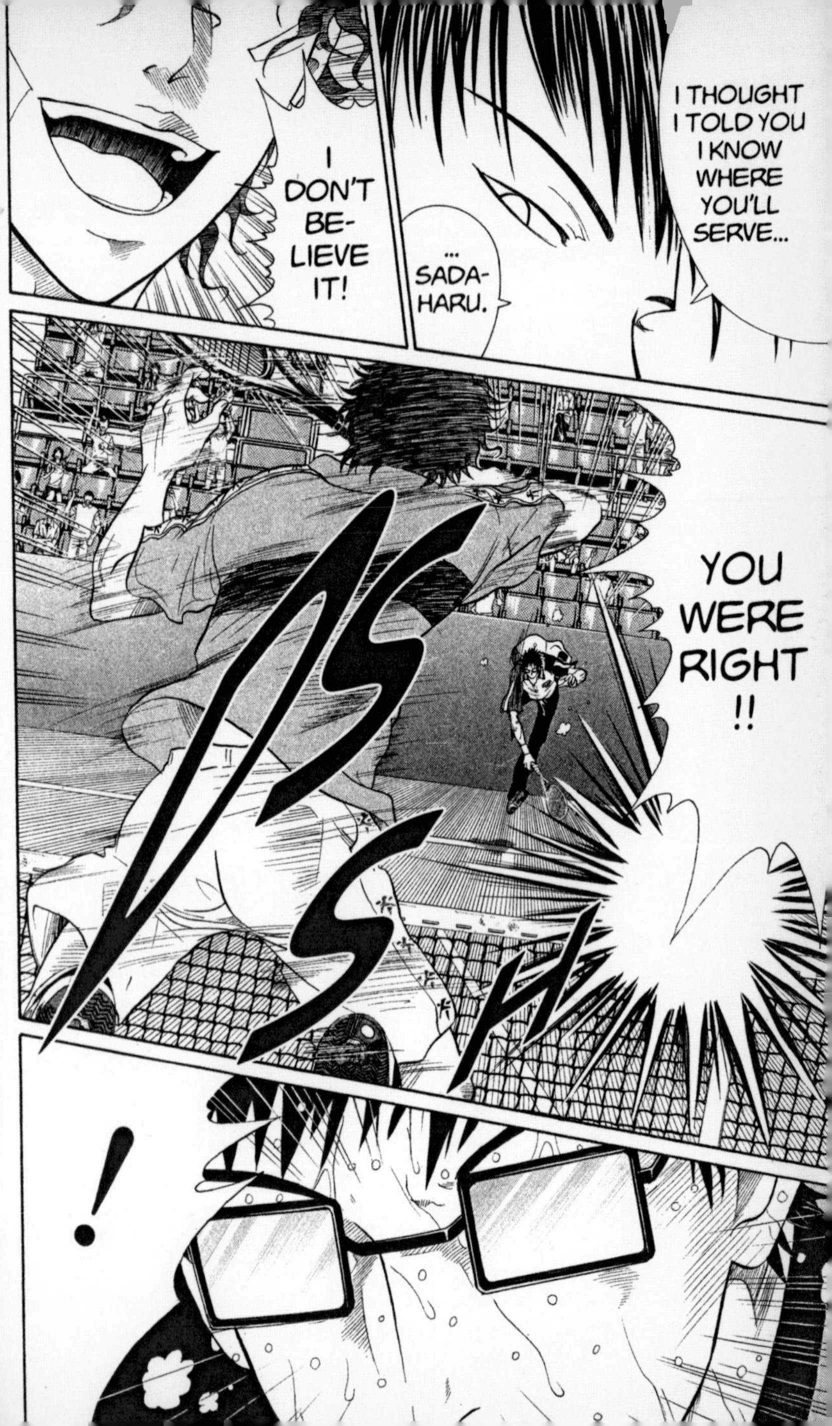
I THOUGHT I TOLD YOU I KNOW WHERE YOU'LL SERVE...
... SADA-HARU.
I DON'T BE-LIEVE IT!
YOU WERE RIGHT !!
!

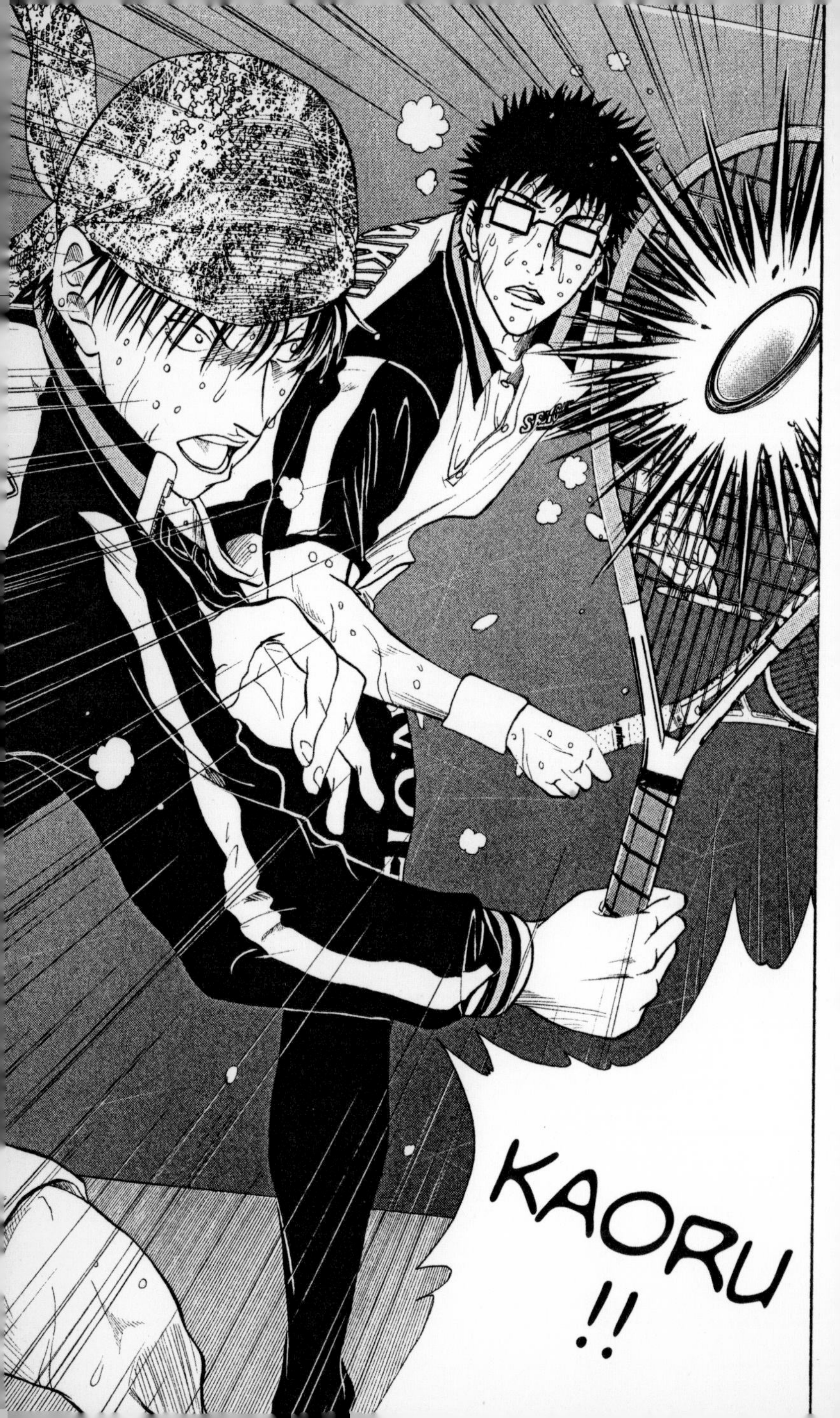
KAORU!!

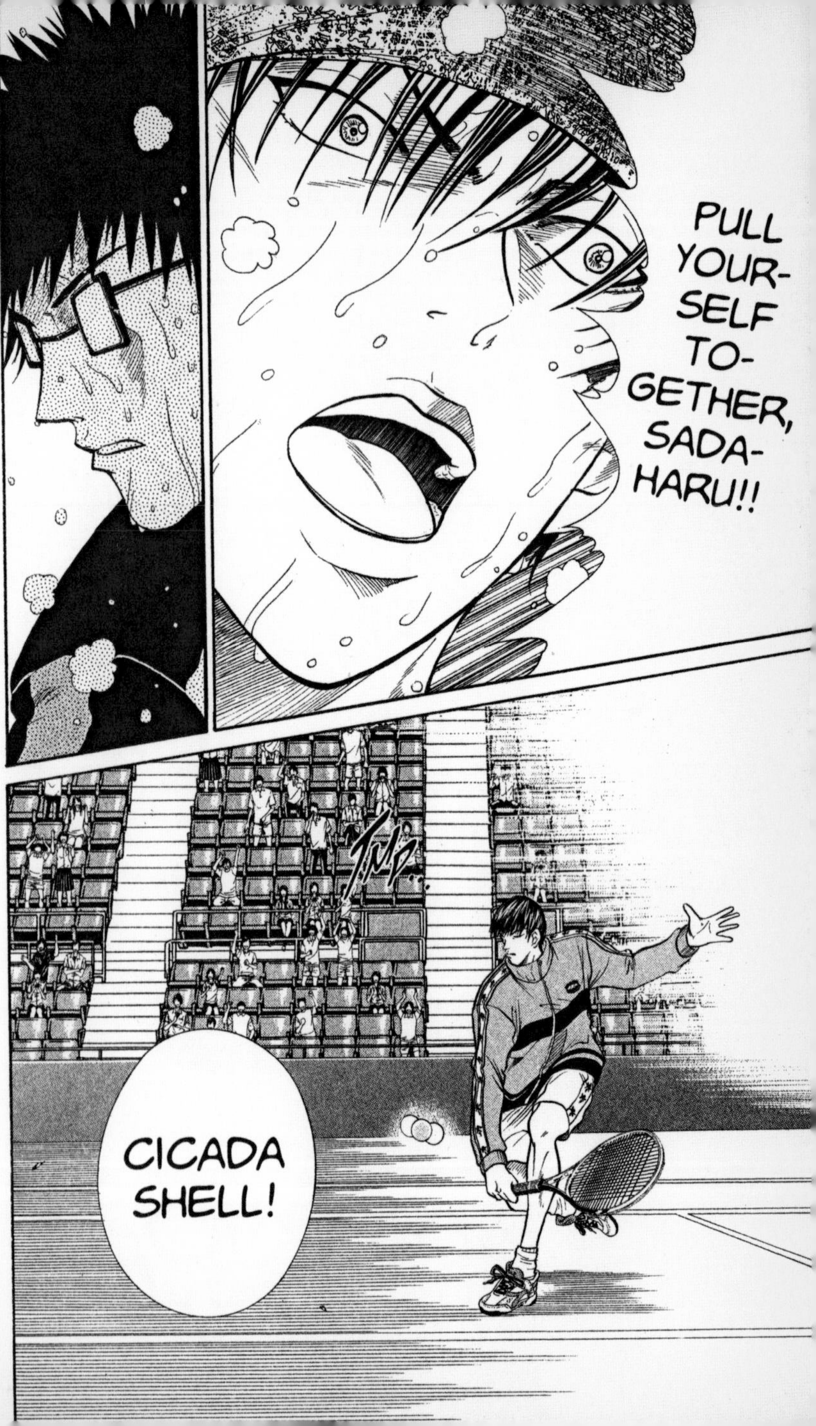
PULL YOURSELF TOGETHER, SADAHARU!!
CICADA SHELL!

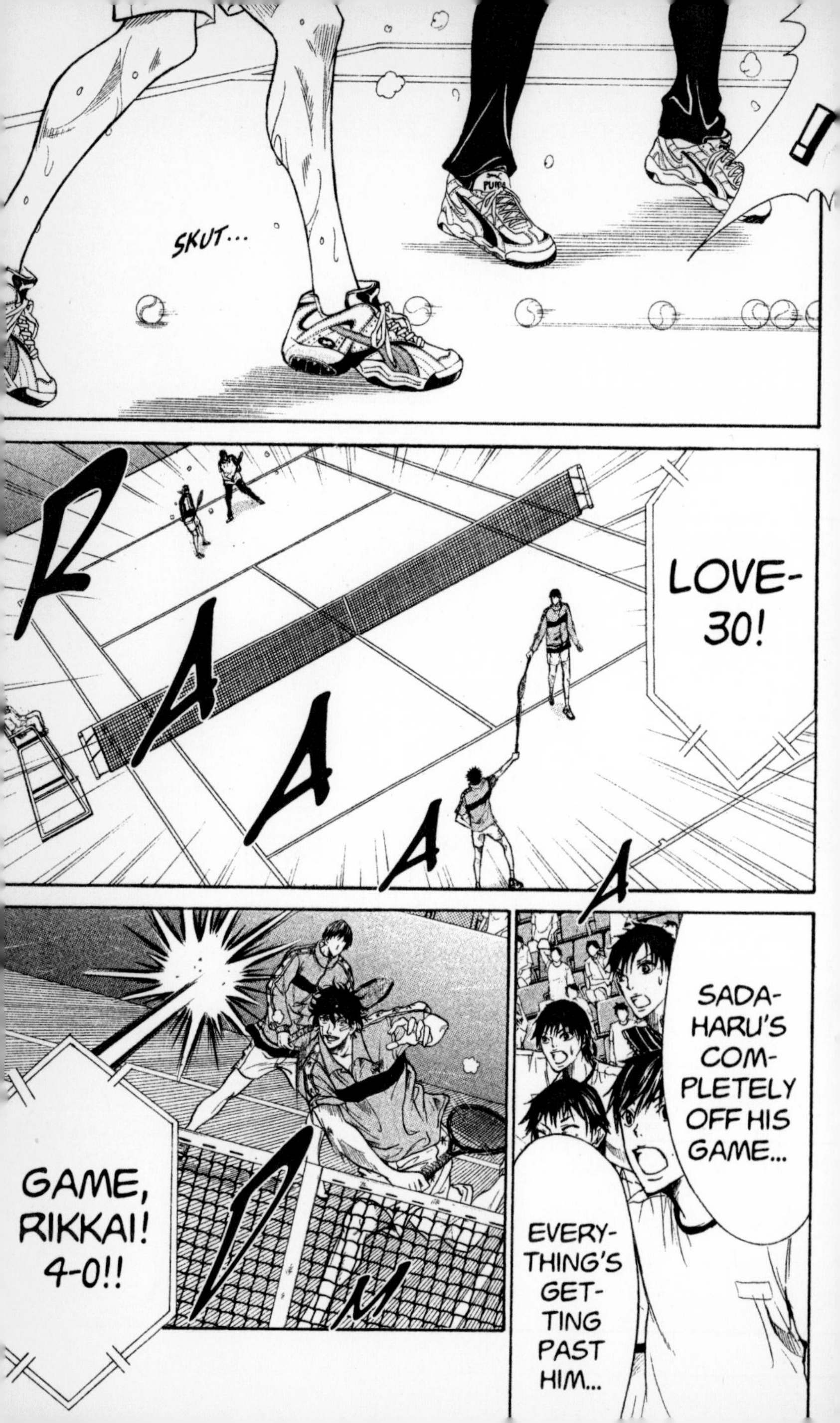
SKUT...
PUMA
LOVE-30!
RAAAAA
SADA-HARU'S COMPLETELY OFF HIS GAME...
EVERYTHING'S GETTING PAST HIM...
GAME, RIKKAI! 4-0!!

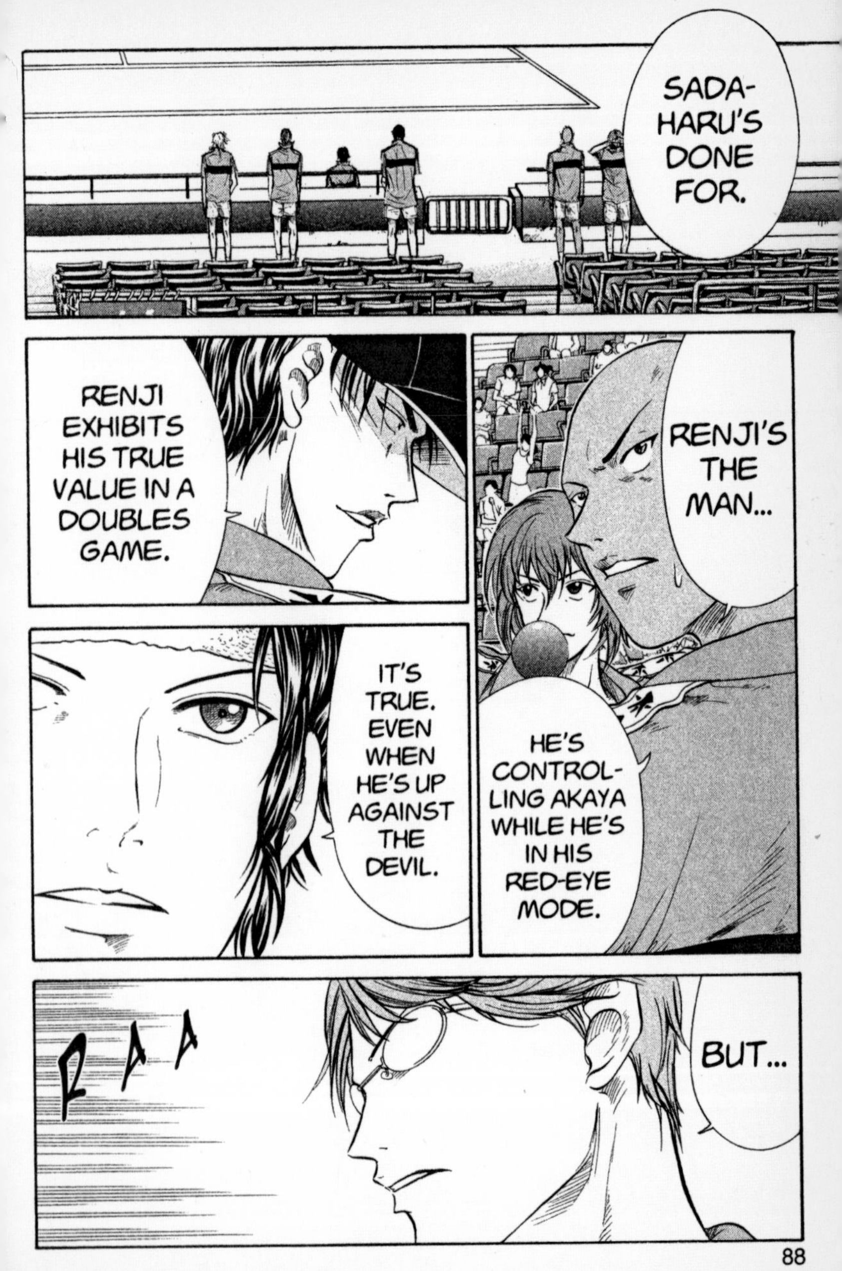
SADA-HARU'S DONE FOR.
RENJI'S THE MAN...
HE'S CONTROL-LING AKAYA WHILE HE'S IN HIS RED-EYE MODE.
RENJI EXHIBITS HIS TRUE VALUE IN A DOUBLES GAME.
IT'S TRUE. EVEN WHEN HE'S UP AGAINST THE DEVIL.
BUT...
RAA

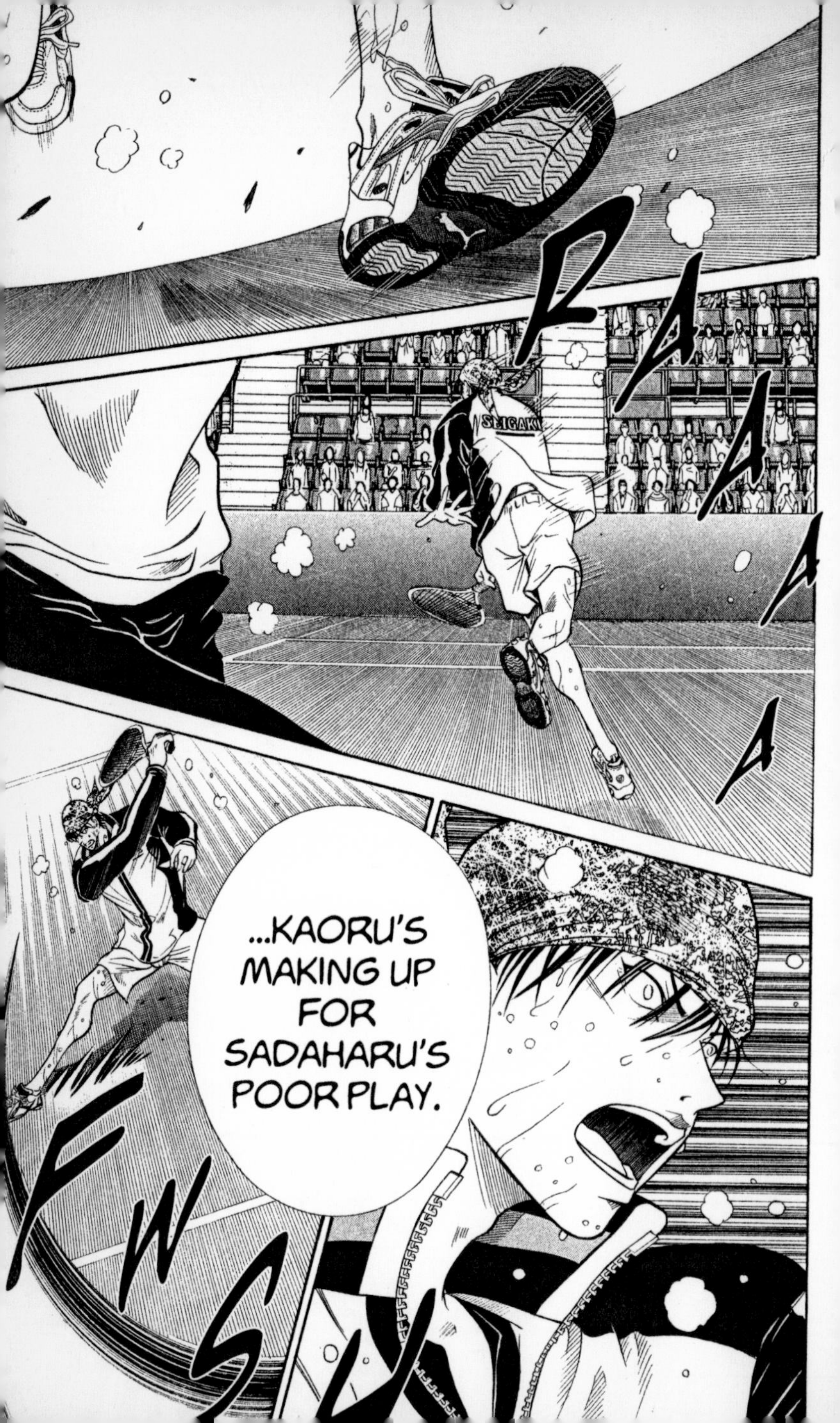

PA A A A A
SEIGAKU
...KAORU'S MAKING UP FOR SADAHARU'S POOR PLAY.
FWSH

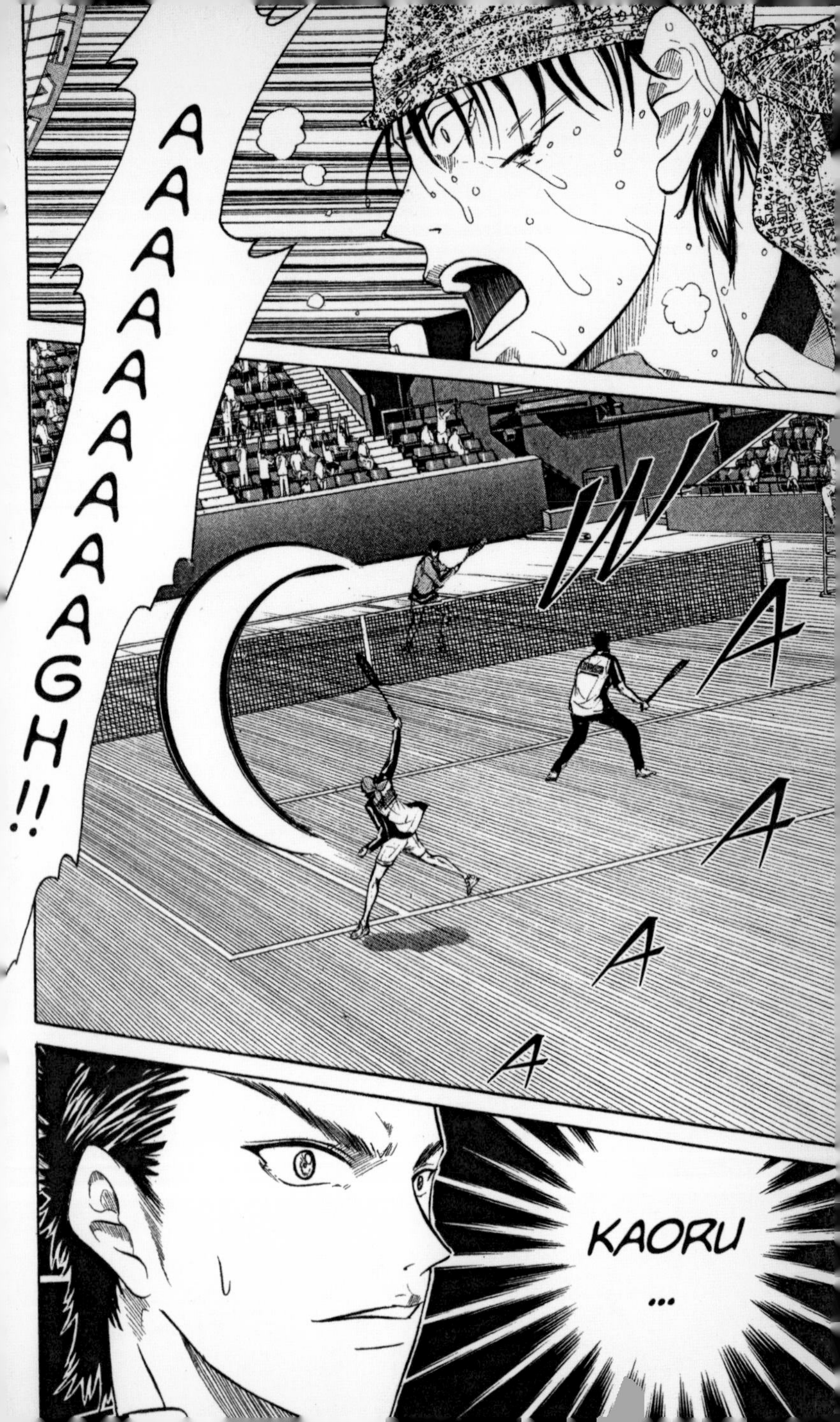
AAAAAAAAAAAAAGH!!
WAAAA
KAORU ...

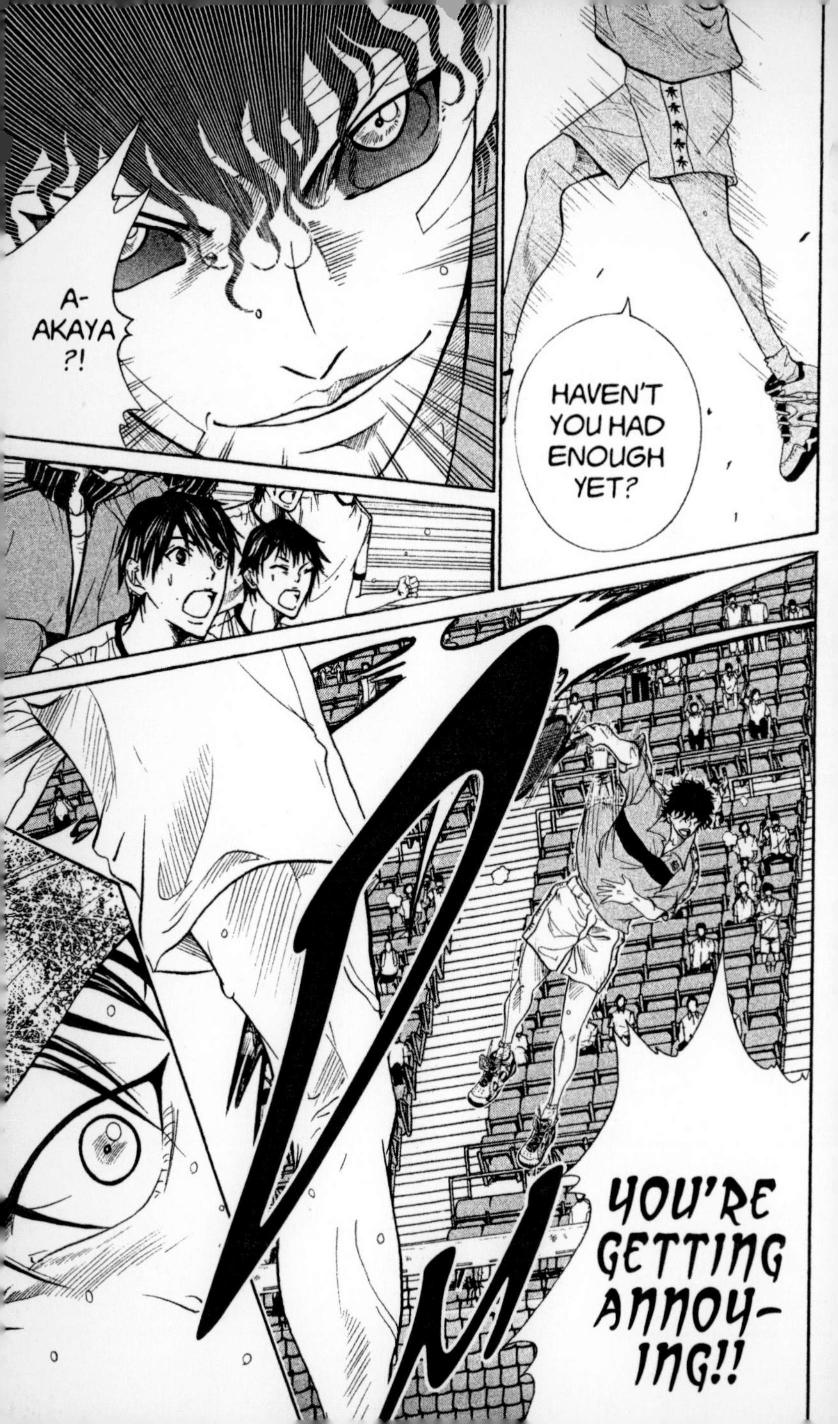
HAVEN'T YOU HAD ENOUGH YET?
A-AKAYA?!
YOU'RE GETTING ANNOY-ING!!

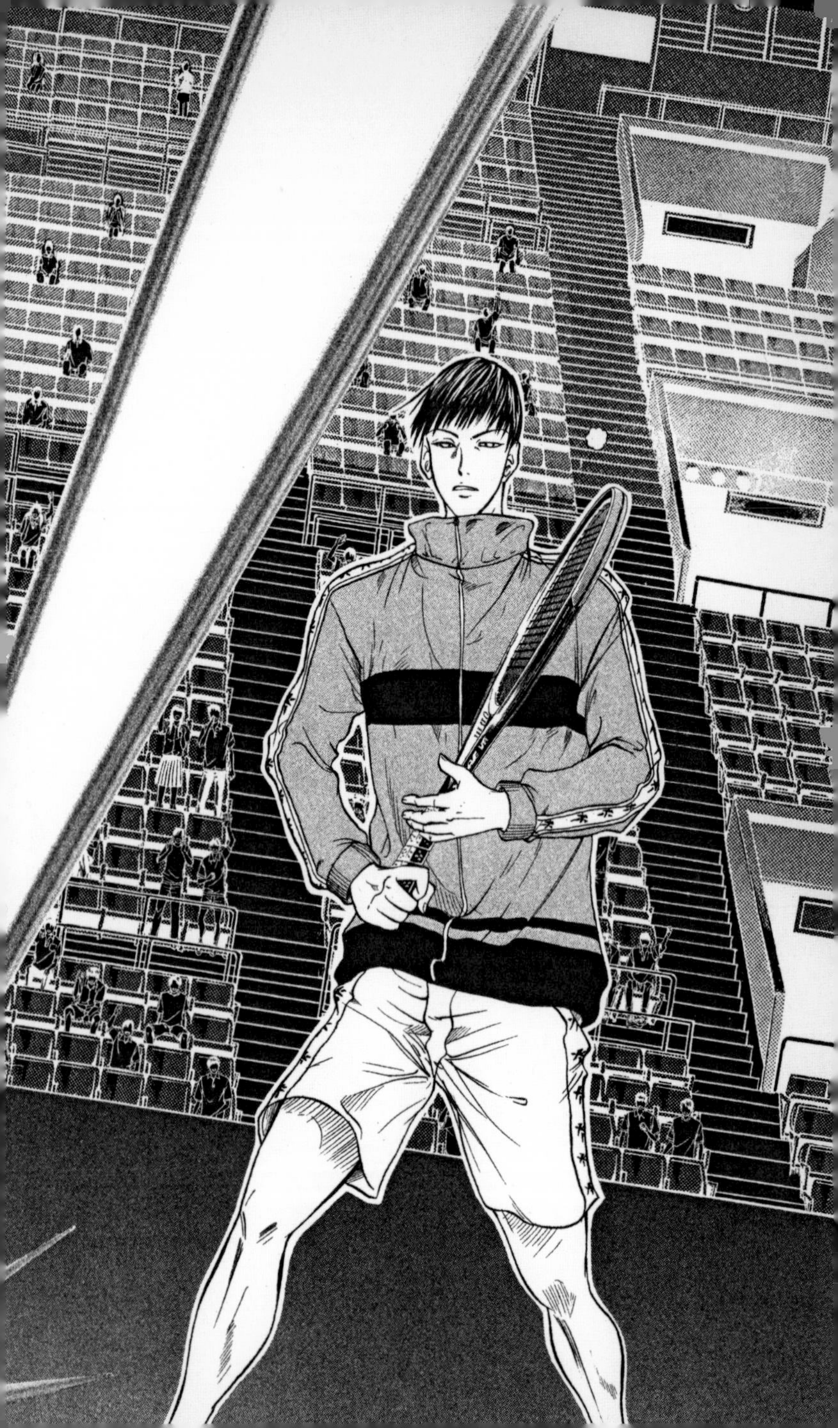

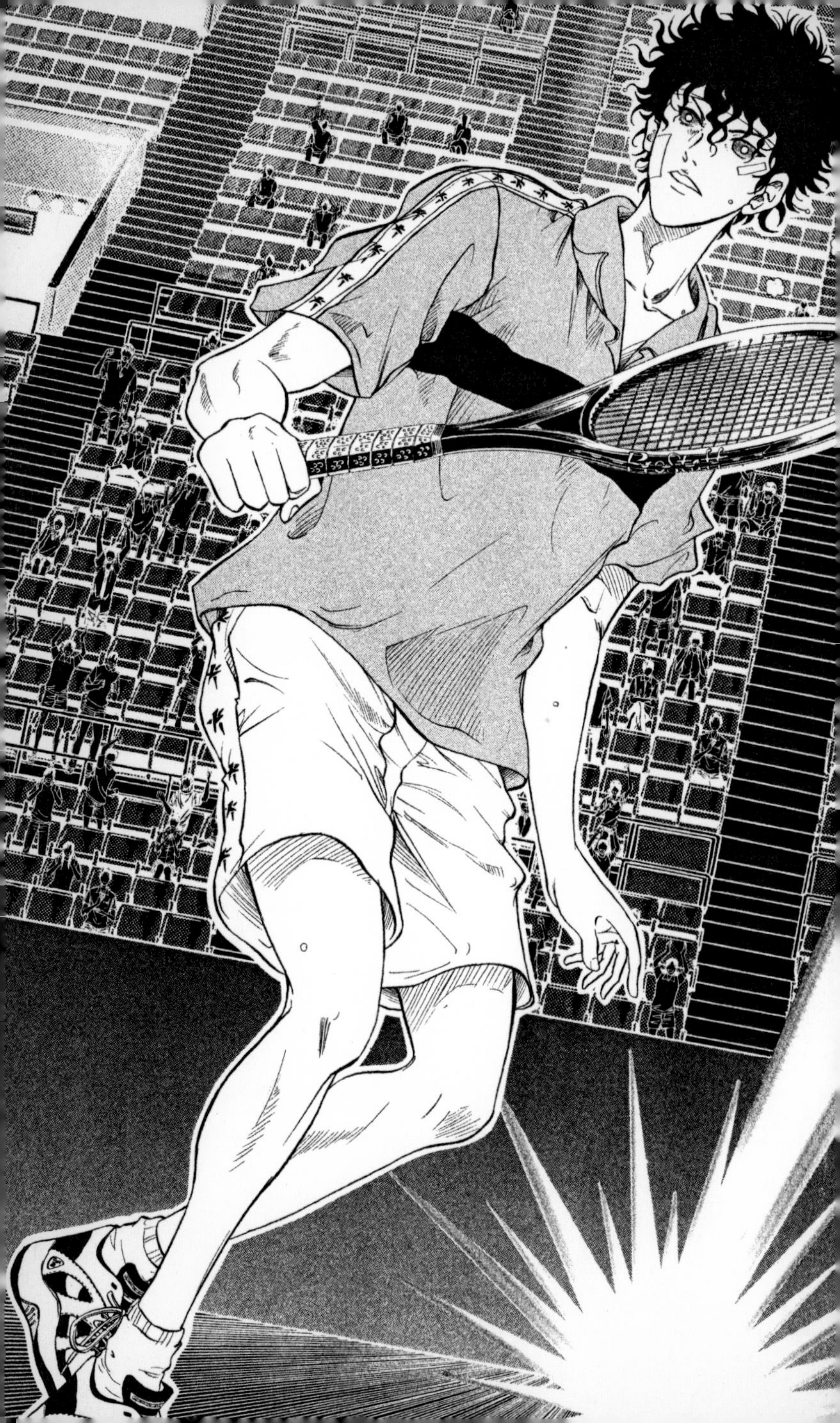

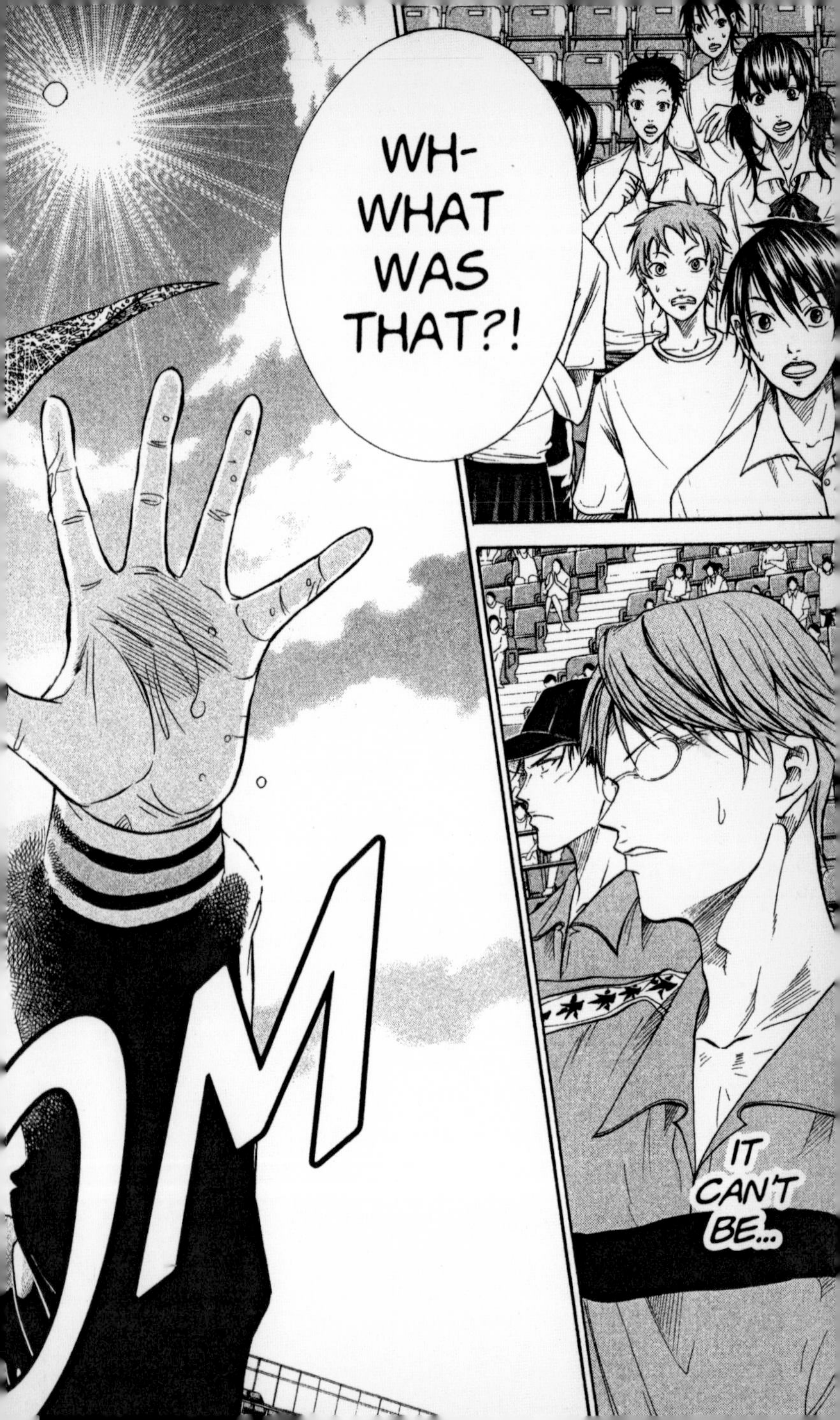
WH- WHAT WAS THAT?!
IT CAN'T BE...
M

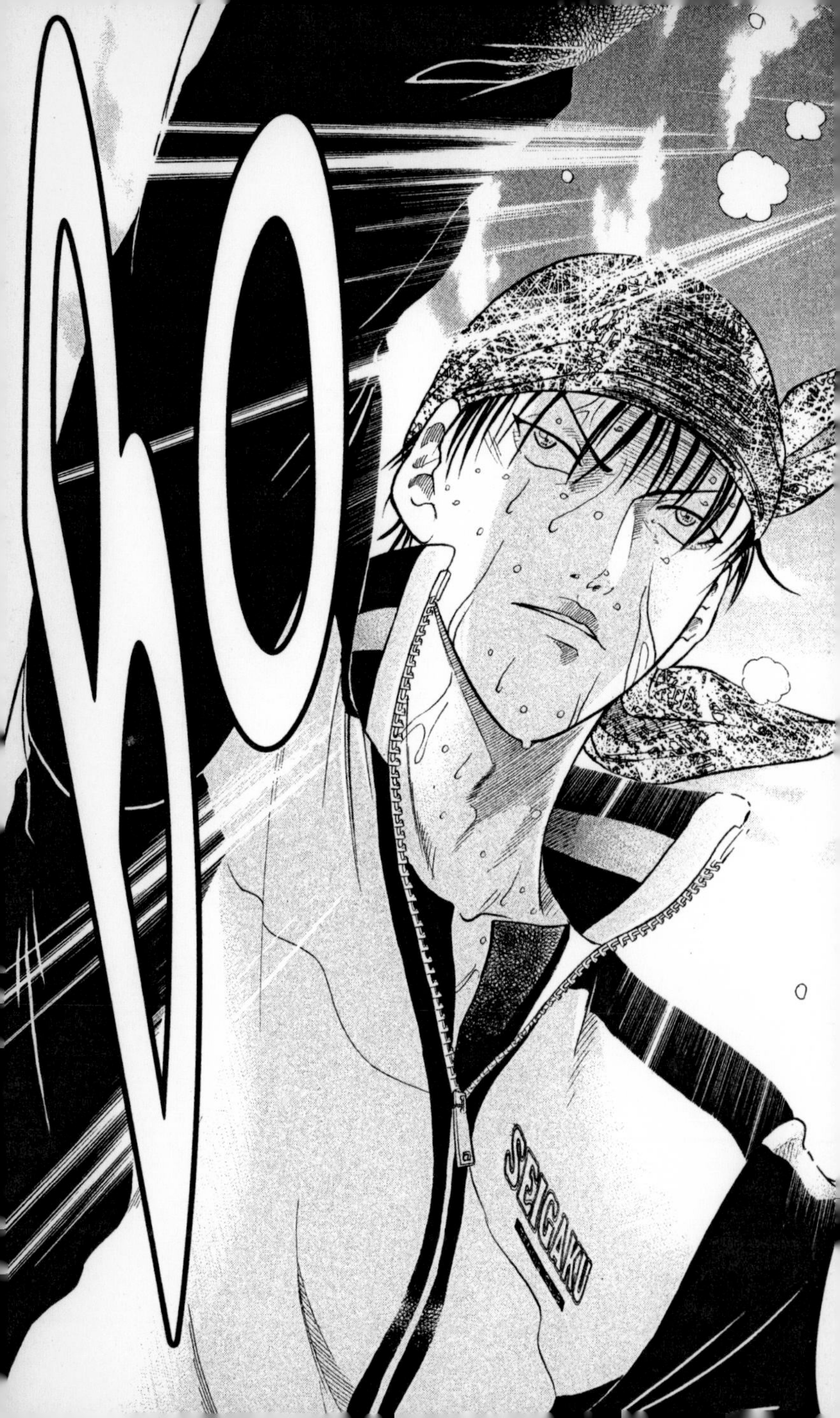
SEIGAKU

テニスの王子様

THE PRINCE OF TENNIS

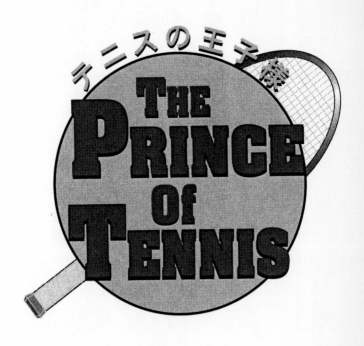

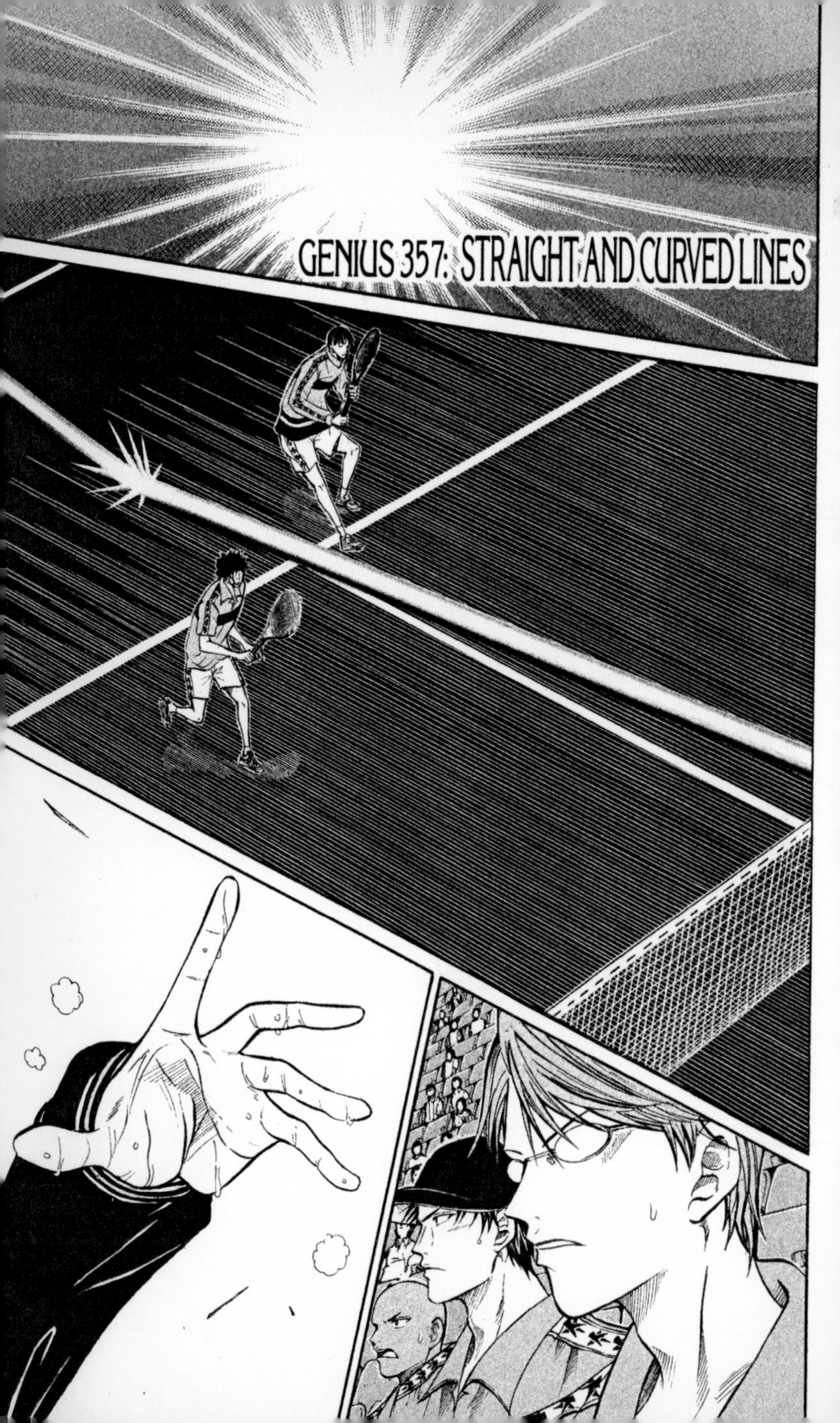
GENIUS 357: STRAIGHT AND CURVED LINES

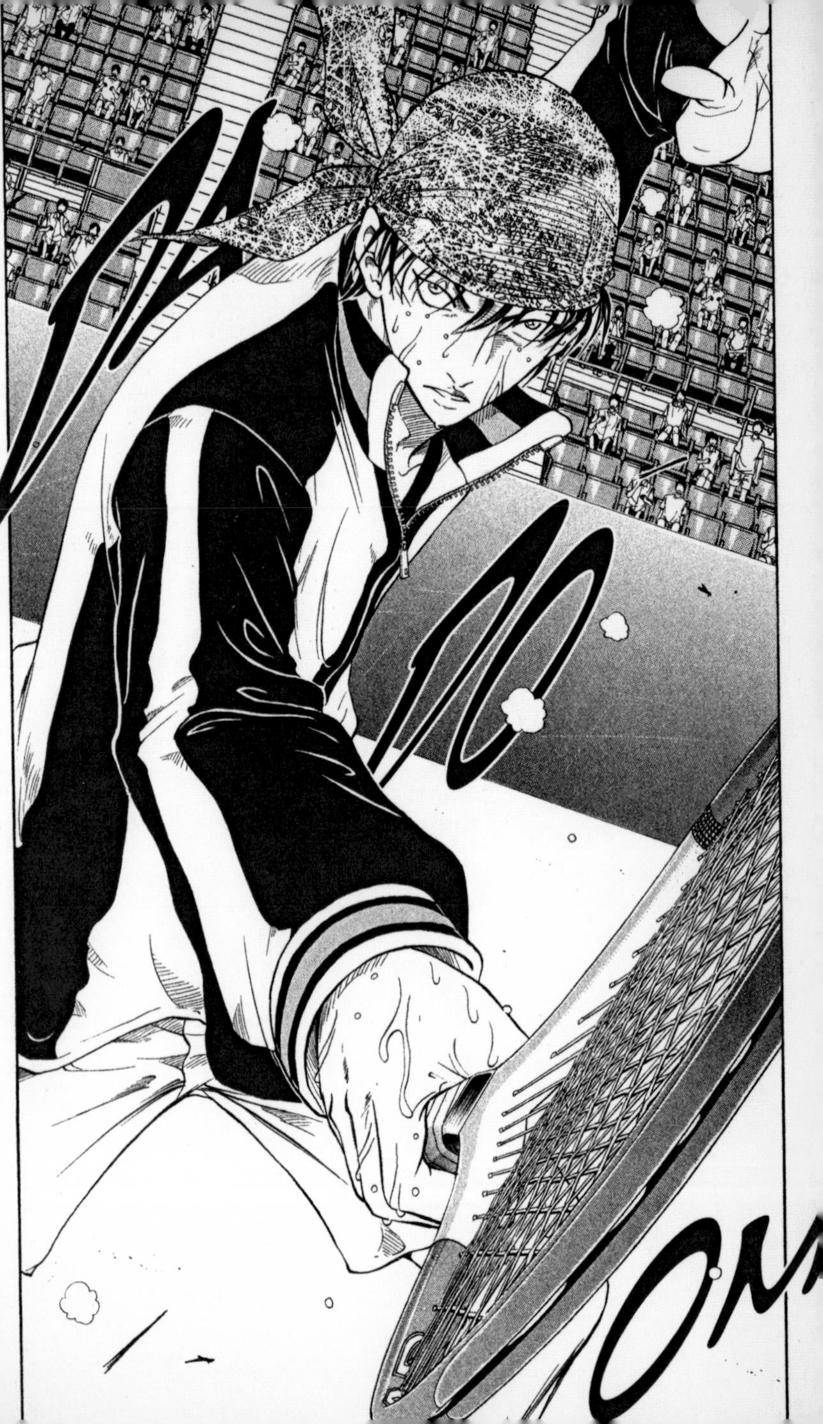

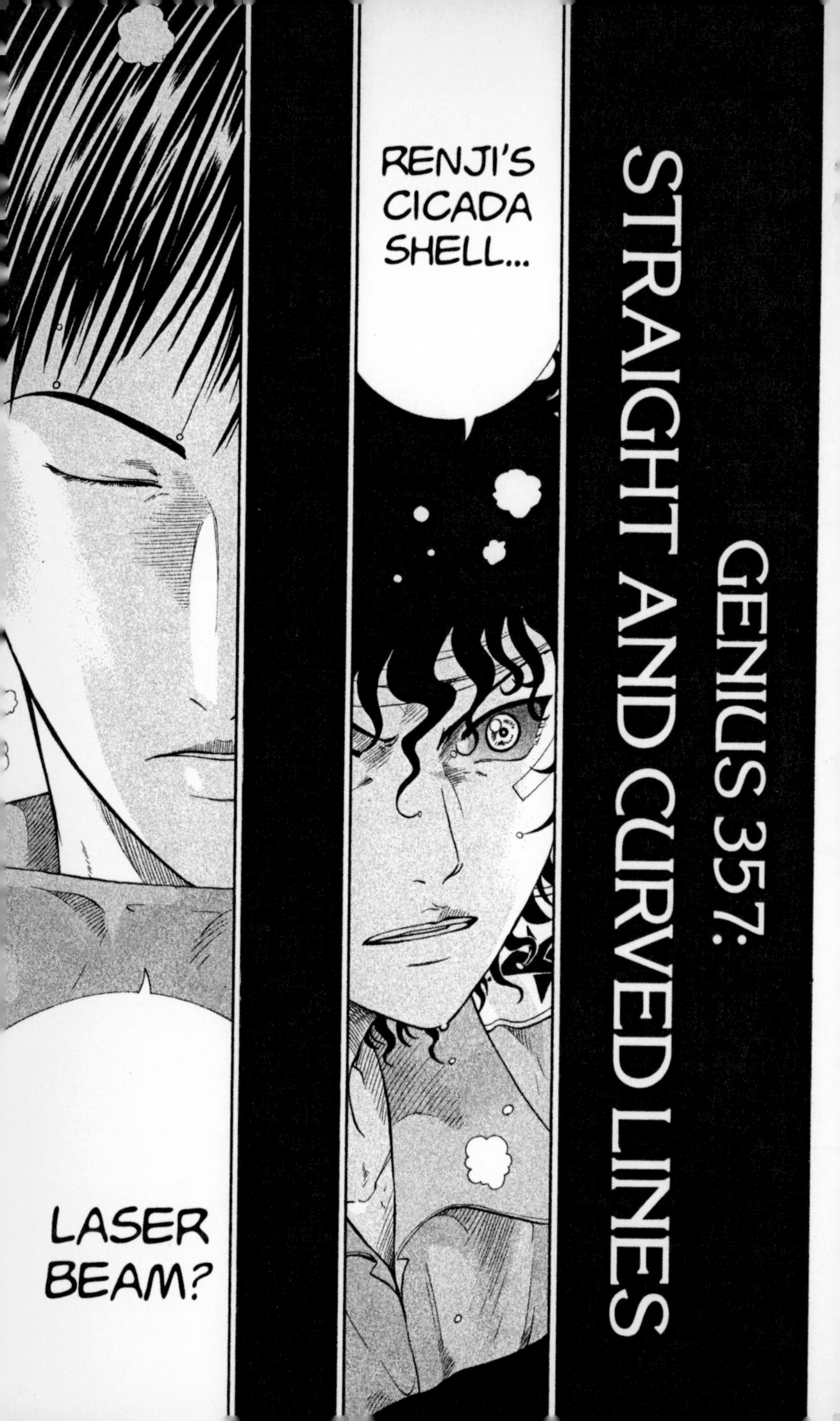
GENIUS 357:
STRAIGHT AND CURVED LINES
RENJI'S CICADA SHELL...
LASER BEAM?

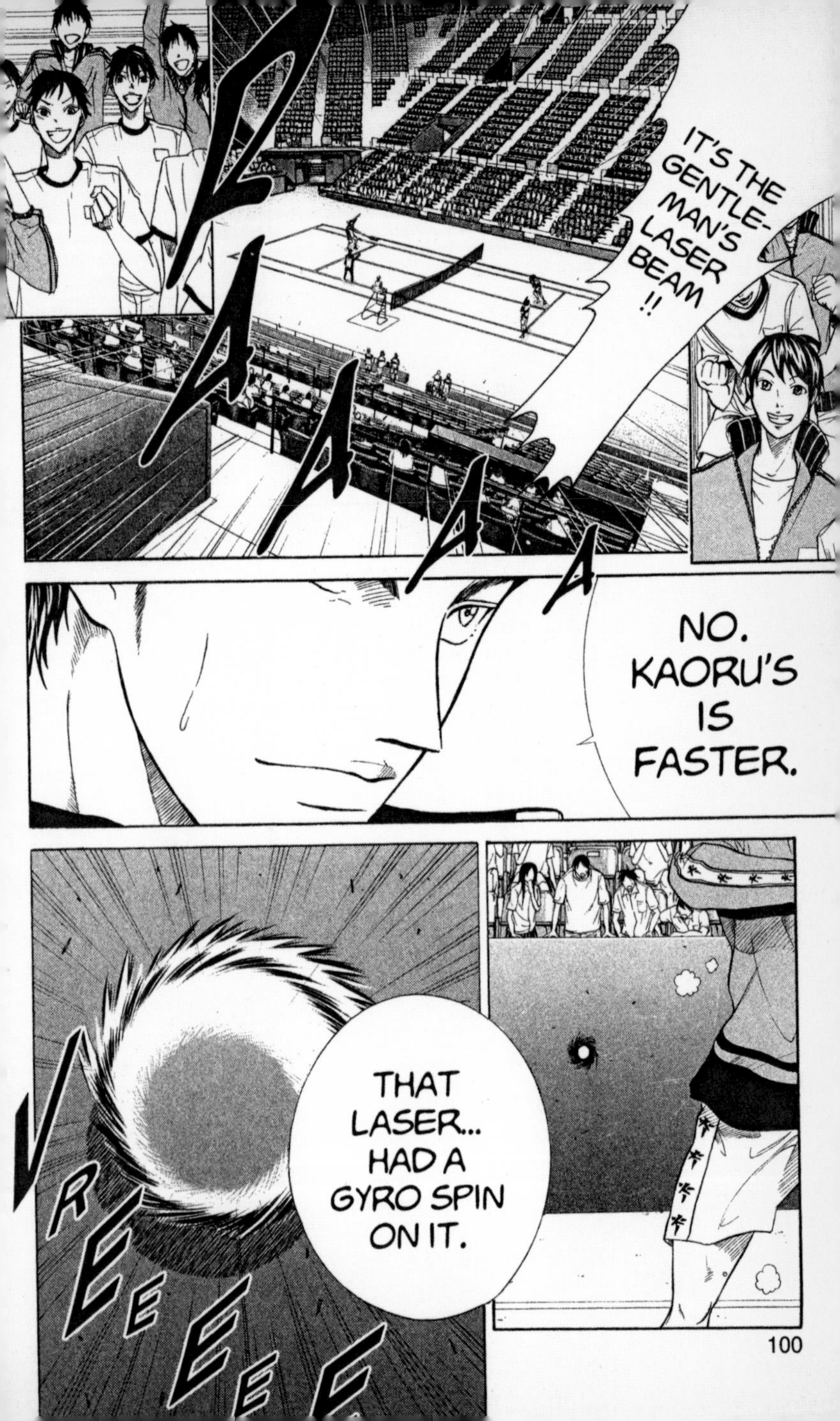
IT'S THE GENTLE-MAN'S LASER BEAM!!
NO. KAORU'S IS FASTER.
THAT LASER... HAD A GYRO SPIN ON IT.

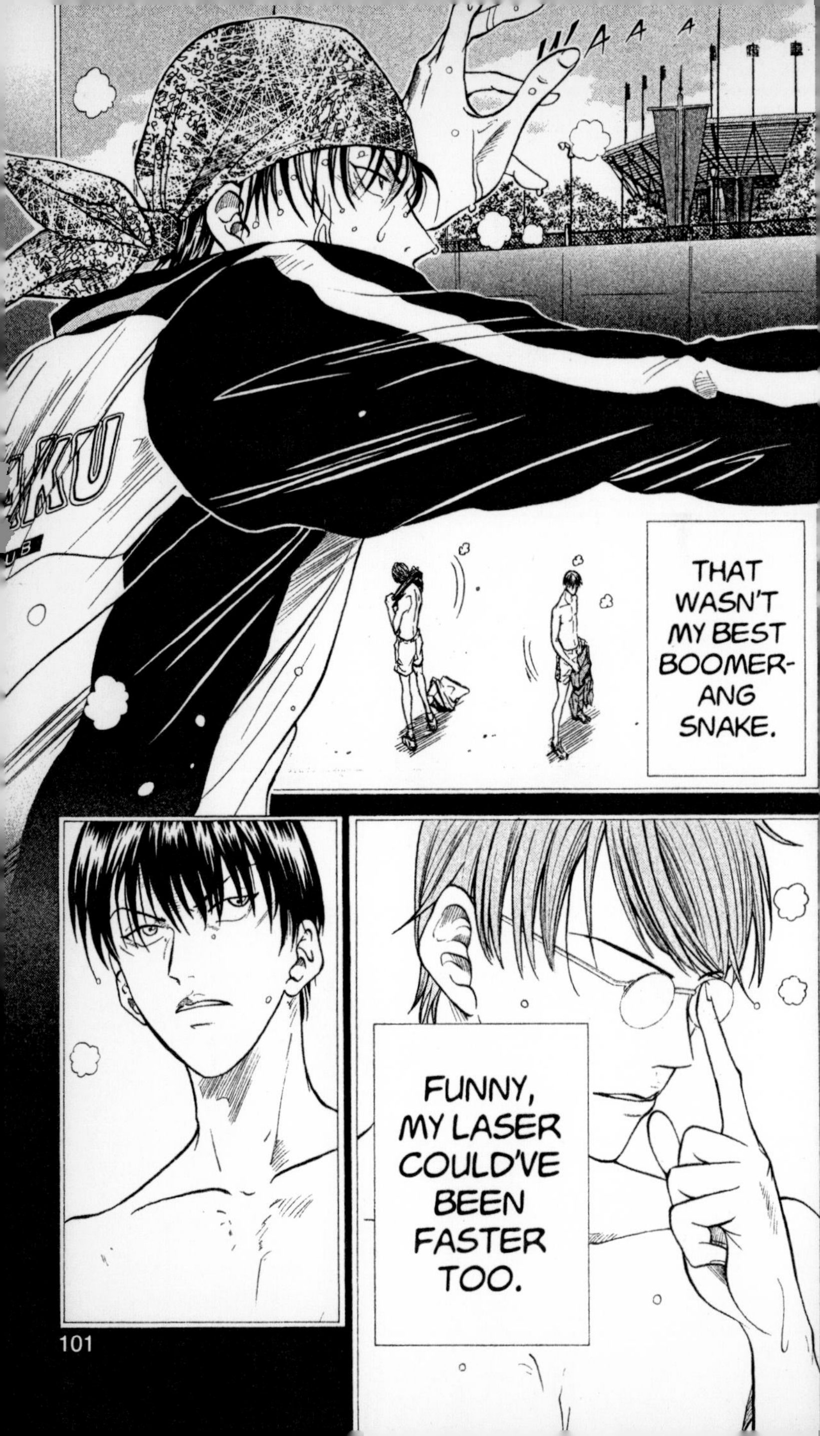
THAT WASN'T MY BEST BOOMERANG SNAKE.
FUNNY, MY LASER COULD'VE BEEN FASTER TOO.

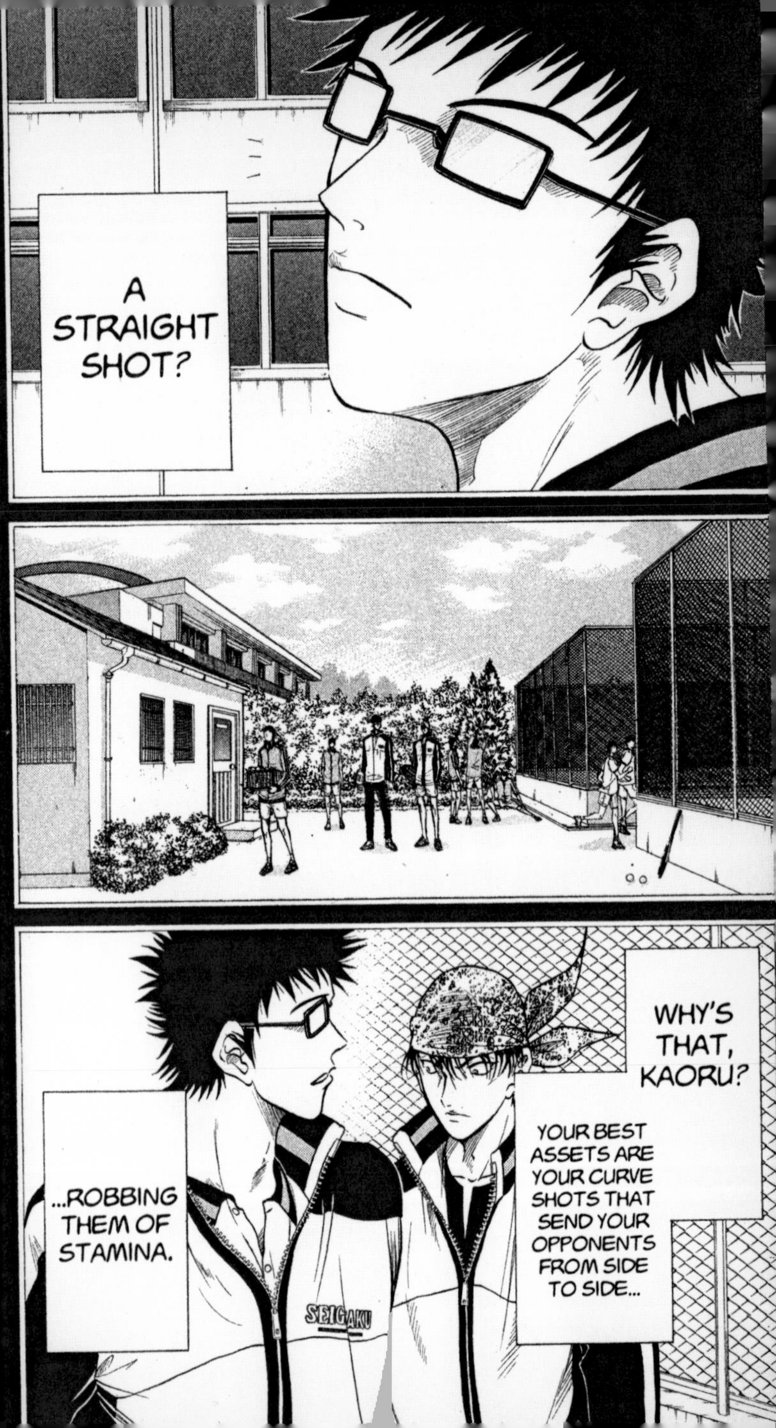
A STRAIGHT SHOT?
WHY'S THAT, KAORU?
YOUR BEST ASSETS ARE YOUR CURVE SHOTS THAT SEND YOUR OPPONENTS FROM SIDE TO SIDE...
...ROBBING THEM OF STAMINA.
SEIGAKU

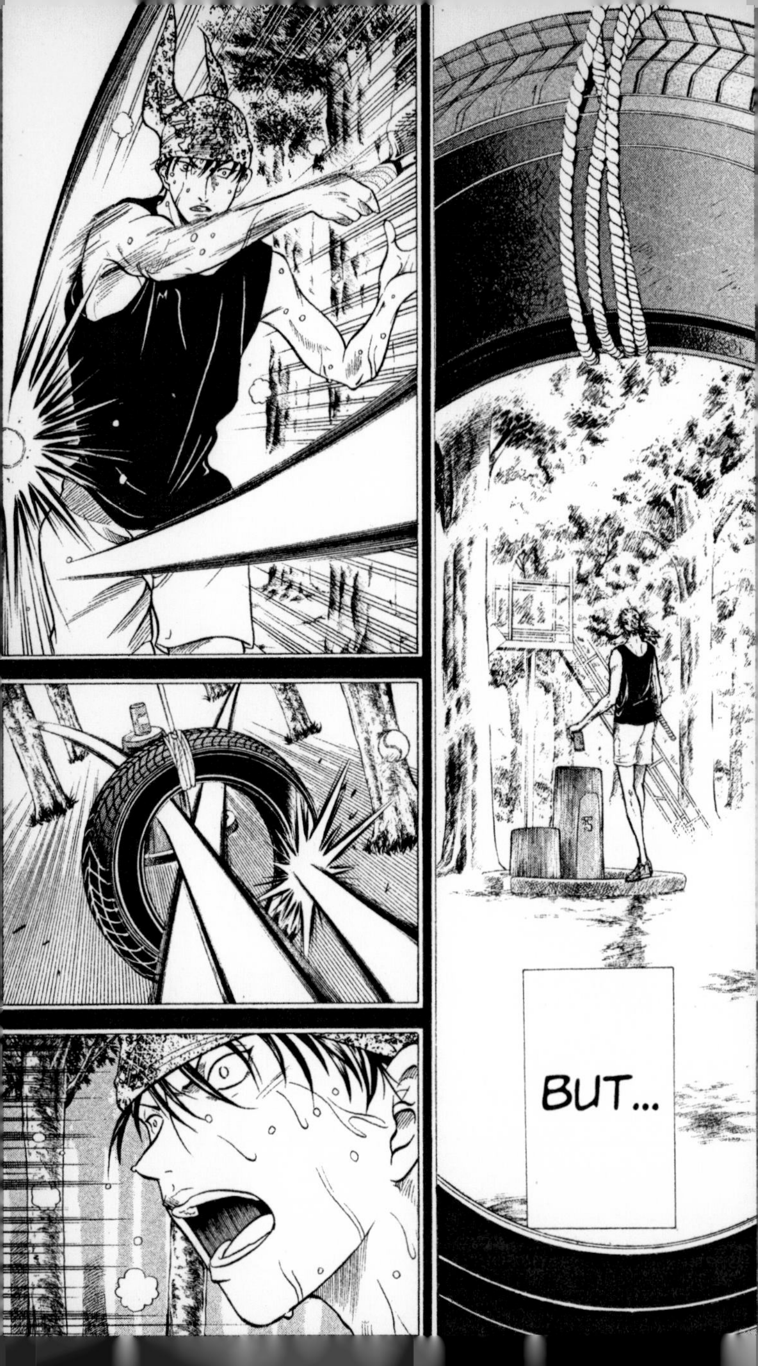
BUT...

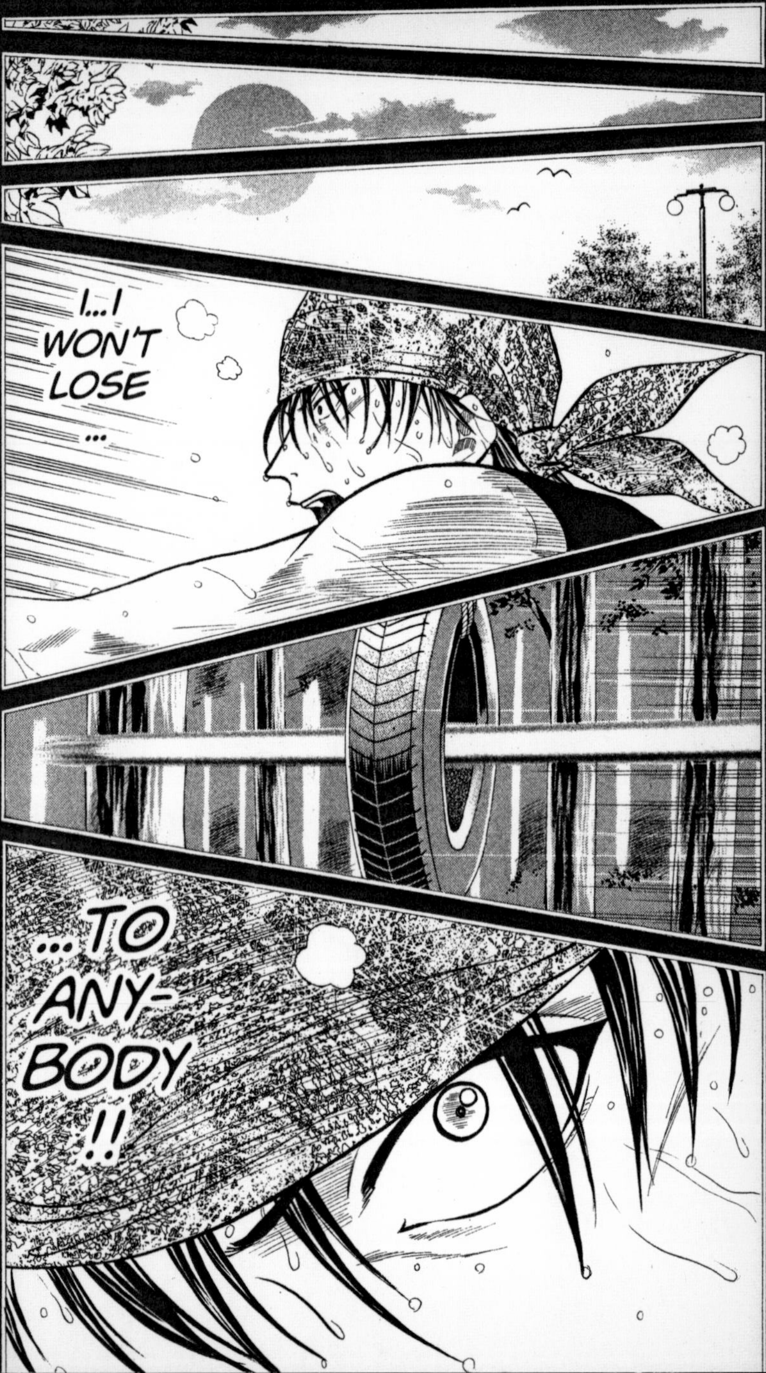
I...I WON'T LOSE ...
...TO ANY-BODY !!

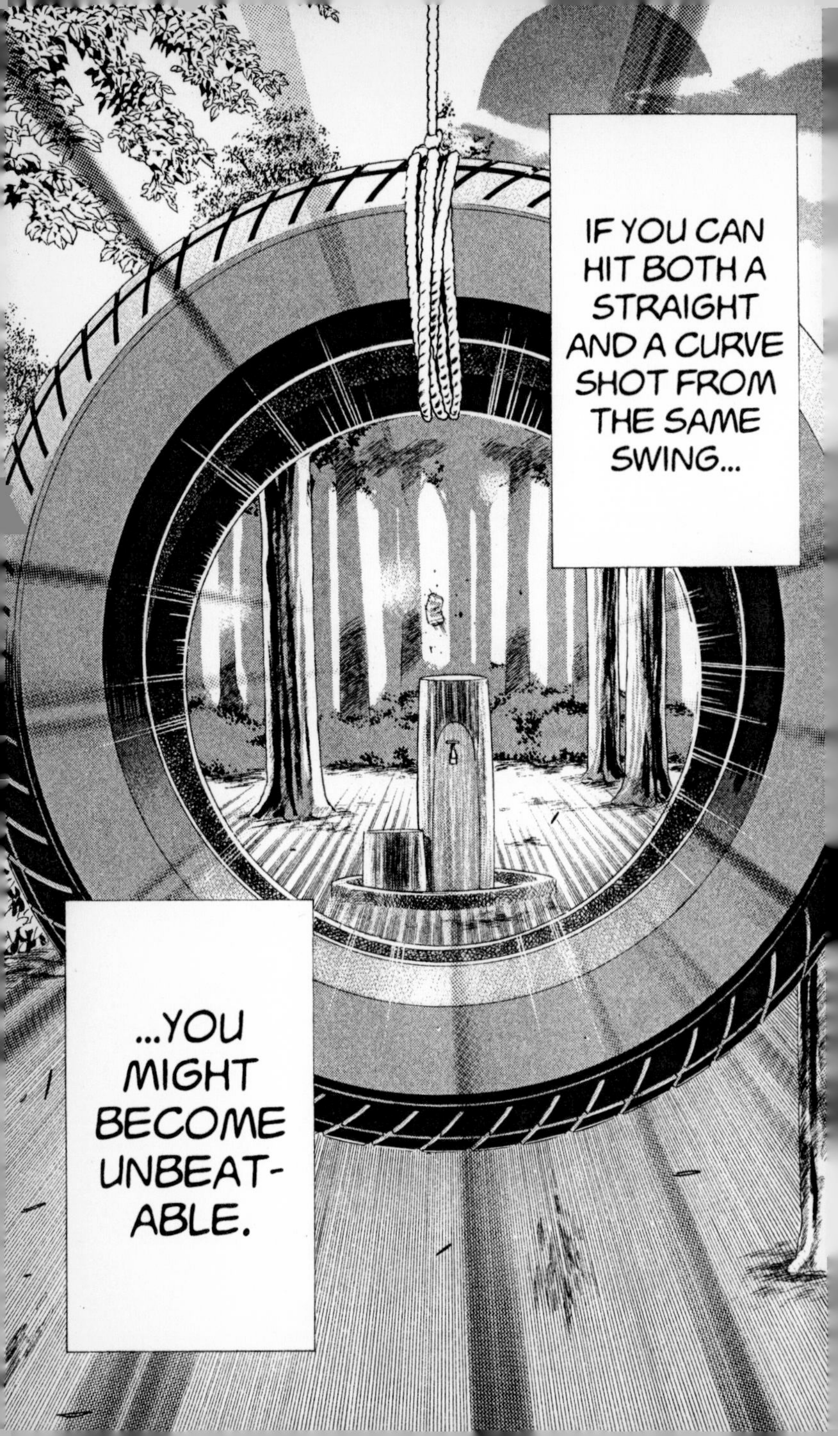
IF YOU CAN HIT BOTH A STRAIGHT AND A CURVE SHOT FROM THE SAME SWING...
...YOU MIGHT BECOME UNBEAT-ABLE.

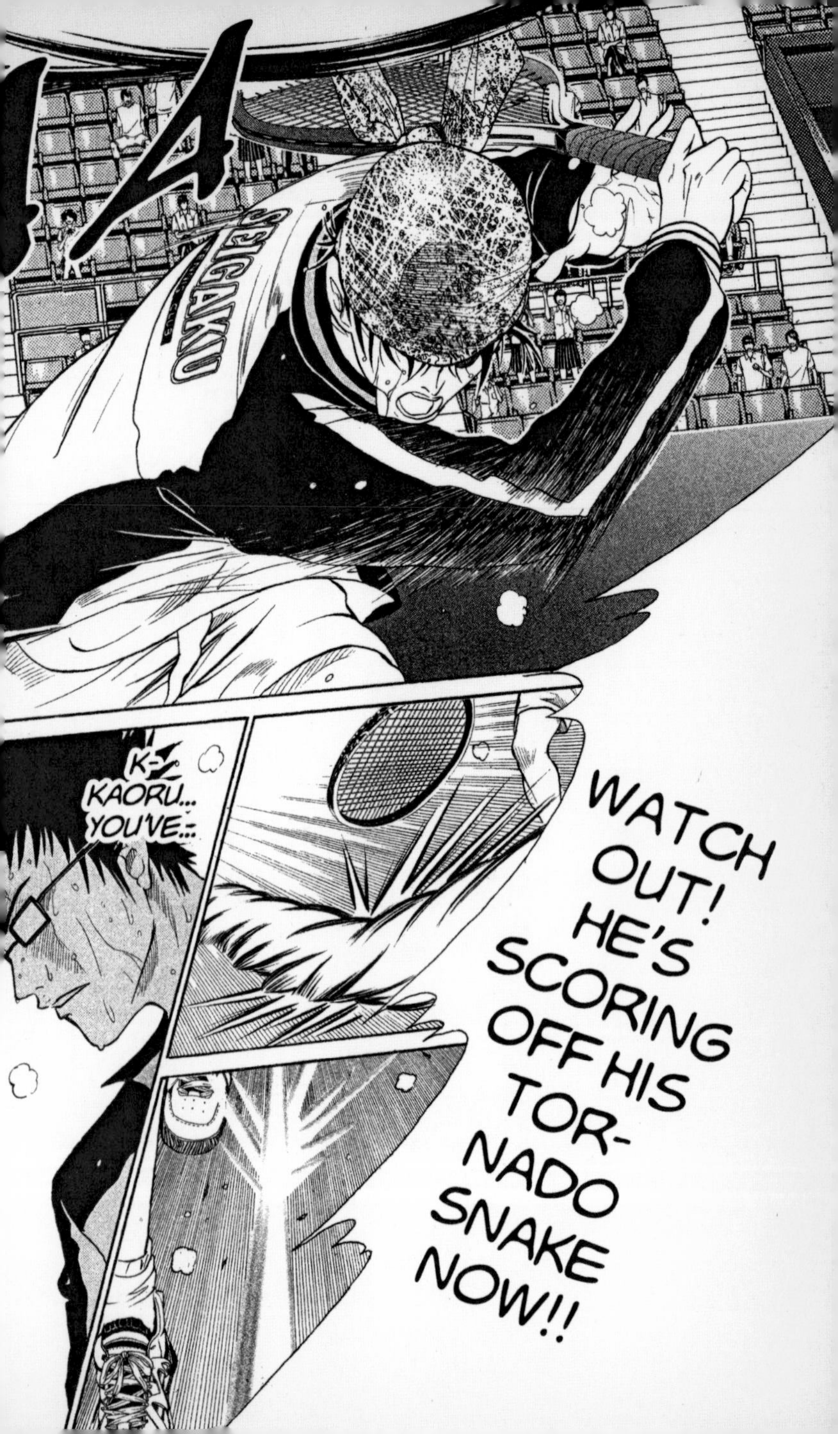

SEIGAKU
WATCH OUT! HE'S SCORING OFF HIS TOR-NADO SNAKE NOW!!
K-KAORU... YOU'VE...

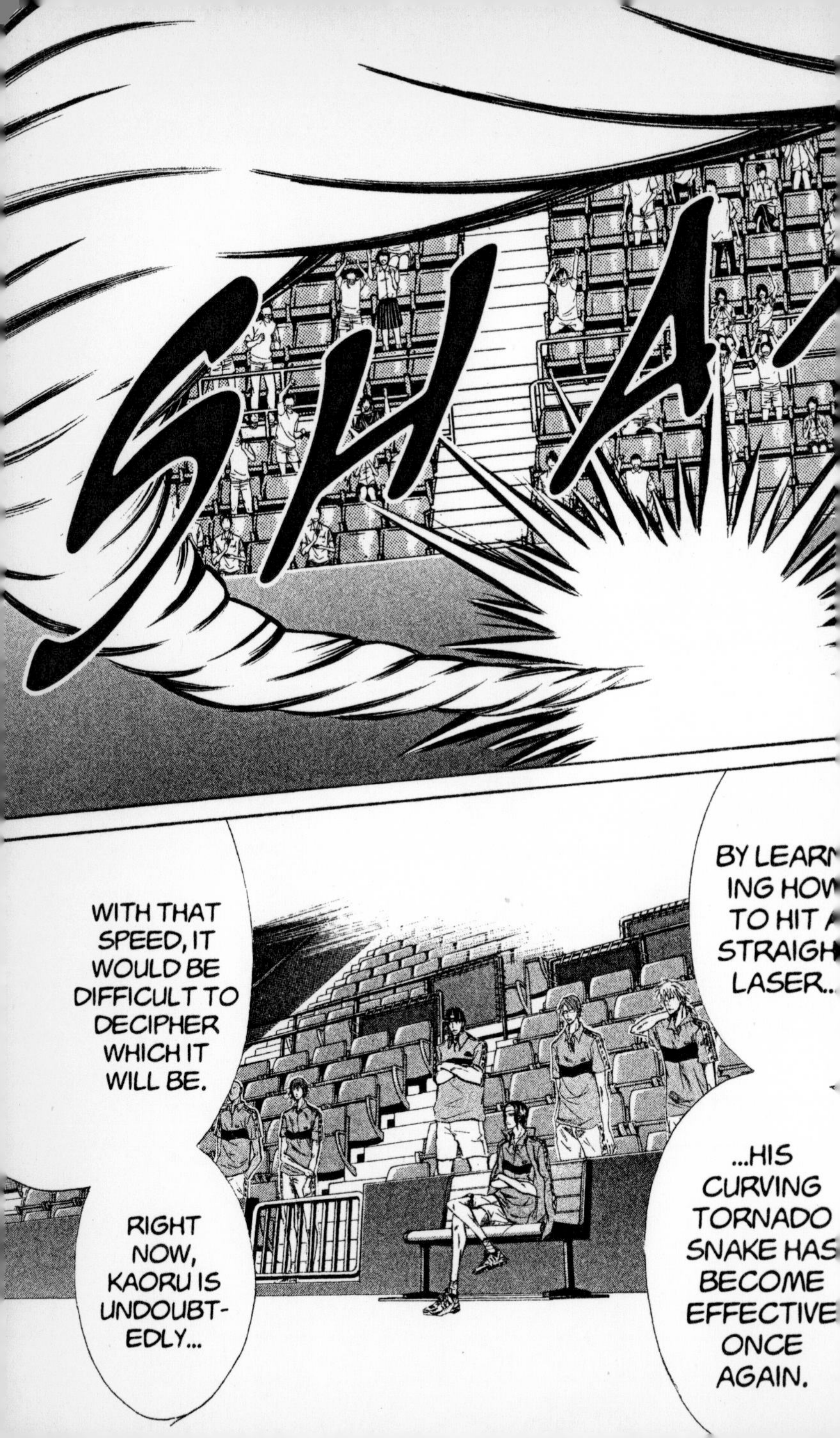
SHA
BY LEARN ING HOW TO HIT A STRAIGH LASER...
...HIS CURVING TORNADO SNAKE HAS BECOME EFFECTIVE ONCE AGAIN.
WITH THAT SPEED, IT WOULD BE DIFFICULT TO DECIPHER WHICH IT WILL BE.
RIGHT NOW, KAORU IS UNDOUBT-EDLY...

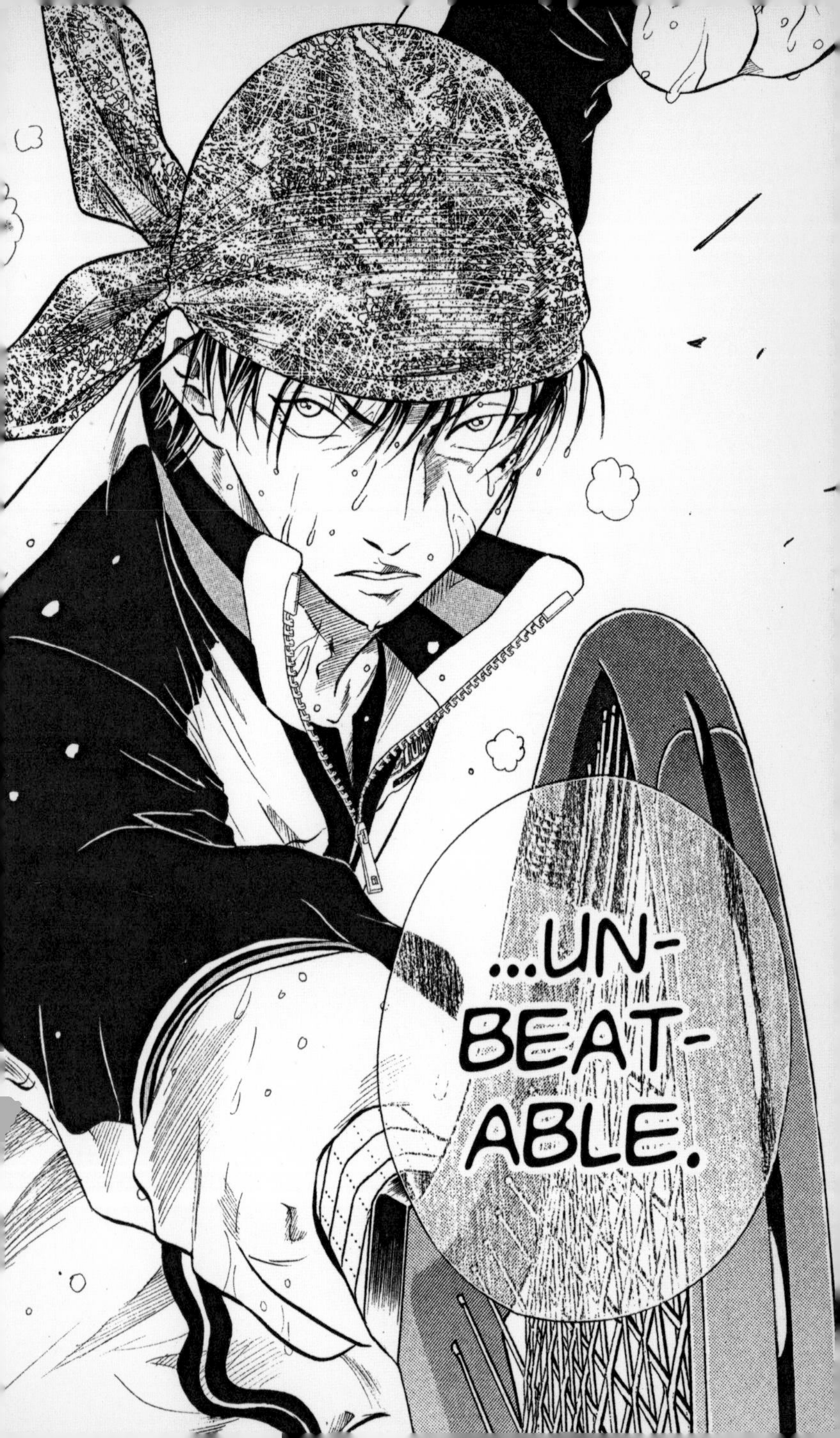
...UN-
BEAT-
ABLE.

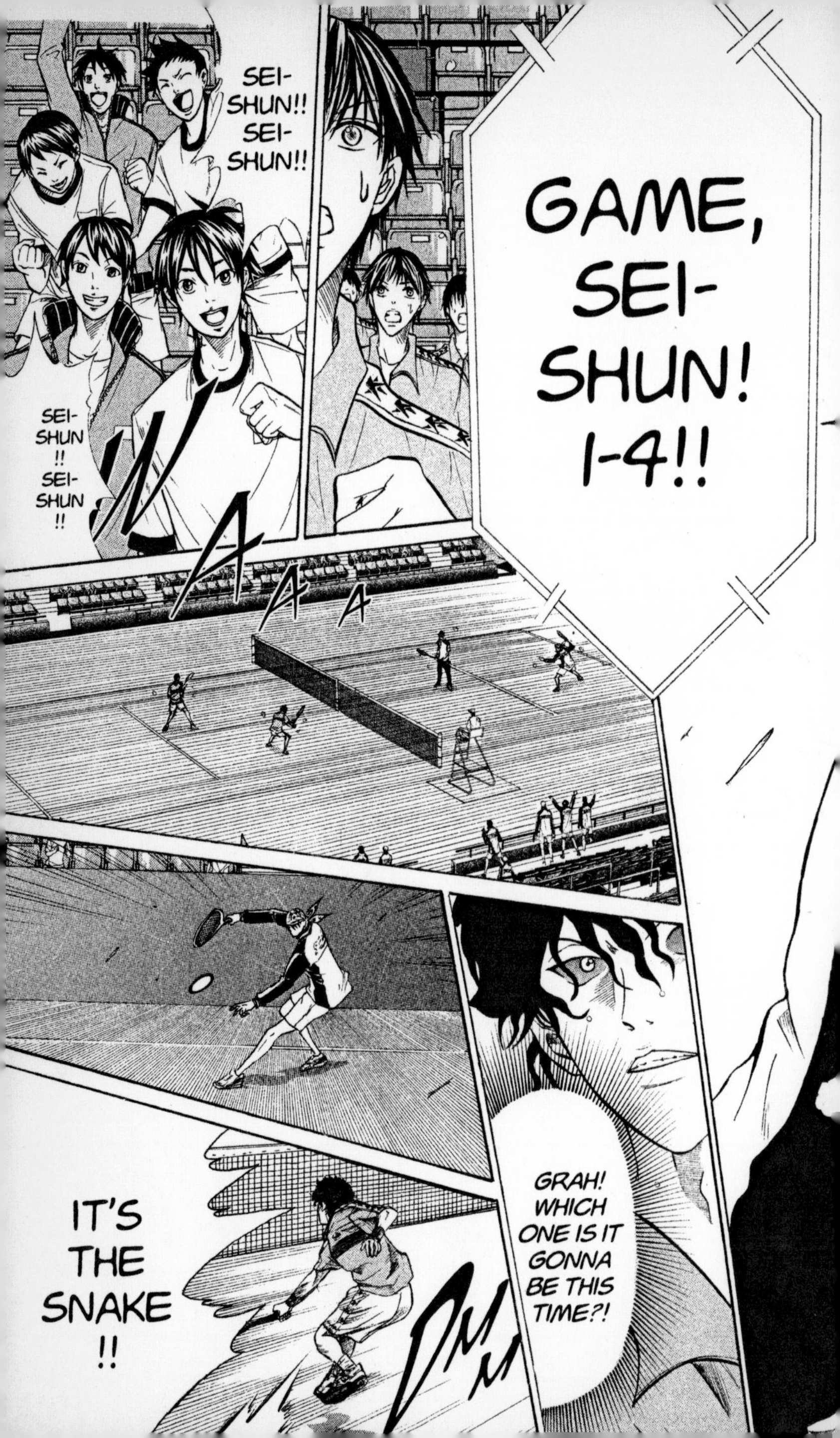
GAME, SEI-SHUN! 1-4!!
SEI-SHUN!! SEI-SHUN!!
SEI-SHUN!! SEI-SHUN!!
WAAA
GRAH! WHICH ONE IS IT GONNA BE THIS TIME?!
IT'S THE SNAKE!!

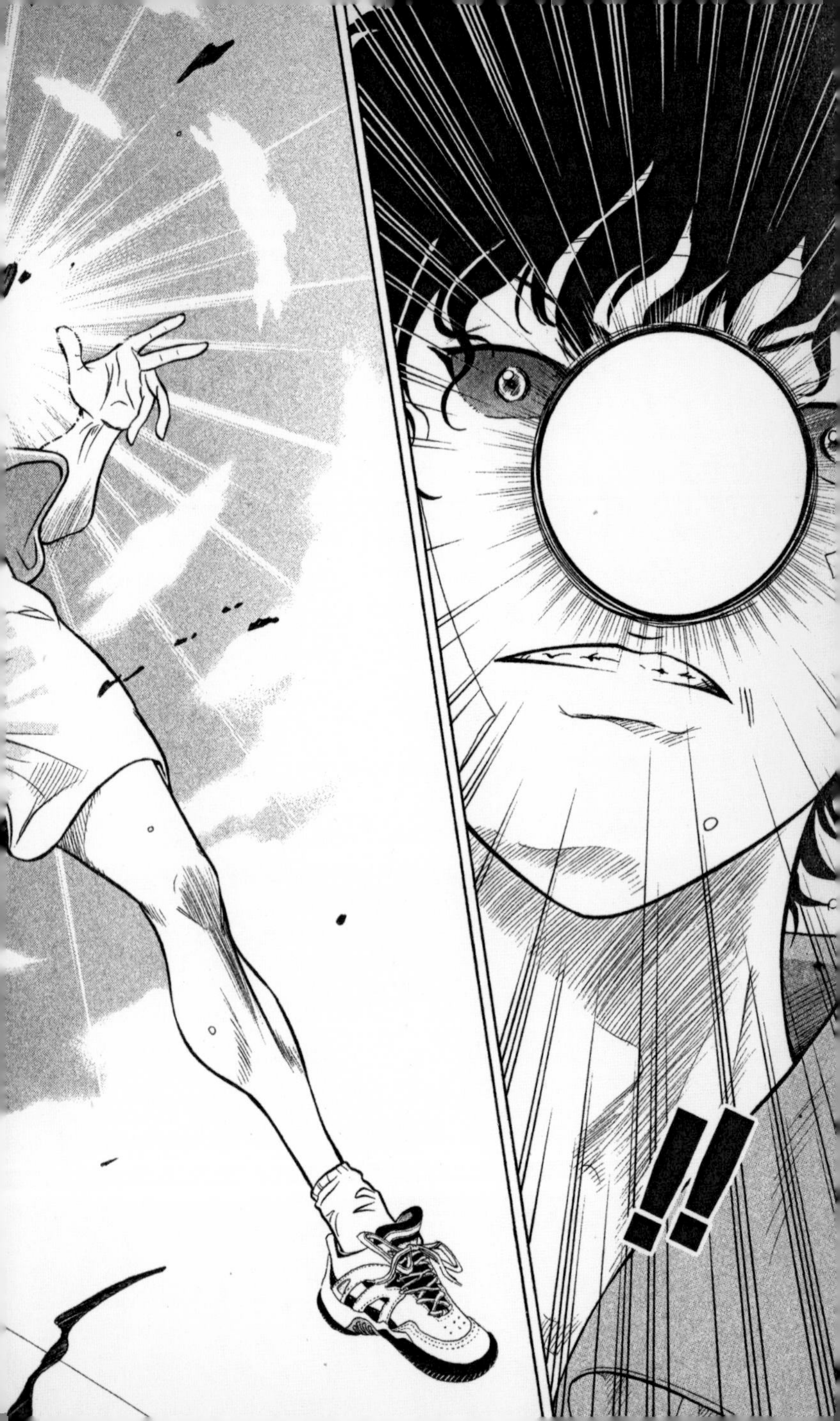
!!

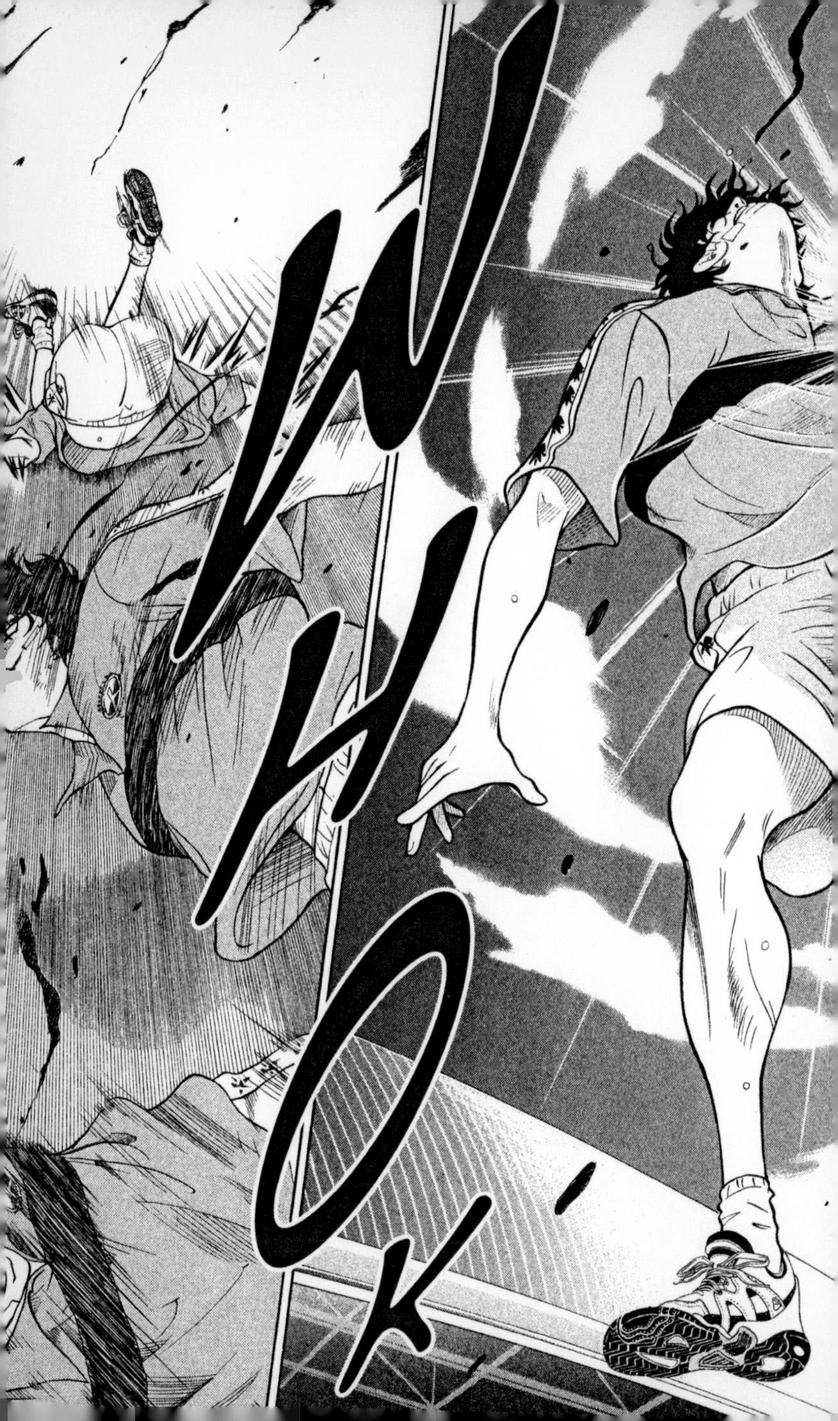

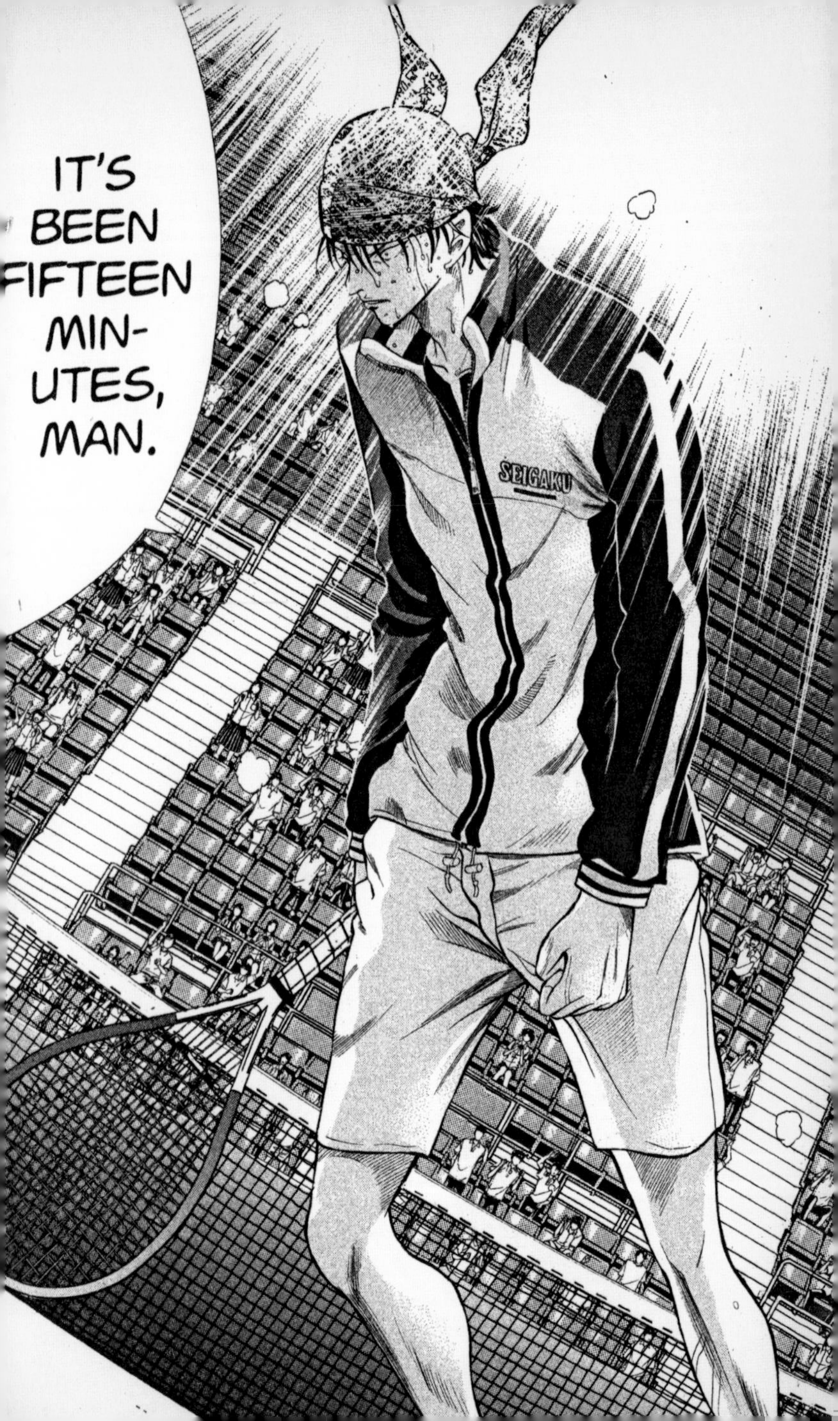
IT'S BEEN FIFTEEN MIN-UTES, MAN.
SEIGAKU

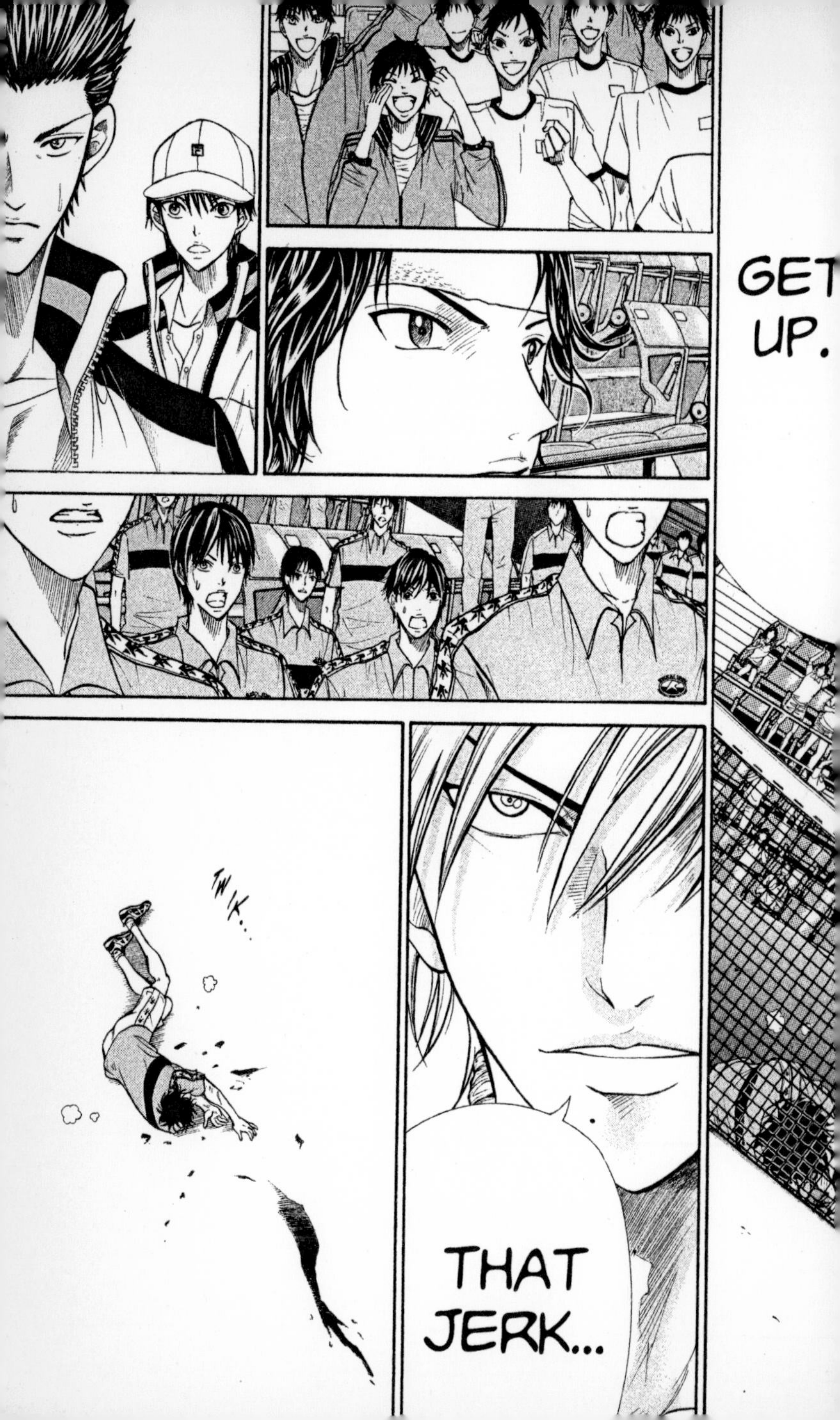
GET UP.
THAT JERK...
TWIK...

テニスの王子様

THE PRINCE OF TENNIS

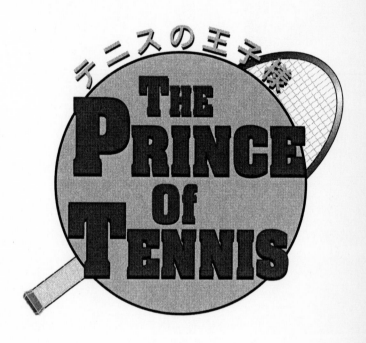

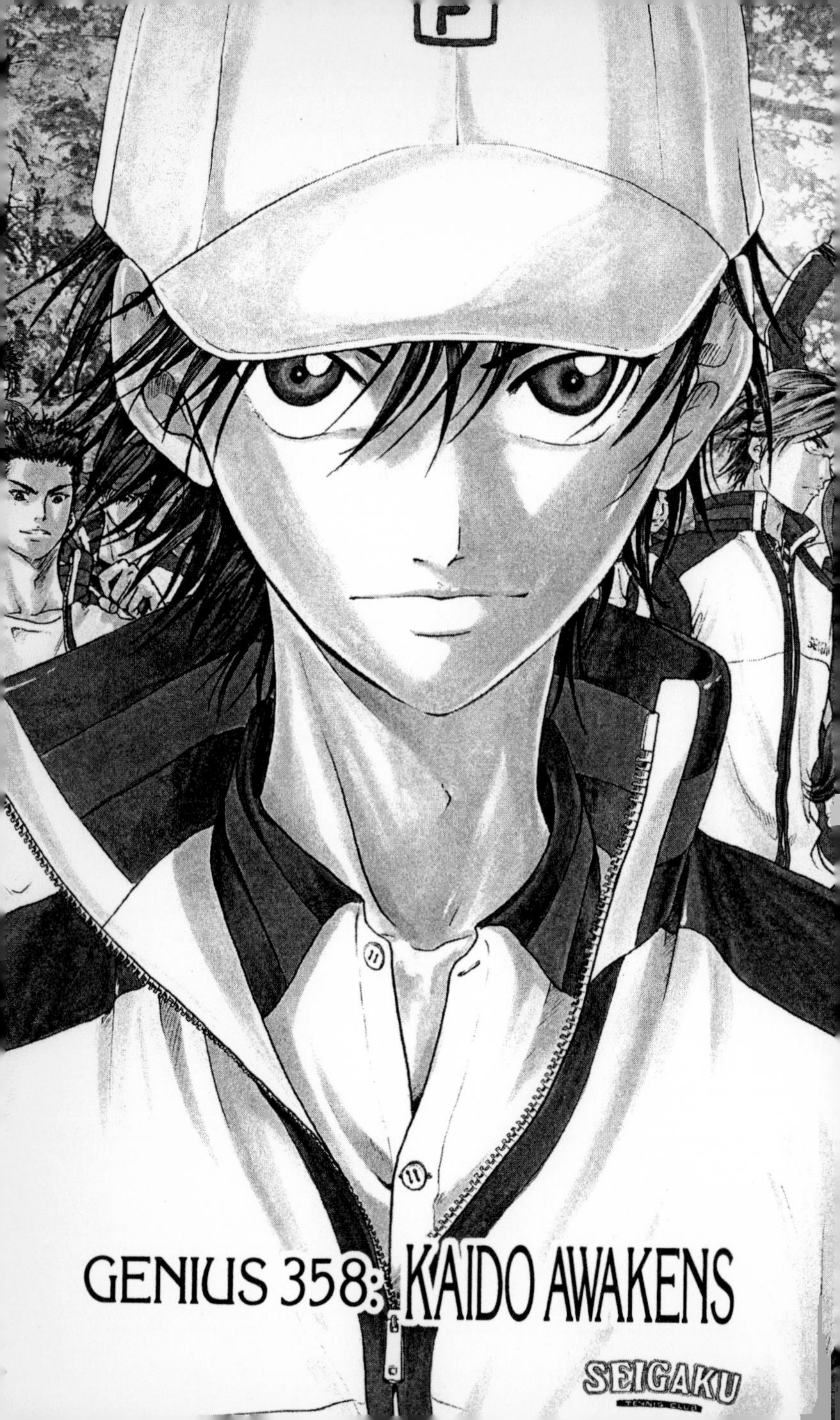
SEIGAKU

GENIUS 358: KAIDO AWAKENS

テニスの王子様

THE PRINCE OF TENNIS

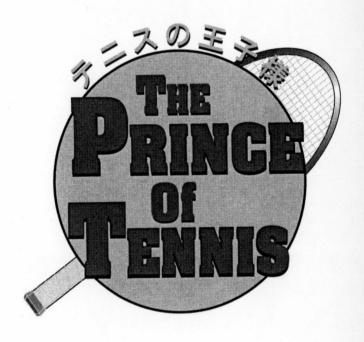

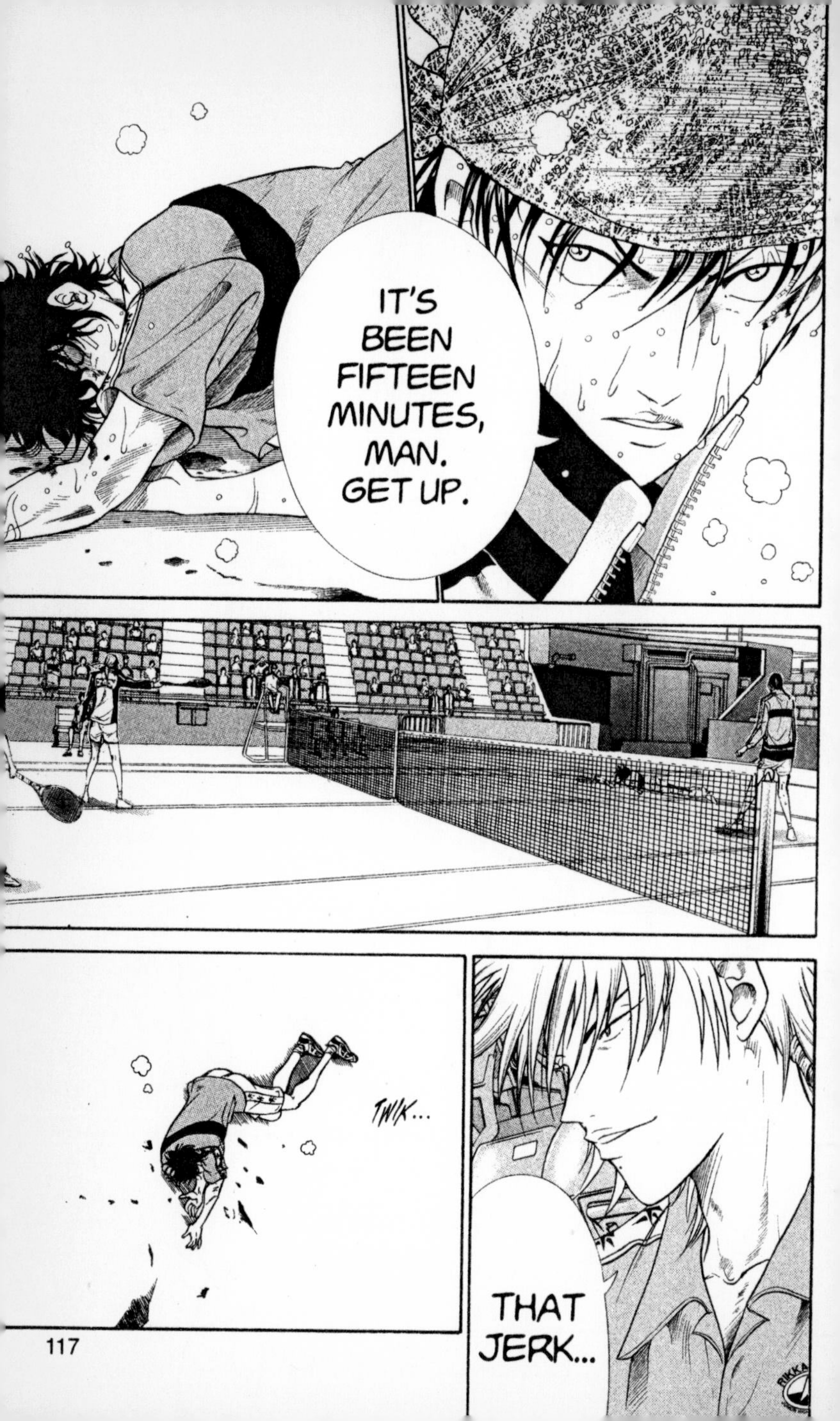
IT'S BEEN FIFTEEN MINUTES, MAN. GET UP.
THAT JERK...
TWIK...
RIKKA

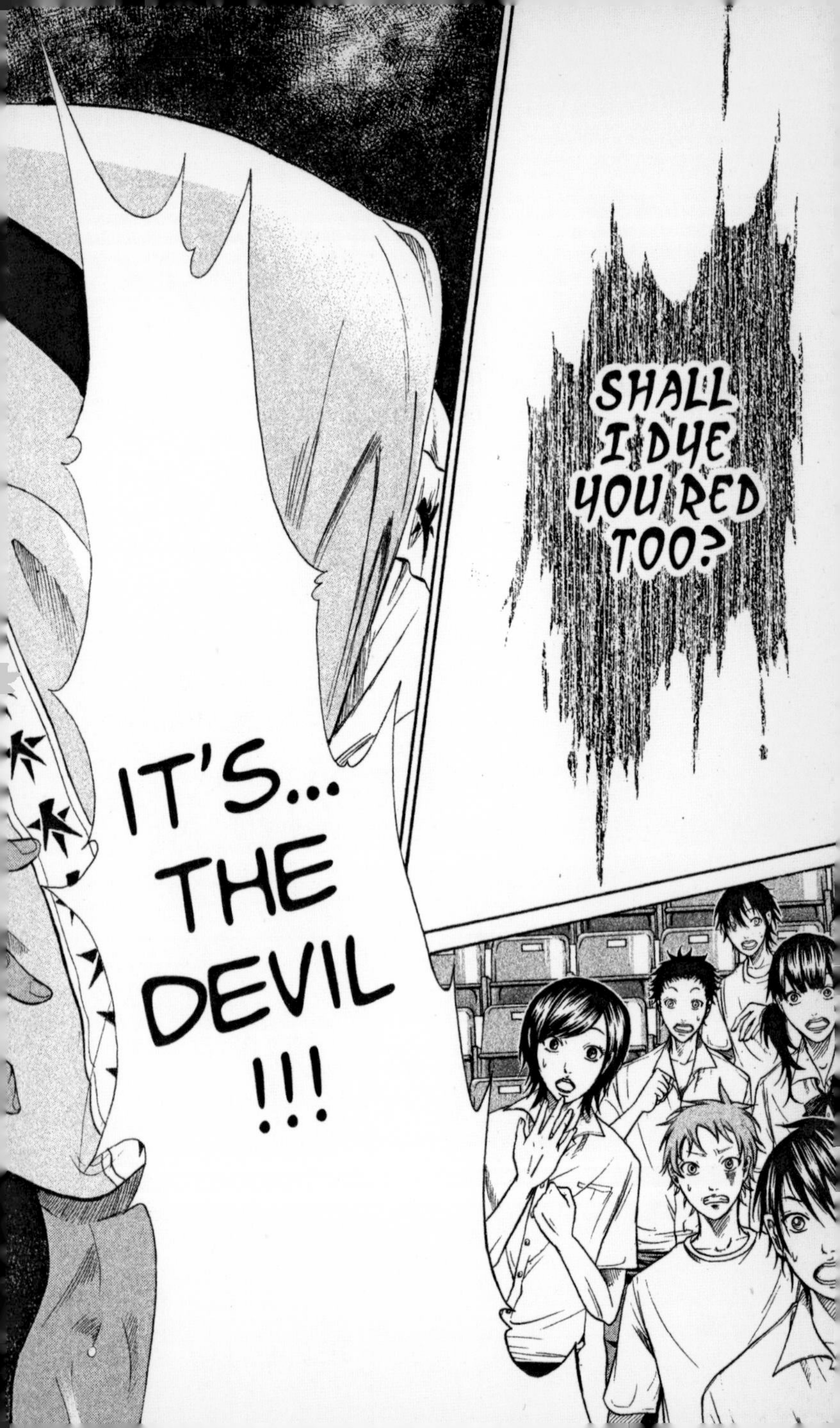
SHALL I DYE YOU RED TOO?
IT'S... THE DEVIL!!!

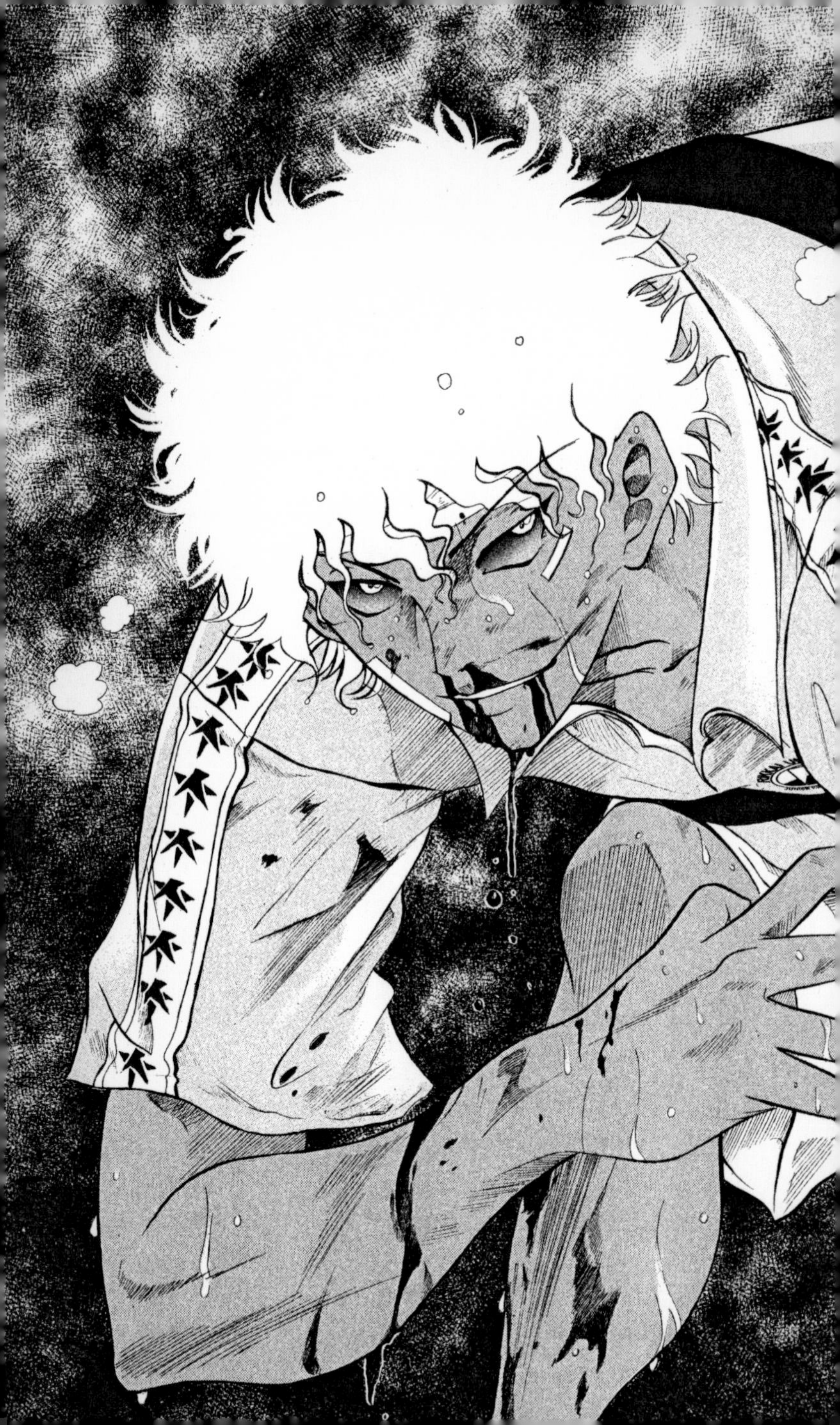

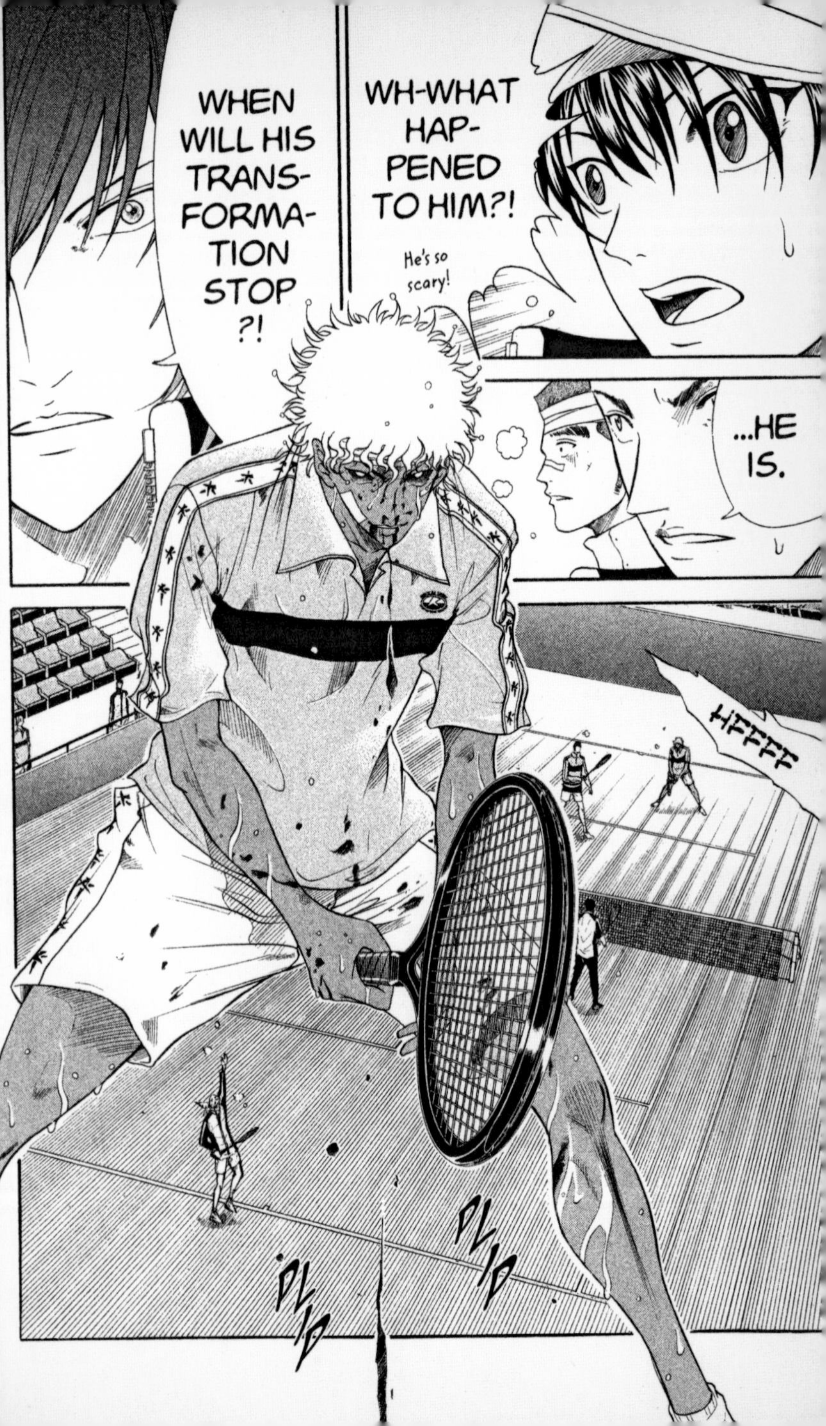
WH-WHAT HAP-PENED TO HIM?!
He's so scary!
...HE IS.
WHEN WILL HIS TRANS-FORMA-TION STOP ?!
HFFFF
DLIP
DLIP

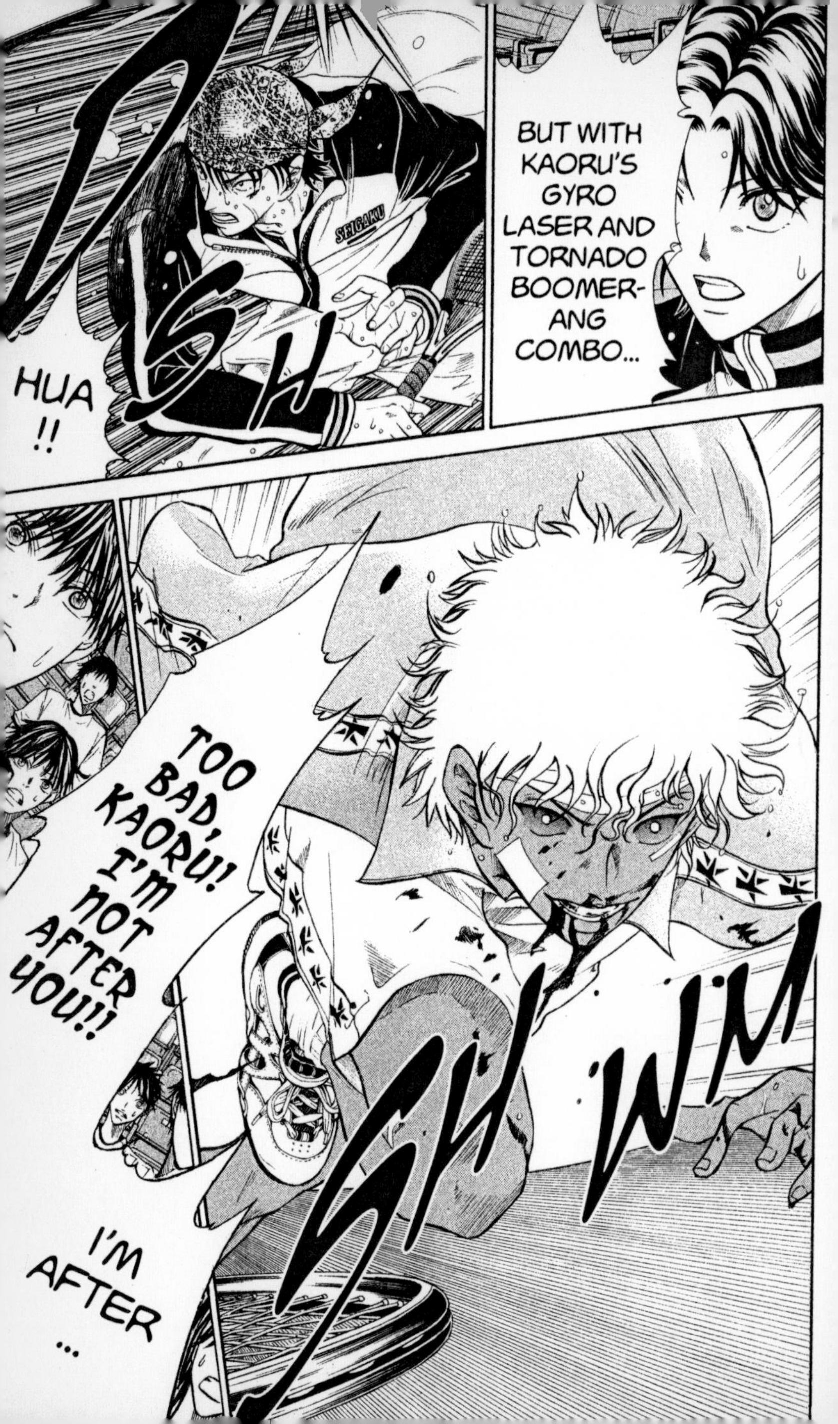
BUT WITH KAORU'S GYRO LASER AND TORNADO BOOMER-ANG COMBO...
HUA!!
TOO BAD, KAORU! I'M NOT AFTER YOU!!
SHWM
I'M AFTER ...

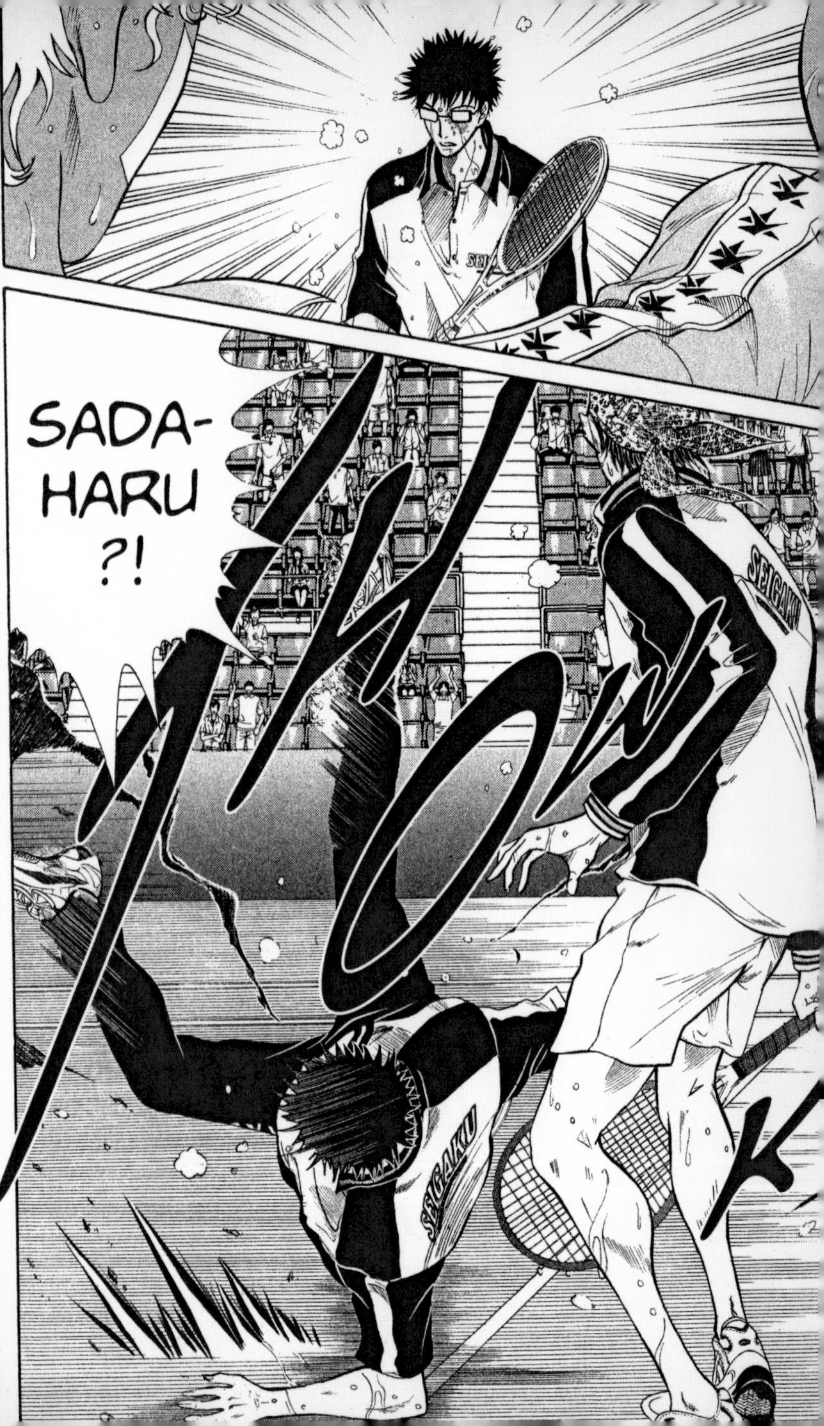
SADA-
HARU
?!

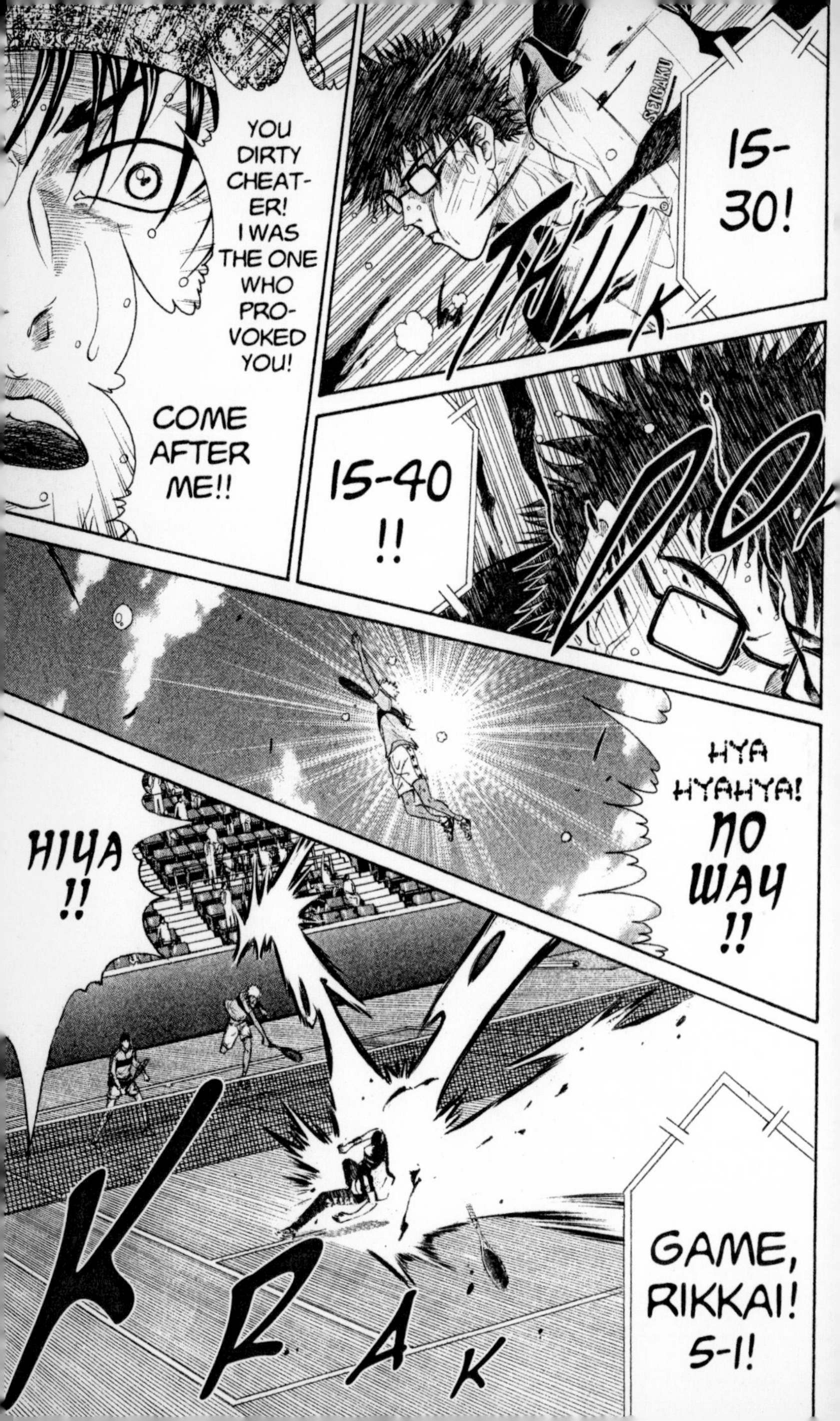
SEIGAKU
15-30!
THUNK
15-40 !!
YOU DIRTY CHEATER! I WAS THE ONE WHO PROVOKED YOU!
COME AFTER ME!!
HYA HYAHYA! NO WAY!!
HIYA !!
GAME, RIKKAI! 5-1!
KRAK

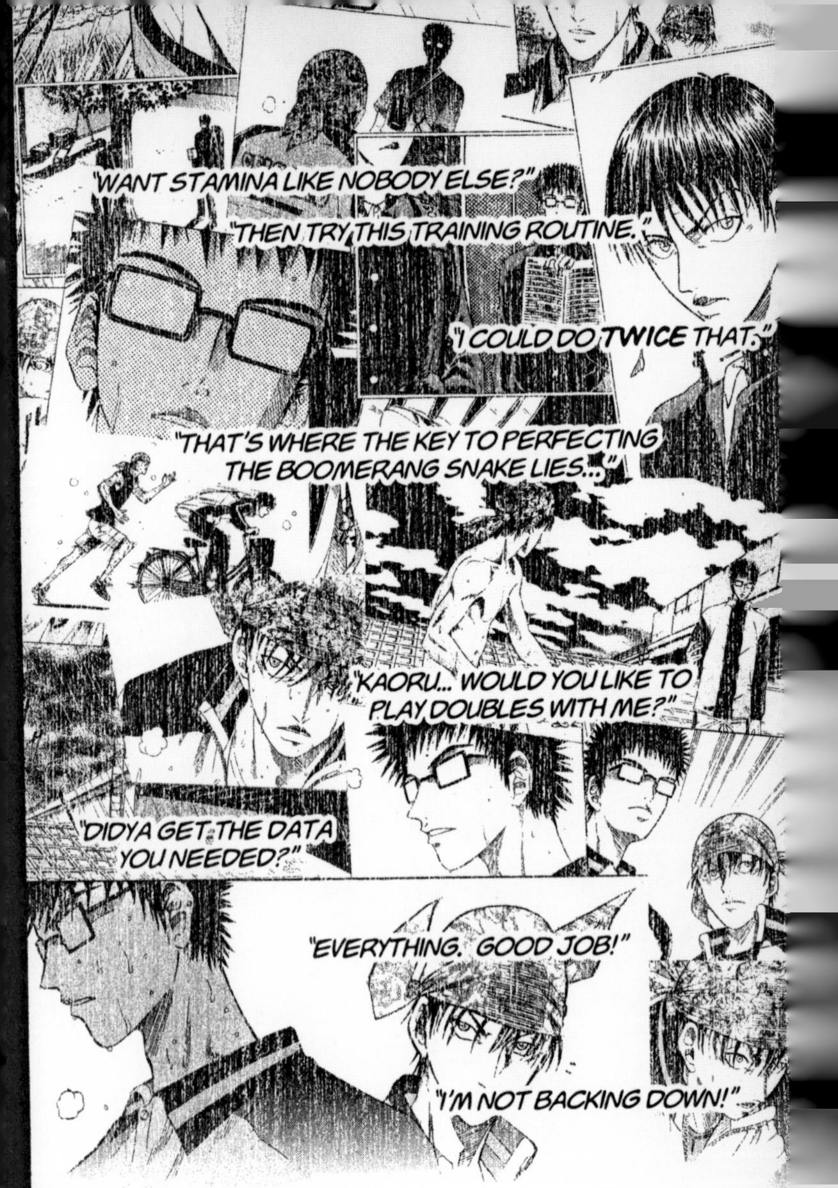
"WANT STAMINA LIKE NOBODY ELSE?"
"THEN TRY THIS TRAINING ROUTINE."
"I COULD DO TWICE THAT."
"THAT'S WHERE THE KEY TO PERFECTING THE BOOMERANG SNAKE LIES..."
"KAORU... WOULD YOU LIKE TO PLAY DOUBLES WITH ME?"
"DIDYA GET THE DATA YOU NEEDED?"
"EVERYTHING. GOOD JOB!"
"I'M NOT BACKING DOWN!"

"KAORU TAUGHT ME ABOUT TENACITY AND MENTAL STRENGTH."

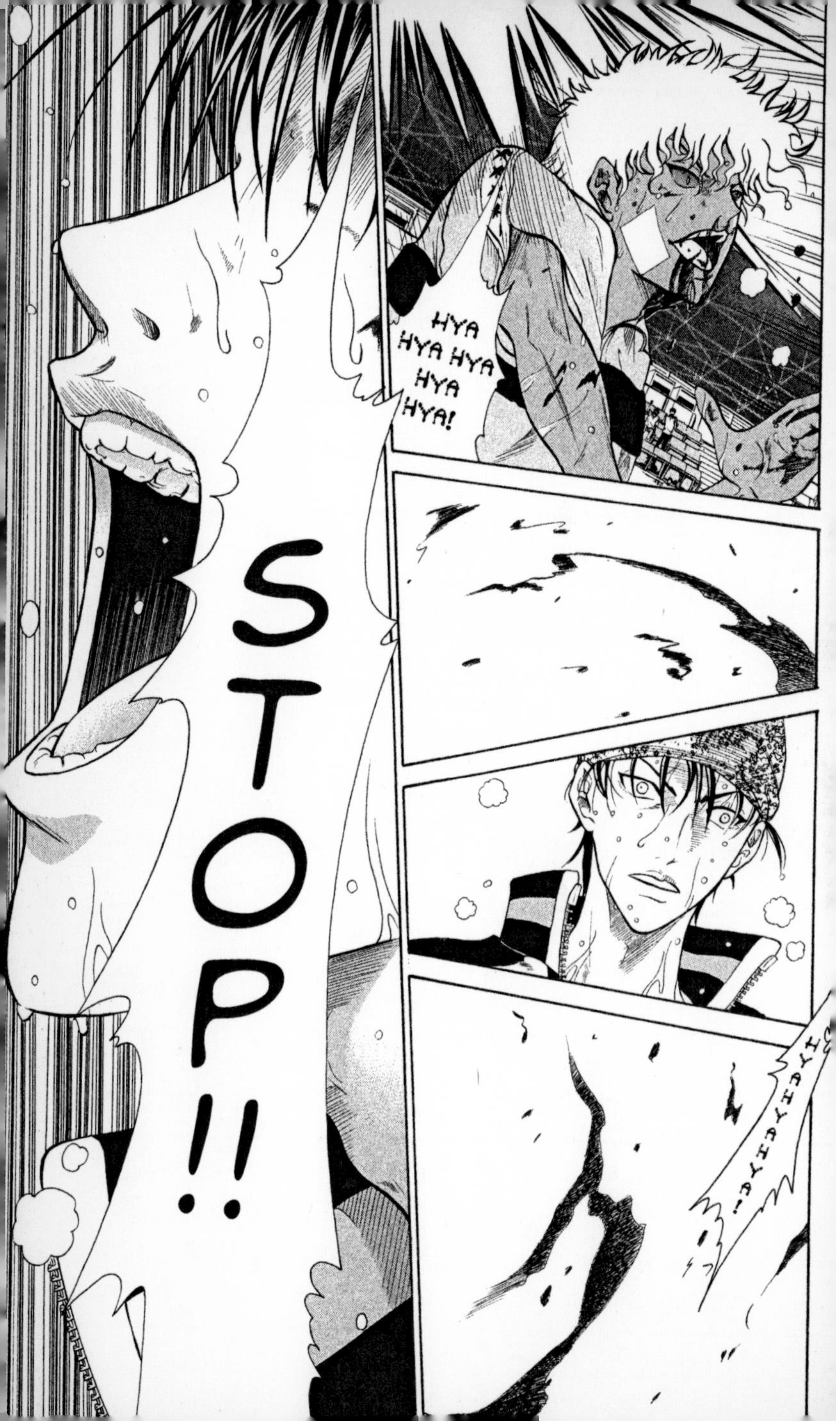
HYA HYA HYA HYA HYA!
STOP!!
HYAHYAHYA!

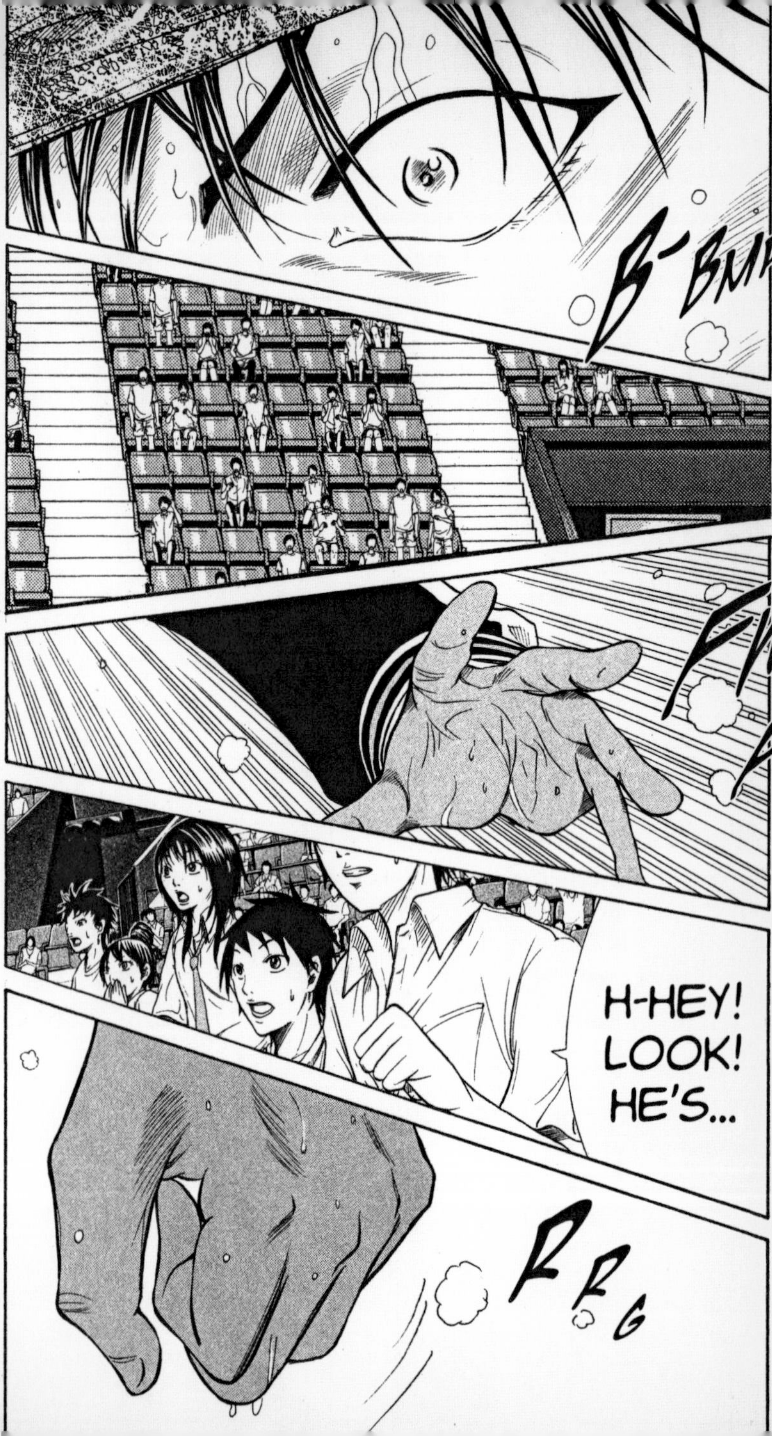
B-BMP
FWP
H-HEY! LOOK! HE'S...
RRG

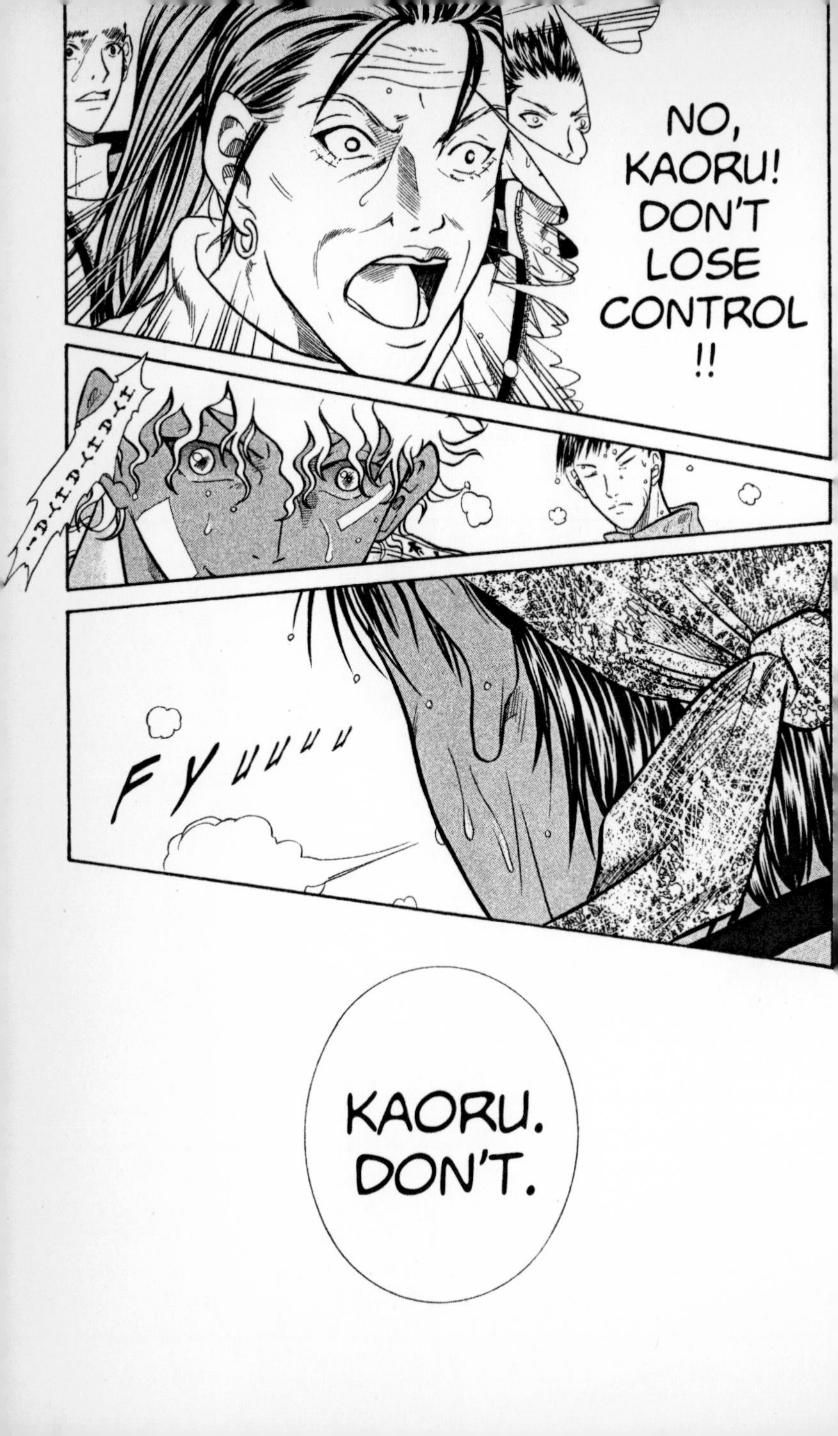
NO, KAORU! DON'T LOSE CONTROL !!
FYuuuu
KAORU. DON'T.

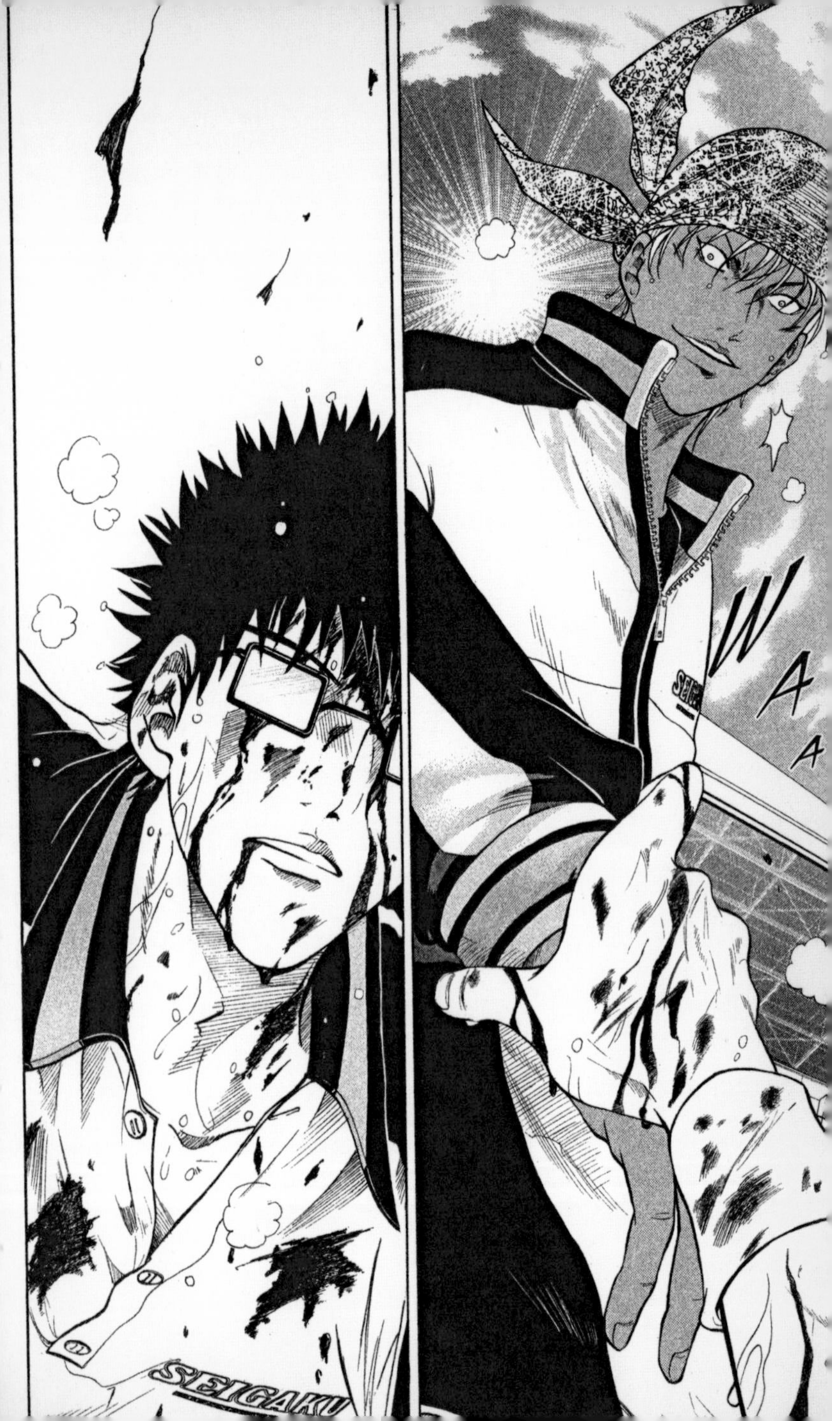
WAA
SEIGAKU

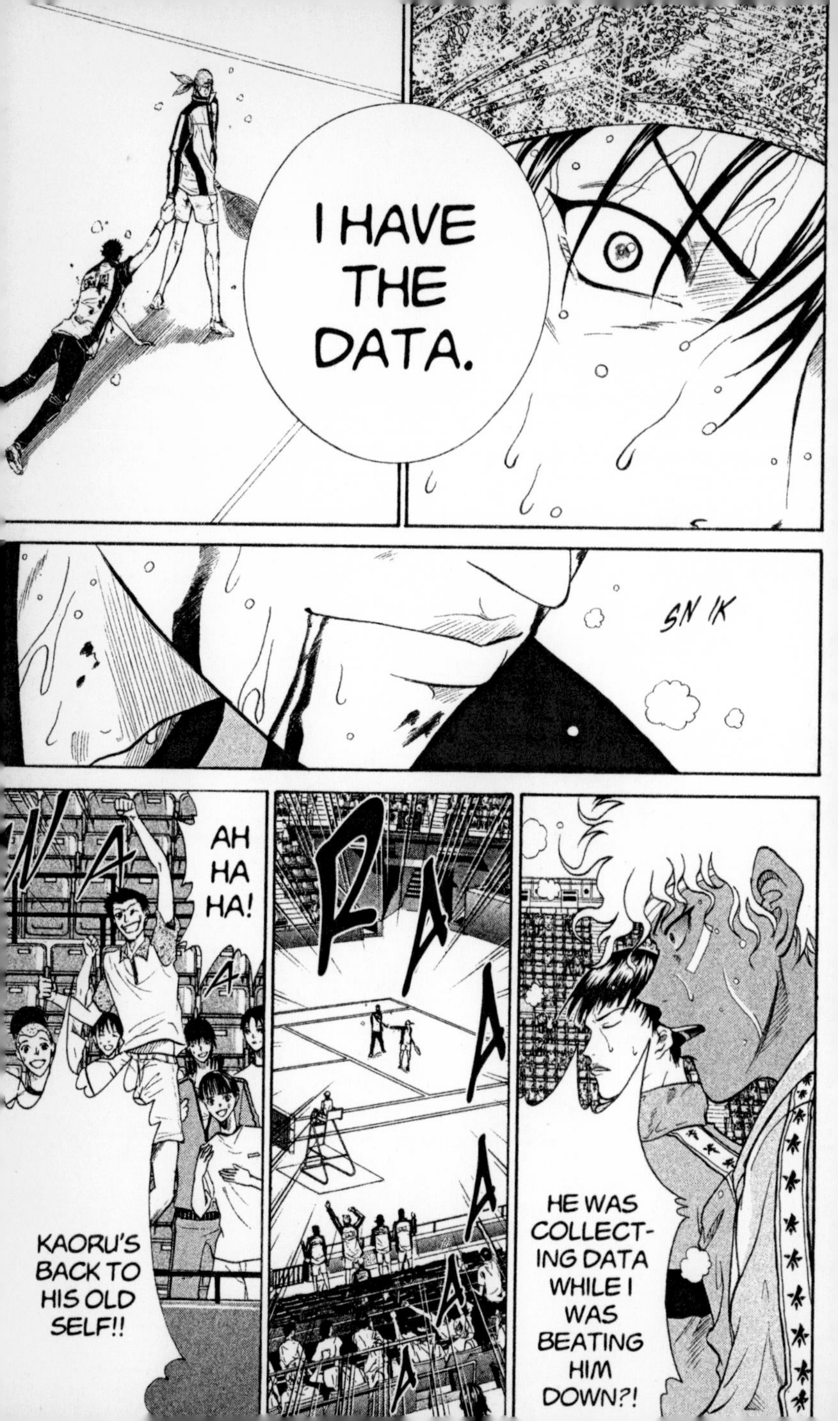
I HAVE THE DATA.
SN IK
HE WAS COLLECT-ING DATA WHILE I WAS BEATING HIM DOWN?!
AH HA HA!
KAORU'S BACK TO HIS OLD SELF!!

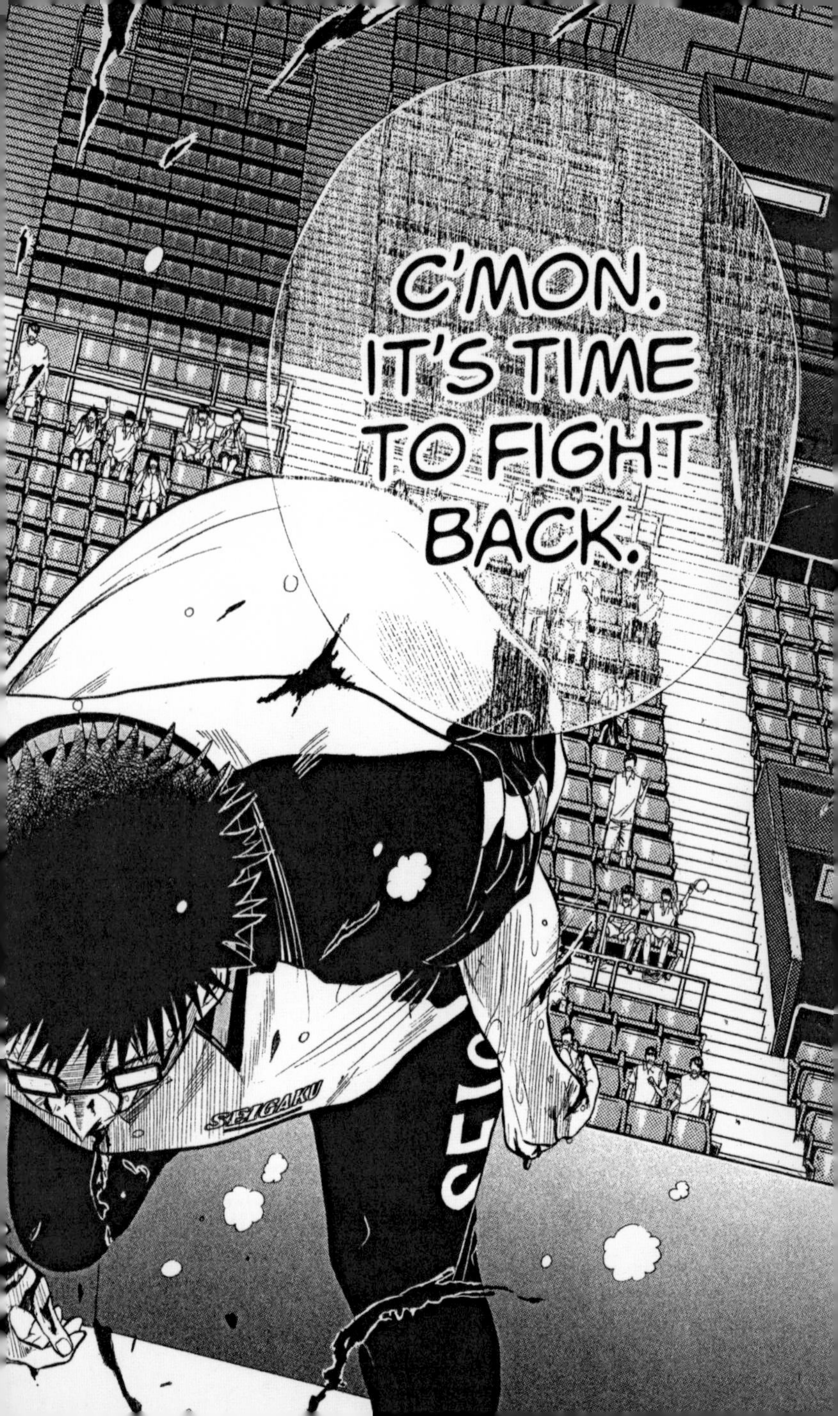
C'MON. IT'S TIME TO FIGHT BACK.
SEIGAKU

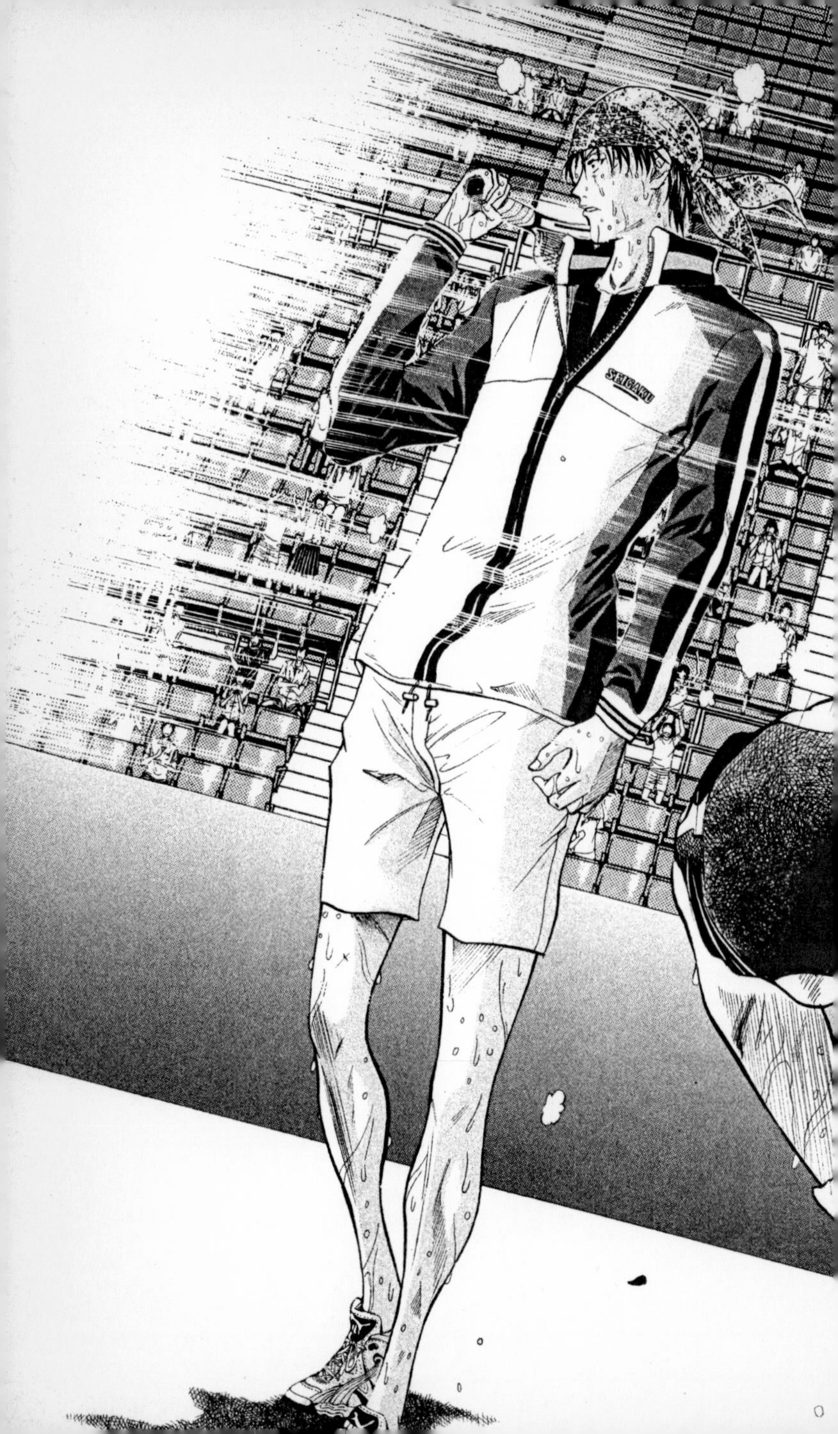
SEIGAKU

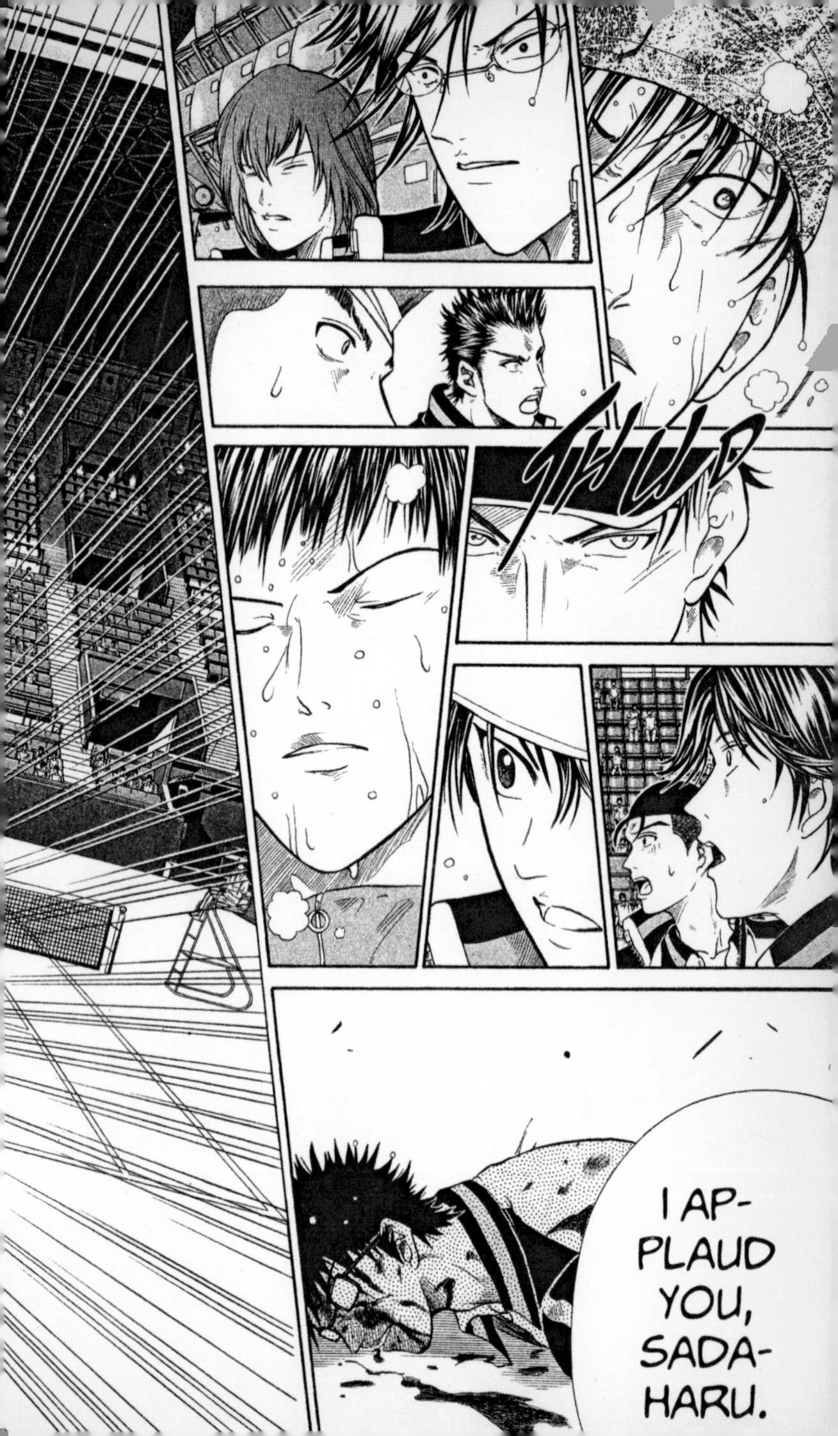
THUD
I AP-
PLAUD
YOU,
SADA-
HARU.

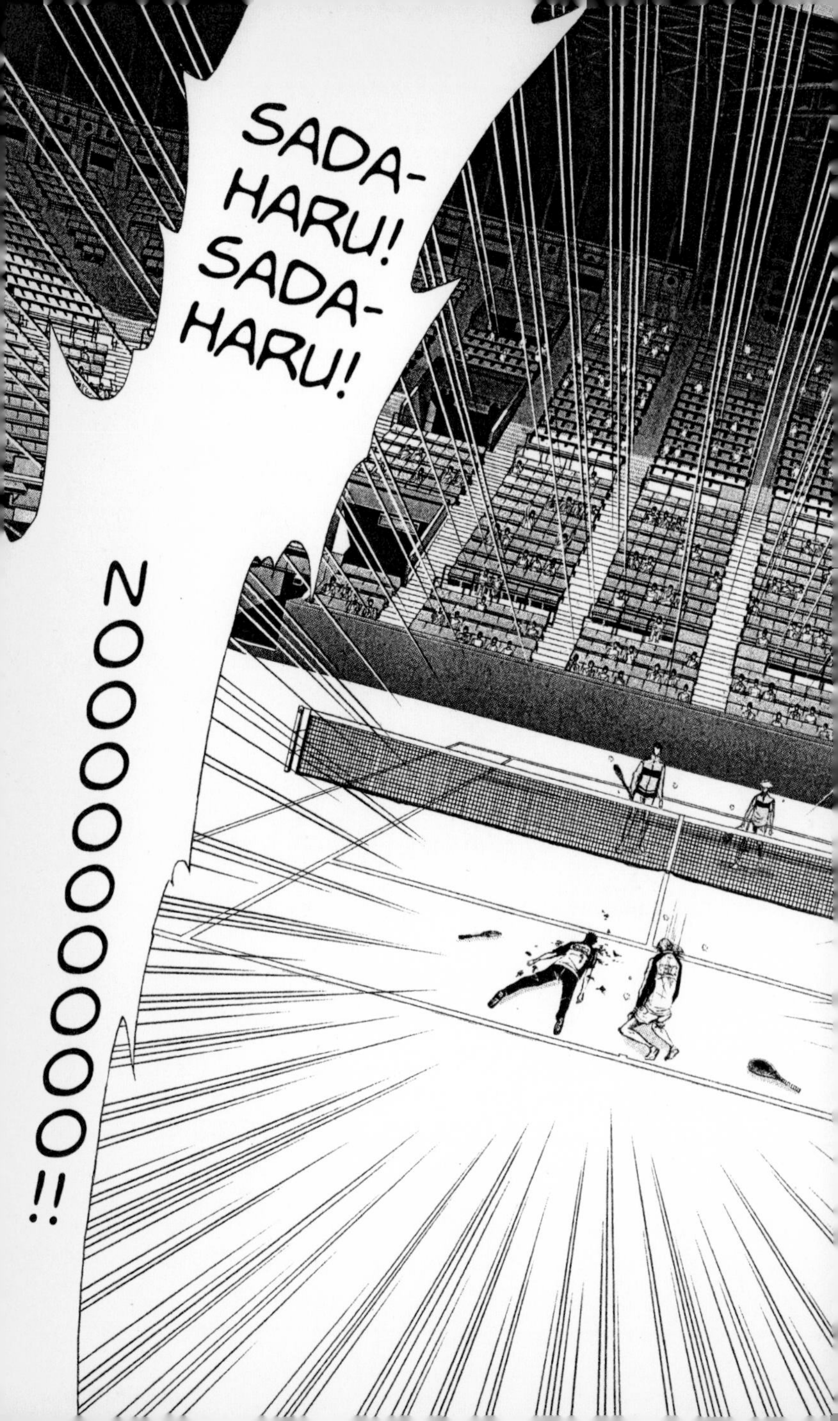
SADA-HARU! SADA-HARU!
NOOOOOOOOOOO!!

テニスの王子様

THE PRINCE OF TENNIS

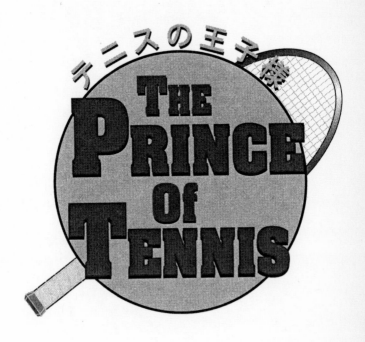

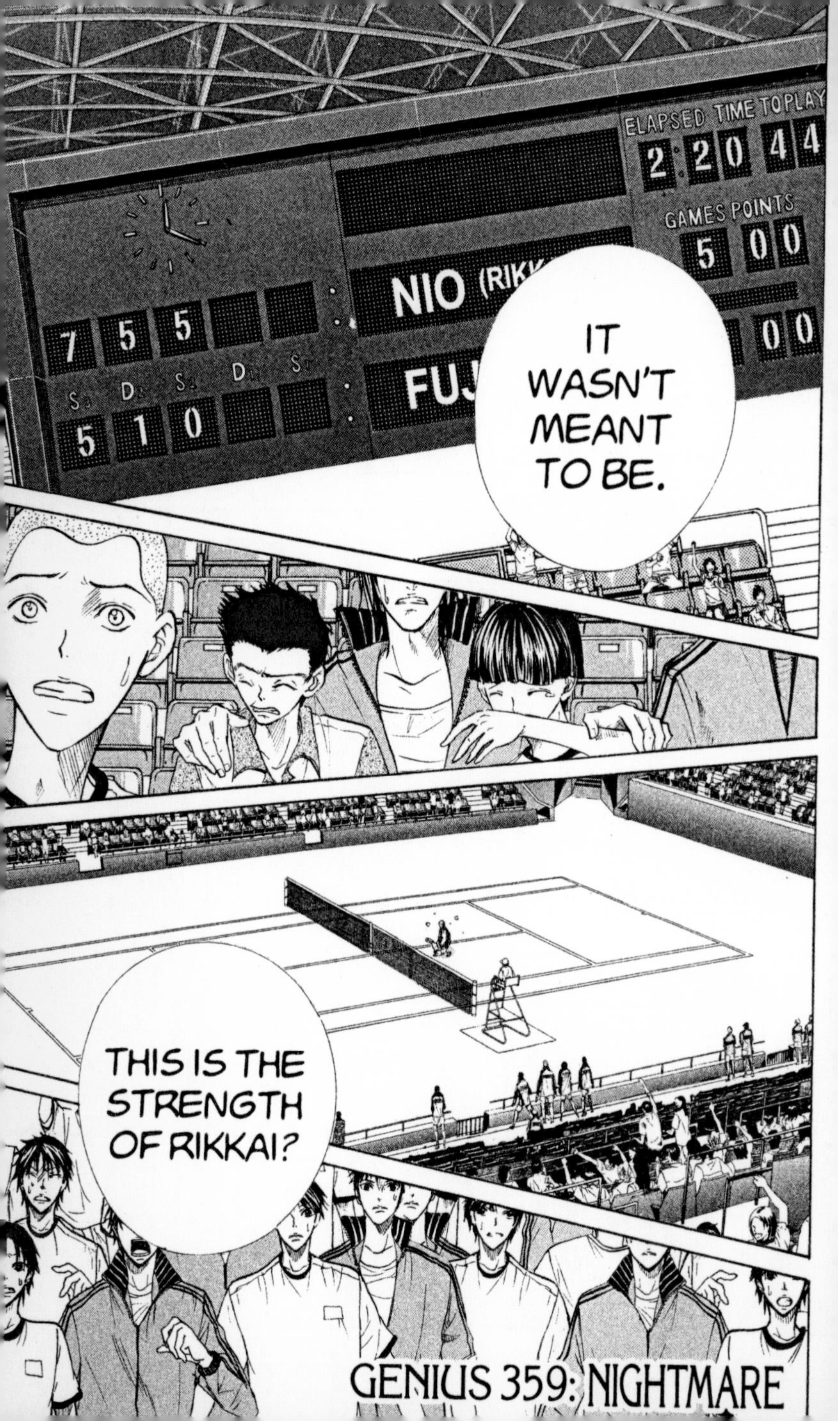
ELAPSED TIME TOPLAY
2 20 44
GAMES POINTS
5 00
NIO
IT WASN'T MEANT TO BE.
THIS IS THE STRENGTH OF RIKKAI?
GENIUS 359: NIGHTMARE

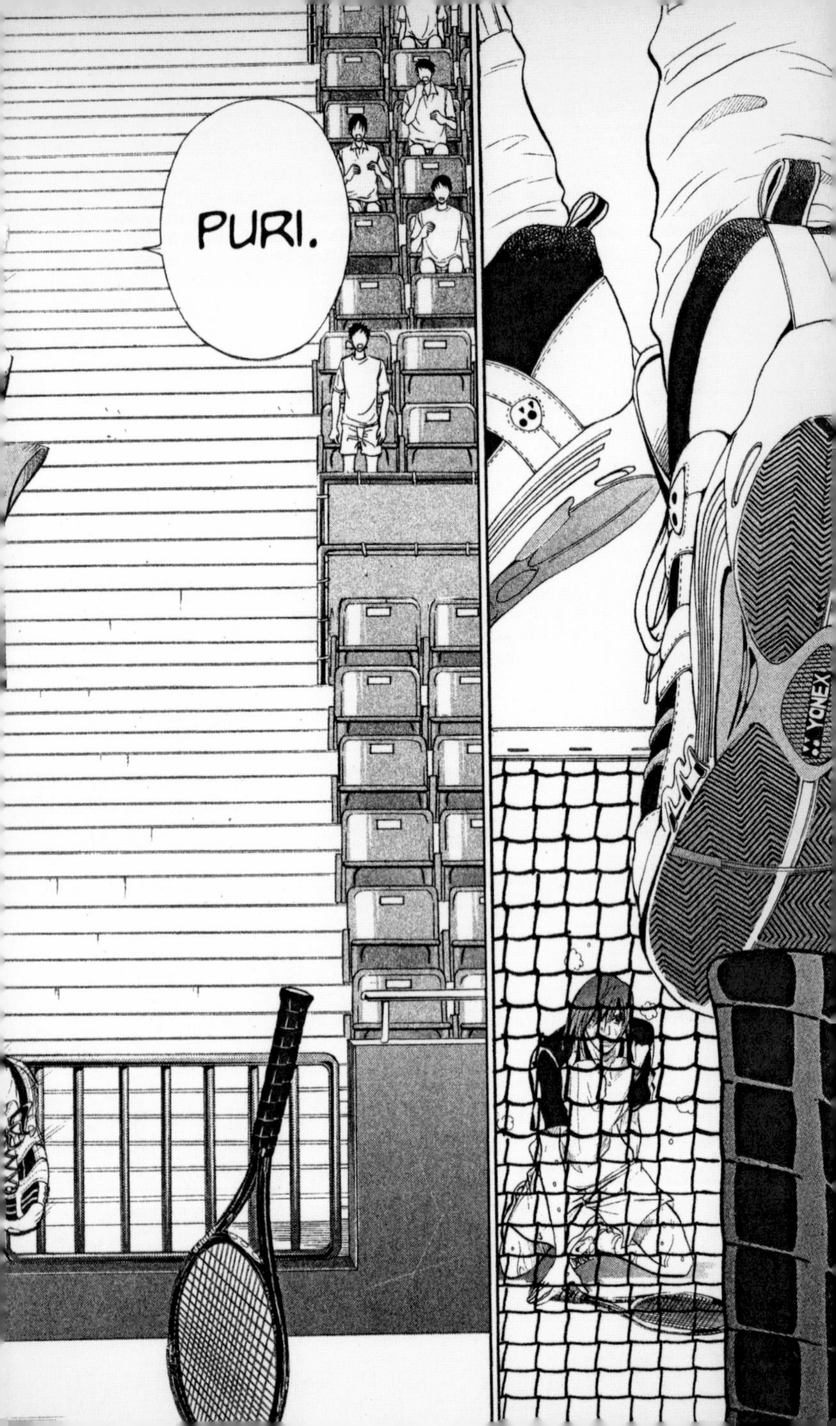
PURI.
YONEX

GENIUS 359: NIGHTMARE

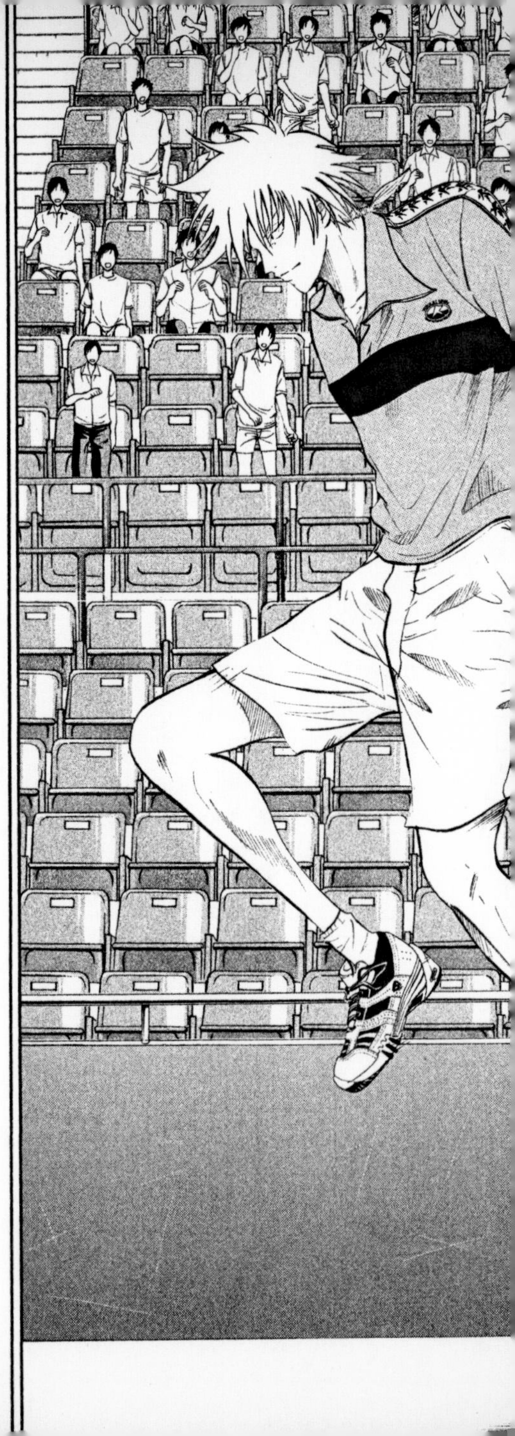

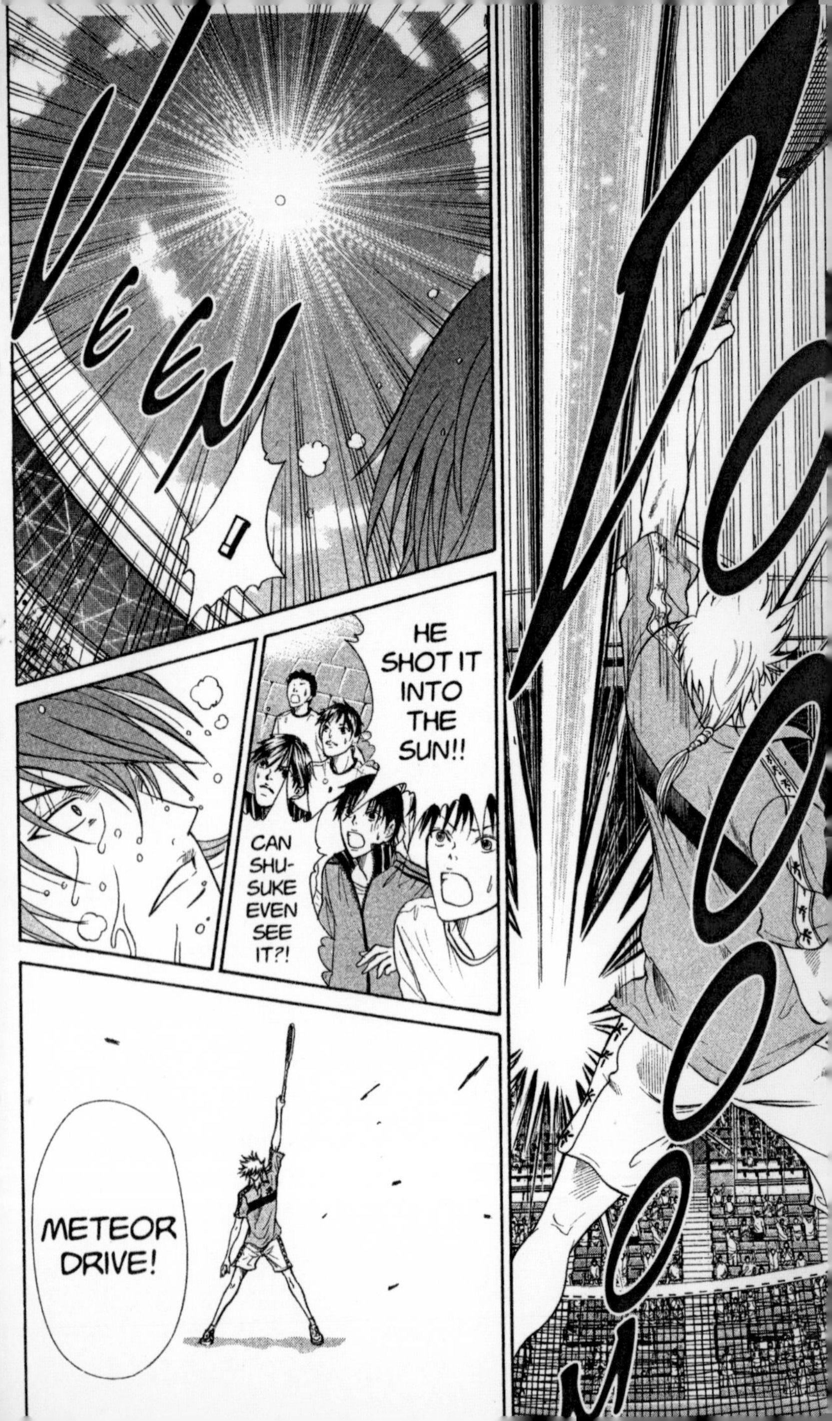
HE SHOT IT INTO THE SUN!!
CAN SHU-SUKE EVEN SEE IT?!
METEOR DRIVE!

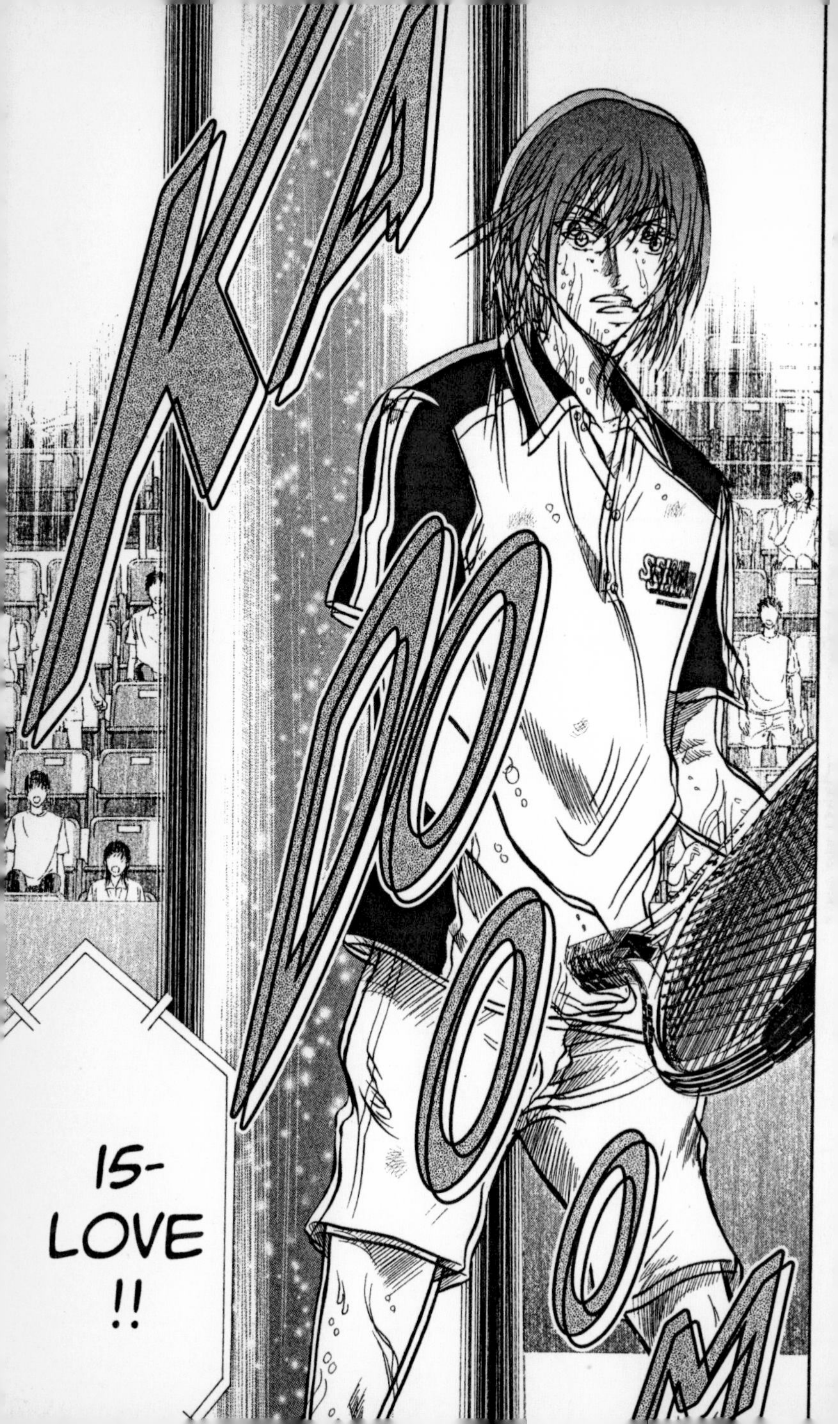
KABOOOOM
15-
LOVE
!!

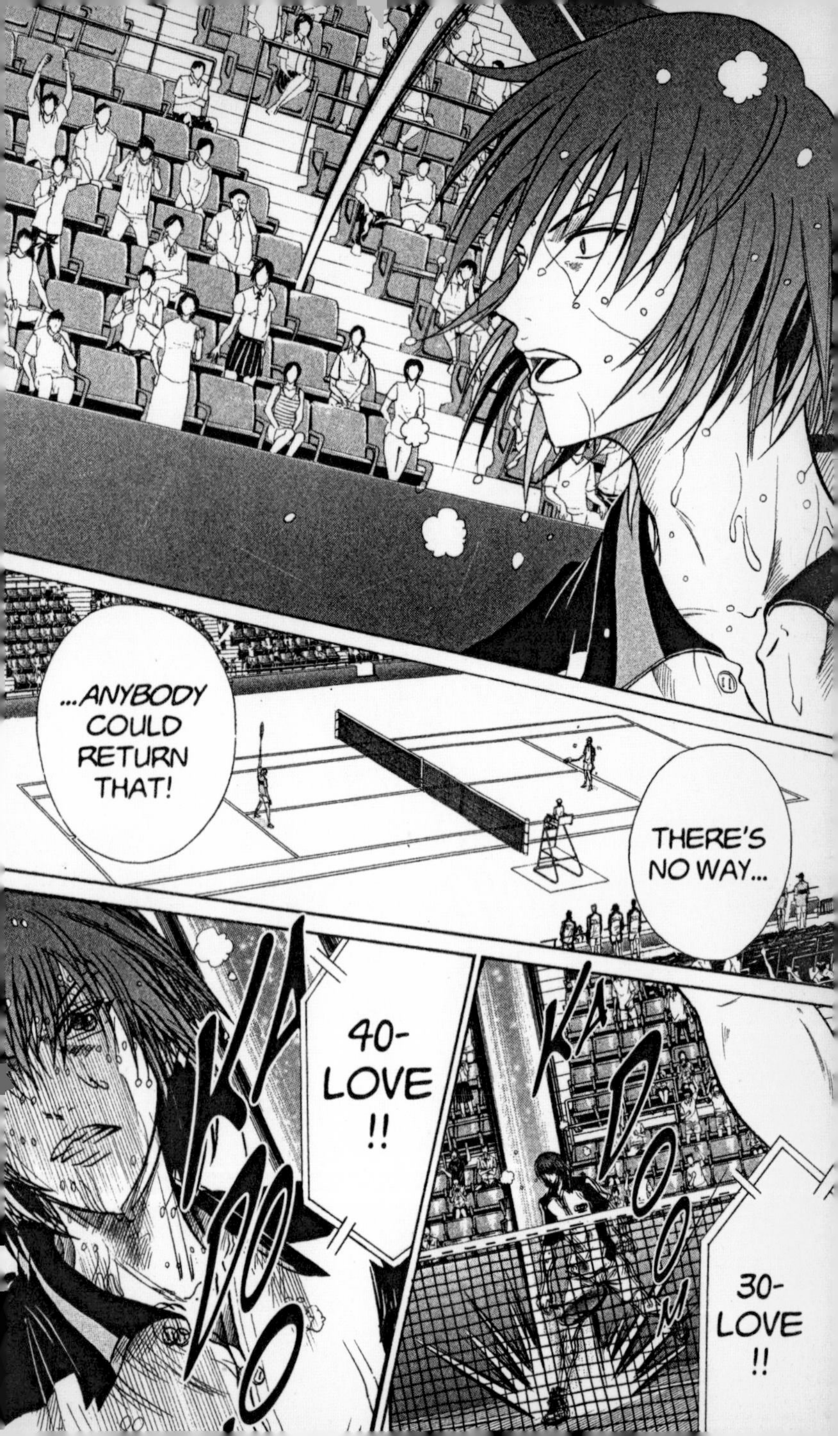
THERE'S NO WAY...
...ANYBODY COULD RETURN THAT!
30-LOVE!!
40-LOVE!!

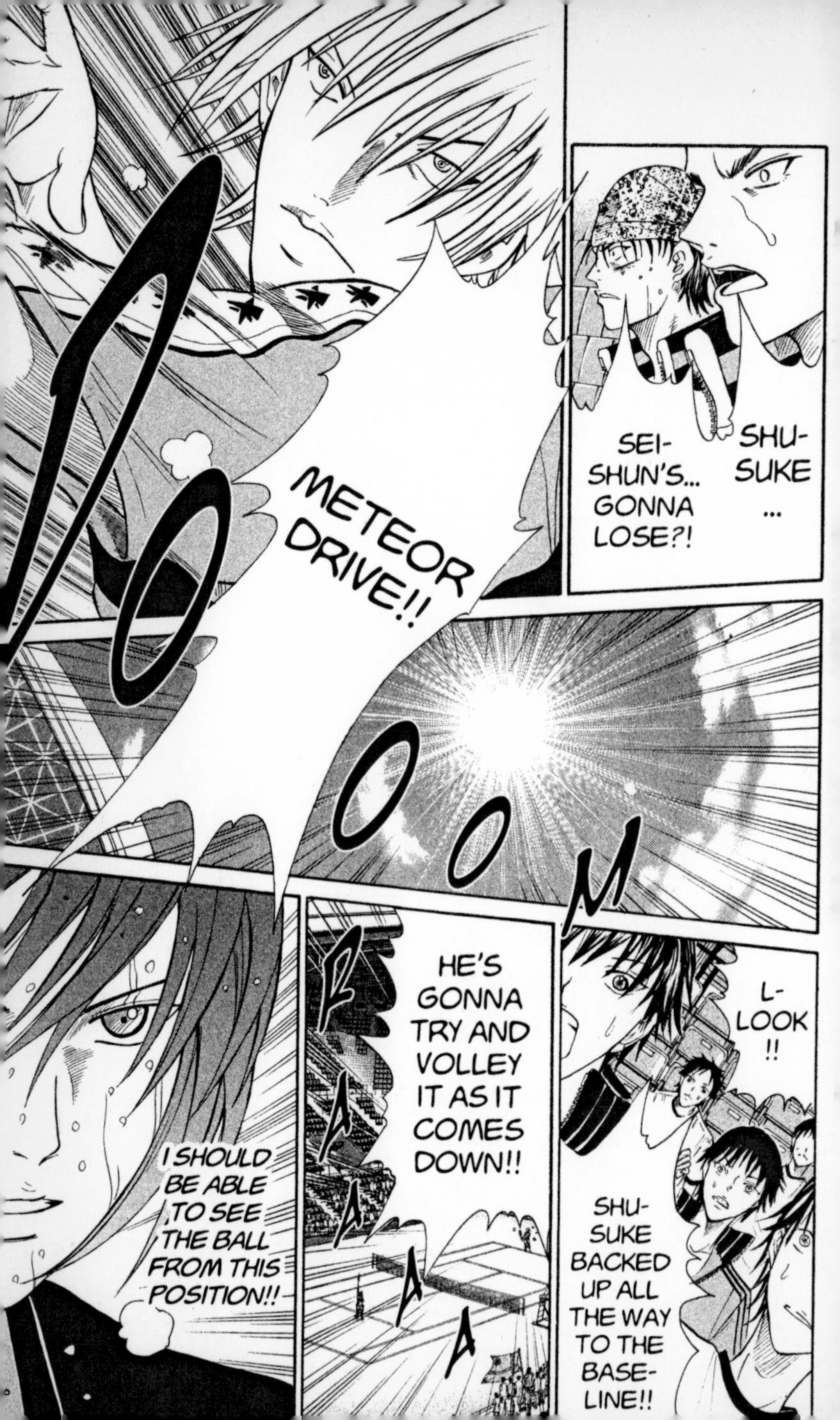
SHU-SUKE...
SEI-SHUN'S... GONNA LOSE?!
METEOR DRIVE!!
DOOOM
L-LOOK!!
SHU-SUKE BACKED UP ALL THE WAY TO THE BASE-LINE!!
HE'S GONNA TRY AND VOLLEY IT AS IT COMES DOWN!!
I SHOULD BE ABLE TO SEE THE BALL FROM THIS POSITION!!

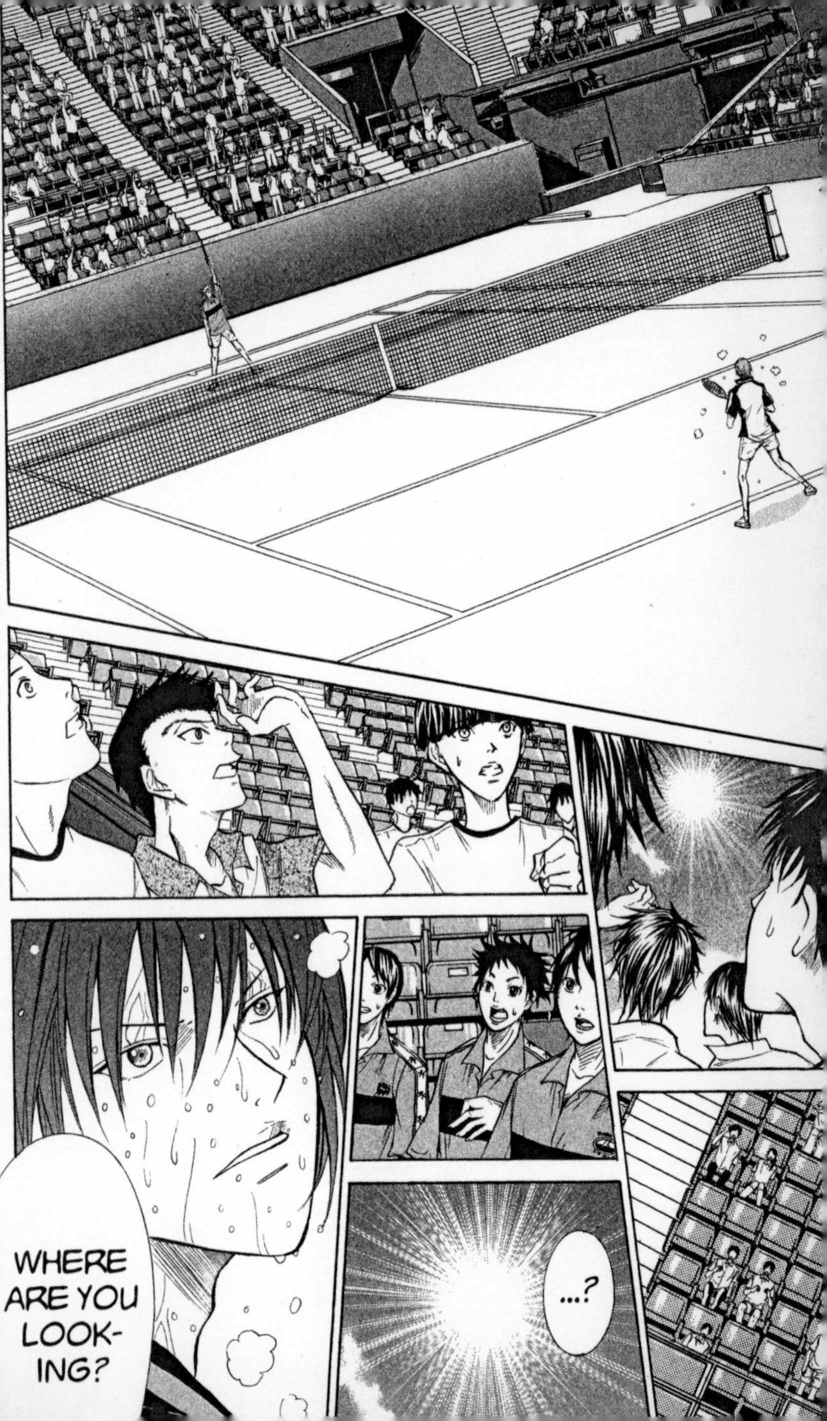
...?
WHERE ARE YOU LOOKING?

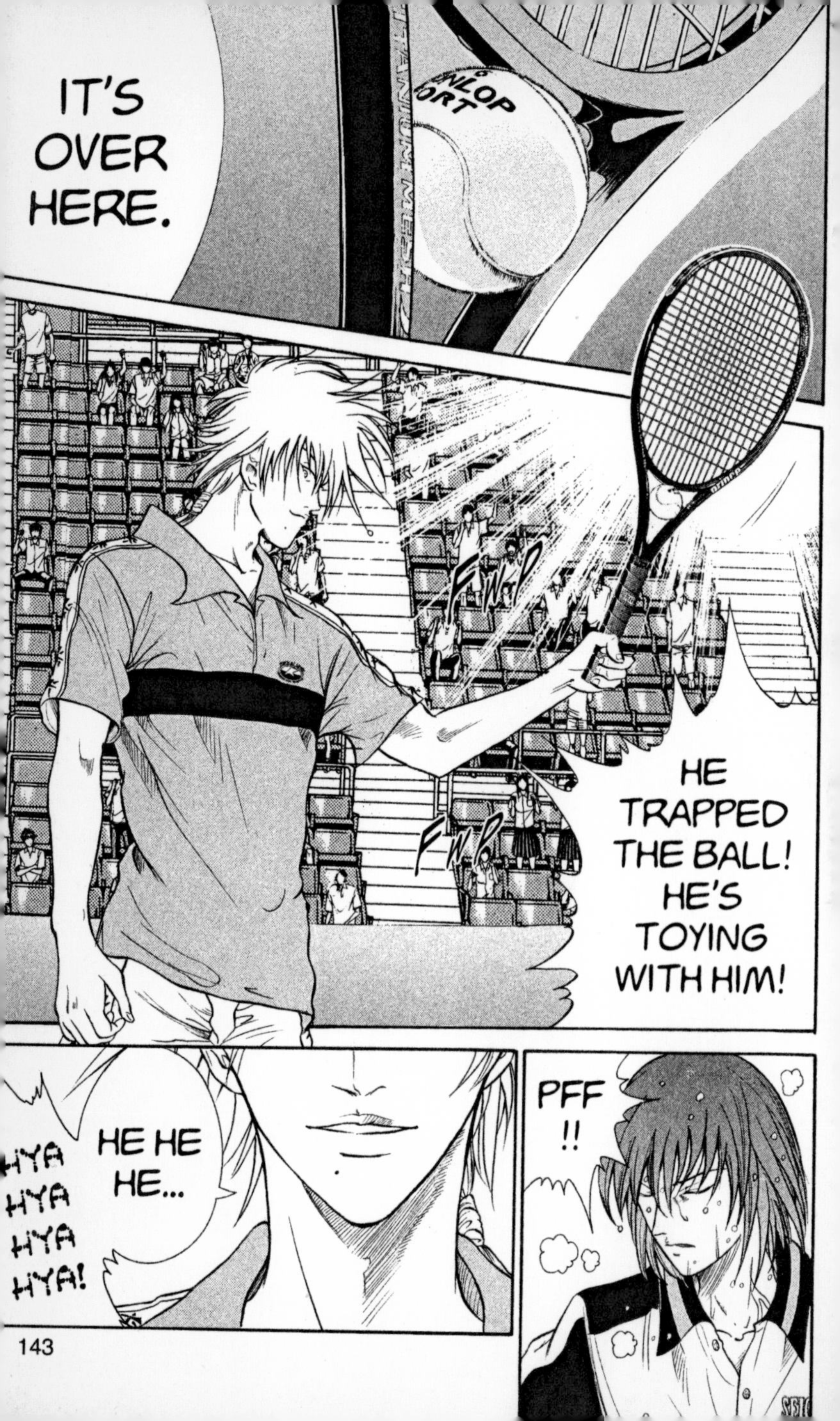
IT'S OVER HERE.
FWP
FWP
HE TRAPPED THE BALL! HE'S TOYING WITH HIM!
PFF !!
HE HE HE...
HYA HYA HYA HYA!

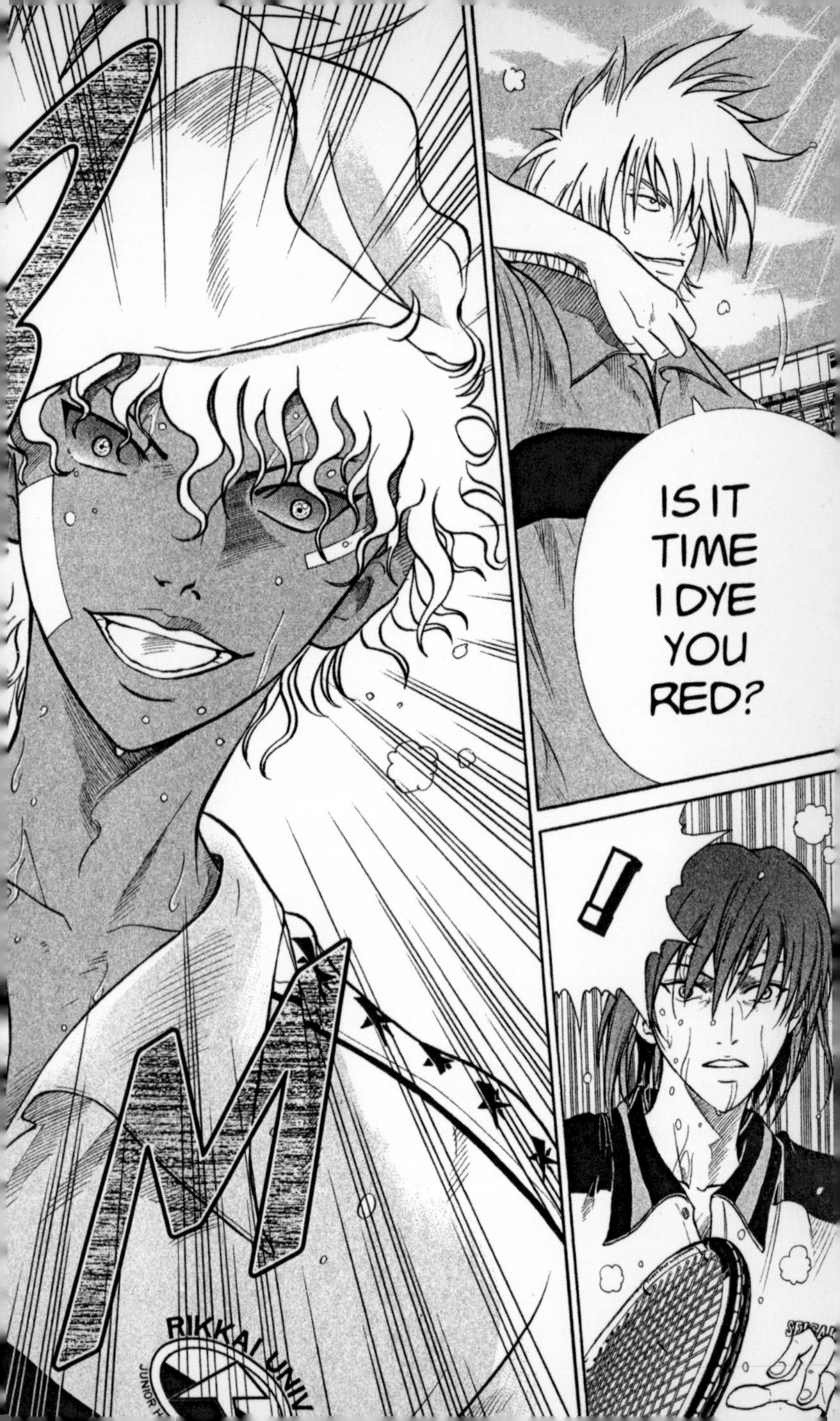
IS IT TIME I DYE YOU RED?
!
RIKKAI UNIV

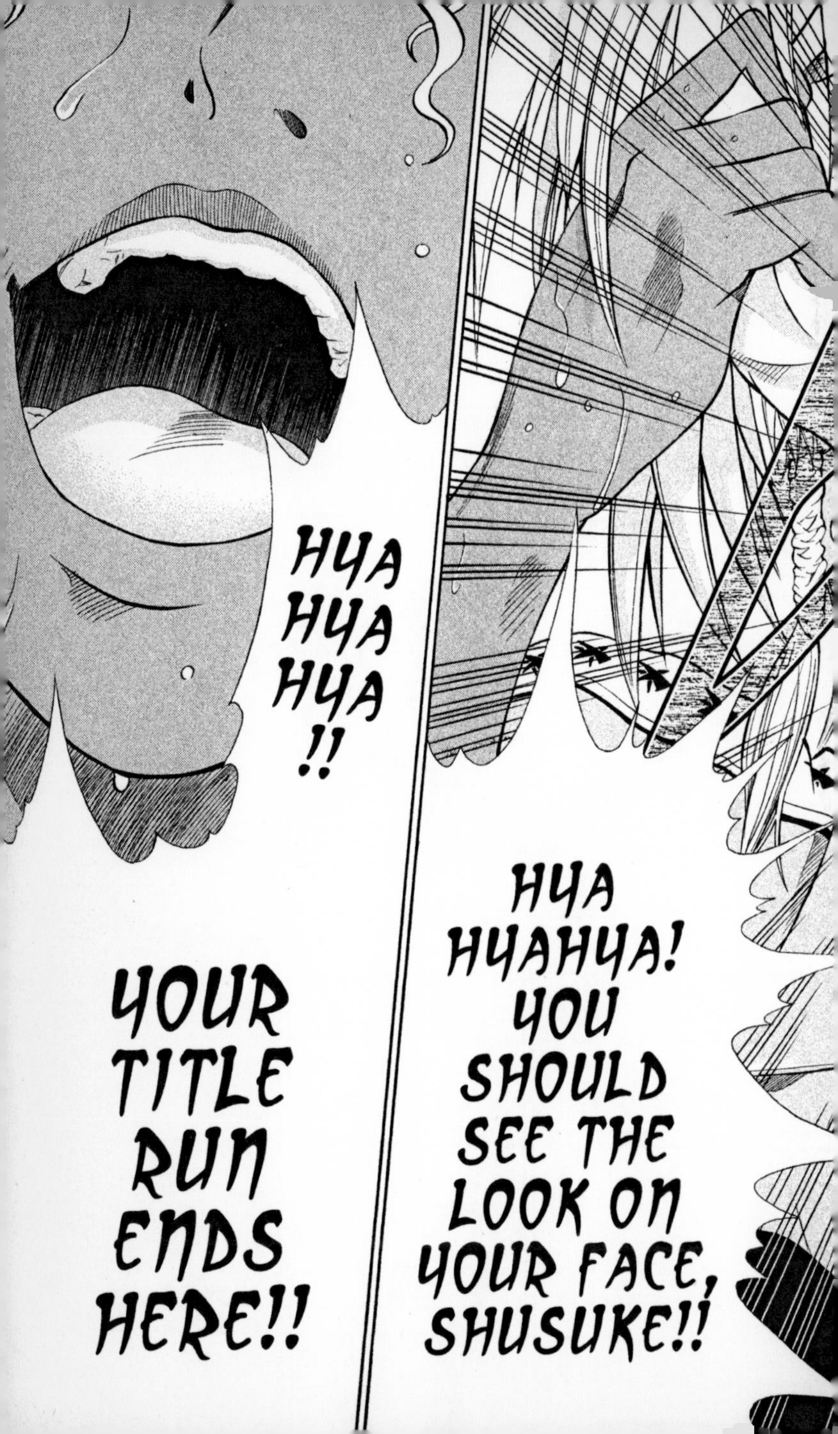
HYA HYAHYA! YOU SHOULD SEE THE LOOK ON YOUR FACE, SHUSUKE!!
HYA HYA HYA!!
YOUR TITLE RUN ENDS HERE!!

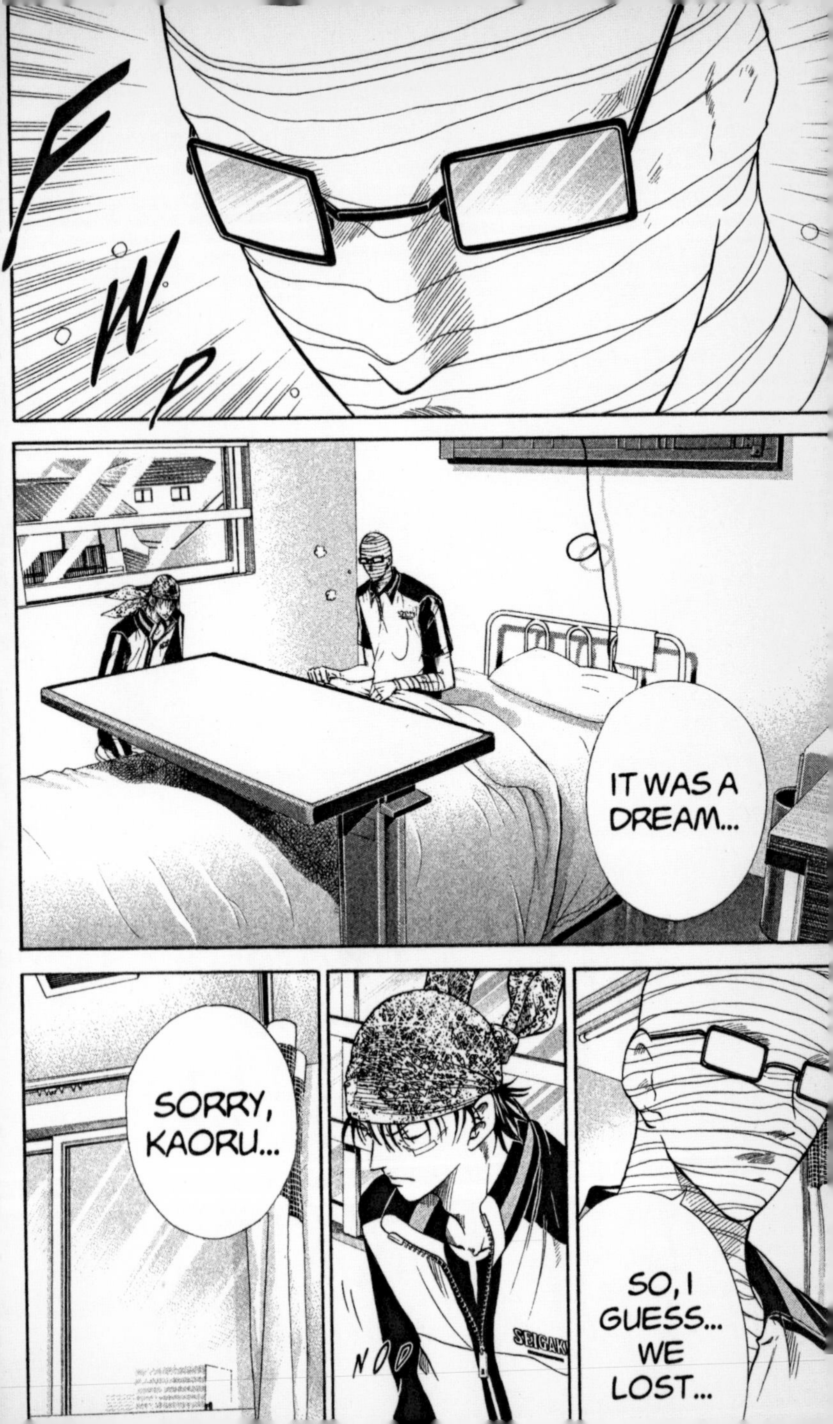
FWP
IT WAS A DREAM...
SO, I GUESS... WE LOST...
NOD
SEIGAKU
SORRY, KAORU...

READ THIS WAY

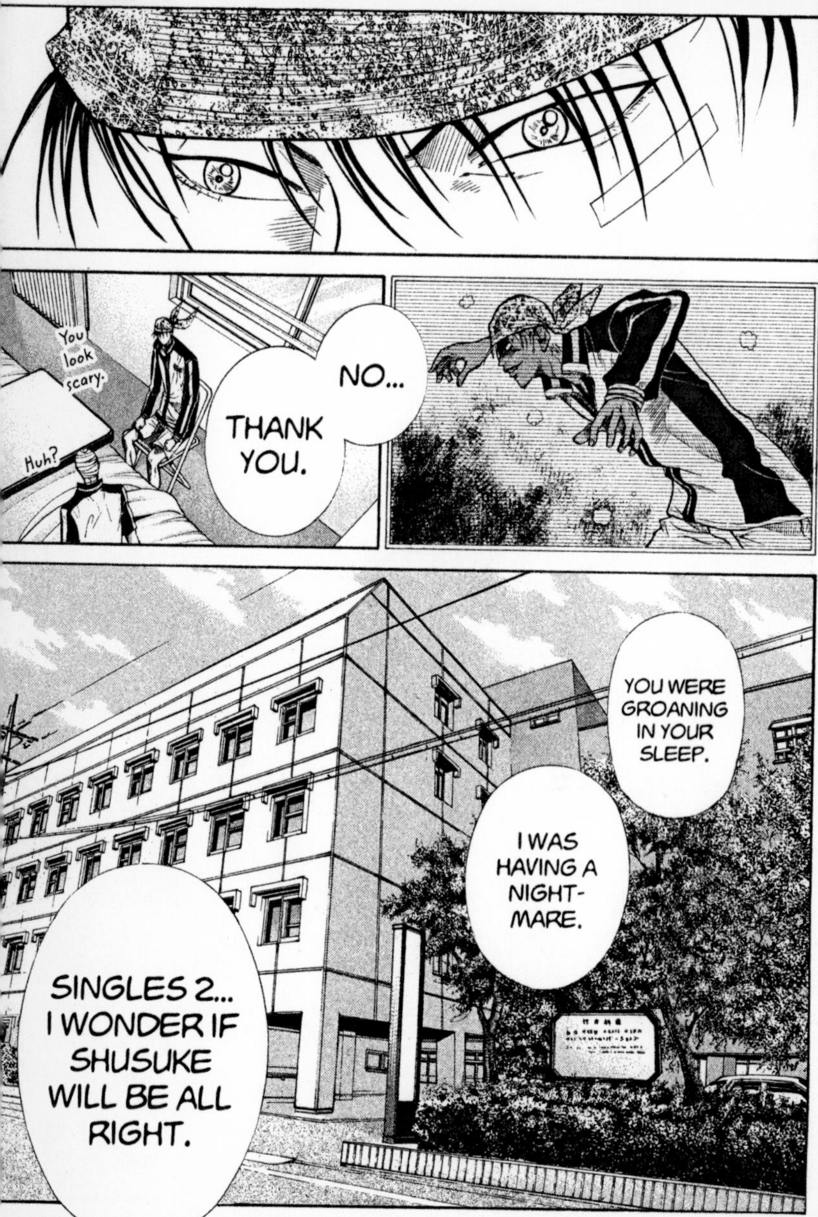
NO... THANK YOU.
You look scary.
Huh?
YOU WERE GROANING IN YOUR SLEEP.
I WAS HAVING A NIGHT-MARE.
SINGLES 2... I WONDER IF SHUSUKE WILL BE ALL RIGHT.

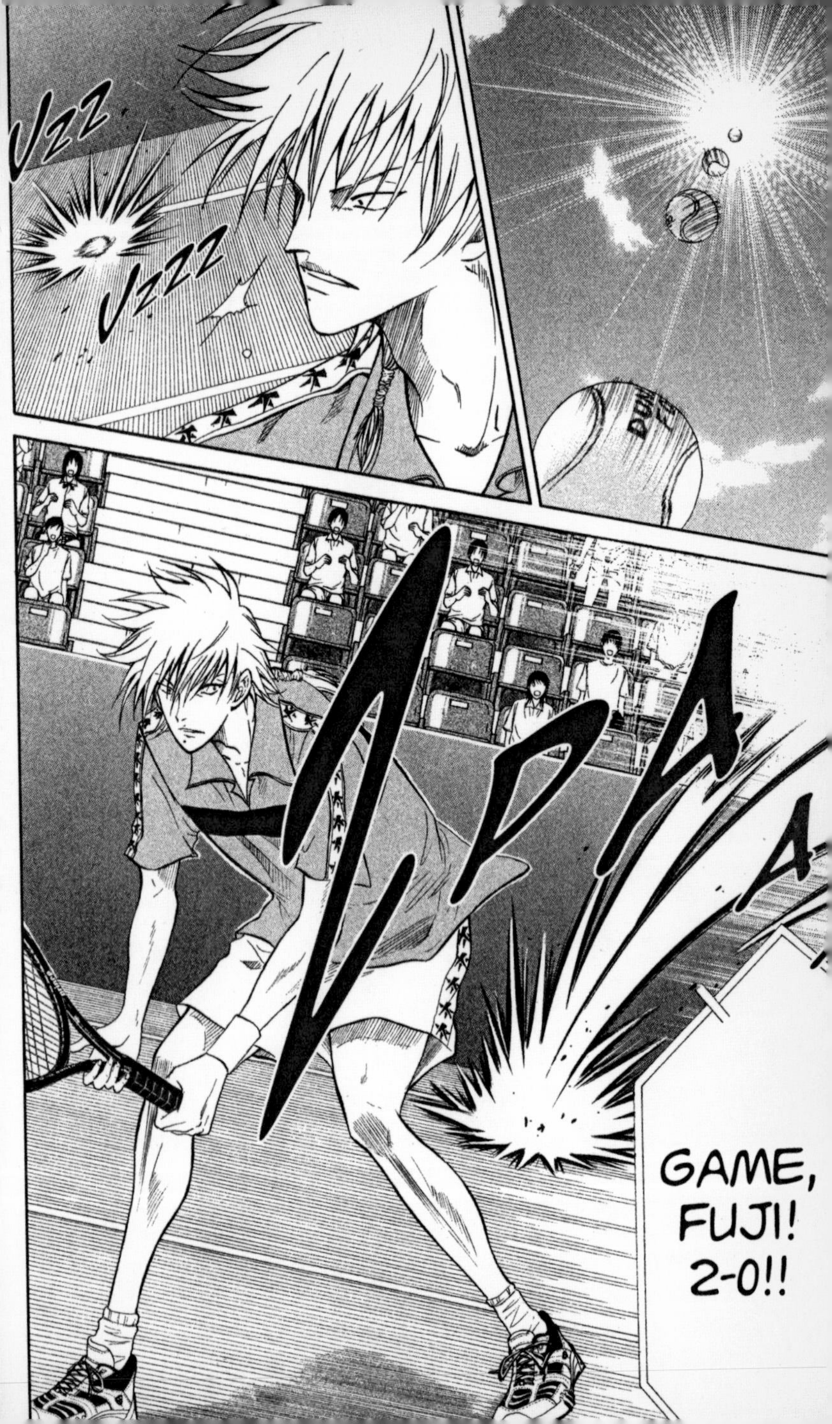
VZZ
VZZZ
GAME, FUJI! 2-0!!

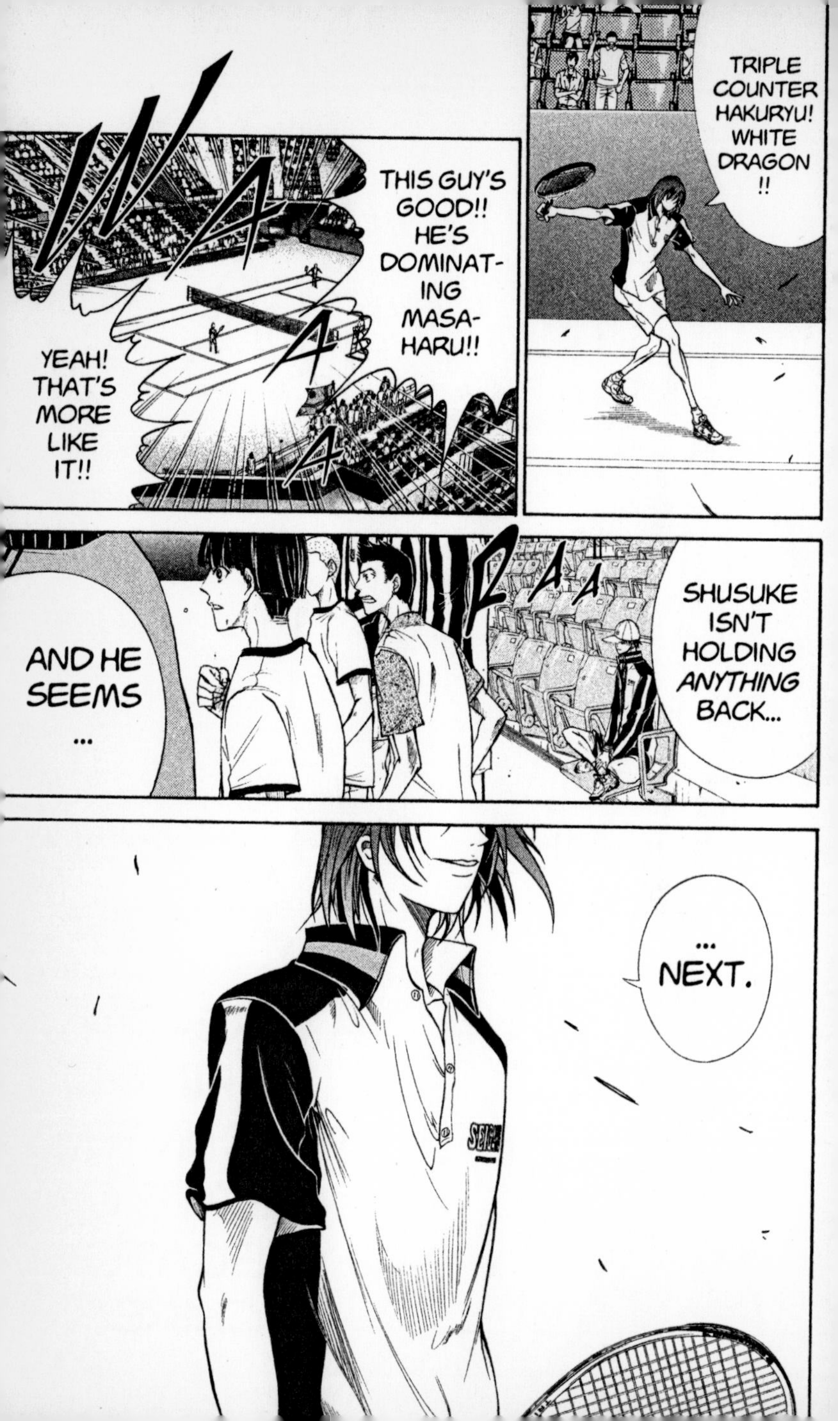
TRIPLE COUNTER HAKURYU! WHITE DRAGON !!
THIS GUY'S GOOD!! HE'S DOMINAT-ING MASA-HARU!!
WAAA
YEAH! THAT'S MORE LIKE IT!!
SHUSUKE ISN'T HOLDING ANYTHING BACK...
RAA
AND HE SEEMS ...
... NEXT.

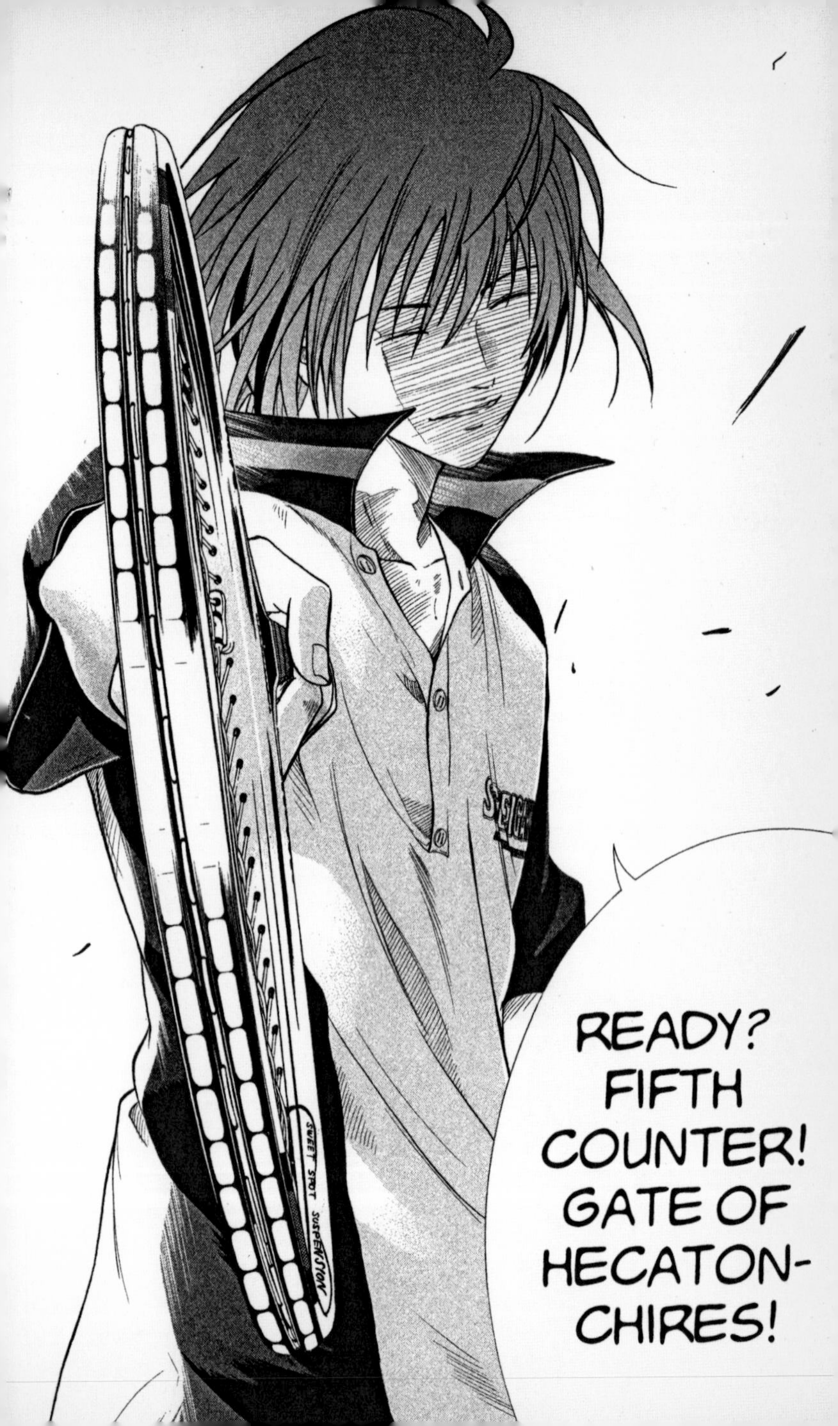
READY? FIFTH COUNTER! GATE OF HECATON-CHIRES!
SWEET SPOT SUSPENSION

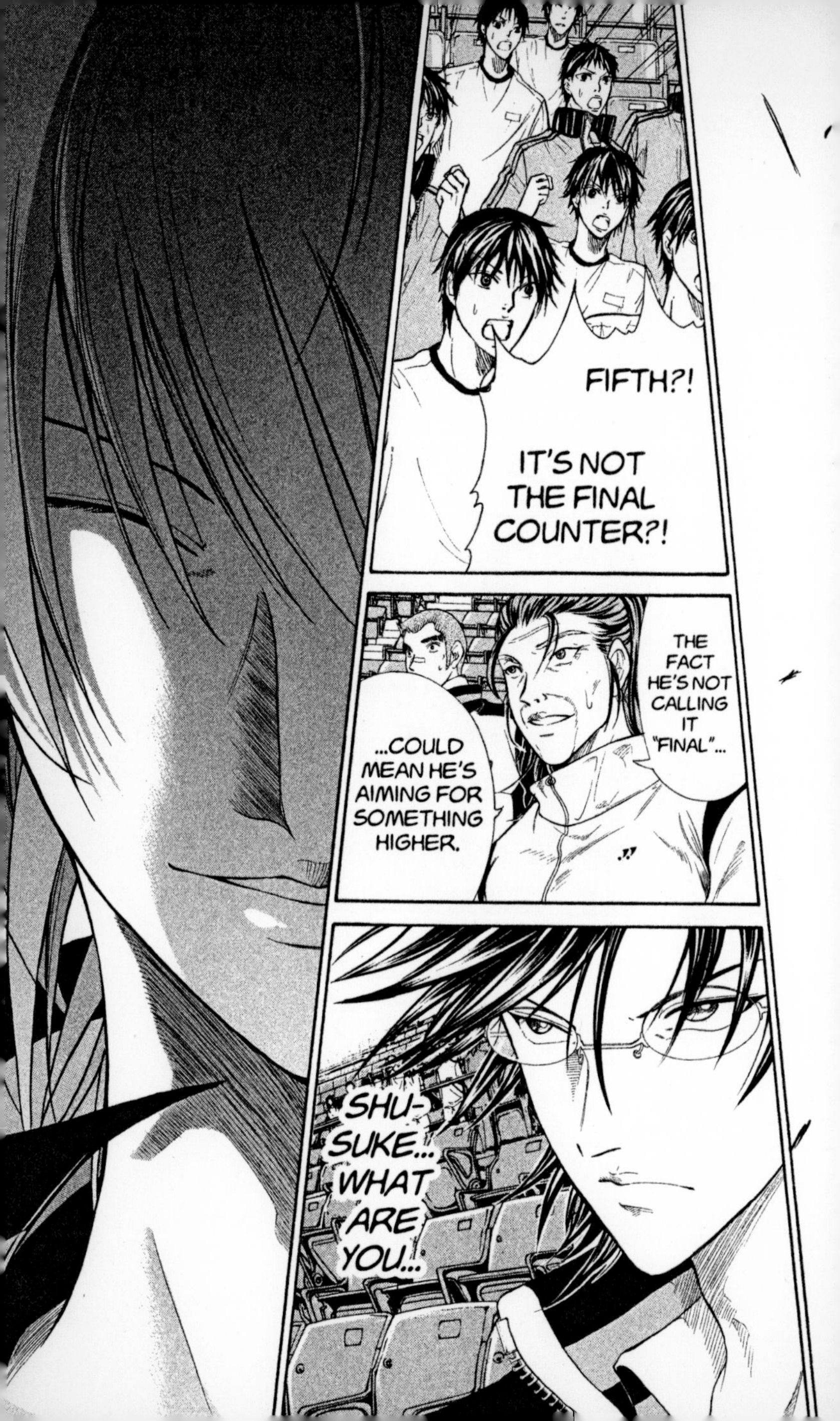
FIFTH?!
IT'S NOT THE FINAL COUNTER?!
THE FACT HE'S NOT CALLING IT "FINAL"...
...COULD MEAN HE'S AIMING FOR SOMETHING HIGHER.
SHU-SUKE... WHAT ARE YOU...

テニスの王子様

THE PRINCE OF TENNIS

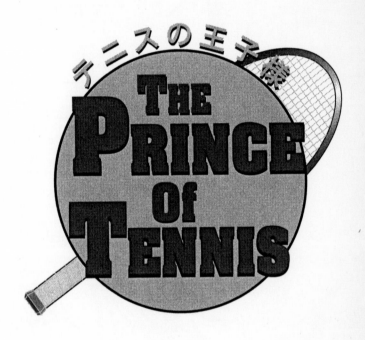

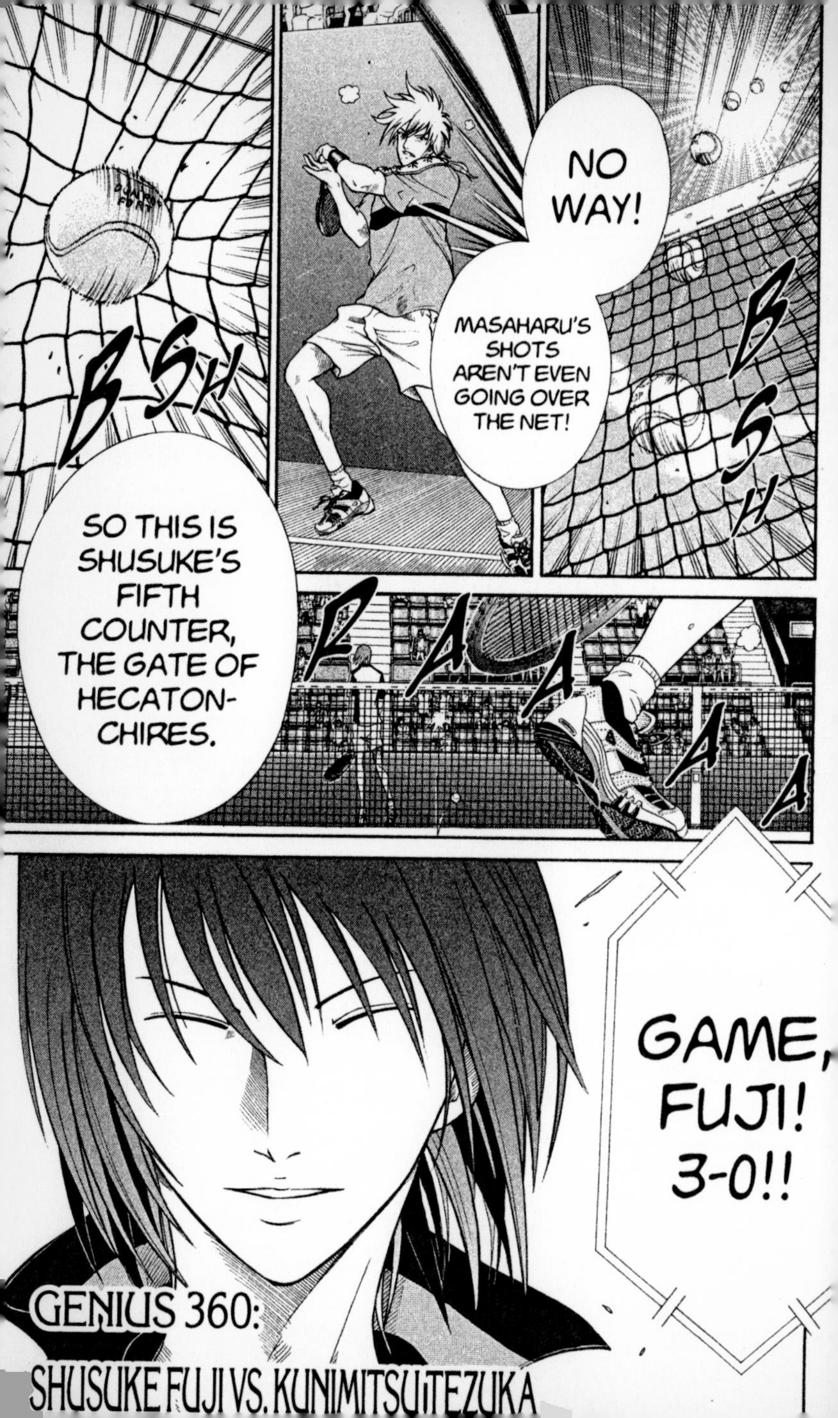
BSSH
NO WAY!
MASAHARU'S SHOTS AREN'T EVEN GOING OVER THE NET!
BSH
SO THIS IS SHUSUKE'S FIFTH COUNTER, THE GATE OF HECATON-CHIRES.
RAAAA
GAME, FUJI! 3-0!!
GENIUS 360:
SHUSUKE FUJI VS. KUNIMITSU TEZUKA

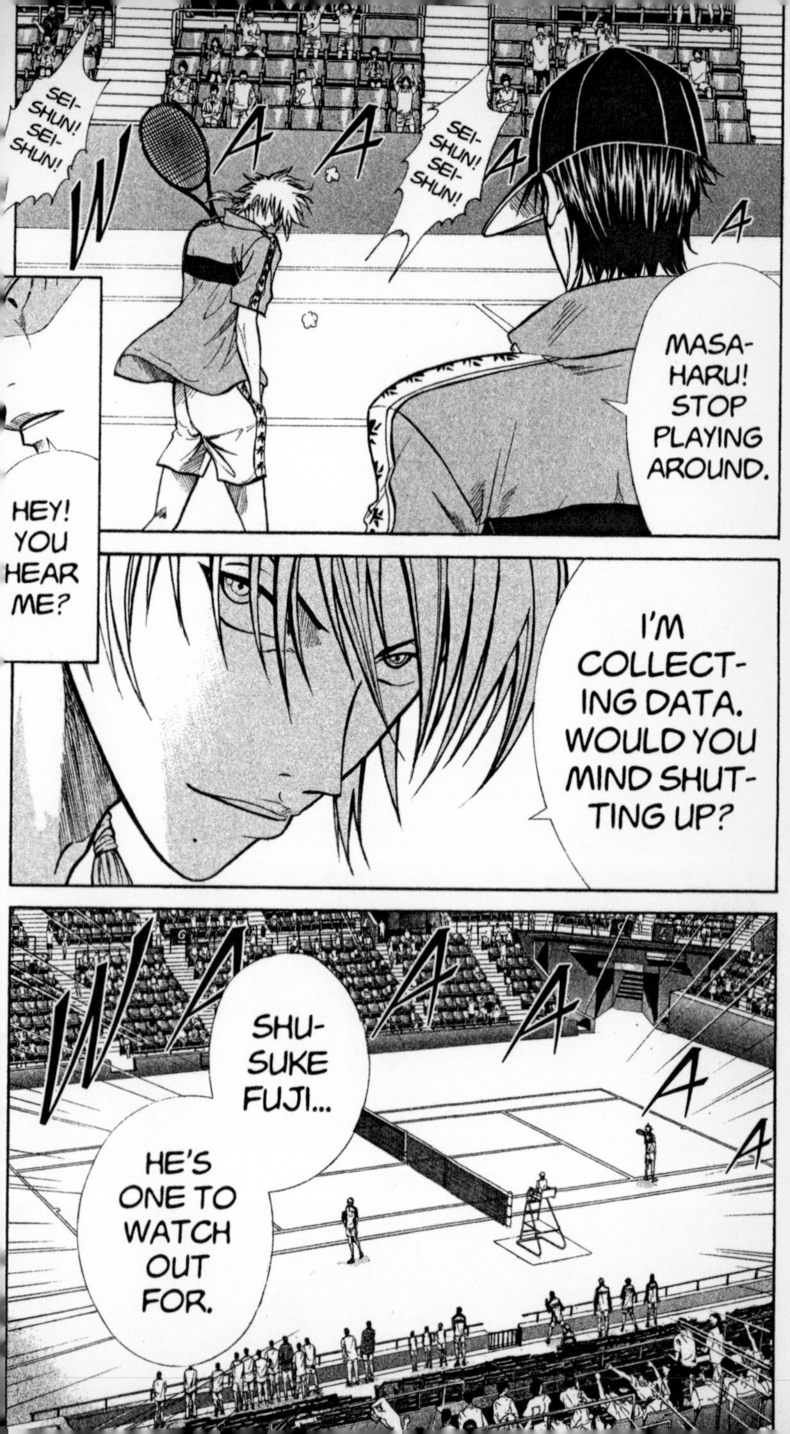
WAAAA
SEI-SHUN! SEI-SHUN!
SEI-SHUN! SEI-SHUN!
MASA-HARU! STOP PLAYING AROUND.
HEY! YOU HEAR ME?
I'M COLLECT-ING DATA. WOULD YOU MIND SHUT-TING UP?
WAAAAA
SHU-SUKE FUJI...
HE'S ONE TO WATCH OUT FOR.

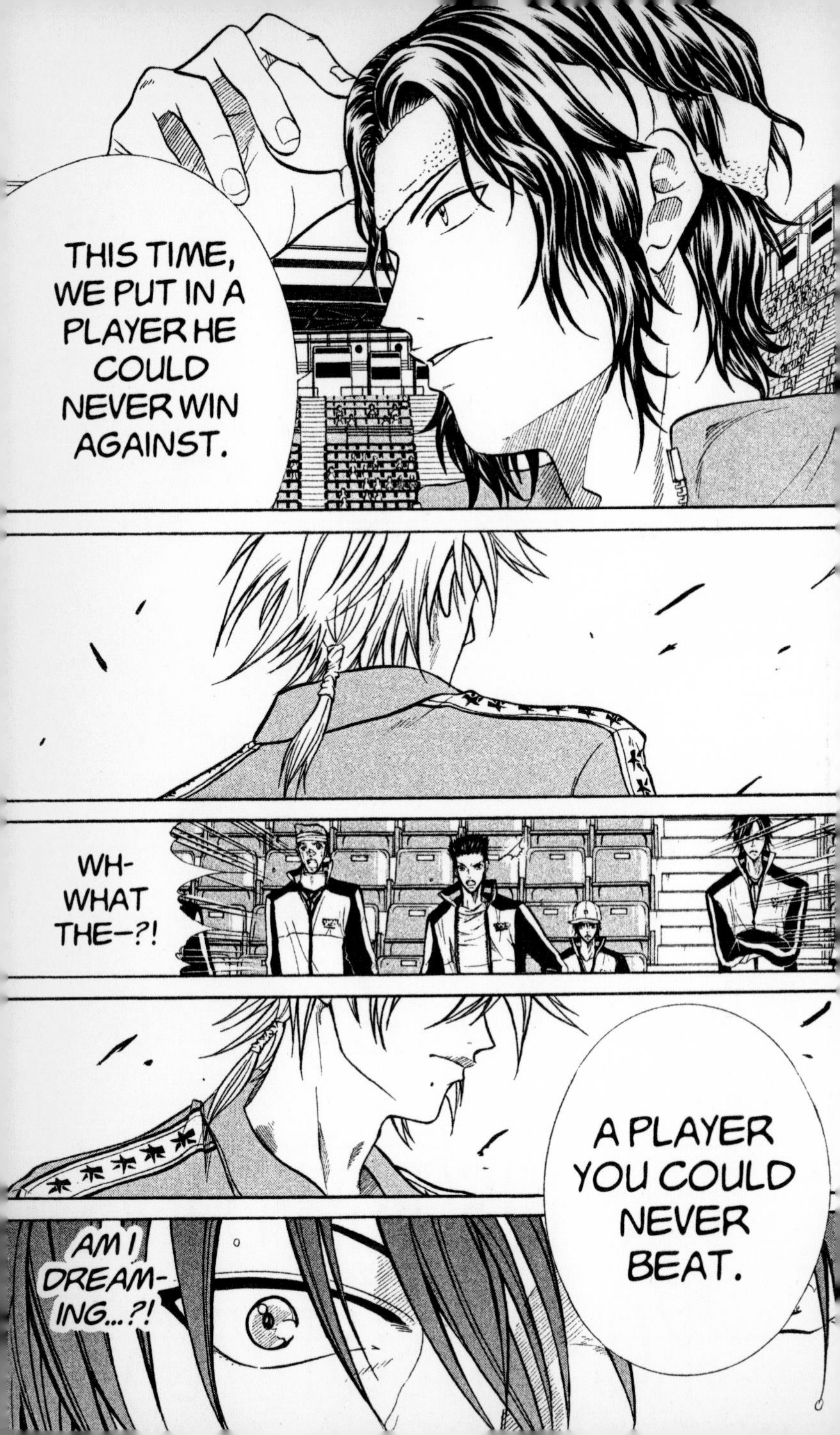
THIS TIME, WE PUT IN A PLAYER HE COULD NEVER WIN AGAINST.
WH- WHAT THE--?!
A PLAYER YOU COULD NEVER BEAT.
AM I DREAMING...?!

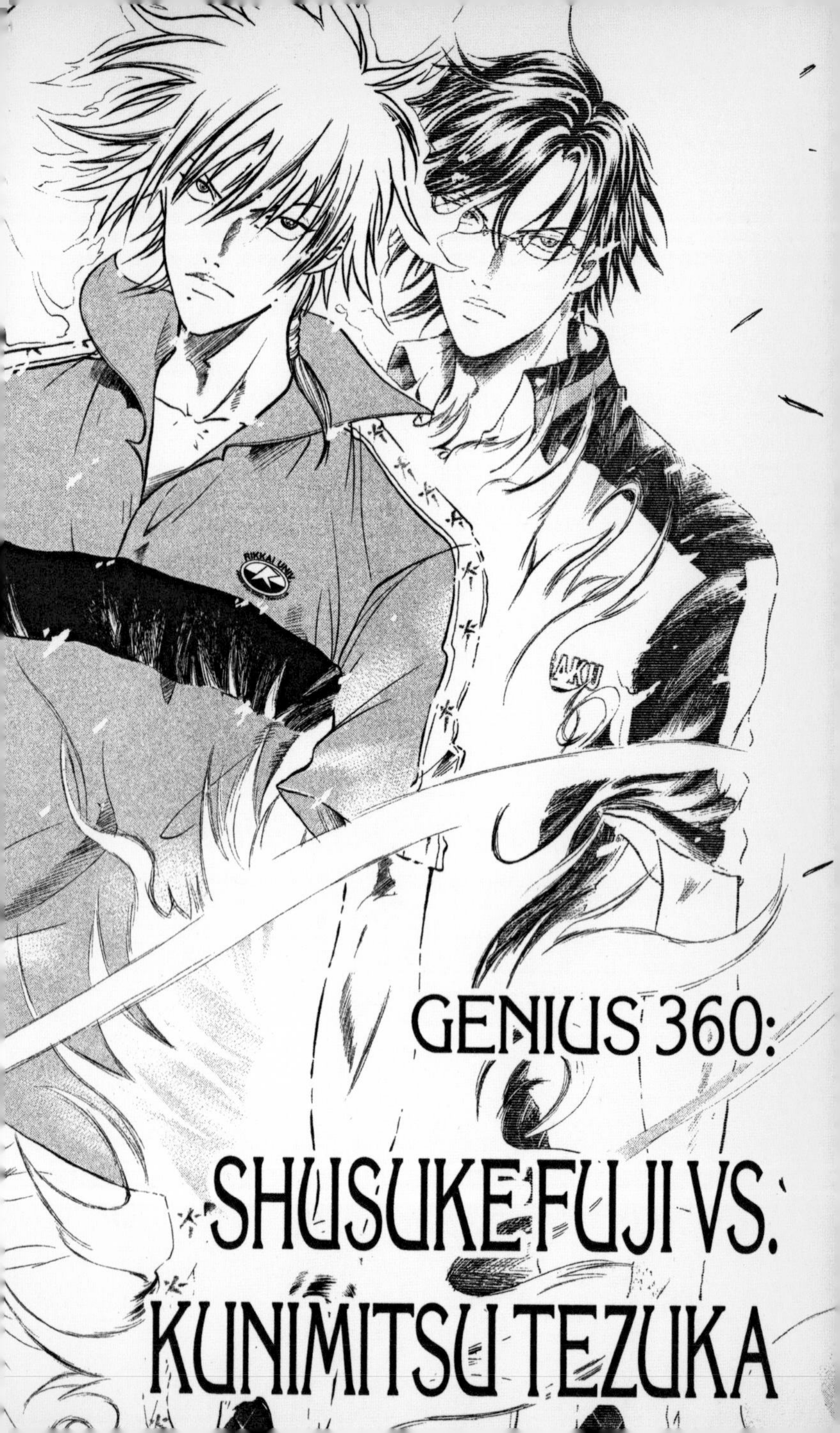
RIKKAI UNIV
GENIUS 360:
SHUSUKE FUJI VS.
KUNIMITSU TEZUKA

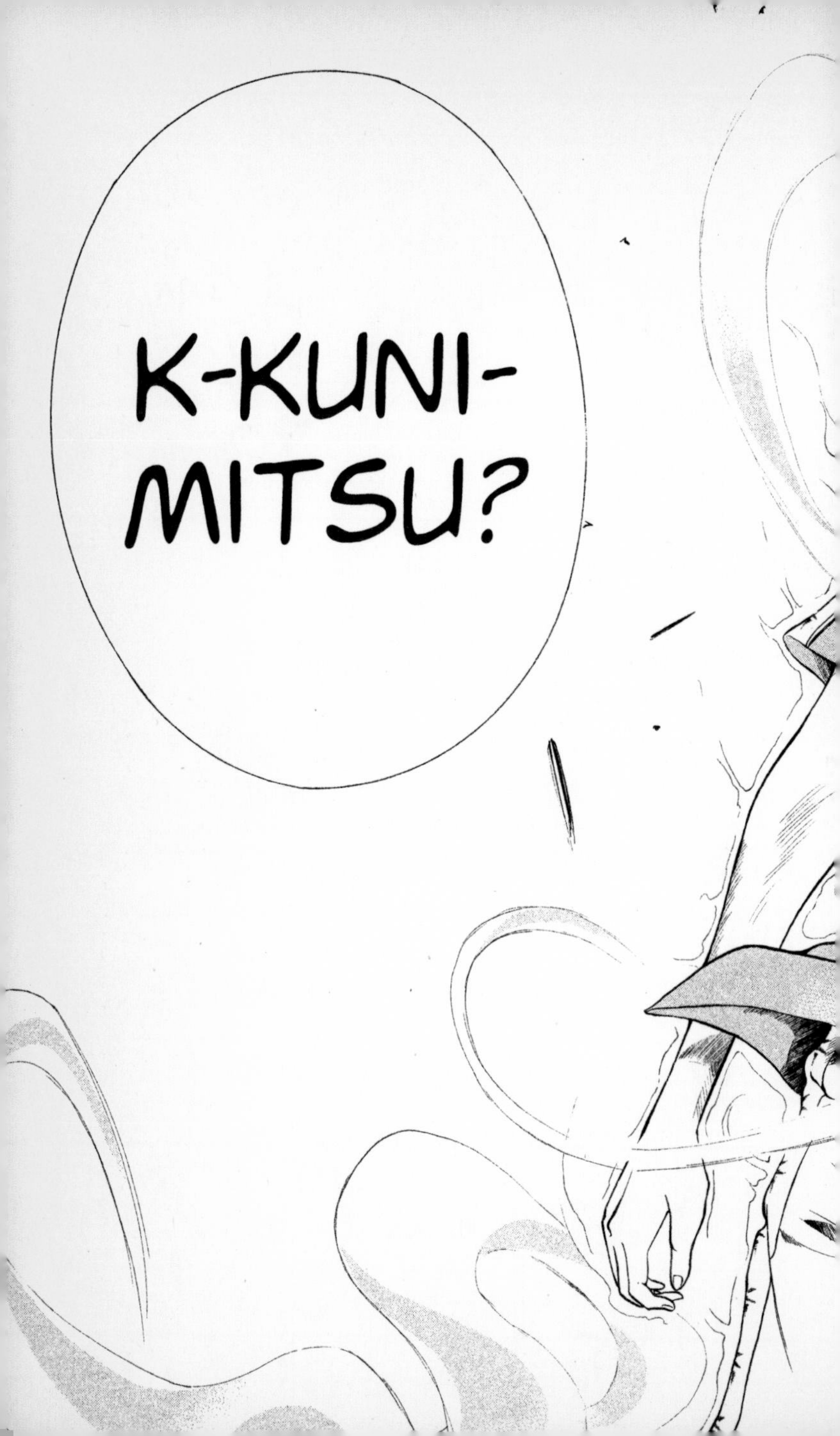
K-KUNI-MITSU?

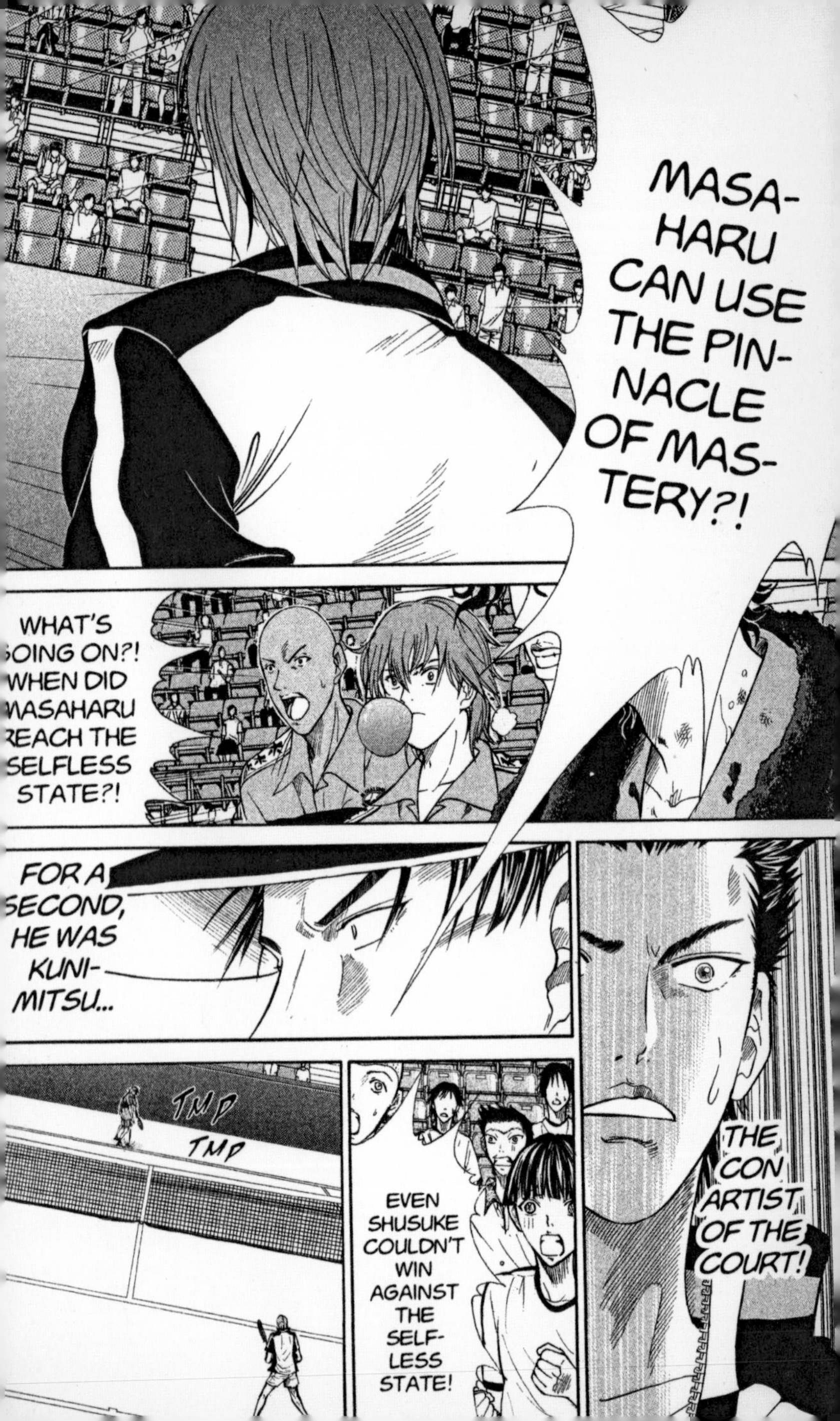
MASA-HARU CAN USE THE PIN-NACLE OF MAS-TERY?!
WHAT'S GOING ON?! WHEN DID MASAHARU REACH THE SELFLESS STATE?!
THE CON ARTIST OF THE COURT!
FOR A SECOND, HE WAS KUNI-MITSU...
EVEN SHUSUKE COULDN'T WIN AGAINST THE SELF-LESS STATE!
TMP
TMP

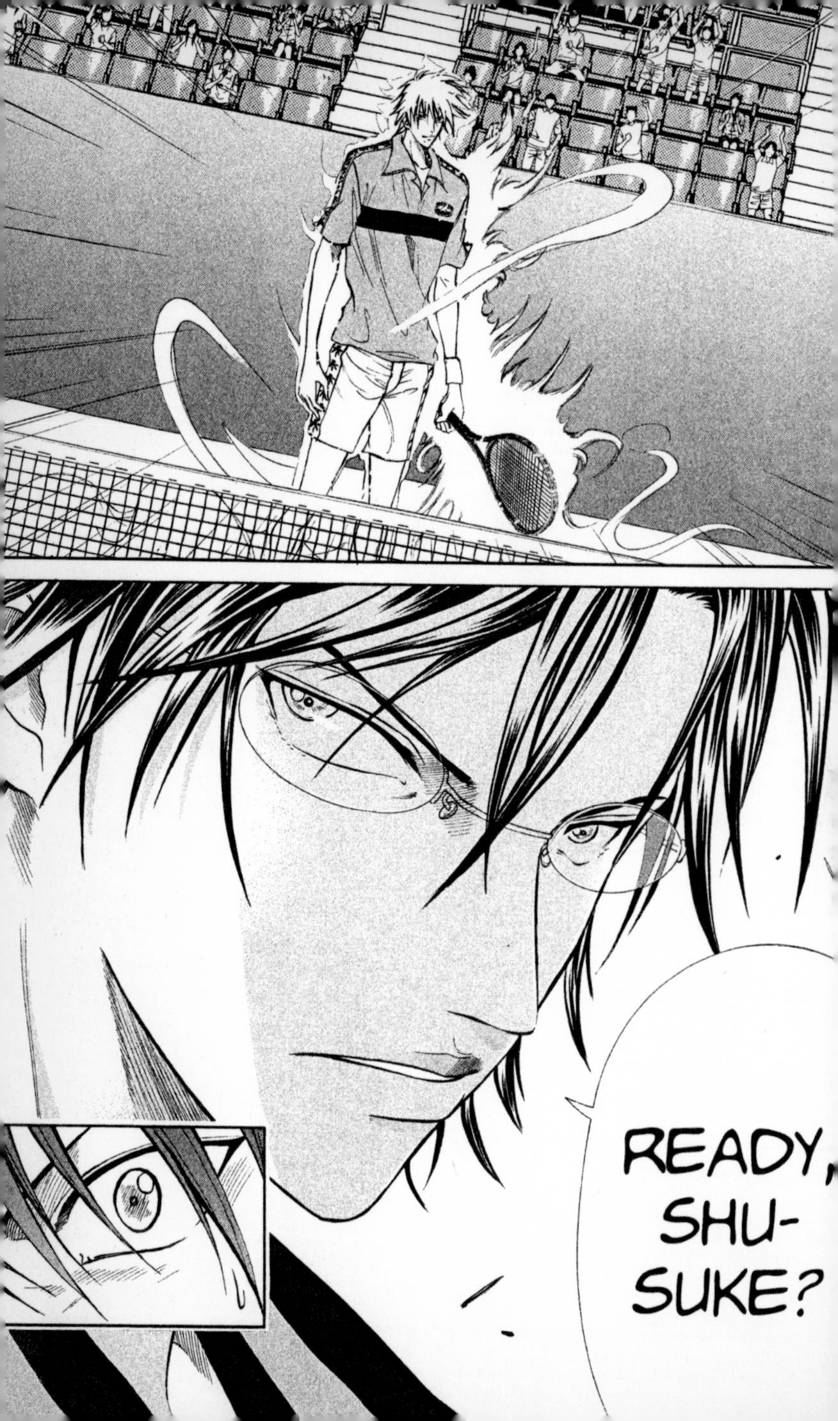
READY, SHU-SUKE?

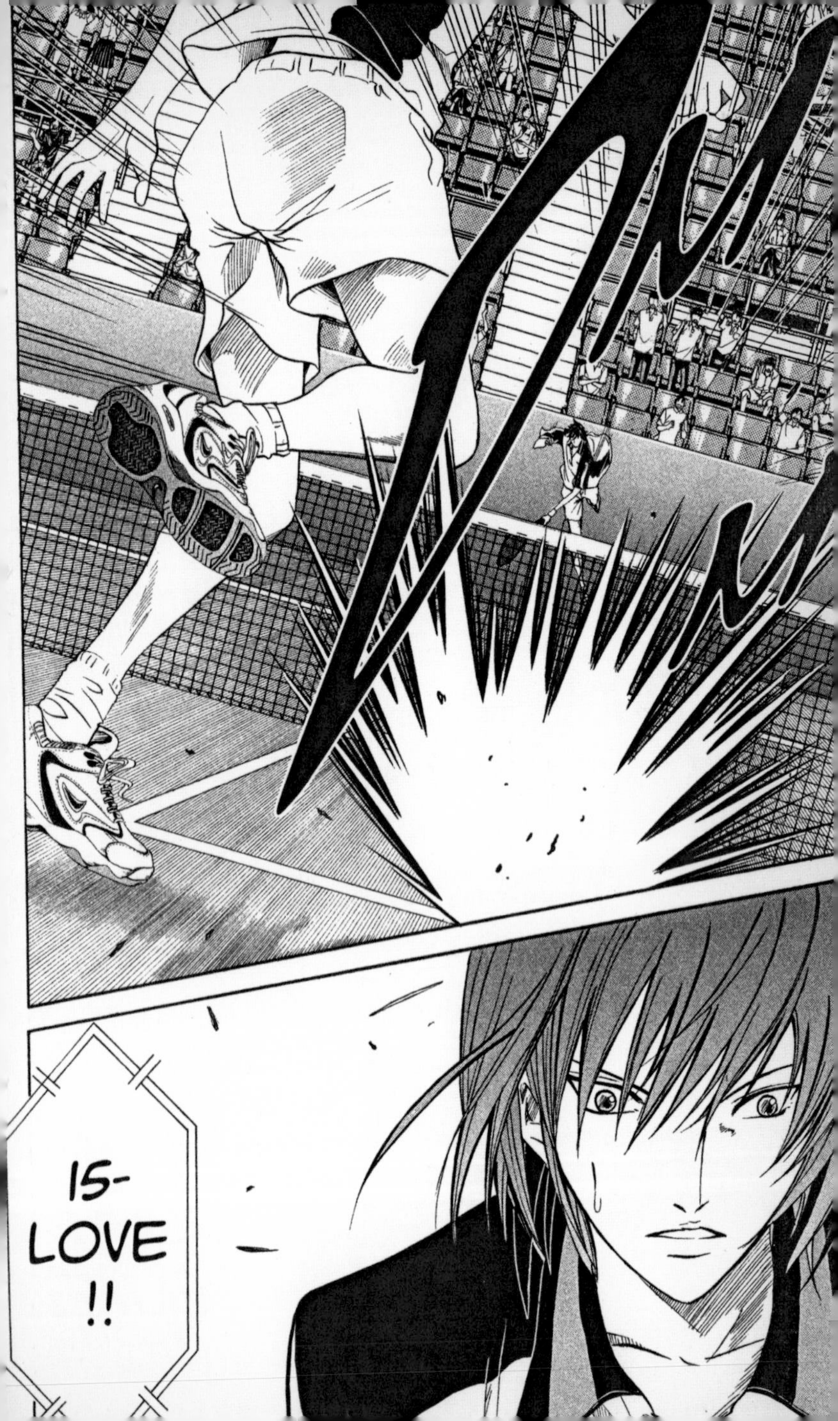
15-LOVE !!

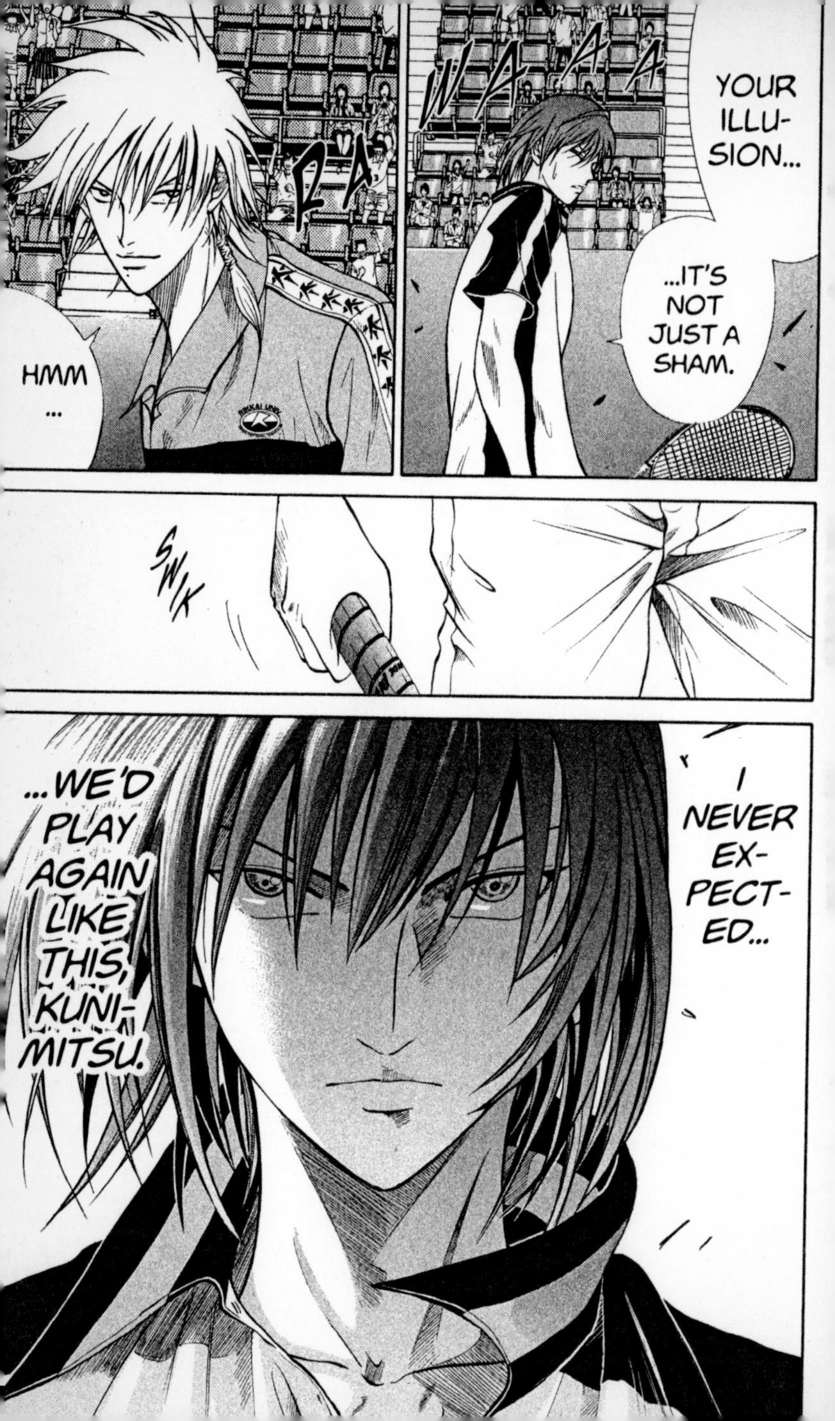
WAAAA
YOUR ILLUSION...
...IT'S NOT JUST A SHAM.
RA
HMM ...
SWIK
I NEVER EXPECTED...
...WE'D PLAY AGAIN LIKE THIS, KUNIMITSU.

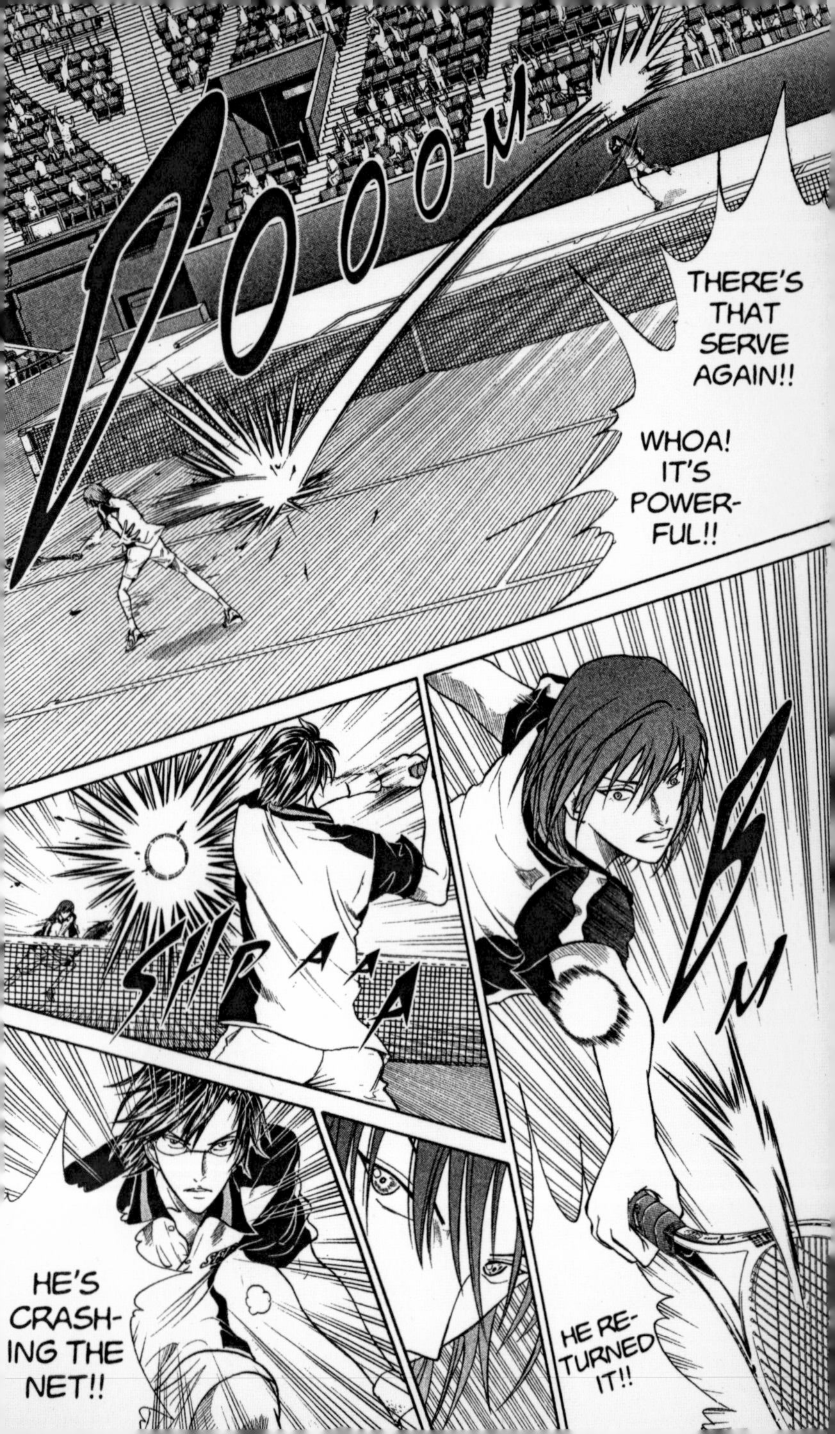
ZOOOM
THERE'S THAT SERVE AGAIN!!
WHOA! IT'S POWER-FUL!!
SWM
HE RE-TURNED IT!!
SHPAAA
HE'S CRASH-ING THE NET!!

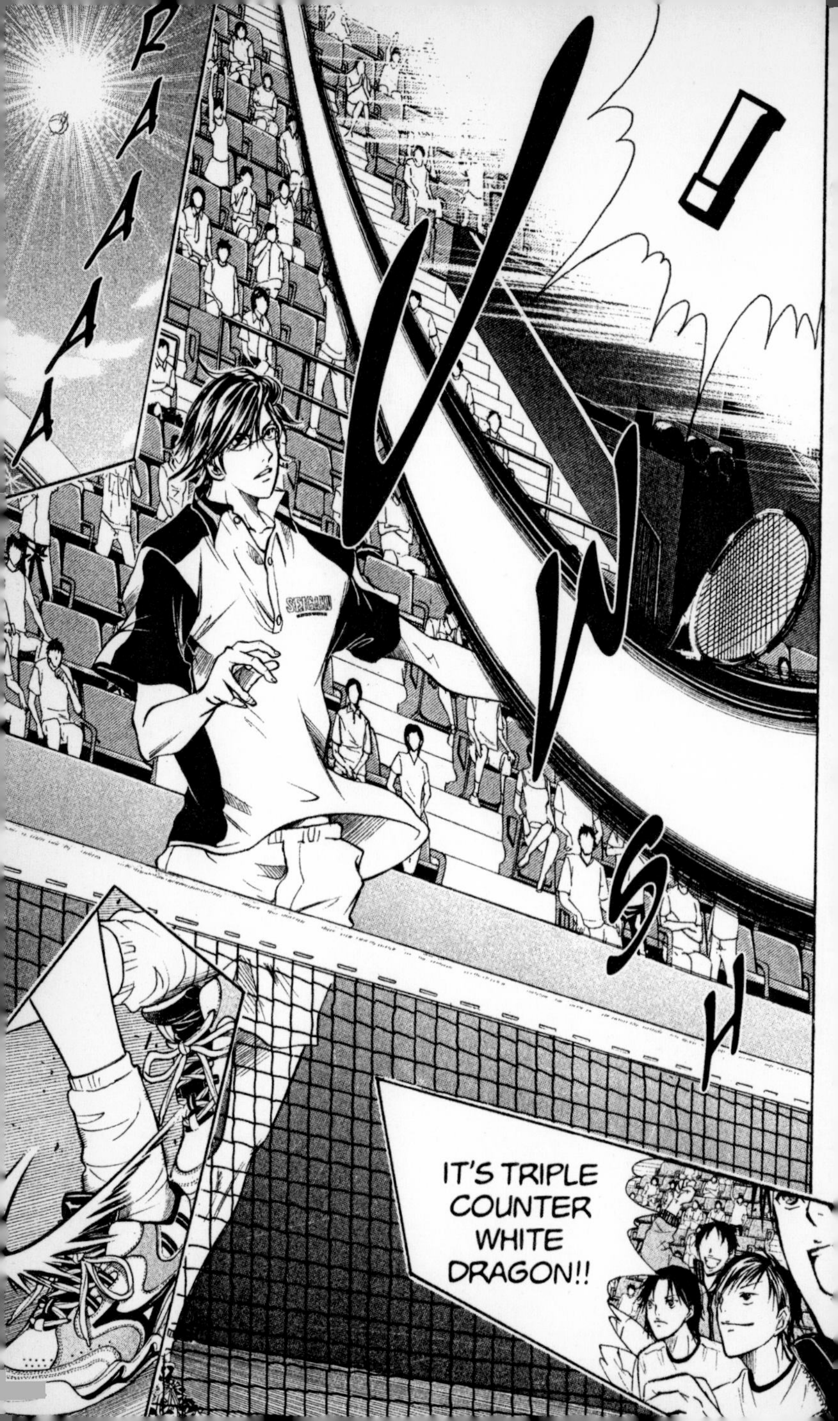
PAAAAA
IT'S TRIPLE COUNTER WHITE DRAGON!!

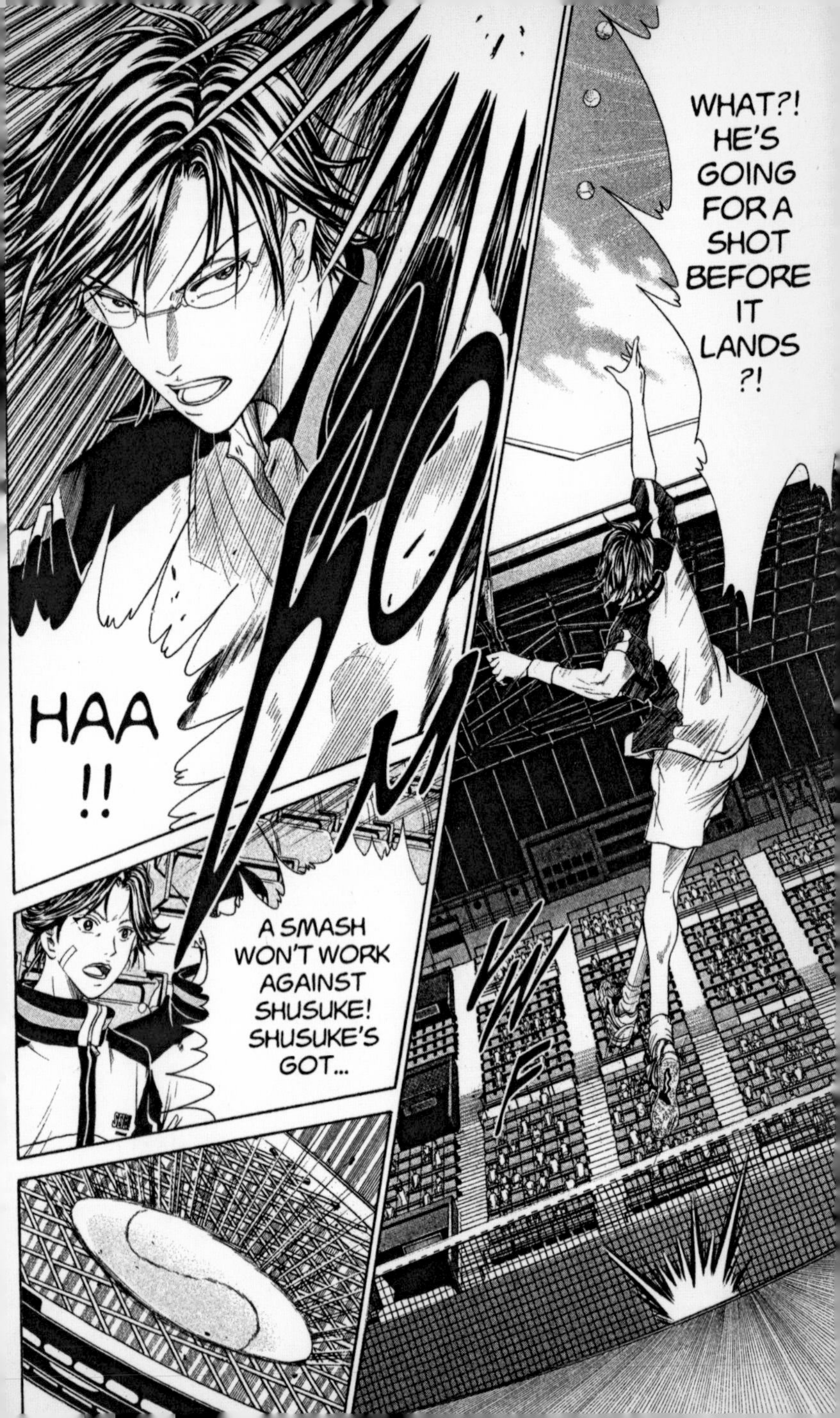
WHAT?! HE'S GOING FOR A SHOT BEFORE IT LANDS ?!
HAA !!
A SMASH WON'T WORK AGAINST SHUSUKE! SHUSUKE'S GOT...

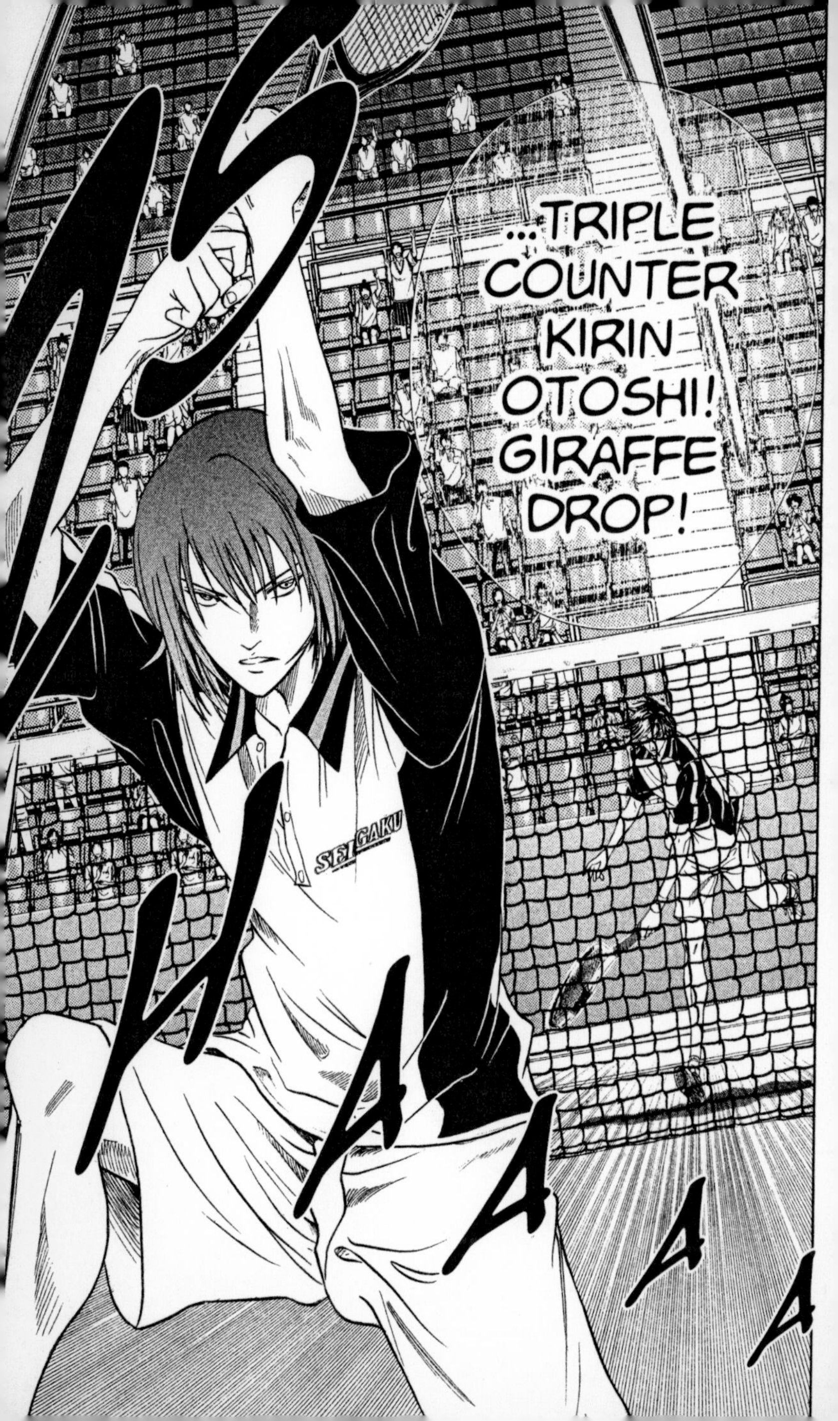
...TRIPLE COUNTER KIRIN OTOSHI! GIRAFFE DROP!

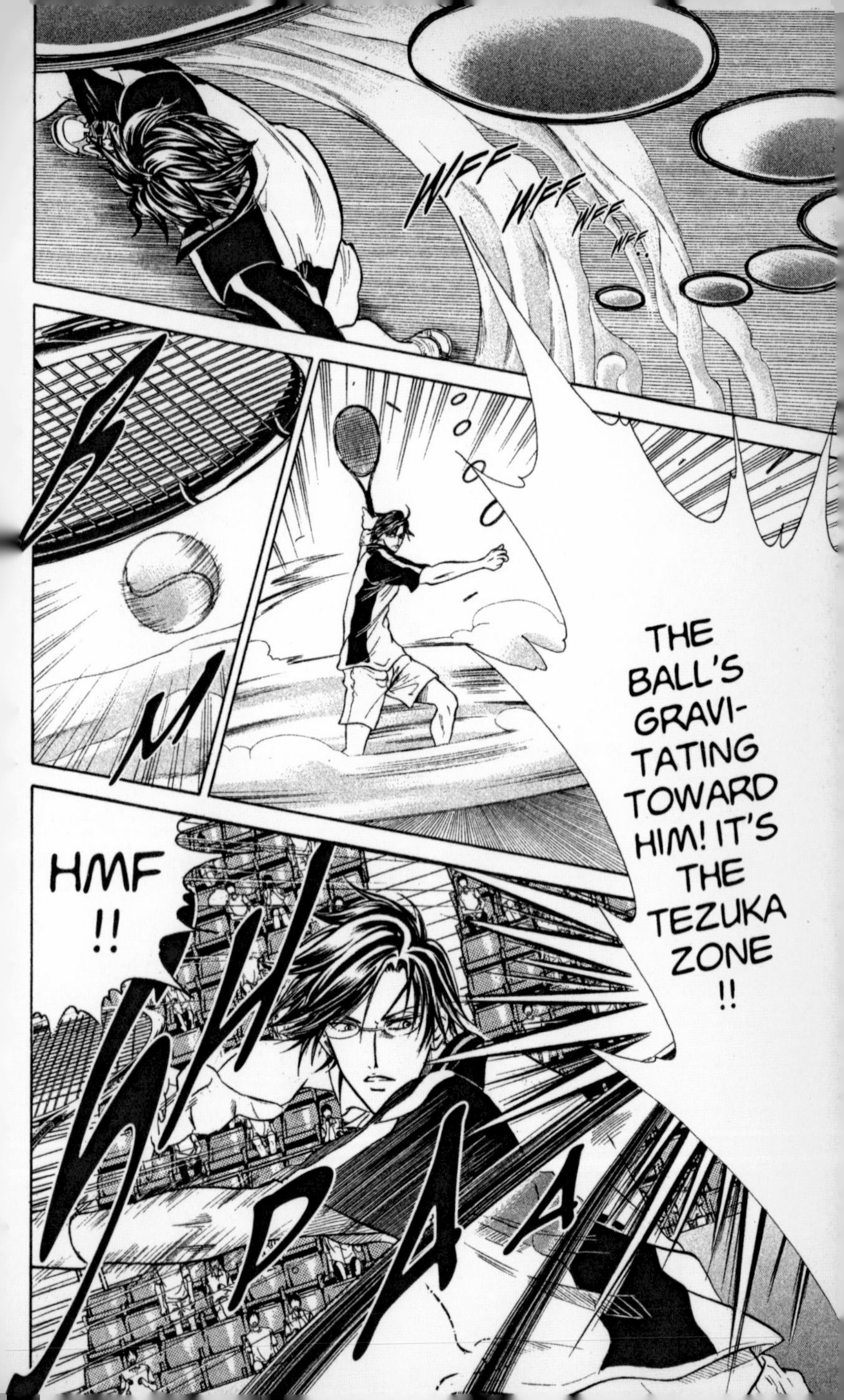
WFF WFF WFF WFF...
THE BALL'S GRAVITATING TOWARD HIM! IT'S THE TEZUKA ZONE !!
HMF !!

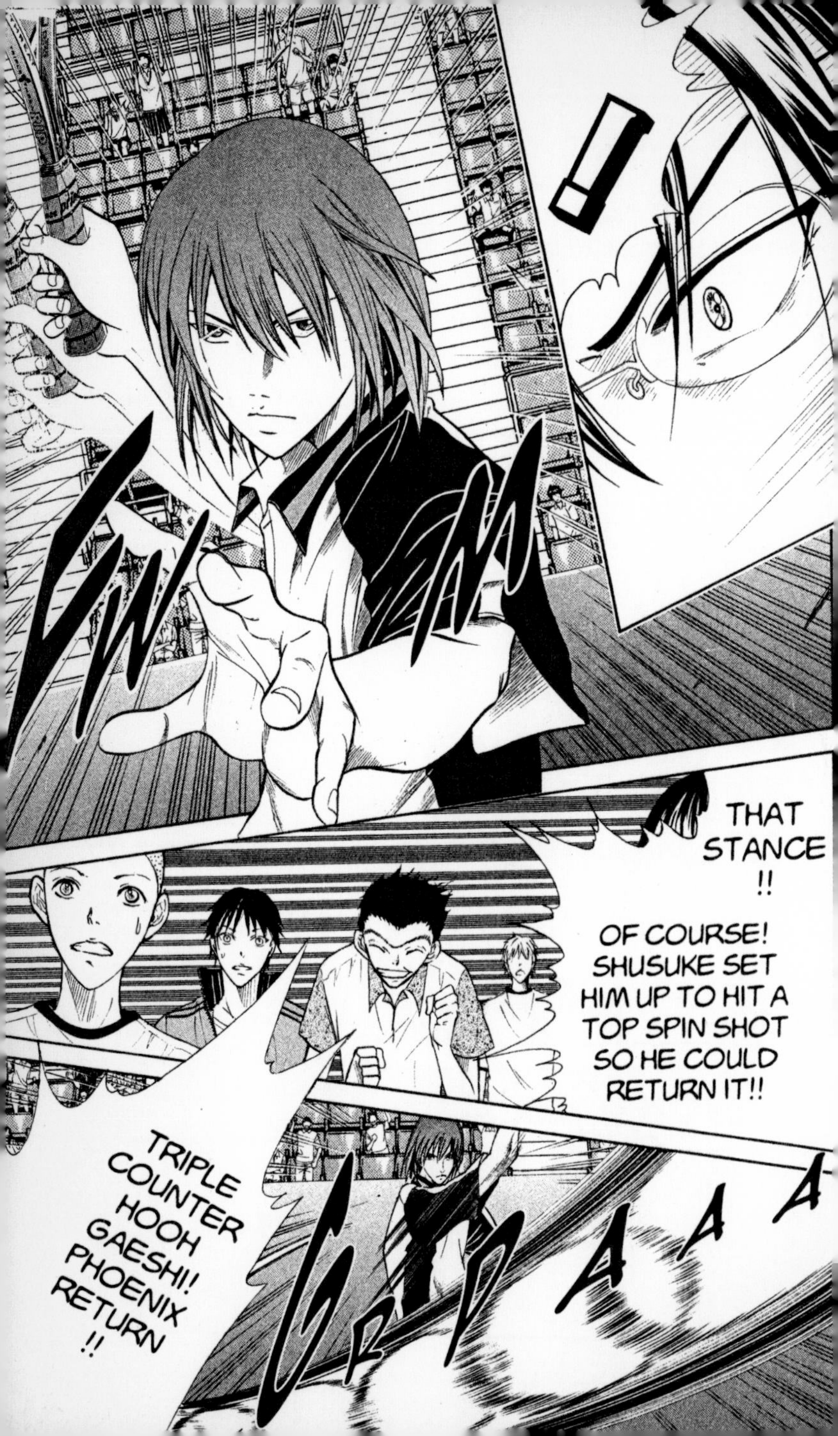
!
THAT STANCE !!
OF COURSE! SHUSUKE SET HIM UP TO HIT A TOP SPIN SHOT SO HE COULD RETURN IT!!
TRIPLE COUNTER HOOH GAESHI! PHOENIX RETURN !!

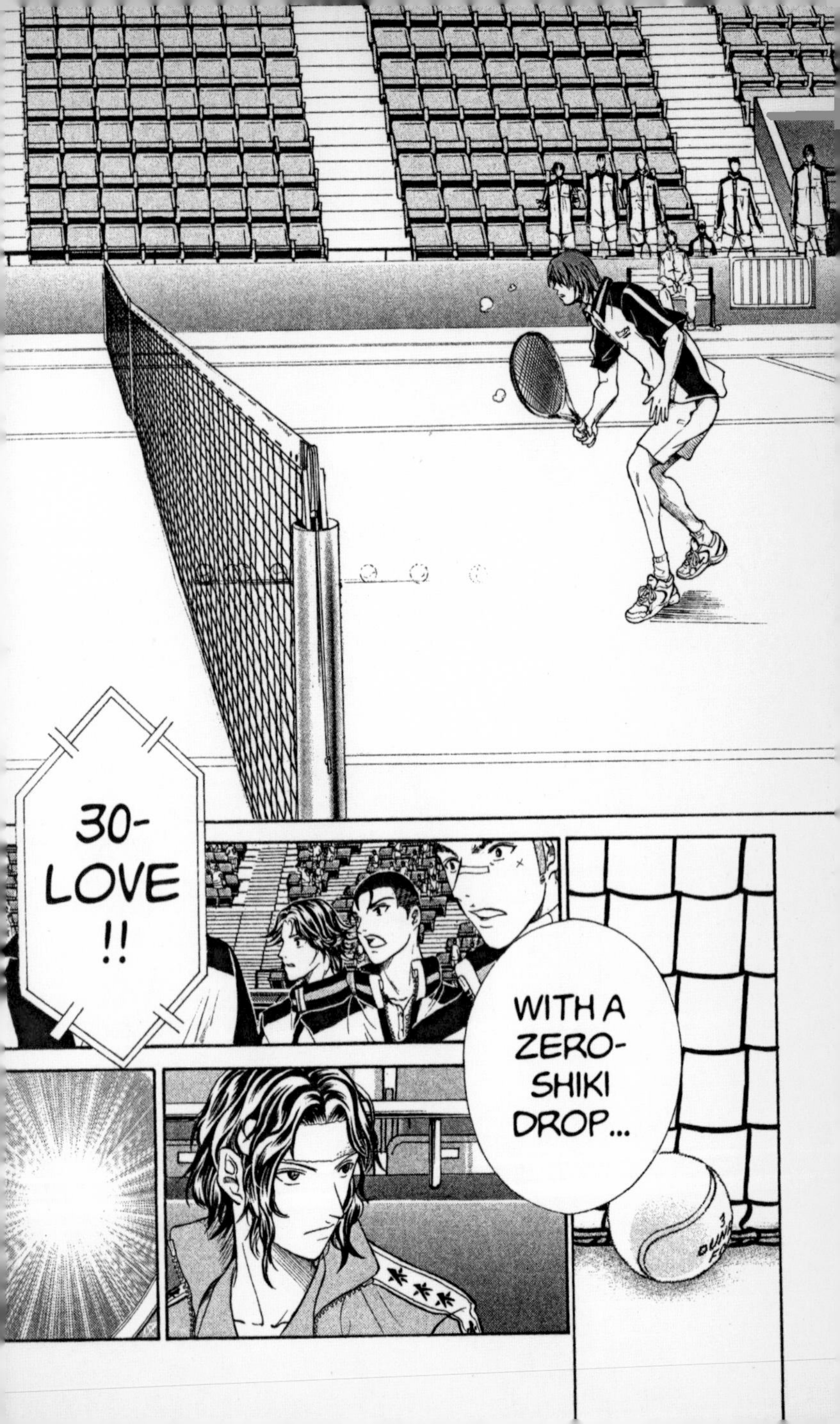
30-LOVE!!
WITH A ZERO-SHIKI DROP...

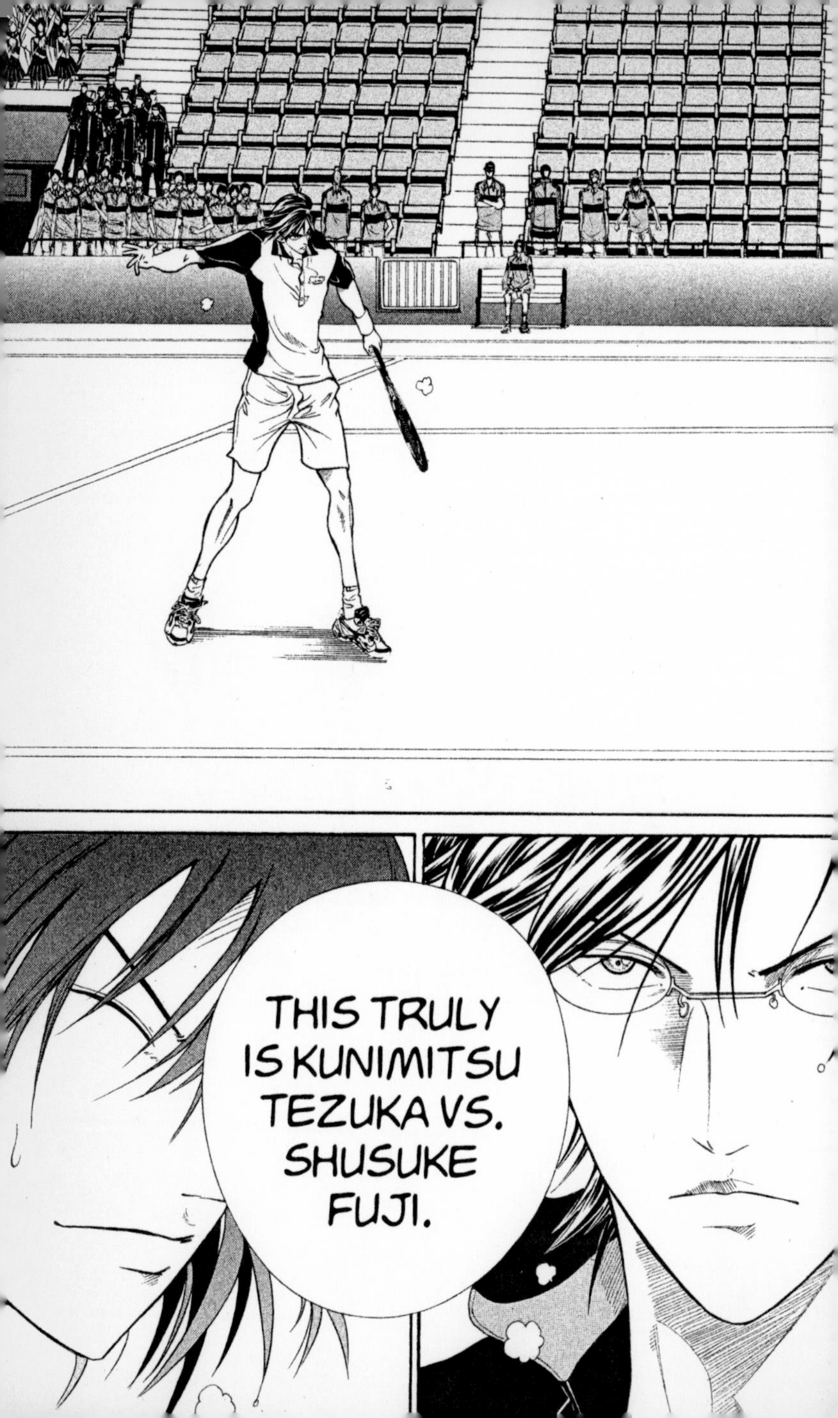
THIS TRULY IS KUNIMITSU TEZUKA VS. SHUSUKE FUJI.

テニスの王子様

THE PRINCE OF TENNIS

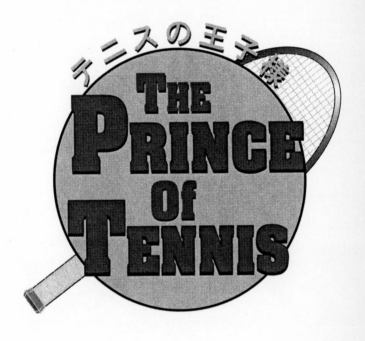

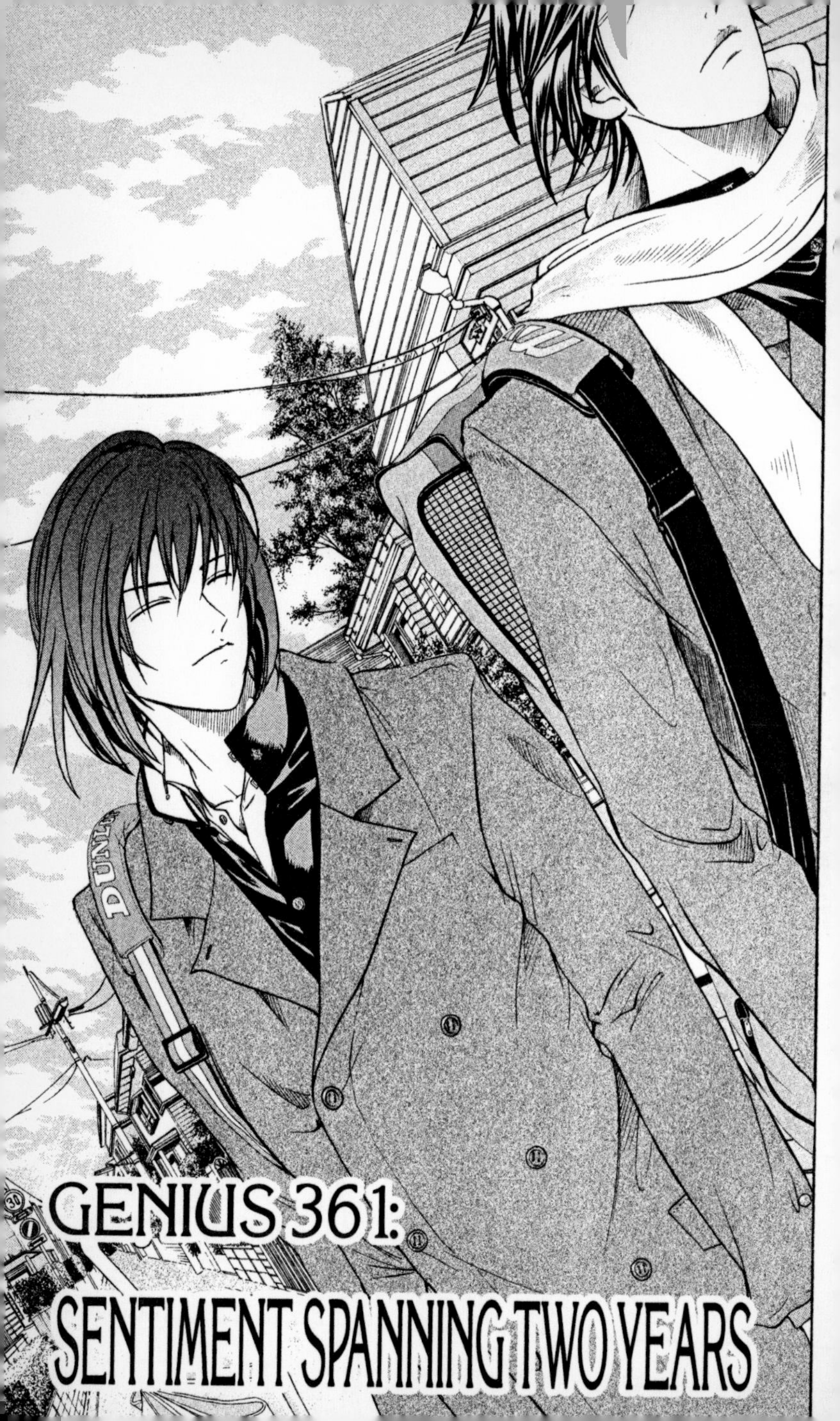
GENIUS 361:
SENTIMENT SPANNING TWO YEARS

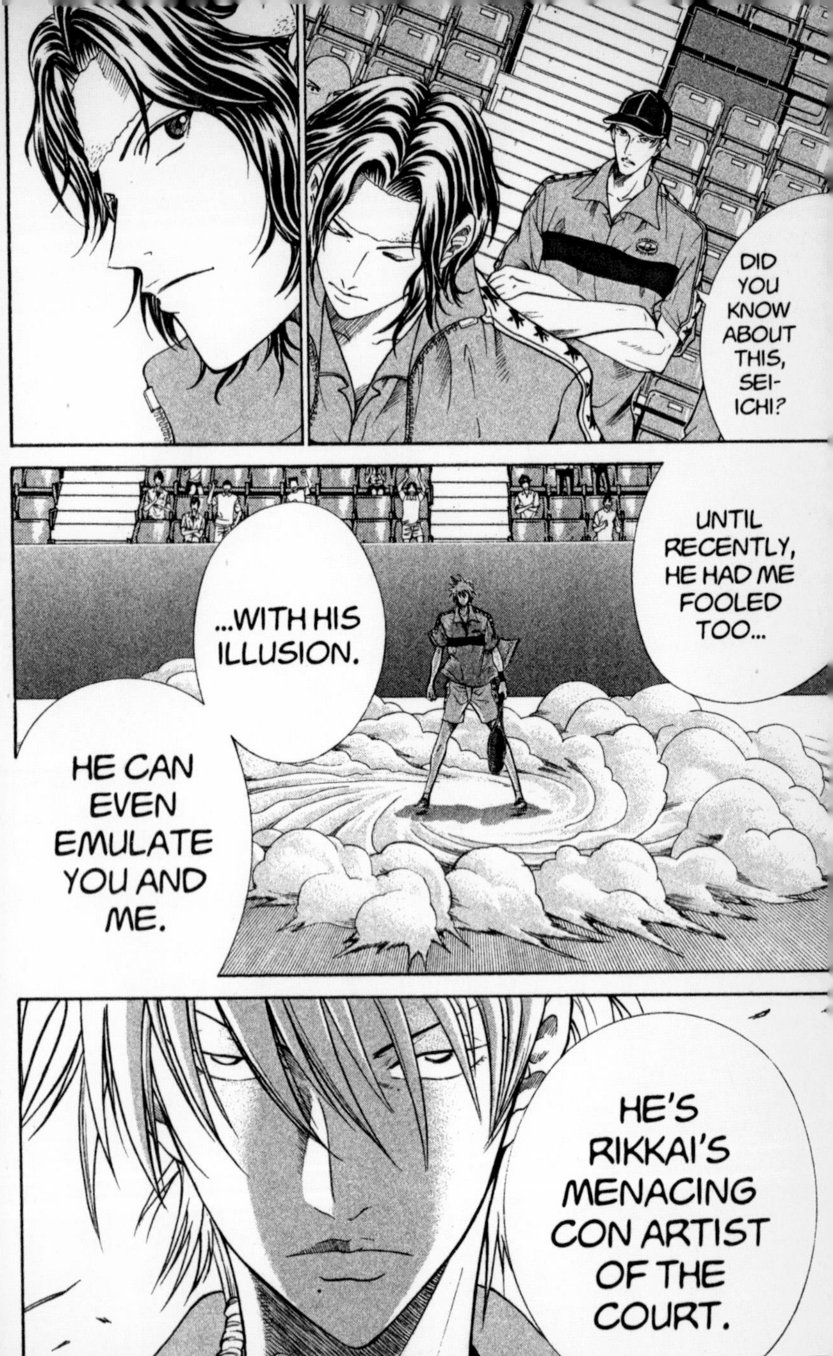
DID YOU KNOW ABOUT THIS, SEI-ICHI?
UNTIL RECENTLY, HE HAD ME FOOLED TOO...
...WITH HIS ILLUSION.
HE CAN EVEN EMULATE YOU AND ME.
HE'S RIKKAI'S MENACING CON ARTIST OF THE COURT.

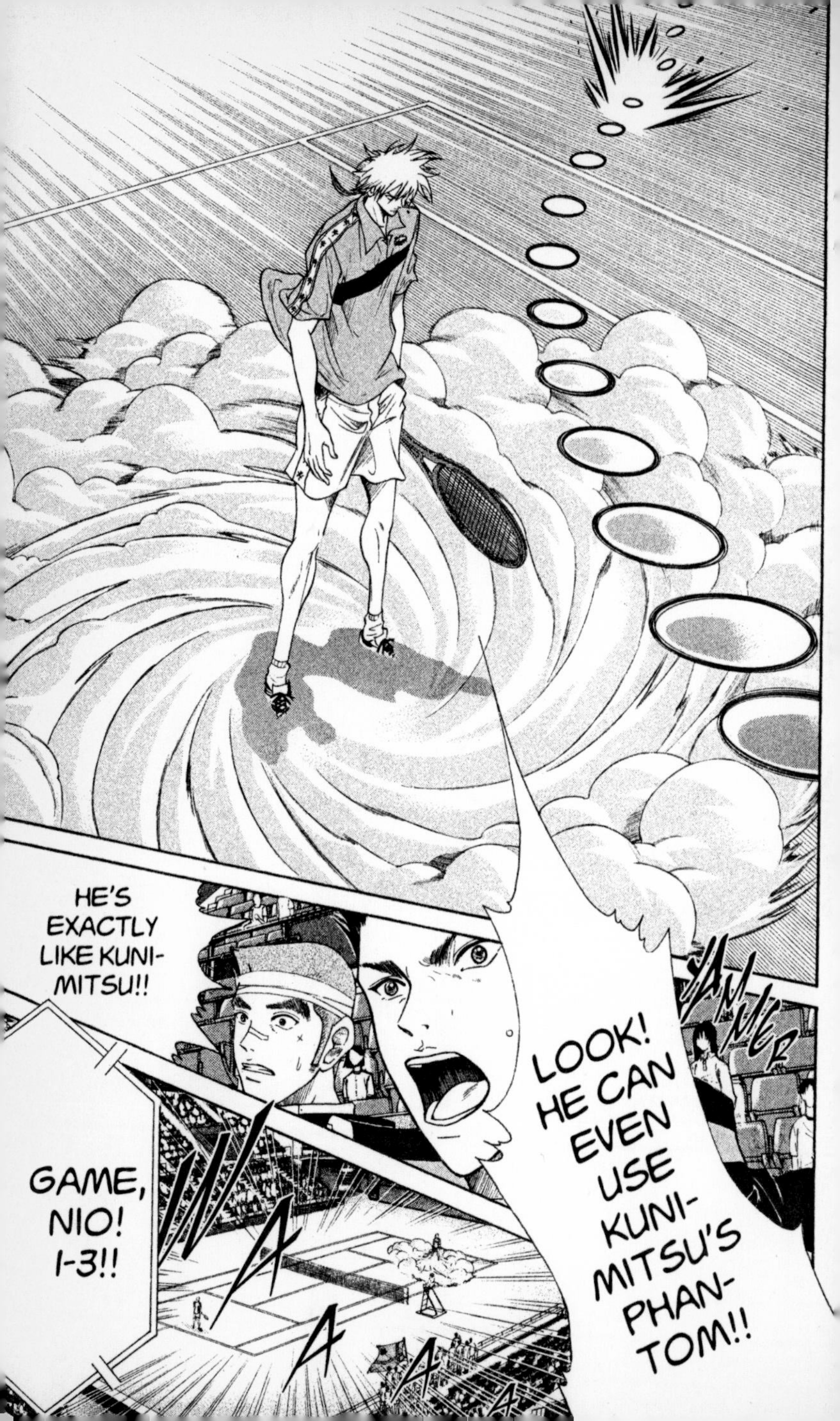

LOOK! HE CAN EVEN USE KUNI-MITSU'S PHAN-TOM!!
HE'S EXACTLY LIKE KUNI-MITSU!!
GAME, NIO! 1-3!!

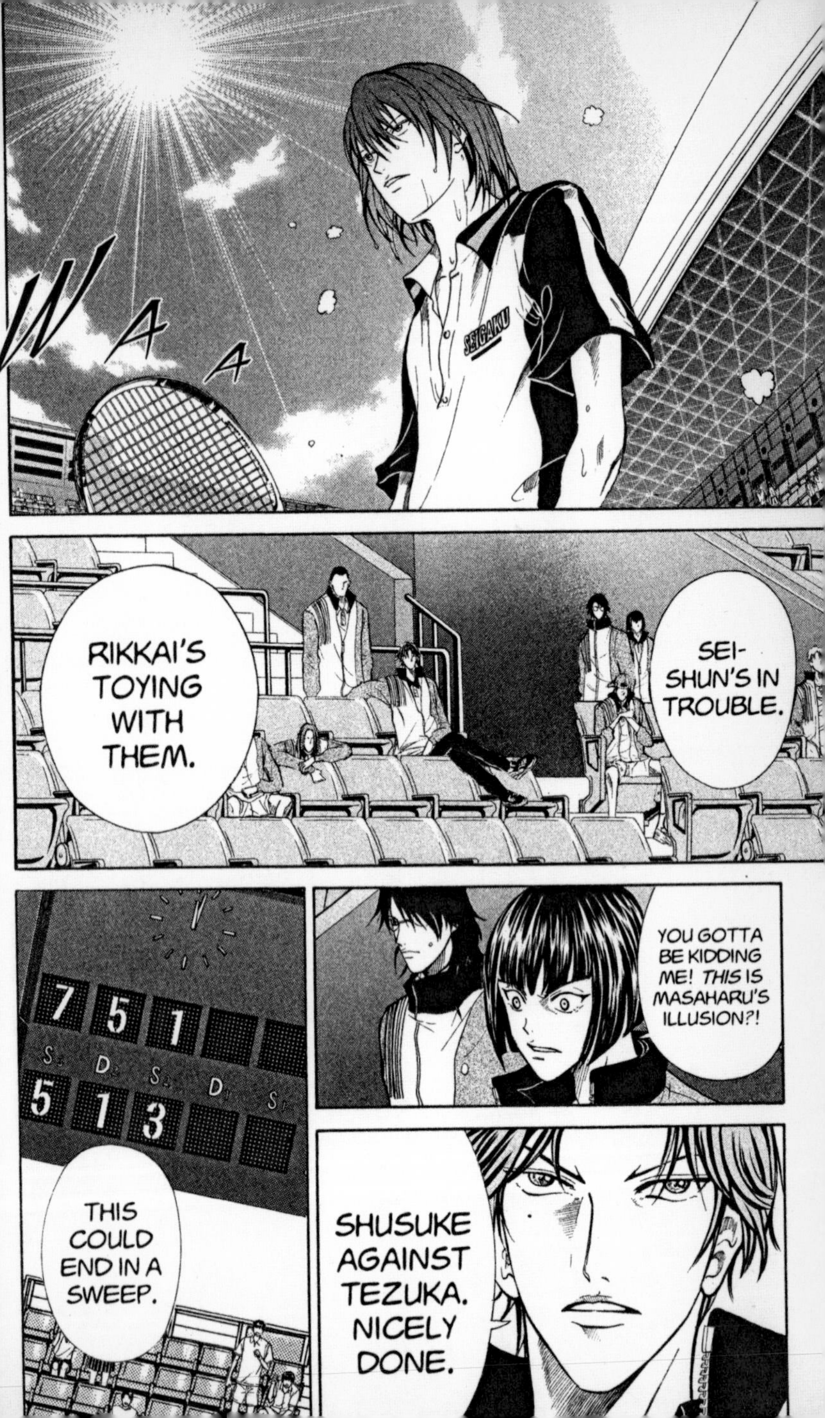
WAAA
SEI-SHUN'S IN TROUBLE.
RIKKAI'S TOYING WITH THEM.
YOU GOTTA BE KIDDING ME! *THIS* IS MASAHARU'S ILLUSION?!
SHUSUKE AGAINST TEZUKA. NICELY DONE.
7 5 1
5 1 3
THIS COULD END IN A SWEEP.

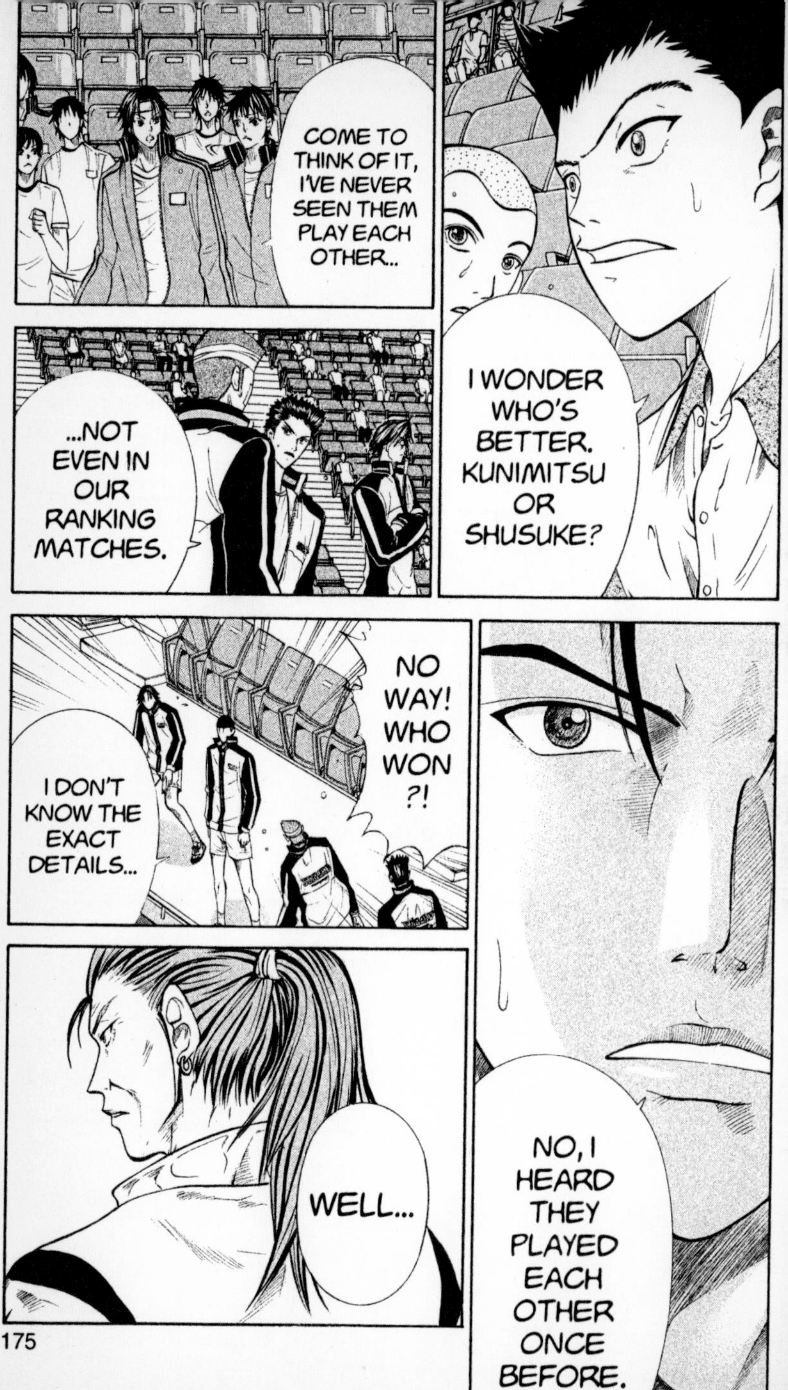
I WONDER WHO'S BETTER. KUNIMITSU OR SHUSUKE?
COME TO THINK OF IT, I'VE NEVER SEEN THEM PLAY EACH OTHER...
...NOT EVEN IN OUR RANKING MATCHES.
NO, I HEARD THEY PLAYED EACH OTHER ONCE BEFORE.
NO WAY! WHO WON?!
I DON'T KNOW THE EXACT DETAILS...
WELL...

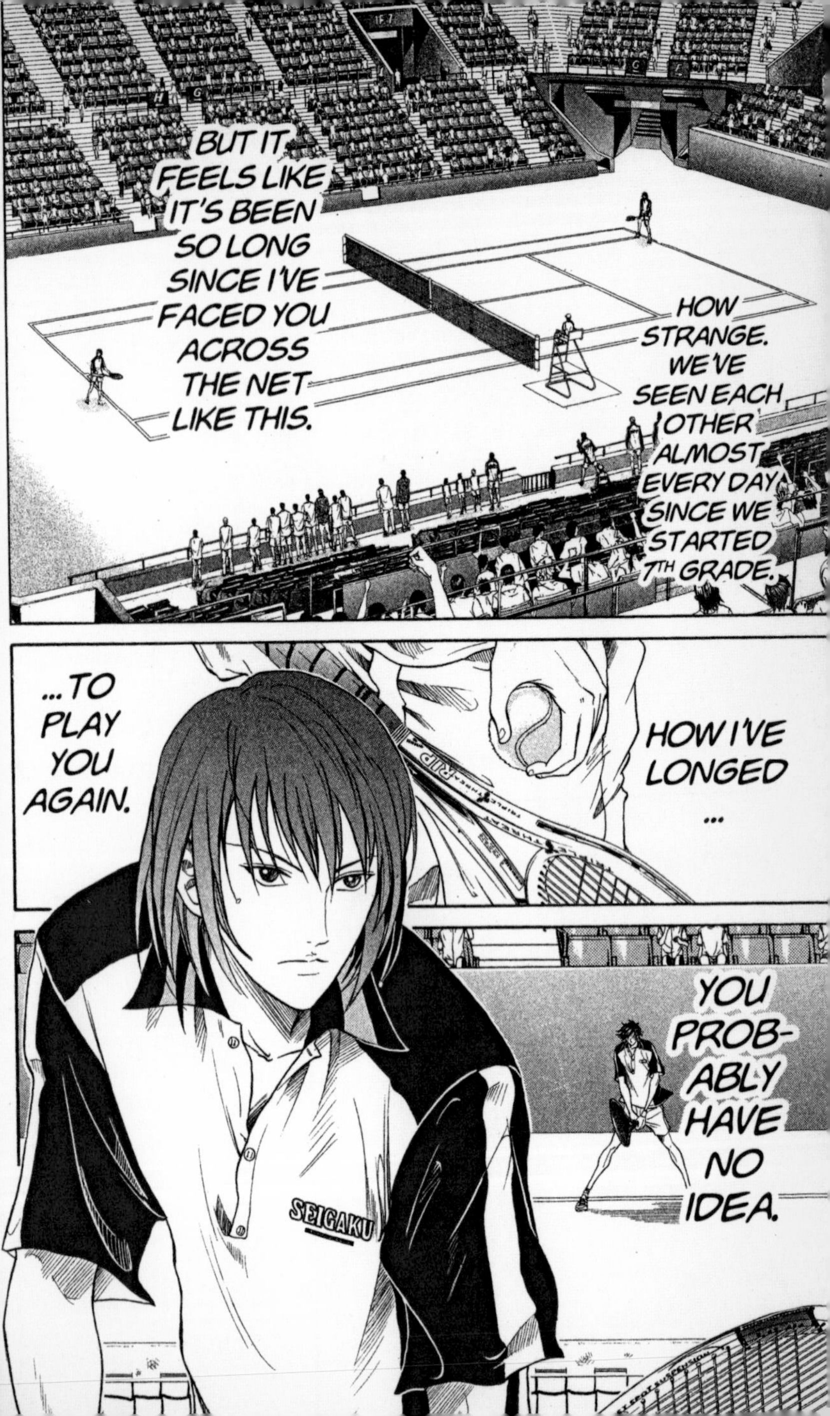
HOW STRANGE. WE'VE SEEN EACH OTHER ALMOST EVERY DAY SINCE WE STARTED 7TH GRADE.
BUT IT FEELS LIKE IT'S BEEN SO LONG SINCE I'VE FACED YOU ACROSS THE NET LIKE THIS.
HOW I'VE LONGED ...
...TO PLAY YOU AGAIN.
YOU PROB-ABLY HAVE NO IDEA.
SEIGAKU

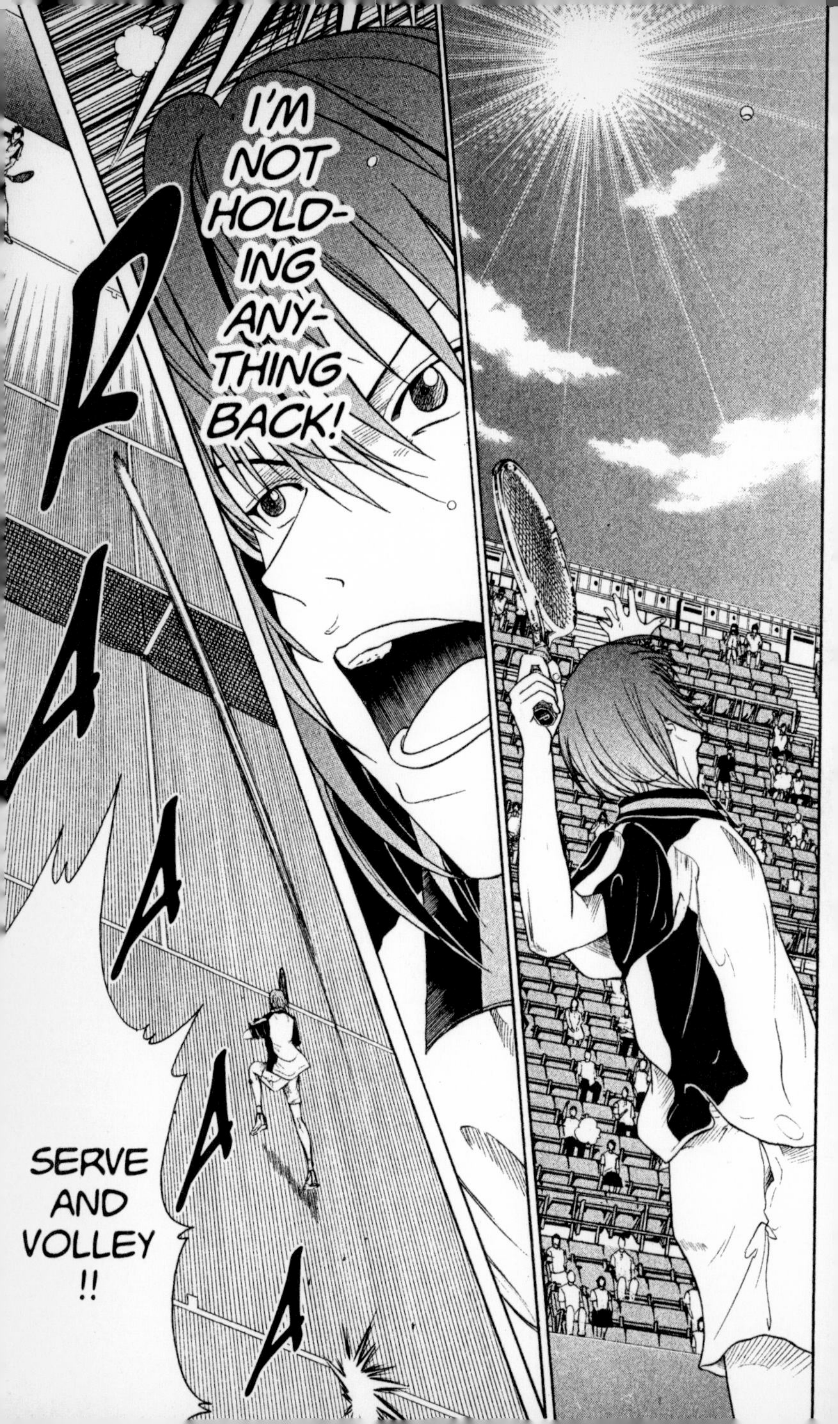
I'M NOT HOLD-ING ANY-THING BACK!
SERVE AND VOLLEY !!

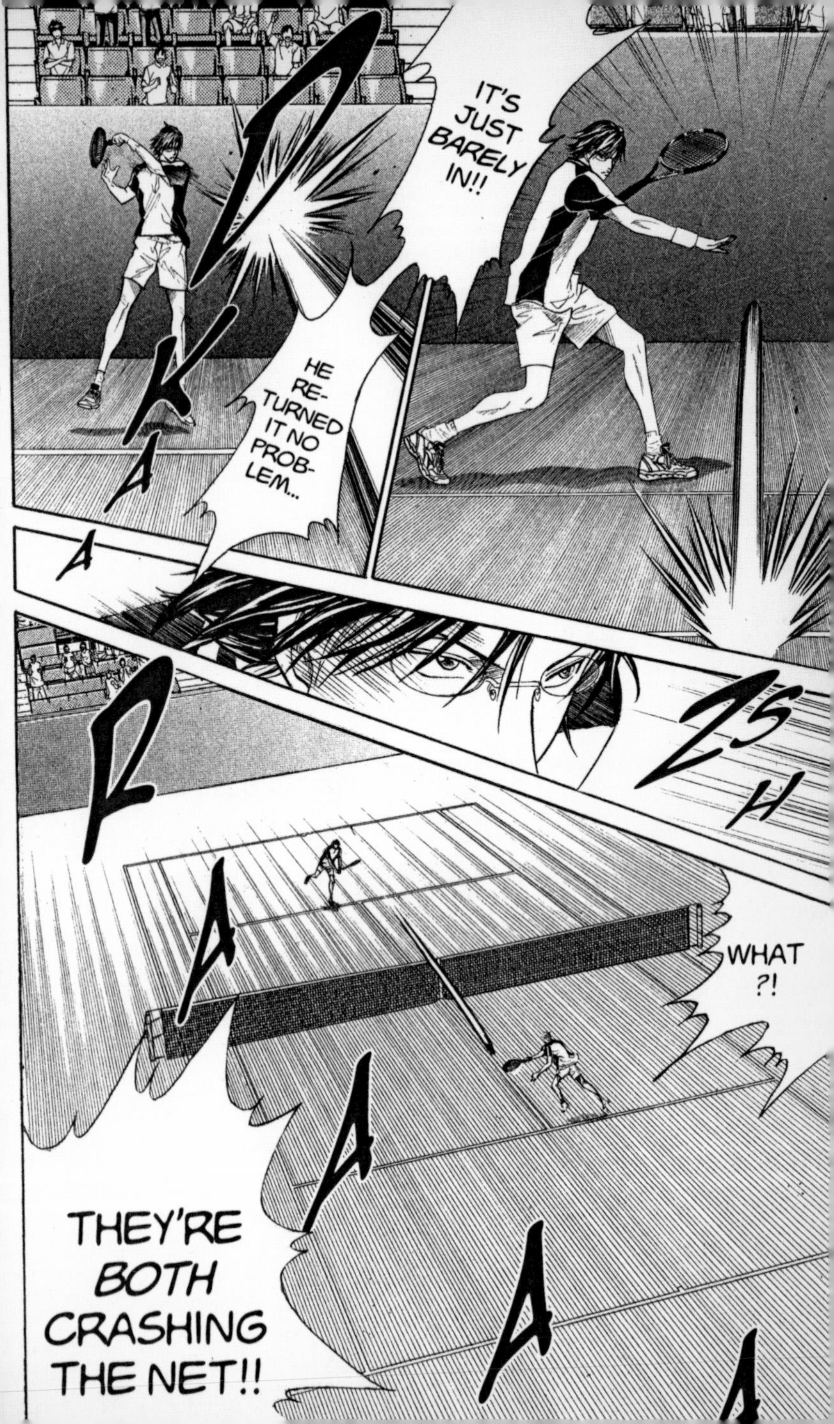
IT'S JUST BARELY IN!!
HE RE-TURNED IT NO PROB-LEM...
DKAA
ZSH
WHAT?!
THEY'RE BOTH CRASHING THE NET!!

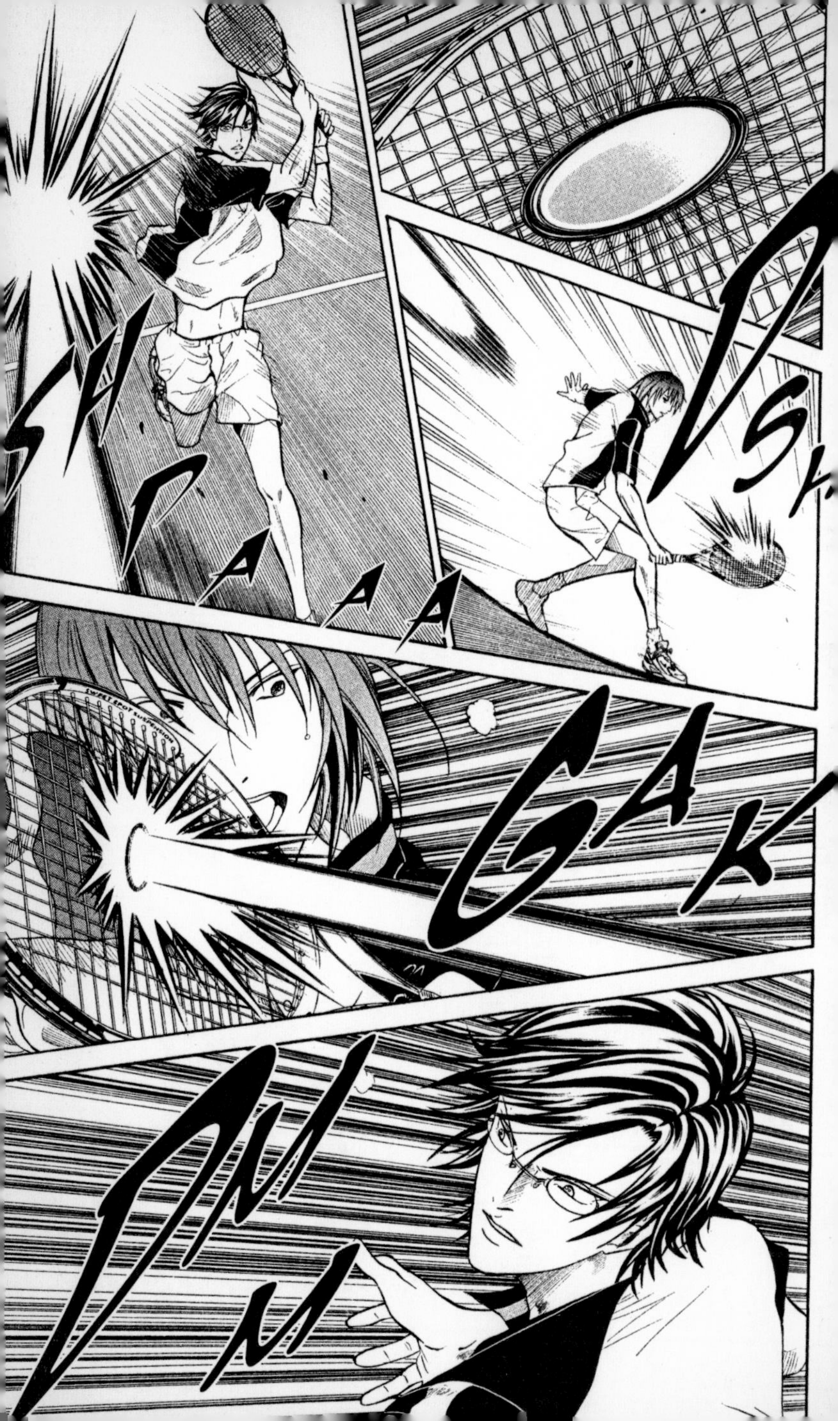
VSH
SHPAAA
SWEET SPOT SUSPENSION
GAK!

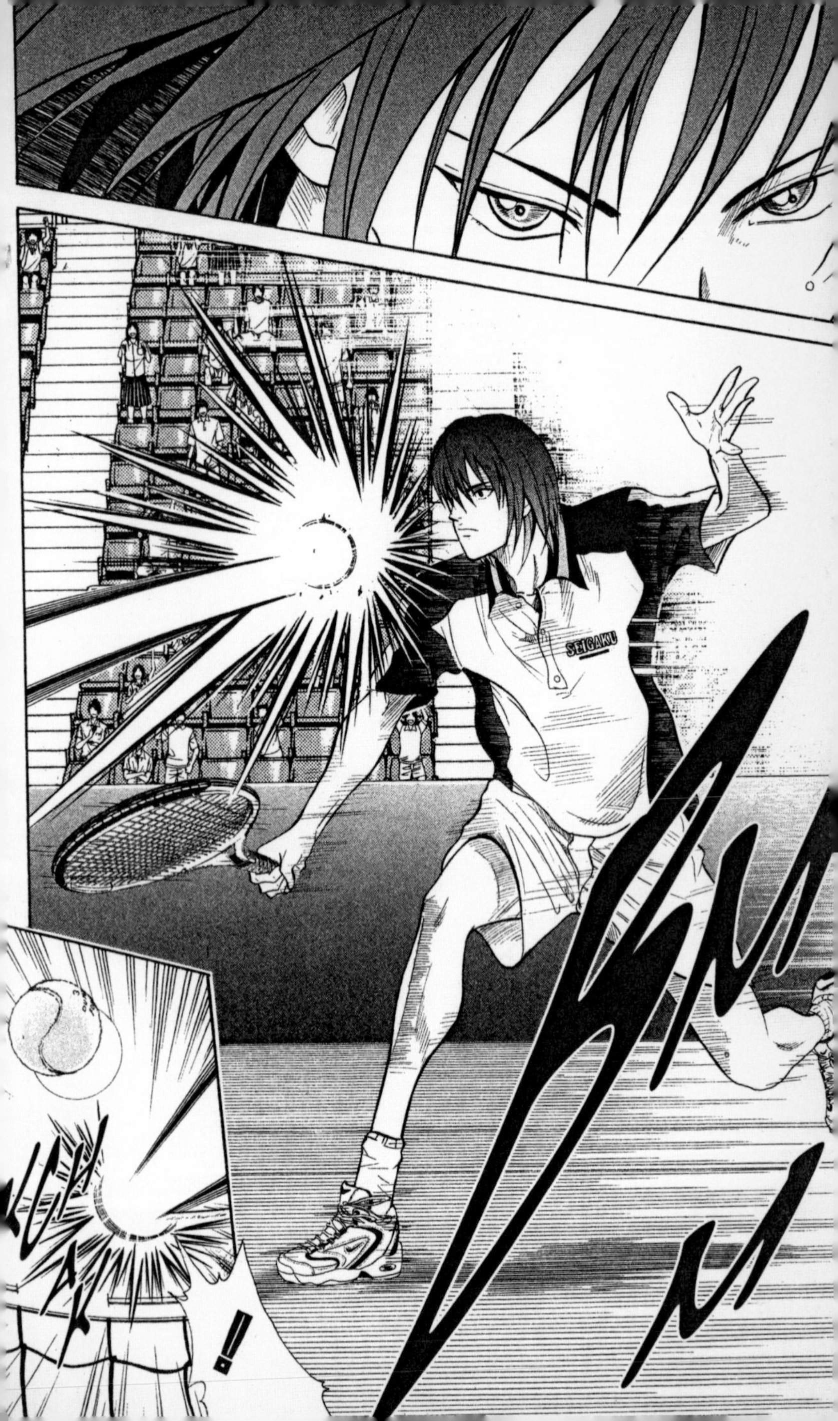
!
SEIGAKU
!

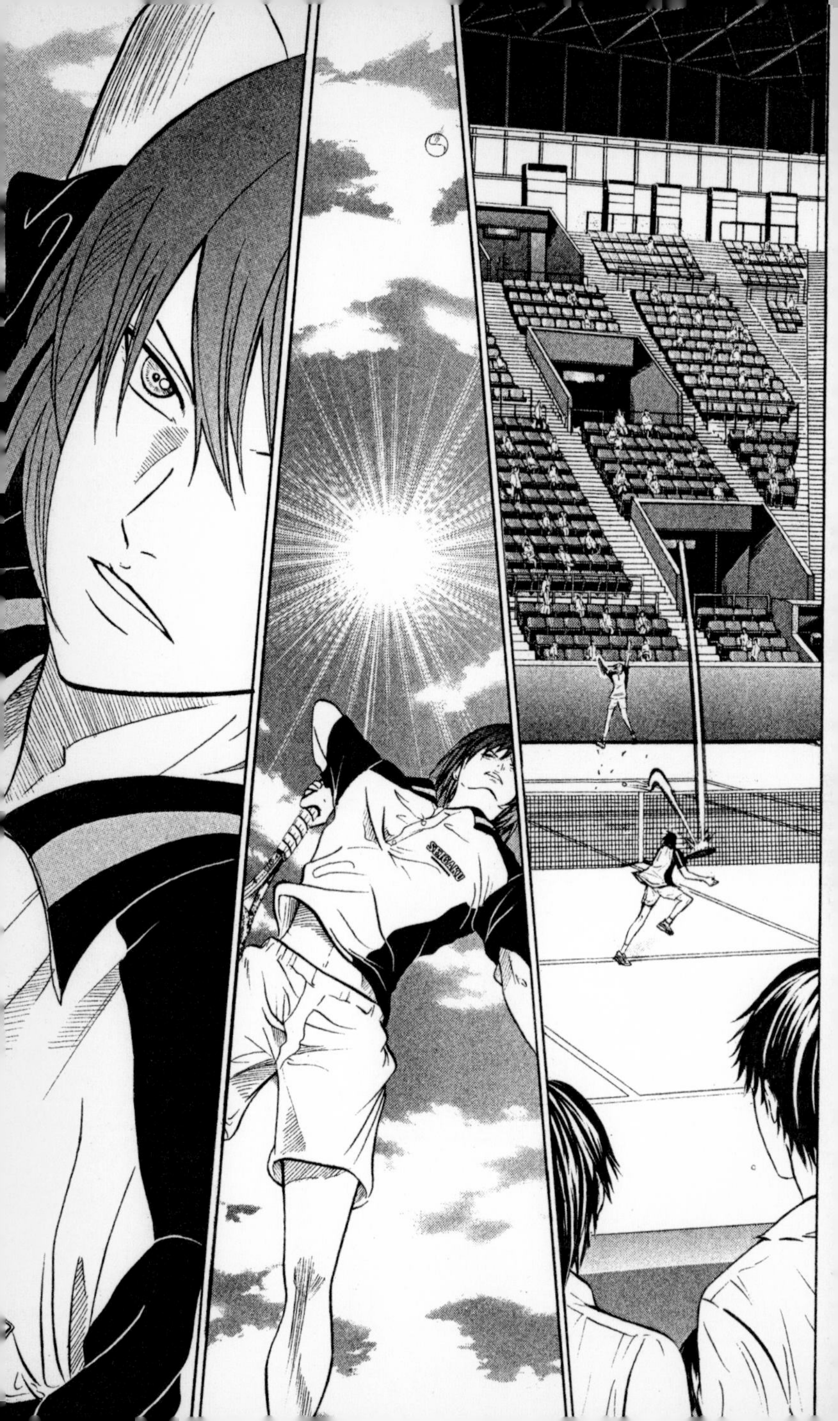
SEIGAKU

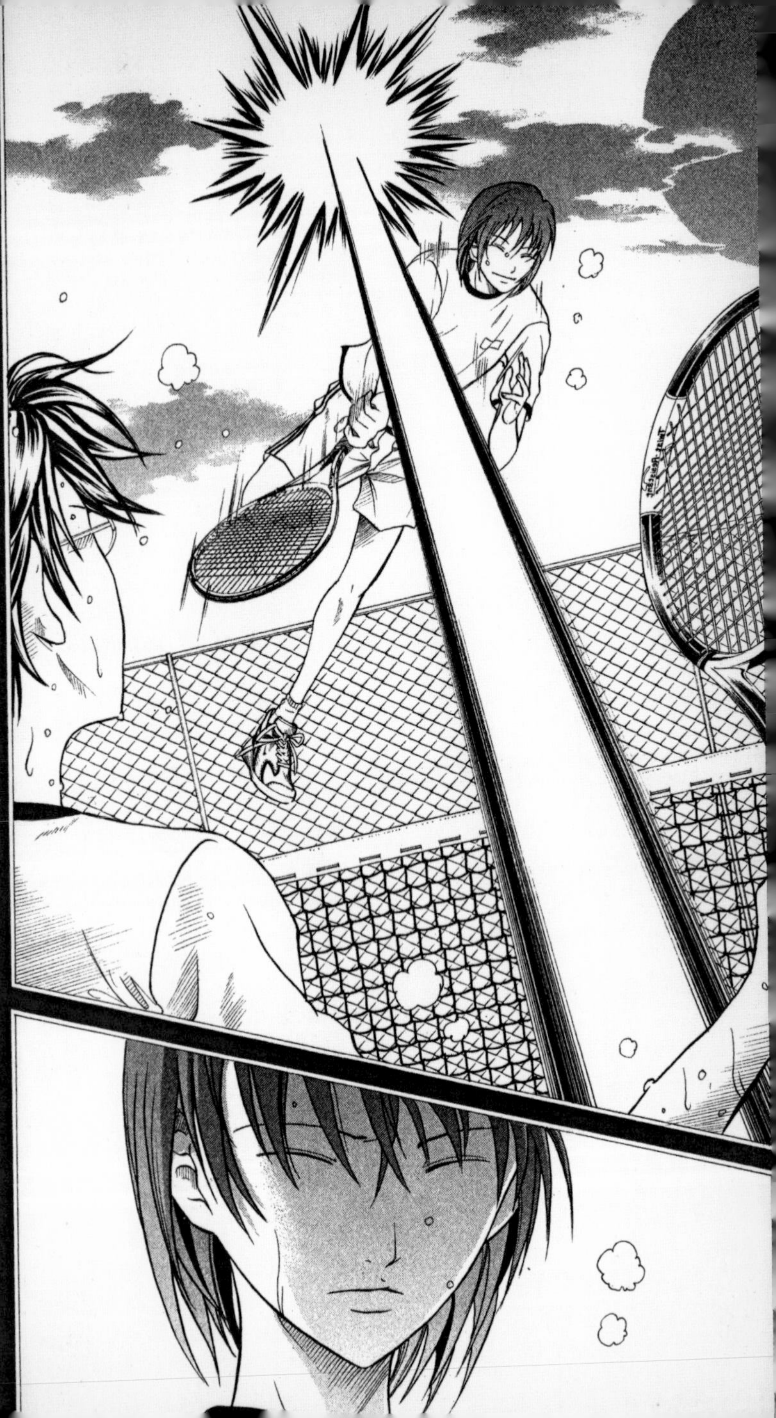

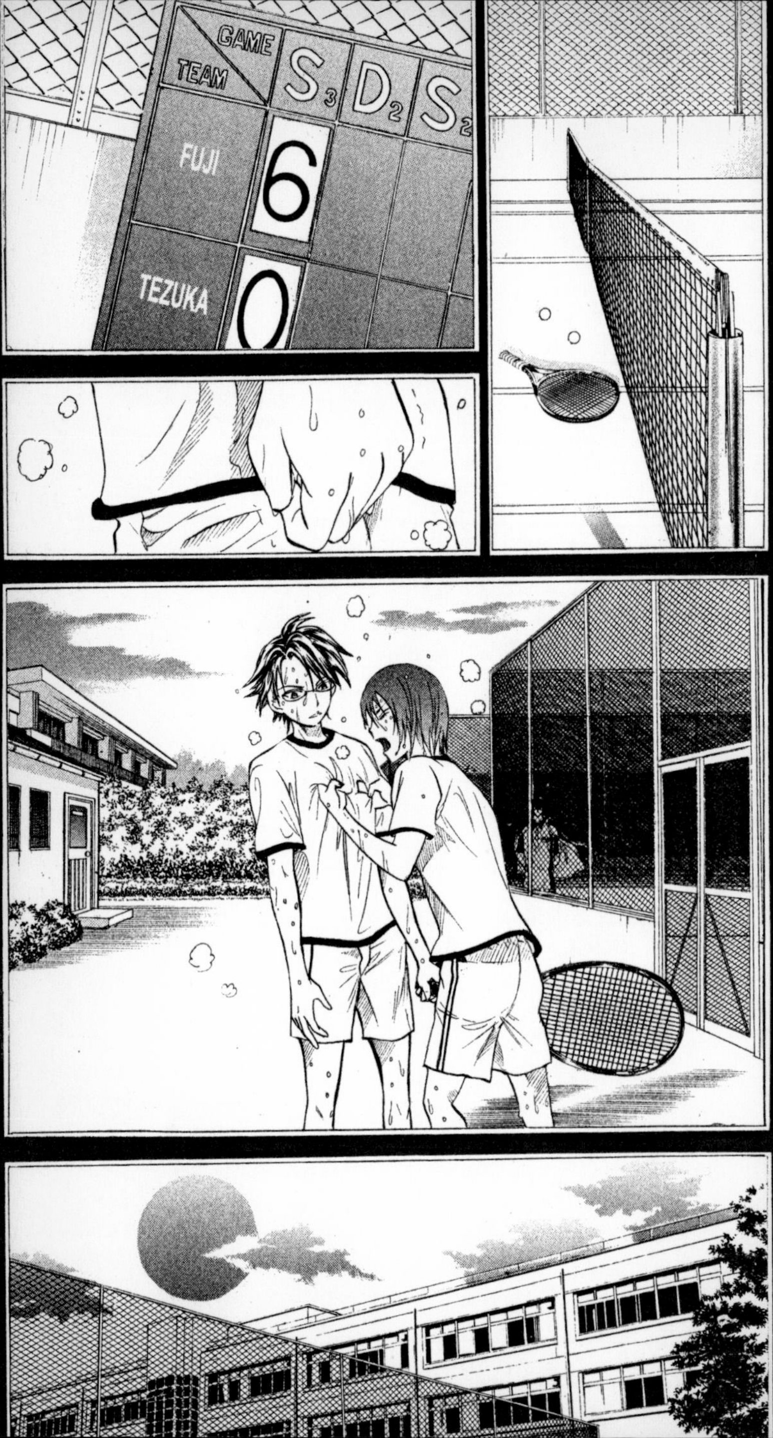
GAME
TEAM
S3
D2
S2
FUJI
6
TEZUKA
0

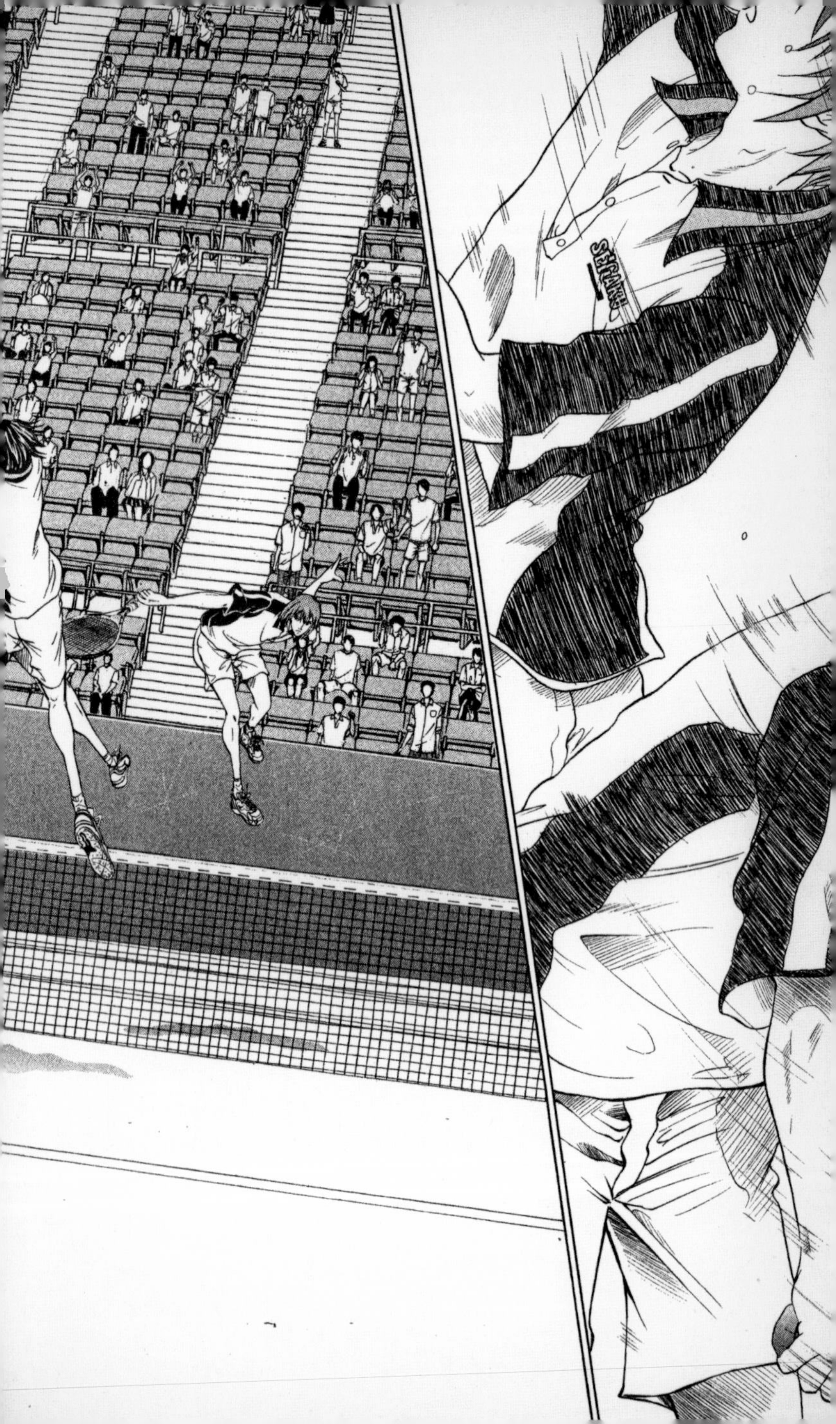
SEIGAKU

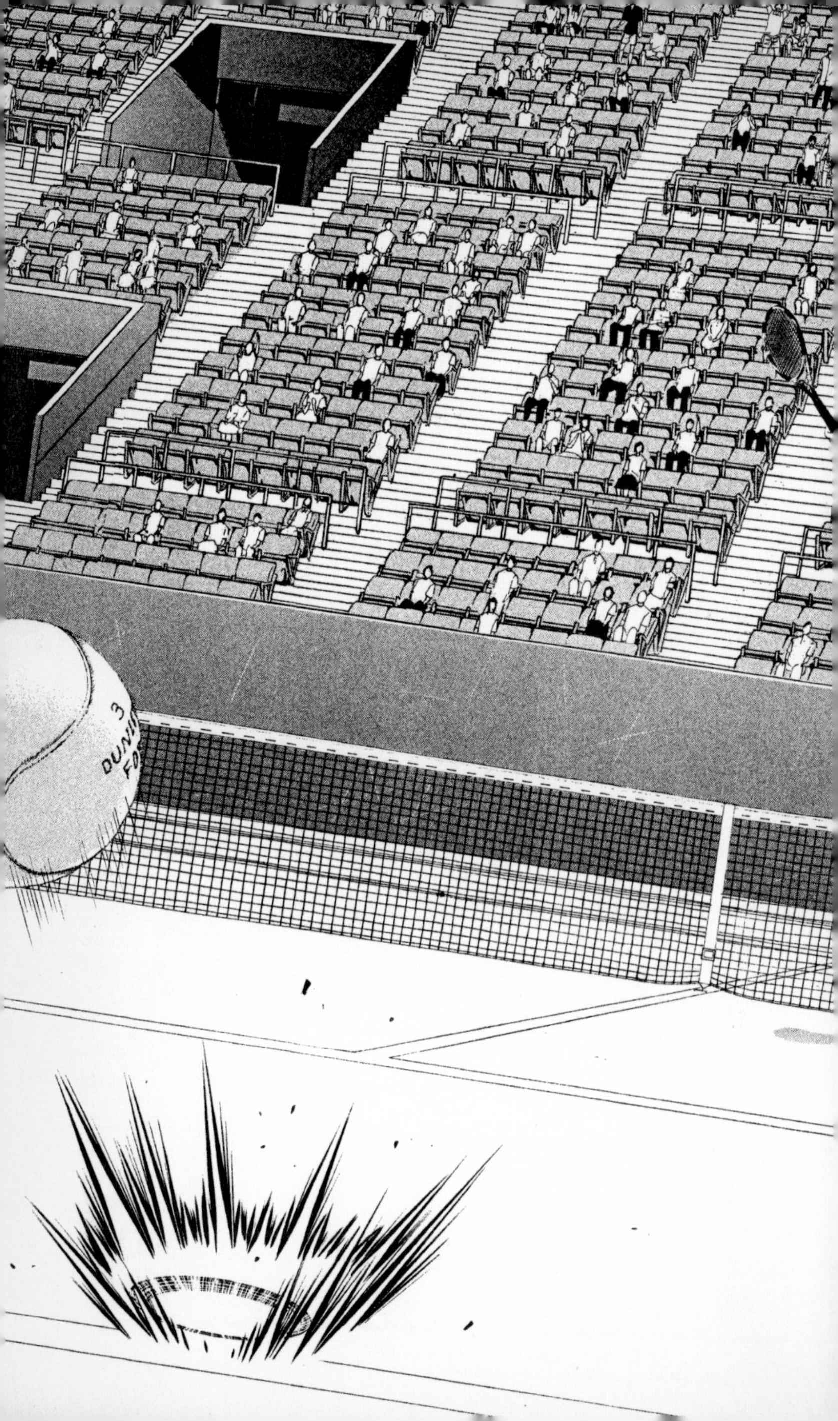

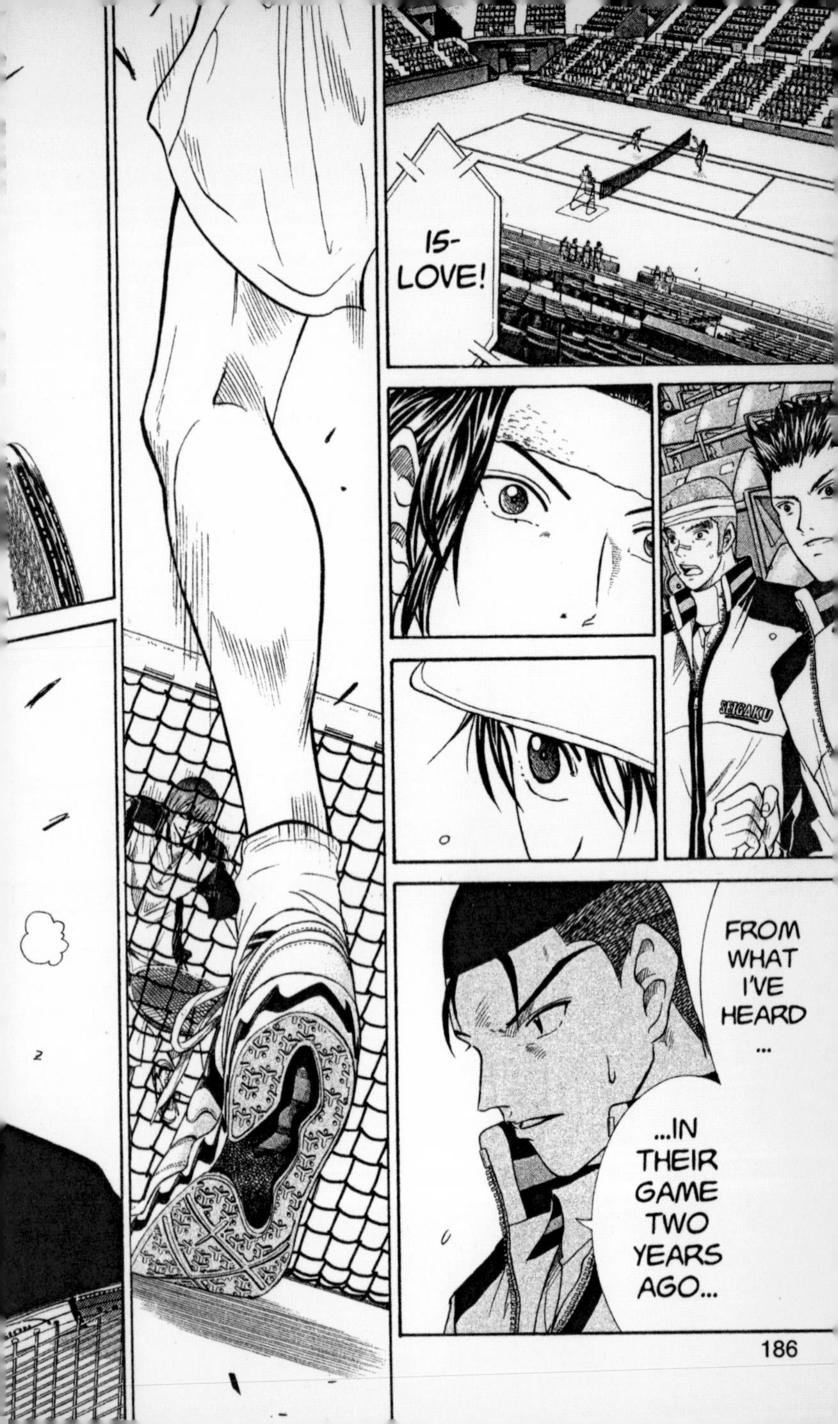
15-LOVE!
SEIGAKU
FROM WHAT I'VE HEARD...
...IN THEIR GAME TWO YEARS AGO...

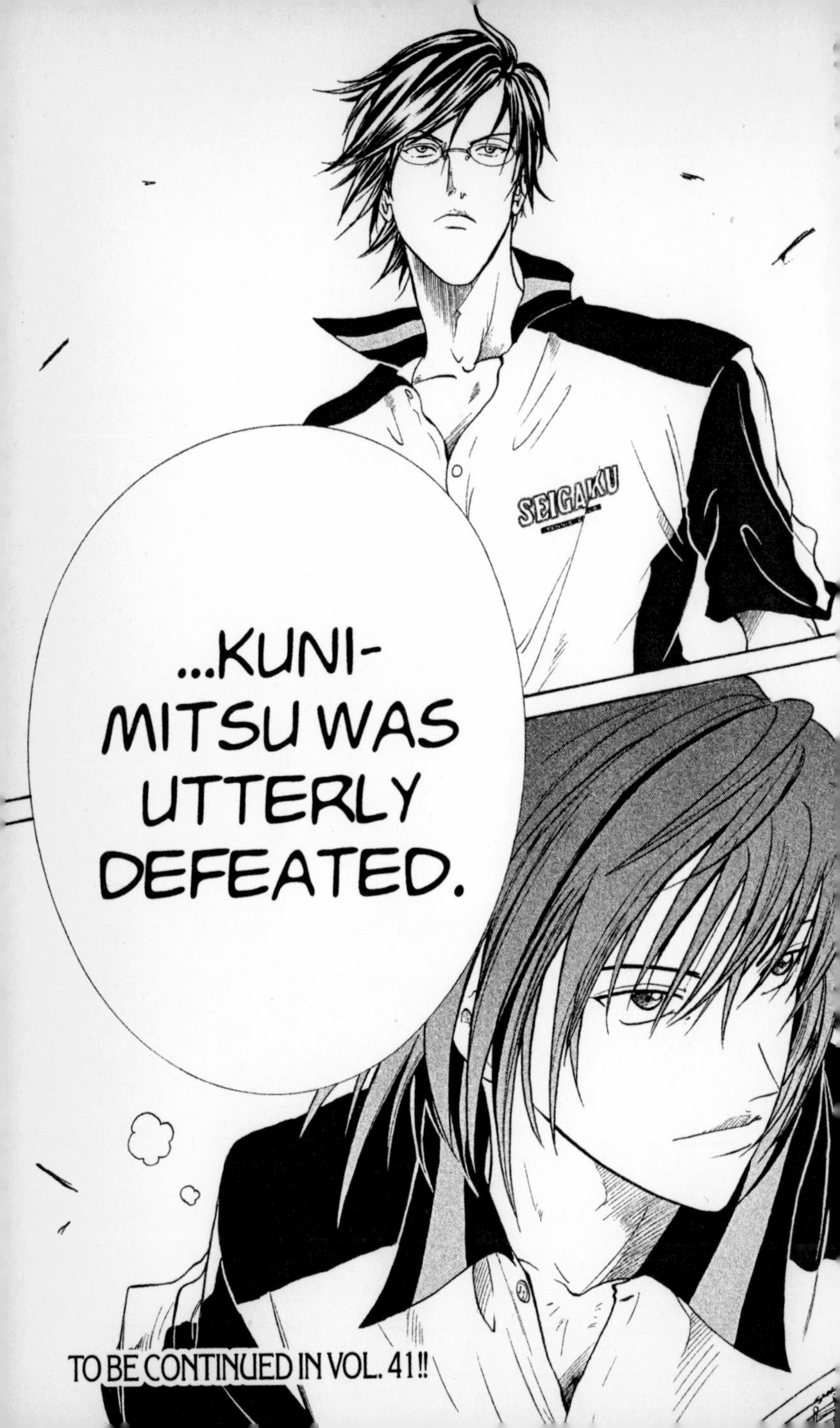
...KUNI-MITSU WAS UTTERLY DEFEATED.
SEIGAKU
TO BE CONTINUED IN VOL. 41!!

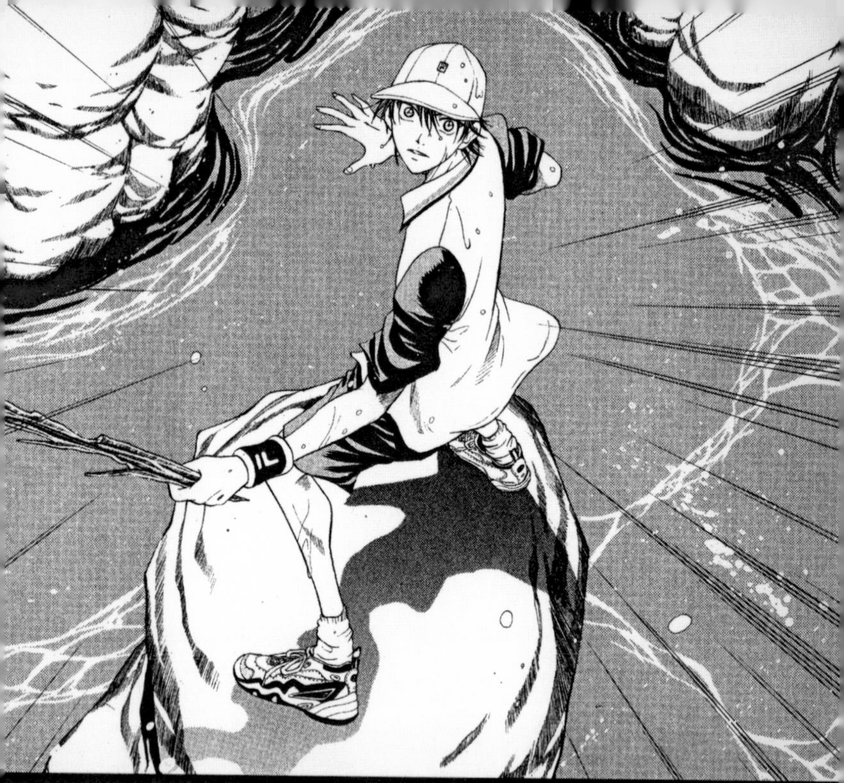

Final Showdown!
The Prince vs. the Child of the Gods

Shusuke battles Rikkai's Nio, the tricky "Con Artist of the Court." Just when it looks like Shusuke will be able to thwart Nio's devious ploy, Nio packs a punch that goes straight for Shusuke's weakness. Meanwhile, Momo is doing everything he can to help Ryoma overcome his amnesia in time to face the dreaded Seiichi Yukimura, aka "Child of the Gods." Will Ryoma recover in time?

Available April 2011!

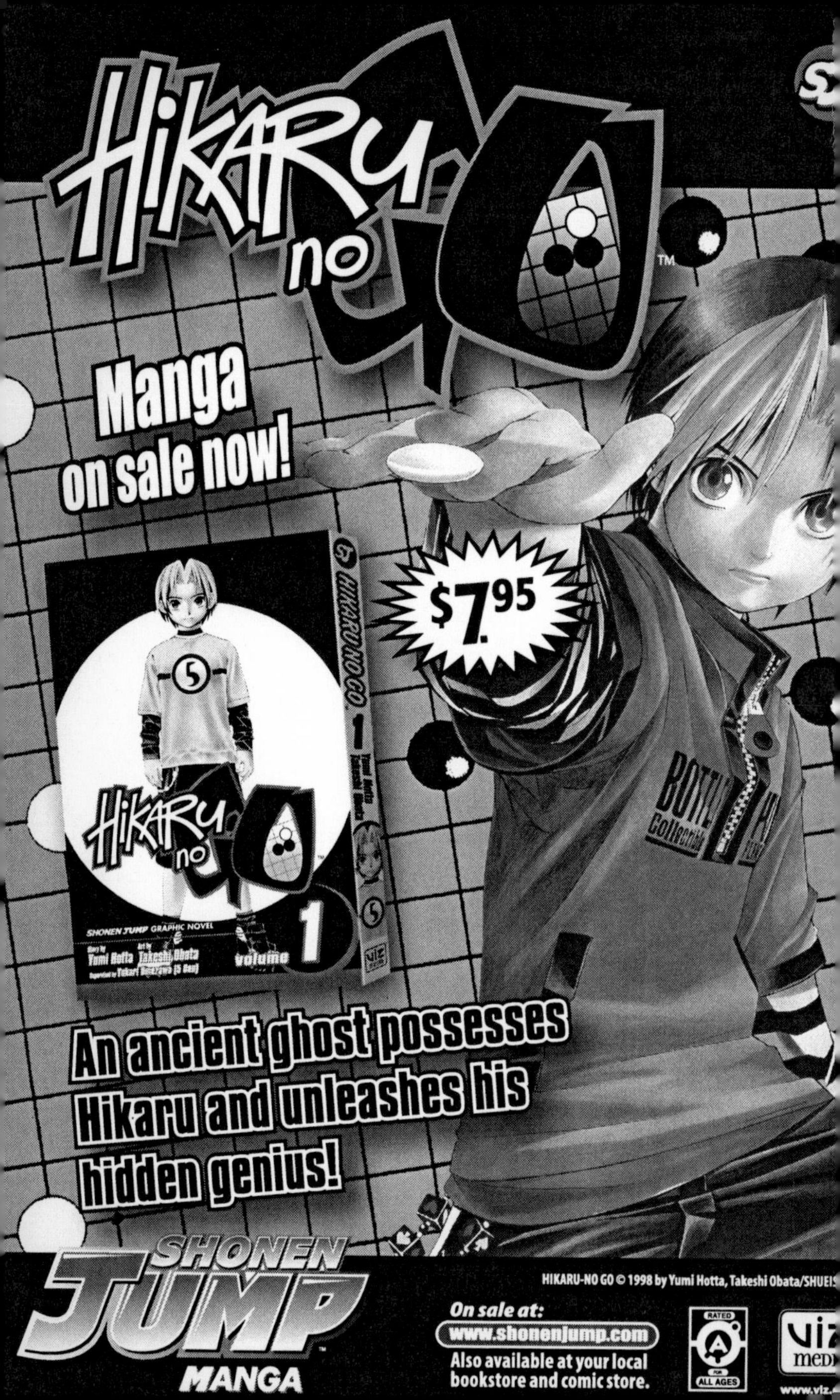
Hikaru no Go™
Manga on sale now!
$7.95
HIKARU NO GO 1
Hikaru no Go™
SHONEN JUMP GRAPHIC NOVEL
Yumi Hotta Takeshi Obata
volume 1
An ancient ghost possesses Hikaru and unleashes his hidden genius!
SHONEN JUMP™ MANGA
HIKARU-NO GO © 1998 by Yumi Hotta, Takeshi Obata/SHUEIS
On sale at:
www.shonenjump.com
Also available at your local bookstore and comic store.
RATED A FOR ALL AGES

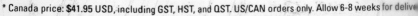